An Et

# An Ethics of Dissensus

POSTMODERNITY, FEMINISM,
AND THE POLITICS OF
RADICAL DEMOCRACY

EWA PŁONOWSKA ZIAREK

Stanford University Press
Stanford, California 2001

Stanford University Press
Stanford, California

© 2001 by the Board of Trustees of the
Leland Stanford Junior University

Printed in the United States of America
on acid-free, archival-quality paper

Library of Congress Cataloging-in-Publication Data
Ziarek, Ewa Plonowska
    An ethics of dissensus : postmodernity, feminism, and
the politics of radical democracy / Ewa Plonowska Ziarek.
    p.  cm.
    Includes bibliographical references and index.
    ISBN 0-8047-4102-6 (alk. paper)
    ISBN 0-8047-4103-4 (pbk. : alk. paper)
    1. Ethics, Modern—20th century.   2. Postmodernism.
3. Feminist ethics.   4. Democracy— Moral and ethical
aspects.   I. Title.
    BJ324.P67 Z53    2001
    170—dc21                                    00-067943

Original Printing 2001


Typeset by BookMatters in 10.5/12 Bembo

*To Jasia, Carol, and Rita,
whose friendship, wisdom, and amazing intelligence
were the inspiration for this project.*

# Contents

# Acknowledgments

IT IS MY PLEASURE to thank many colleagues and friends who read and commented on various parts of this book. In particular, I am indebted to Kate Baldwin, Robert Bernasconi, Rosalyn Diprose, Thomas Flynn, Graham Hammill, Cyraina Johnson-Roullier, Dalia Judovitz, Katherine O'Brien O'Keeffe, Diane Perpich, Hilary Radner, T. Denean Sharpley-Whiting, and Krzysztof Ziarek for their helpful comments and criticisms. I am especially grateful to Penelope Deutscher, who read the manuscript in its entirety and offered invaluable suggestions for revision. Her generous comments have made this a better book. I would also like to thank Kurt Schreyer and Carolyn Bitzenhofer for their help in preparing the final version the manuscript for publication. I am especially grateful to Henry Sussman for having faith in this project. Finally, I want to express my gratitude to Maria Tomasula for her generous permission to use the reproduction of her painting, *My Alba*, for the cover.

Grateful acknowledgment is made to the Institute of Scholarship in Liberal Arts at the University of Notre Dame for a summer research stipend that helped me to complete the chapter on Levinas.

A section of Chapter 5 appeared in the special issue of *Diacritics* 28 (1998): 60–75, devoted to the thought of Luce Irigaray. An earlier version of the first part of Chapter 1, entitled "Between the Visible and the Articulable: Matter, Interpellation, and Resistance in Foucault's *Discipline and Punish*," appeared in *Resistance, Flight, Creation: Feminist Enactments of French Philosophy*, ed. Dorothea Olkowski (Ithaca, N.Y.: Cornell University Press, 2000), reprinted by the permission of the publisher, Cornell University Press.

# An Ethics of Dissensus

# An Ethics of Dissensus
## Postmodernity, Feminism, and the Politics of Radical Democracy

To theorize the political, to politicize the theoretical, are such vast aggregative asymmetrical undertakings; the hardest lesson is the impossible intimacy of the ethical.

—Gayatri Chakravorty Spivak,
"French Feminism Revisited: Ethics and Politics"

Sexual difference entails the existence of a sexual ethics, an ethics of the ongoing negotiations between beings whose differences, whose alterities, are left intact but with whom some kind of exchange is nonetheless possible.

—Elizabeth Grosz, *Volatile Bodies*

We must discover—produce—justice. It is here that the real political burden and trajectory of the postmodern is to be found: the search for a just politics, or the search for just a politics.

—Thomas Docherty, *Postmodernism*

*An Ethics of Dissensus* presents ethics as a contested terrain and stresses the important, although often occluded, role of sexual and racial differences in this contestation. To underscore this conflictual articulation of ethics, I deploy the neologism "dissensus" (from the Latin *dissensio*, disagreement, struggle; the opposite of consensus) to refer to the irreducible dimension of antagonism and power in discourse, embodiment, and democratic politics. I use this neologism instead of a more common "dissension" to preserve not only the inverted reference to consensus but also the carnal implications of *sensus* in its double significance as meaning and sensibility. Although I stress its diverse configurations, "ethics" in this book refers primarily to the seemingly irreconcilable dilemma of freedom and obligation—or what I call the "ethos of becoming" and the "ethos of alterity." In the context of postmodernity I propose to reformulate this dilemma in the following way: although emphasis on the historical constitution of subjectivity contests the notion of freedom as an unquestionable attribute of the autonomous self, freedom is still presupposed, implicitly or explicitly, in all postmodern discussions of agency, resistance, and the transformation of the social forms of life beyond their present limitations.[1] And although the postmodern critique of universal reason and the concomitant dispersal of discourse question the notion of responsibility grounded in obedience to moral law, this critique nonetheless allows us to articulate what Emmanuel Levinas calls an "anarchic obligation," one that signifies a nonappropriative relation to the Other. What interests me in this dilemma is whether obligation based on respect for alterity and accountability for the Other's oppression can motivate resistance and the invention of the new modes of life. By contesting the binary opposition between freedom and responsibility, I propose to redefine freedom in relational terms as an engagement in transformative praxis motivated by the obligation for the Other. I will argue that such a redefinition is made possible by the ethico-political significance of sexuality and embodiment.

As the unavoidable yet productive dissonance among these three terms—antagonism, freedom, obligation—suggests, the ethics of dissensus does not transcend political and subjective antagonisms (as some feminist critics fear[2]) but rather articulates the difficult role of responsibility and freedom in democratic struggles against racist and sexist oppression. By opposing the conservative political work performed by privatized moral discourse, which reduces social antagonisms to the apolitical experience of good and evil, the ethics I propose elaborates a sense of freedom and responsibility in political life without grounding politics in a normative discourse. By emphasizing the agency of historically constituted subjects, the imperative of ethical judgment in sociopolitical conflicts, responsibility for others without the assurance of normative criteria, and the ethical significance of embodiment, the ethics of dissensus both moves beyond the impasses of the debates about the stakes of postmodernity and provides an important alternative to the communitarian and liberal conceptions of democracy. I pursue the relevance of these ethical concerns for a feminist politics of radical democracy, which rejects the rationalist and universalist framework and posits instead discursive operations of power and social antagonism as the irreducible dimension of democratic politics.

My articulation of such an ethics grows out of several interrelated questions: What kind of challenge does sexual and racial difference pose for postmodern ethics? What is the relation between ethical obligations irreducible to the law and feminist interpretations of embodiment, passion, and eros? How can we negotiate between ethical responsibility for the Other and democratic struggles against domination, injustice, and inequality, on the one hand, and the internal conflicts within the subject, on the other? What are the implications of postmodern ethics for the agonistic politics of radical democracy? I pursue these questions in my engagements with a number of writers ranging from Jacques Derrida, Emmanuel Levinas, Patricia Williams, Jean-François Lyotard, Michel Foucault, bell hooks, Cornel West, Claude Lefort, Ernesto Laclau, and Chantal Mouffe, to Jacques Lacan, Frantz Fanon, Julia Kristeva, and Luce Irigaray. Despite the different trajectories of their thinking and diverse disciplinary affiliations, the writers discussed in this book share the conviction that the limits of rationality and universalism disclosed in different ways by feminist and postmodern theories do not foreclose ethics but, on the contrary, renew it and intensify its political significance. As Drucilla Cornell has persuasively demonstrated, the limits in question preserve a nonviolent relation to the Other and open a possibility of "reimagining our forms of life."[3]

Yet, if the limits of universality do not prevent ethical reflection, they nonetheless necessitate a radical rethinking of ethics in the context of the dispersal of antagonisms and the radical contingency of power in democracy, on the one hand, and the paradoxical condition of being a sexed, embodied subject, on the other. When considered in relation to antagonism and sexuality, the notion of the limit not only dramatizes the impossibility of achieving full racial, sexual, or political identity, thus opening these identities to contestation, but also calls into question the disembodied notions of citizenship, rights, and democratic community. By challenging the desexualized subject of ethics and politics, the limits of universal reason raise a difficult question about how to think about ethical responsibility in the double context of embodiment and antagonism.

As Lawrence Buell, the editor of the 1999 special issue of *PMLA*, entitled "Ethics and Literary Study," observes, "Ethics has gained new resonance in literary studies during the past dozen of years," approaching the status of "the paradigm-defining concept that textuality was for the 1970s and historicism for the 1980s."[4] Yet, despite this growing concern with ethics in literary and cultural studies, Continental philosophy, and critical theory, several crucial omissions have constrained the discussions of postmodern ethics from the outset. First, the most influential studies of the conflicting relation between postmodernity and ethics (Bauman, Caputo, Critchley, Rajchman, Scott, and others[5]) usually do not consider the challenges of feminist theory to their claims and thus risk not only the exclusion of women's contributions to ethical reflection but also the perpetuation of the disembodied character of ethical subjectivity and liberal citizenship. Second, although the relation between postmodernism and feminism has received significant critical attention from feminist critics, the issue of ethics has been elided in most discussions of this subject. For instance, two of the most influential and representative anthologies in this field, *Feminism/Postmodernism* and *Feminism and Postmodernism*, contain no reference to ethics whatsoever.[6] Focused on the question of politics, the feminist confrontations with postmodernity not only ignore the centrality of ethics in postmodern critiques of rationality and domination but, in fact, reenact a modern split between the ethical and the political initiated by Enlightenment philosophy.[7] Third, despite the influential work of Drucilla Cornell, bell hooks, Rosalyn Diprose, Tina Chanter, and Rey Chow,[8] most feminist work that *does* address the problem of ethics (the most characteristic example of which is still the continuing debate on the "ethics of care" versus the "ethics of justice"[9]) often ignores the epistemological and political challenges of postmodernism.[10] As the Blackwell anthology, *Ethics: A Feminist Reader*, illustrates too well, although the feminist articulations of ethics rightly contest the concealment of power relations by traditional morality, the proposed ethical alternatives—the moral reflection based on the specificity of female experience,[11] ethics of freedom,[12] or the ethical visions of oppositional communities[13]—are often insufficient because they do not take into account the postmodern critique of the terms, such as freedom, experience, community, and value, upon which these alternatives rest. Finally, as bell hooks, Katie Cannon, Michele Wallace, Patricia Hill Collins, and Zillah R. Eisenstein[14] point out, most postmodern and feminist ethical reflections ignore the specific challenges to ethics emerging from democratic struggles against racial and sexist oppression.[15] According to bell hooks, "Racism allows white women to construct feminist theory and praxis in such a way that it is far removed from anything resembling radical struggle."[16] By ignoring the question of race and racism, feminist ethics runs the risk of being "far removed" from radical intervention despite all the claims to the contrary.

By addressing these exclusions in contemporary debates, my theory of the feminist ethics of dissensus displaces ethical reflection onto territories hardly recognized by traditional morality: the realm of the body, race, and sexuality, on the one hand,[17] and the realm of the *polemos* understood both as the discursive operation of power and the libidinal economy of the drive, on the other.[18] Consequently, such an ethics does not aspire to a neutral position transcending power and embodiment, provided for instance by normative criteria, but rather articulates the difficult role of responsibility and freedom in democratic struggles. In fact, I argue that neither the agonistic politics of difference without ethics nor the grand theory of a normative justice that transcends conflict are viable options for feminist theory today. By rejecting these binary oppositions, the ethics of dissensus I propose might at first glance appear contradictory because postmodern feminist politics and moral philosophy (both the liberal tradition running from Kant to Rawls and Habermas's ethics of communicative action) seem to be conflicting, if not mutually exclusive. Yet, despite all the worries and criticisms to the contrary, this paradoxical pursuit of ethics within democratic struggles leads neither to an internal contradiction nor to political quietism but confronts us, in Gayatri Spivak's words, with the experience of "the impossible."[19] In place of obedience to the moral law or construction of normative criteria enabling us to judge the outcome of political struggles in advance, such an "impossible" ethics calls for infinite accountability for justice without the final assurance of norms—it articulates responsibility that never ceases to obligate us to find the means of expression and compensation for forgotten wrongs.

Since it does not transcend politics, an ethics of dissensus reopens what Moira Gatens calls "the rather awkward question of the connection between *polis* and *ethos*."[20] At stake in this "agitated passage," to use Lyotard's phrase, between the feminist politics and the ethics of difference is neither the assimilation of ethics to politics nor a recovery of ethics as a new "ground" of politics but rather an elaboration of a different concept of alterity missing in most articulations of feminist politics. In postmodern political vocabularies, the category of the Other, most frequently associated with women and people of color, is synonymous with objectification, exclusion, and domination. It is either a negative foil for the identity of those who count as political subjects or a fetishistic screen for the projection of social antagonisms.[21] In this context, the task of feminist politics of difference has been to transform the institutional conditions of inequality and to demand the status of the subject for those who have been so "othered." By embracing the struggle against the interlocking forms of domination based on class, gender, and race as an irreducible goal of feminist politics, I accept Chantal Mouffe and Ernesto Laclau's point that such politics requires the formations of hegemonic links among different forms of antagonisms.[22] Yet, I also argue that to challenge domination, it is necessary not only to create hegemonic coalitions and reclaim subjecthood for the oppressed but also, as bell hooks reminds us, to transform the nature of the self/Other relation beyond objectification. Perhaps the most significant limitation of the feminist politics of difference is that it has failed to articulate this alternative model of intersubjective relations. Consequently, what is at stake in the proximity between the politics and ethics of difference is an elaboration of the nonappropriative relation to the Other that is based on responsibility and accountability rather than on power and knowledge.[23]

The question of obligation and accountability brings an element of the unconditional into the radical contingency of democratic politics. "Contingency" refers here to the arbitrariness and groundlessness of historically constituted power arrangements and subjective identities. Let me stress that the contingency of democratic politics—what Claude Lefort defines as the institution of the empty place of power—needs to be defended as an enabling condition of contestation and refiguration of existing power relations. Consequently, by raising the question of the unconditional in democratic politics I do not want to recover a moral foundation for politics but, on the contrary, to articulate infinite responsibility for justice without the assurance of normative criteria. Levinas and Lyotard call this responsibility anarchic because it is not based on any prior principle and thus remains unlegitimated and ungrounded. Although the specific forms such responsibility should take in political life are always open to question and contestation, obligation itself is unconditional, in the sense that it cannot be derived from these debates but is always already presupposed by them. Manifesting itself merely as vigilance, urgency, and commitment to justice, accountability is a motivating force of political contestation and action.

To articulate the place of anarchic responsibility in the feminist politics of difference, I negotiate between obligation for the Other and the agency of the subject, between responsibility and the struggles against sexist, racist, and class oppression, and finally, between the desire for justice and embodiment, affect, and sexuality. In so doing, I reformulate the project of the feminist politics of difference. My revision of agonistic politics is based on four crucial interventions. First, it takes into account the limit cases of antagonism—what Lyotard calls the "differends"—that lack the means of expression and resolution and thus cannot be a part of hegemonic formations. Second, it negotiates between the proliferation of social antagonisms and the conflictual negativity represented by the libidinal economy of the drive. Third, it supplements the hegemonic articulation of struggle and resistance with the necessity of justice based on the obligation for the Other. Fourth, it reconceptualizes ethical obligation in the context of embodiment, sexuality, and the negativity of the drive. I argue that the enabling tension between unconditional responsibility and the radical contingency of democratic politics prevents the deterioration of feminist politics either into an indifferent struggle of heterogeneous forces without ethical stakes, or into its opposite, the utopian vision of justice transcending the antagonisms of race, class, sexuality, and gender.

In order to elaborate the interventions of the feminist ethics of dissensus, it is crucial to foreground the split between two different lines of ethical inquiry—what I call the ethos of becoming and the ethos of obligation—within postmodernism itself. The first trajectory is best represented by the work of Nietzsche, Deleuze, and Foucault; the second one by Levinas, Derrida, and, to a certain degree, Lyotard. Although both trajectories depart from the notion of morality as the universal system of law and norms, they represent different approaches to freedom, alterity, and obligation. For Levinas, Derrida, and Lyotard, the ethical significance of alterity persistently escapes social systems of signification and, in this sense, marks transcendence as a break in discourse, whereas for Nietzsche, Foucault, and Deleuze, otherness is contained within the endless variations on the plane of immanence. To clarify this difference, it might be useful to recall John Caputo's distinction between two kinds of ethics—between Nietzschean heteromorphism and Levinasian heteronomy. In its celebration of diversity, difference, and power, heteromorphism, Caputo claims, puts forward the claim of freedom but cannot accommodate an obligation to the Other or respond to any external claim: "In heteromorphism, the aim is freedom from inhibition and blockage, freedom from the weight of being, from the weight of values . . . from everything that weights the will down. . . ." In the Levinasian heteronomic ethics, by contrast, "freedom is suspect, suspended, held in question, because it is aggressive, self-accumulative, and eventually, finally murderous. Heteronomism wants to let the other be free while one is oneself held hostage."[24]

Originating in the gap between heteromorphism and heteronomy, immanence and transcendence, love and *polemos*, freedom and obligation, a feminist ethics of dissensus cannot disregard either of these claims. Paradoxically, what allows us to think through the disjunction between the two main ethical trajectories of postmodernism and find the means to negotiate between them is the issue most frequently disregarded in postmodern discussions, namely, an analysis of sexuality in the context of the interlocking systems of racial and sexist oppression. By adopting the feminist psychoanalytical perspective proposed by Kristeva and Irigaray, I see sexuality as the limit of the multiple identifications of the subject. Such an approach to sexuality allows us to interpret the failure of identity not only as an effect of antagonistic relations with others but also as a result of the internal negativity of the sexed subject. By maintaining sexuality as the limit of social positions, the feminist ethics of dissensus enables the transformation of the existing power relations and, at the same time, prevents the paranoid reification of the social and subjective antagonisms in the figure of the Other.

I begin to investigate the disjunction between the ethos of becoming and the ethos of obligation by juxtaposing two influential yet diametrically opposed thinkers: Michel Foucault and Emmanuel Levinas. The main question I raise in my engagement with Foucault is how resistance, freedom, and ethical agency are possible under the conditions of disciplinary regime and how they need to be redefined. On the basis of Foucault's work, I argue that the diagnosis of the formative role of disciplinary power in the constitution of political identities and in the materialization of the sexed and racial bodies not only makes the question of antagonism central to feminist reformulation of ethics but also contests the disembodied character of democratic politics. Consequently, to elaborate a model of resistance irreducible to the demand for recognition or the liberation of repressed identities, we need to account for the causality of the disciplinary power and for the disjunction in its materialization. Building on the work of Wendy Brown, Judith Butler, and Gilles Deleuze, who in different ways have explored the possibilities of agency in Foucault's work, I argue that the conditions of resistance to disciplinary regime emerge from the relation to the outside (or the limit) of historical formation and from the intensification of divergence within the embodied subjects. Subsequently, however, I shift my discussion from the negative thought of resistance to an aesthetics of existence in order to elaborate a model of experimental praxis aiming to surpass the historical limits of bodies, discourses, and sexuality. Irreducible to the practices of self in private life, this model of transformation not only emphasizes the futural dimension of democratic politics but also shifts the ethos of democratic struggles from the liberation of repressed identities to an invention of new modes of life, eroticism, and social relations. Grounded in the intensification of erotic pleasure as well as in "patiently documentary" genealogical critique, freedom in this context is not an attribute or a transferable possession of the subject but a situated praxis aiming to overcome historically sedimented identities and create modes of being that are still "improbable."

Although the practice of transgression allows us to intervene into existing power relations, it reaches its limit in the context of the nonappropriative relations to the Other: it cannot account for what Foucault describes as the problematic of friendship and the ethical concern for the sexual partner. To move beyond this limitation, I renegotiate the ethos of becoming in the context of the radical reformulation of ethical responsibility proposed by Emmanuel Levinas. No longer concerned with the autonomy of the subject or the universality of moral law, such an anarchic responsibility is based on the affirmation of the irreducible alterity and the asymmetry of the Other.[25] At stake in this shift is a productive tension between the transformative political praxis and ethical obligation, between the disruptive temporality of becoming and the anarchic signification of otherness, and, finally, between political and ethical significance of embodiment.

Drawing on the work of Robert Bernasconi, Drucilla Cornell, Simon Critchley, Tina Chanter, and Jacques Derrida, among others, I address what I consider to be still the most challenging task emerging from Levinas's work: the necessity of contextualizing ethical obligation, which, as the infinite movement toward the Other, exceeds, nonetheless, all contextual bounds. Toward this end, I reread Levinas's ethics in context of Luce Irigaray's and Patricia Williams's thought. Such an encounter between Levinas's ethics, feminist theory of sexual difference, and race theory is motivated by three main concerns: first, I want to rearticulate Levinas's concept of "anarchic" obligation and sensibility in the context of feminist articulations of sexuality and embodiment. If in Chapter 1 I discuss bodies as the site of the materialization of power and resistance, in Chapter 2 I develop the ethical structure of embodiment, which disrupts the familiar oppositions between matter and form, passivity and activity, constituted and constituting character of history. Second, by engaging Levinas's and Williams's essays on human rights in the light of Claude Lefort's and Chantal Mouffe's theories of democracy, I analyze the role of ethical respect for the Other in proliferating democratic struggles against racial, sexist, and class oppression. By departing from the philosophical model of politics in *Totality and Infinity* and *Otherwise than Being*, I redefine Levinas's concept of the political in the context of the performative politics of race and rights and, conversely, rethink the performative in the context of ethical obligation. Finally, by contesting Levinas's concept of homosocial fraternity, I discuss the significance of ethical and sexual passions for the conception of a heterogeneous democratic community.

In Chapter 3, "Toward an Ethics of Dissensus: Lyotard's Agonistic Politics and the Pursuit of Justice," I argue for the necessity of supplementing the hegemonic politics of radical democracy with obligation and ethical judgment. If in my engagement with Levinas, I reinscribe ethical responsibility, which for Levinas remains exterior to politics and war, within *polemos*, in this chapter I rethink antagonism in the light of ethics. Although Lyotard has been frequently criticized (not only by the proponents of deliberative democracy but also by Mouffe and Laclau) for the uncritical embracing of the fragmentation and contingency of postmodern culture, his emphasis on the irreducible antagonism in political life not only does not prevent coalition politics but, in fact, opens an inquiry into the possibility of an ethics of radical democracy. By juxtaposing Lyotard with Ernesto Laclau's and Chantal Mouffe's work, I claim that the politics of radical democracy cannot be based only on the hegemonic consolidation of dispersed struggles against manifold forms of oppression; rather, it has to be articulated in the gap between the ethos of becoming and the ethos of alterity, between the futural temporality of political praxis and the anarchic diachrony of obligation. This redefinition of democratic politics allows us to encounter ethics not outside *polemos* but in the midst of the extreme form of antagonism— what Lyotard calls the "differend"—which cannot be articulated within hegemonic formations but which nonetheless imposes an obligation to respond to the obliterated wrongs. Patricia Williams's trenchant analysis of injustices caused by racist and sexist oppression is a compelling example of such a differend, where the suffered wrong is prevented from being signified by the racial neutrality of justice that claims to redress it.[26]

Confronted with erased wrongs, the central difficulty the politics of democracy has to address is the limit of both communicative rationality and hegemonic politics represented by the differend. What enables us to respond and redress these nonsignifiable wrongs is an indeterminate ethical judgment proceeding without criteria. Consequently, the politics of radical democracy not only has to articulate equivalence among diverse struggles but also assume obligation for a just judgment without an assurance of the normative principles of justice. Finally, through the juxtaposition of Lyotard's work and Mae Gwendolyn Henderson's influential essay, "Speaking in Tongues: Dialogics, Dialectics, and the Black Woman Writer's Literary Tradition," I argue that such a judgment bears a necessary relation to embodiment, conceived not only as a site of struggle and regulation but also as the limit, or the remainder, of that regulation.

My reading of Lyotard's negotiation between *polemos* and obligation opens a space for the elaboration of a feminist ethics that neither renounces intervention into multiple structures of oppression nor forgets the burden of ethical responsibility for the Other. In Chapter 4, "The Libidinal Economy of Power, Democracy, and the Ethics of Psychoanalysis," I begin to elaborate such an ethics by examining Kristeva's work in the context of recent psychoanalytic critiques (advanced by such diverse theorists as Claude Lefort, Chantal Mouffe, Slavoj Žižek, Drucilla Cornell, and Joan Copjec) of the liberal subject endowed with natural rights prior to its social determination. In my engagement with Kristeva I articulate two crucial aspects of the feminist ethics of dissensus: what I call, in a supplement to Judith Butler's recent project, the libidinal economy of power and "the psychic life" of ethics. By stressing the inseparability of sociosymbolic order from the libidinal economies of drive and affect, I move the analysis of the "psychic life of power" beyond the problem of identifications, predominant in Judith Butler's, Ernesto Laclau's, and Chantal Mouffe's political theories, toward the question of fantasy, *jouissance*, and the irreducible negativity within the subject at odds with its social positionality. In so doing, I rethink antagonisms and the instability of social relations in democracy in the context of the subject's conflicting relation to "the Other within" and ask under what conditions it can function either as a condition of responsibility or as an exacerbation of social conflict. This redefinition of the constitutive antagonism in democracy in the light of Kristeva's heterogeneous and conflicted subject, split between desire and drive, signifier and affect, questions Lefort's thesis about disincorporation of power in democracy and contests the disembodied character of citizenship separated from the affective and libidinal dimension of intersubjectivity.

The relation between the negativity of the drive and the constitutive antagonism in democracy is a starting point for my second intervention—the elaboration of the "psychic life" of ethics. Through the juxtaposition of Levinas's ethics of responsibility and Kristeva's ethics of "the irreconcilable," I develop a psychoanalytic model of ethical relation to the Other, irreducible either to the narcissistic reflection of the ego Ideal or to the fetishistic embodiment of the abject in social relations. By pushing Kristeva's and Levinas's ethics toward their limits, I define such a model as the interplay between the sublimation of the death drive and the confrontation with the abject as one's own most intimate yet inassimilable alterity. By rethinking the conditions of ethical responsibility in the context of the libidinal economy of the drive, I contest the separation of ethics not only from embodiment and sensibility but also from conflict and sexuality. Kristeva's ethics of democracy is crucial for understanding her formulation of the third generation of feminism. By transcending the dilemma of equality versus difference, this type of feminism opposes the disembodied character of liberal citizenship and, in so doing, inscribes the asymmetry of sexual difference into the heterogeneity of democratic community. By calling for a transformation of the symbolic "under the pressure of social practices," it also emphasizes the ethical responsibility for violence that might accompany the contestation of social identities. Although Kristeva's discussion of democracy and feminism does not engage explicitly the problem of racial difference, I argue that the juxtaposition of her critique of xenophobia and anti-Semitism with Frantz Fanon's discussion of Negrophobia allows us to develop a feminist account of the psychosexual dynamics of race.

In Chapter 5, I rethink postmodern ethics and the politics of radical democracy through the prism of Luce Irigaray's carnal ethics of sexual difference. By reconsidering Irigaray's work in the context of the ethics of dissensus, I propose a theory of sexual difference that still has a political future and ethical relevance for feminism. Although Irigaray's systematic critique of the major philosophical figures—from Plato to Nietzsche, Heidegger, Freud, and Levinas—contests the erasure of sexed bodies not only in the Western philosophical tradition but also in the postmodern theories of ethics and politics, her exclusive focus on sexual difference might entail a different kind of forgetting—the disregard for antagonistic differences among women. Because of this limitation, the theory of sexual difference has been increasingly questioned by such diverse feminist theorists as Hortense J. Spillers, bell hooks, Deborah E. McDowell, Evelynn Hammonds, Valerie Smith, Elizabeth V. Spelman, Judith Butler, and Ellen T. Armour, among others, for its implication in heterosexism and its neglect of women's diversity.[27] In the light of this critique, I argue that feminist ethics needs a theory of sexual difference that is more dynamic, more democratic, and more ethical—a theory capable of foregrounding not only the futurity of democracy and antagonistic differences among women but also ethical respect for alterity in all its

forms. In order to develop such a theory, I engage and radicalize three crucial concepts in Irigaray's work: the labor of the negative; the impossible;
and the work of "disappropriation." By stressing the disappropriation and
the incompleteness of subjective identities, I argue that the labor of the negative accomplished through sexual difference is a condition of social transformation and ethical responsibility in both homo- and heterosexual relations. I elaborate the ethical significance of asymmetrical sexual relations by
negotiating between two kinds of excess: the anarchic force of ethical obligation and the exorbitant *jouissance* of sex; the transcendence of the Other and
the "immediate ecstasy" of flesh. By contesting the oppositions between the
respect for the Other and the becoming of the subject, such a theory of sexual difference allows us to rethink the disjunction between the two main
ethical trajectories of postmodernism and to find the means to negotiate between them.

By reconsidering sexual difference in the context of democratic politics,
I contest the disembodied notion of democratic citizenship, on the one
hand, and criticize Irigaray's inability to address antagonistic differences
among women, on the other. To redress these shortcomings of her work, I
supplement Irigaray's "sexuate rights" with Patricia Williams's performative
politics of race and with Mae Gwendolyn Henderson's discussion of black
female subjectivity.[28] What this juxtaposition of the theories of race and sexuality illustrates is that the future of radical democracy, its precarious space
"in-between," cannot be explained only in terms of antagonistic differences
limiting collective identifications from without but has to be supplemented
by the limits of the subject represented by the sexed body, *jouissance*, and the
discontinuous temporality of becoming. I argue that the rethinking of sexual difference in a double context of ethics and democratic struggles against
sexist and racist oppression enables us to radicalize all three of these areas of
feminist inquiry.

I conclude my discussion of the feminist ethics of dissensus with bell
hooks, whose work in feminism and race theory not only advances one of
the most trenchant critiques of the postmodern discourse of the Other but
also articulates alternative paradigms of ethics and multicultural radical
democracy. Acknowledged as one of the most creative theorists and de-
manding interlocutors of both feminism and postmodernism, hooks raises
doubts whether the postmodern discourse of otherness produced primarily
by white theorists can enhance and support struggles against domination
without interrogating racism. Yet, although she has been widely recognized
for her critique of feminism and postmodernism, her own contributions to
ethics and democratic theory have received less attention. In her theory of
postmodern blackness hooks combines the structuralist diagnosis of interlocking relations of race, gender, and class, with the analysis of the devastat-

ing psychic effects of racial traumas, on the one hand, and with the unapologetic commitment to freedom and ethical vision, on the other. Her discussion of trauma not only foregrounds the intersection of race and sexuality at the limits of discourse but also complicates postmodern theories of resistance, performativity, and freedom. In contrast to the hesitation or even a retreat from the discourses of freedom and ethics in the majority of postmodern analyses of power,[29] hooks argues that ethics constitutes an indispensable framework for both progressive theory and the politics of radical democracy. Like Cornel West and Patricia Hill Collins,[30] she argues that without ethics the institutional analysis of power cannot overcome nihilism, mobilize resistance, or offer hope.

Based on the "subject-to-subject encounter" and the desire for justice as the shared sensibility among oppressed groups, hooks's ethics reformulates responsibility for the Other in terms of accountability for racist, sexist, and economic oppression. This approach to ethics not only contests institutionalized patterns of domination but also stresses a positive significance of difference as a condition of solidarity among diverse groups. By combining the ethical respect for difference with struggle against domination, hooks's work, I argue, provides an important alternative to many postmodern and feminist theories of democracy, in particular, to Laclau's and Mouffe's hegemonic politics based exclusively on social antagonism and its obverse side, Habermas's and Benhabib's idealized communicative rationality. Acknowledging the passionate and ambivalent dimensions of democratic politics, hooks links collective struggles against oppression not only to love and ethical accountability but also to the necessary confrontation with the internal conflict, aggressivity, and the division of the subject.

As this brief synopsis of my main arguments demonstrates, I do not propose a unified seamless ethical theory but, by presenting ethics as a contested terrain, I dramatize a certain unavoidable dispersal of the ethical into a plurality of language games. Since the strength of my approach is not based on a single thread running through all the language games but, as Wittgenstein and Lyotard are fond of saying, on many threads intertwined with each other, the individual chapters can be read either as parts of the overall argument or as specific interventions into ethical debates. By respecting as much as possible differences and discontinuities among diverse discourses I engage in this book, I create out of them a new configuration that allows us to redefine the importance of ethics for feminism. Thus, although I work through heterogeneous articulations of ethics, the multiple links and intersections I construct among them constitute, to use another of Wittgenstein's metaphors, a certain "family resemblance." This structure of my book reflects my conviction that the articulation of a feminist ethics of dissensus has to negotiate in a serious way the conflicting multiplicity of the ethical.

Only through such a negotiation can the modes of inquiry that still proceed in a large degree in isolation from each other—postmodern ethics, feminism, and race theory—be brought together.

*An Ethics of Dissensus* presents the vexed question of ethics as one of the most important legacies of postmodernity. Yet, as bell hooks, Rey Chow, and Kelly Oliver, among others, argue, any articulation of postmodern ethics is seriously handicapped if it does not take into account questions of racial differences and sexuality.[31] To redress these limitations in the contemporary debates on ethics, I claim that it is crucial to articulate both the proximity and the difference between responsibility for an Other and democratic struggles against racist and sexist oppression, freedom and obligation, social antagonisms and the internal conflicts within the subject, erotic love and infinite demands of justice. The unique contribution of my project lies in the fact that by bringing together postmodern ethics, feminism, and race theory, it redefines the relation among freedom, obligation, and antagonism in a double context of embodiment and democratic politics. What emerges from this redefinition is a challenge of ethics for the politics of radical democracy. Although I affirm antagonism and difference as the irreducible dimensions of democratic politics, I argue that the hegemonic model of radical democracy proposed by Mouffe and Laclau is insufficient. Thus, to elaborate what Mouffe calls an "ethics proper to modern democracy," the feminist project of radical democracy has to take into account the sexed body, *jouissance*, and the discontinuous temporality of becoming, on the one hand, and the ethical imperative of judgment and obligation, on the other.

## CHAPTER 1

# Toward an Experimental Ethos of Becoming
## From Docile Bodies to Ethical Agency

THE IMPORTANT ELEMENT of the ethics of dissensus I will develop in this book is the ethos of becoming. By the "ethos of becoming" I mean first of all the task of resistance to power and, second, the transformation of the negative thought of resistance into a creation of the new modes of being. I elaborate this ethos first in the context of Michel Foucault's work and later reconfigure it in the context of Luce Irigaray's ethics of sexual difference and bell hooks's theory of multiracial democracy. I argue that this emphasis on discontinuous becoming shifts the ethical problematic from the concern with the universal norms of ethical behavior to the task of transforming the subjective and social forms of life beyond their present limitations. Consequently, the ethos of becoming poses and redefines the question of agency and freedom of historically constituted subjects: no longer seen as an attribute or a possession of the subject, freedom is conceptualized as an engagement in praxis.[1] Furthermore, since subjective and social transformation occurs on the level of bodies, materiality, and power, the ethos of becoming contests the disembodied subjectivity of traditional ethics.

To articulate a viable theory of the ethics of dissensus—an ethics that does not transcend power relations but intervenes and enables their transformations—I begin with a discussion of the new modalities of power in modernity. For that reason I turn to the work of Foucault, whose diagnosis of the forms of modern power outside state control—what he defines as disciplinary biopower operating on the level of bodies and the life of population—redefines first of all the nature of antagonism and shows its formative role not only in the construction of subjectivities but also in the materialization of bodies. Although Foucault, like Chantal Mouffe and Ernesto Laclau, argues that power relations are constitutive of political identities, he contests the disembodied character of these identities not only in liberal theory but also in the theories of radical democracy. Consequently, I argue that neither

15

the politics of radical democracy nor the ethics of dissensus I develop in this book can disregard racial and sexed bodies as the location of the historical struggles.

Not a sign of a defeatist attitude toward political change, as it is sometimes claimed,[2] the ethos of becoming, I argue, provides a new basis for democratic struggles. In the wake of the disappearance of religious morality and universal law—what Lyotard calls the "crisis of legitimation"—diverse democratic struggles against domination, racism, or homophobia have to articulate an alternative ethos of freedom. Otherwise liberation movements are blocked by the impasse of repressive hypothesis, that is, by the conflation of freedom with the emancipation of true identities or repressed sexualities.[3] As Foucault writes, "Recent liberation movements suffer from the fact that they cannot find any principle on which to base an elaboration of new ethics. They need an ethics, but they cannot find any other ethics than an ethics founded on so-called scientific knowledge of what the self is, what desire is, what the unconscious is, and so on" (GE, 343).[4] Far from offering a privatized ethics, Foucault, like bell hooks and Paul Gilroy, enables us to reconceive the ethos of democratic struggles in terms of a praxis aiming to invent new modes of life, eroticism, and social relations. Referring to Foucault's work, Gilroy underscores the importance of the task to "uncover both an ethics of freedom to set alongside modernity's ethics of the law and the new conceptions of selfhood" constructed from the perspective of race and gender.[5] Such an ethos of freedom attempts to surpass the historically specific power relations diagnosed by the "patiently documentary" genealogical research in order to open up "a manner of being that is still improbable" (FWL, 137).

To articulate how an ethos of freedom is possible under the conditions of disciplinary regime, I begin this chapter with a careful consideration of the causality of disciplinary power and its impact on the constitution of embodied subjectivities. By taking Deleuze's interpretation of Foucault as my point of departure, I argue that the conditions of resistance to disciplinary regime emerge from the relation to the outside (or the limit) of historical formation as well as from the radicalization of the finitude and the dispersion of the embodied subject. Subsequently, however, I shift my discussion from the negative thought of resistance to the experimental ethos of becoming and show its relation to queer eroticism, aesthetics, and political struggles. Beginning with Foucault, I elaborate an ethics that goes beyond the reactive force of resistance toward "the creation of new forms of life, relationships, friendships . . . through our sexual, ethical, and political choices."[6] At stake here is a shift, as Frantz Fanon observed some time ago, from a "reactional" to "actional" subjectivity: "There is always resentment in a *reaction*. . . . To educate man to be *actional* . . . is the prime task of him who, having taken thought, prepares to act."[7]

## Between the Visible and the Articulable: On the Causality of Power and the Materialization of Bodies

Although Foucault's account of power relations—for instance, the procedures of discipline, docility, and surveillance—has been extremely influential in feminist analyses of the normalization of sexed and racial bodies in such contemporary cultural practices as consumerism, fashion, diet, fitness regimes, cosmetic surgery, reproduction,[8] and the technologies of state racism,[9] feminist critics of Foucault have consistently raised objections that this approach to power seems to evacuate psychic space and to eliminate the possibility of agency. From the early anthology *Feminism and Foucault: Reflections on Resistance* to the 1996 collection *Feminist Interpretations of Foucault*, the feminist engagements with Foucault expose the paradoxical achievements of his genealogical critique occurring at the expense of the practical ethos of freedom.[10] Although Foucault frequently proclaims that the ethos of his work is to write the history of the present so that we can experiment with different ways of becoming, such an ethos seems to be realized merely in a negative way: the Foucauldian histories of sexuality and penal system demonstrate time and again the insufficiency of the liberal projects of liberation, whether these refer to sex or to docile bodies.[11] Lois McNay sums up this dilemma rather nicely when she points out, "Despite Foucault's assertions about the immanence of resistance to any system of power, this idea remains theoretically underdeveloped, and, in practice, Foucault's historical studies give the impression that the body presents no material resistance to the operations of power."[12] Or, as Francis Bartkowski argues, what is missing in Foucault's articulation of "power-knowledge-pleasure" is the "fourth term of resistance."[13] Although resistance is affirmed theoretically as the necessary outcome of power conceived in terms of the relation between forces, the historical genealogy of docile individuals threatens to eliminate it as the practical possibility.[14]

This perpetual worry about the impossibility of resistance stems from the lack of explicit reflection on the causality of power in Foucault's work. Despite the significant differences in the arguments about the "usefulness" of Foucault's theory of power for feminism,[15] what is characteristic about the majority of feminist discussions of Foucault is either the assumption that the operation of power is characterized by a continuity of causes and effects, as if causes could manifest themselves in their effects without reserve, for instance, disciplinary power could be actualized in the modern docile individual[16] or, as Judith Butler argues, by the unacknowledged personification of power itself, a displacement of power into the emptied position of the political or ethical agent.[17] On the basis of such a notion of causality attributed to historical formations, Nancy Hartsock, for instance, writes that in Foucault's theory "things move, rather than people, a world in which subjects become obliterated or, rather, recreated as passive subjects."[18] The arguments of this sort are by no means limited to feminist criticism. Consider, for instance, Christopher Norris's claim that the Foucauldian subject is reduced to a "recipient" of heteronomous disciplinary power and thus cannot function as an autonomous agent[19] or Axel Honneth's conclusion that Foucault's work is similar to behaviorism as it represents "psychic processes as the result of constant conditioning."[20] Yet, as David Halperin sardonically remarks in response to these criticisms, the Foucauldian "message" about the lack of resistance "was certainly lost on the AIDS Coalition to Unleash Power, or ACT UP."[21]

Insofar as it perpetuates the notion of the subject as a passive receptacle of power, this reception of Foucault, I argue, is deeply implicated in the utilitarian functionalism—that is, in the very notion of causality which Foucault, following Nietzsche, takes as the main target of his genealogical critique in *Discipline and Punish*. The often-unacknowledged debt to utilitarianism in Foucault criticism is nowhere more apparent than in the concept of causality ascribed to "historical formations." As early as "The Discourse on Language," Foucault has warned his readers that what is at stake in historical genealogy is not "consciousness and continuity (with their correlative problems of liberty and causality)" but events and series: "If it is true that these discursive, discontinuous series have their regularity . . . it is clearly no longer possible to establish mechanically causal links or an ideal necessity among their constitutive elements" (DL, 231). Foucault follows here rather closely Nietzsche's critique of utility in *On Genealogy of Morals*. In his reflection on the genealogical method, Nietzsche deplores the naivete of seeking the origin of punishment in its utility. "The calculus of utility" is deeply problematic because it focuses exclusively on the reactive forces and forgets the endless transformations of things toward new ends in the context of the changing relations of power:

One had always believed that to understand the demonstrable purpose, the utility of a thing, a form, or an institution, was also to understand the reason why it originated. . . . Thus one also imagined that punishment was devised for punishing. But purposes and utilities are only *signs* that a will to power has become master of something less powerful and imposed upon it the character of a function; and the entire history of a "thing," an organ, a custom can in this way be a continuous sign-chain of ever new interpretations . . . whose causes do not even have to be related to one another but, on the contrary, in some cases succeed and alternate with one another in a purely chance fashion.[22]

In contrast to this Nietzschean insistence on the discontinuity of cause and utility in the genealogy of morals, utilitarianism, let us recall, in its instrumental conception of the social Good and the utility of pleasure aims to control social relations through the manipulation of causes. By ascribing a proper function even to human waste, Jeremy Bentham's project of panopticon is one of the paradigmatic examples of how the utilitarian notion of causality eliminates contingency for the sake of efficiency and calculability. As Jacques-Alain Miller notes, utilitarian functionalism, based on the logical homology of visibility, law, and language, enables the continuous derivation of causes and effects and the calculation of means and ends.[23] If we substitute "historical formations" for "causes" and "docile individuals" for "effects" we might get a general schema of the predominant Anglo-American criticism of Foucault, which Joan Copjec calls "historicist": "The social system of representation is conceived as lawful, regulatory, and on this account the cause of the subject, which the former subsumes as one of its effects. The subject is assumed to be virtually there in the social and to come into being by actually wanting what social laws want it to want."[24]

In order to theorize the ethos of resistance under the conditions of disciplinary regime, I would like to turn to Gilles Deleuze, who provides one of the most provocative, and, from the feminist point of view, most productive interpretations of the "profound Nietzscheanism" in Foucault's work. By bringing Deleuze into dialogue with feminist criticism, in particular, with the work of Wendy Brown, Judith Butler, and Jana Sawicki, who in different ways have explored resistance in Foucault's work, I argue that the possibility of resistance is located in the disjunction at the very center of the historical formation—in the rift between the forms of visibility and the forms of signification. Unlike utilitarianism's insistence on the homology of language and visibility, Deleuze argues that Foucault discovers in *Discipline and Punish* the disjunction between prison and law, and on the basis of this disjunction he theorizes the "irrational" rift in "historical formation" itself. Reformulating his earlier distinction of "discursive formations" and "nondiscursive practices" in *The Archeology of Knowledge*,[25] Foucault gives in the figure of panopticism a positive articulation of "the non-discursive" as a form of visibility, that is, the historically variable constructions of space, which determine specific modes of perception, practice, and normalizing judgment.[26] Foucault overcomes utilitarian functionalism not only by situating the social utility of pleasure in the context of the disciplinary technologies of bodies but, even more so, by stressing the noncoincidence between the forms of visibility and the forms of discourse at the center of disciplinary formation.

As an immanent cause, force relations are neither visible nor discursive. It is on the level of their actualization in the historical formation that they constitute the historically specific "art of space" and a form of discourse. In the case of the disciplinary society, power constitutes the architectural panopticon as a form of visibility, and delinquency as a new form of articulation. As Foucault repeatedly argues, the disciplinary organization of visibility and the discourse of penal law do not have the same genealogy, nor the same object of punishment, nor the same form. Deleuze evokes Foucault's earlier study of Magritte's famous painting, "This is not a pipe," to underscore the heterogeneity between the prison form and the law form, as if visibility and discourse constituted two different semiotic systems: "Prison as the visibility of crime does not derive from penal law as a form of expression but evolves from something completely different, which is 'disciplinary' not judicial; while penal law, for its part, produces its statements of 'delinquency' independently of prison as though it were always led to say, in a certain way, that this *is not* a prison."[27]

By replacing an earlier mode of visibility, which Foucault defines as a "society of spectacle," disciplines invent new, analytical, and useful spaces modeled on the precise partitioning and distribution characteristic of the town afflicted with plague. Yet, if disciplinary power establishes a new mode of visibility through the reversal of spectacle, its discursive actualization is even more complex since it proceeds through the inversion rather than replacement of the law. Indeed, as Peg Birmingham suggests, "These two heterogeneous but inseparable views [juridical and disciplinary] of power together characterize modern political life."[28] The inversion of the law is nowhere more evident than in "double foundation"—"juridico-economic" and "technico-disciplinary"—of the right to punish (*DP*, 233). Within the disciplinary regime, the function of punishment is expressed, on the one hand, as a deprivation of liberty exercised in the same manner on all members of the society and, on the other hand, as the rehabilitation of individuals. In contrast to formal equality and symmetrical contractual obligations suggested by the juridical form, the disciplinary content—delinquency—excludes reciprocity and institutes in its place asymmetries of domination and the hierarchical classification of isolated individuals. Thus, disciplinary power institutes a new mode of articulation by "parasitically" usurping the juridical form for the expression of new content (delinquency) that is not only incompatible with the law but functions as a "counter-law" (*DP*, 224). What we encounter in *Discipline and Punish* is not only a disjunction between visibility and articulation but also a rift within discourse itself, that is, the noncoincidence of institutionalized content (delinquency as a pathological mode of being) and juridical forms (forms of exchange and contract). These rifts are both the condition of the actualization of power within historical formation and, as Foucault's example of prison revolts suggests, the possibility of resistance.

For Deleuze what brings the forms of visibility and discourse into contact and enables their mutual capture and combinations in various types of knowledge is the Foucauldian concept of power as "an immanent dispersed cause." Even though Deleuze stresses the immanence of cause (power relations) in the sociohistorical field, he presupposes neither continuity nor calculability of causes and effects. The realization of cause (power) within the institutional framework and within specific formations of knowledge accomplishes, on the one hand, an integration of force relations that otherwise remain "unbalanced, heterogeneous, unstable" and without form (*HS*, I:93). Yet, on the other hand, this process of integration is also a differential splitting into the visible and articulable forms of knowledge. In other words, cause can be realized only by splitting and doubling the form of its realization: "Things can be realized only through doubling or dissociation. . . . Between the visible and the articulable a gap or disjunction opens up . . . where the informal diagram [of forces] is swallowed up and becomes embodied instead in two different directions that are necessarily divergent and irreducible" (*F*, 38).

What emerges from Deleuze's reading of Foucault is the contrast between forces (potentiality) and forms of power/knowledge (the actualized power relations), evocative, despite Deleuze's protests to the contrary, of the Nietzschean inflection of Heidegger's distinction between Being and beings. In this sense, as Maurice Blanchot remarks, the actualization of power proceeds not only through the doubling of visible and articulable form but also through the withdrawal of force, which in itself is neither visible nor articulable. This excess or withdrawal of force from the visible and articulable forms that it produces and in which it is actualized constitutes a certain "outside" of the historical formation. Forces, as Foucault puts it, constitute "moving substrate" of the states of power—substrate which are never accessible in themselves but constitute "power's condition of possibility" (*HS*, I:93). The relation to this outside is a condition not only of resistance but also of the emergence of a new configuration of power. Thus, although it is correct to say that in the disciplinary society power relations dominate the entire social field, I argue that the withdrawal of force constitutes an outside of that field as the possibility of resistance.

In the end, I would like to suggest briefly certain parallels between Deleuze's and Blanchot's concept of the outside as the irreducible residue of social formation and Judith Butler's notion of "the psychic remainder" in her recent study of the psychic life of power. It seems to me that the withdrawal of force in the process of its historical realization indeed leaves the remainder on the level of subject formation. Thus, although it is important to stress that the outside of the historical formation does not have a psychic status, the withdrawal of force does explain why historically constituted subjects can, in Judith Butler's words, be "nevertheless haunted by an inassimilable remainder, a melancholia that marks the limits of subjectivation."[29] To put it differently, there can be a limit to subjectivation only because the social "life of power" itself is marked and redoubled by what cannot be assimilated in the process of its actualization.

The crucial question for the feminist ethics of dissensus is how this notion of resistance is linked to embodiment. I am particularly interested in the consequence of the split between the visible and the articulable for the historical constitution of bodies. Indebted, as Elizabeth Grosz argues, to Nietzsche's "physiological investigation" of the origin of morality and the social contract in the body inscribed by pain,[30] Foucault not only presents the body as the location of historical struggles but changes the very notion of bodily subjection: the subjection of the body "is not only obtained by instruments of violence or ideology; it can also be direct, physical, pitting force against force, bearing on material elements and yet without involving violence."[31] Neither violence (acting through the destruction of a body) nor ideology (acting on the level of consciousness), disciplinary power establishes within bodies a specific relation of force. In "Nietzsche, Genealogy, History," Foucault generalizes the effects of power in terms of "inscription" so that the body can indeed be defined as "the inscribed surface of events," "totally imprinted by history" (NGH, 148). Although feminist critics from Susan Bordo, Elizabeth Grosz, and Judith Butler to Naomi Zack have found the political investment of racial and sexed bodies by power relations one of the most productive aspects of Foucault's work, few have attempted to problematize such "investment" in the context of the possible disjunction between visible and articulable bodies.

By analyzing the disjunction between different modalities of bodily materialization in Foucault's work, I want to complicate, on the one hand, Claude Lefort's famous thesis about the disincorporation of power in democracy and, on the other, to account for the possibility of resistance and transformation of power relations on the level of bodies. Lefort argues in *The Political Forms of Modern Society* that democracy dissolves the corporeality of power and, in so doing, exposes both the indetermination of the subject and the antagonistic character of social relations. Unlike the ancien régime, where political power is incarnated in the double body of the king, power in democracy is instituted as an empty place, impossible to occupy.[32] Referring to Nietzsche's location of the origins of social contracts in the subjugation of bodies, Foucault, however, is rather skeptical about the disincorporation of power in a democratic regime. Although he gives in the figure of panopticism his own analysis of the institutionalization of the empty place of power, he argues that what corresponds to such an empty place is not only the intensification of the disciplinary regulation of bodies but also the emergence of biopower focused on the administration of life of the population. As Judith Butler points out, for Foucault the emergence of modern biopower is inseparable from the formation of matter, which she calls "the process of materialization": "Here the body is not an independent materiality that is invested by power relations external to it, but it is that for which materialization and investiture are coextensive."[33] This notion of embodiment as the materialization of power makes it impossible to conceive of either ethics or democratic politics transcending racial and sexed bodies.

Drawing on Foucault's model of disciplinary power, feminist critics and critical race theorists have analyzed contemporary technologies of the normalization of racial and sexed bodies ranging from fashion, diet, and fitness regimes to plastic surgery and reproductive technologies. As Susan Bordo suggests, the disciplinary ascetic ideal manifests itself in popular feminine culture as an infinitely "malleable," perfectible "plastic body"—a body divided into "target zones," each submitted to different regimes of exercise, makeup, or corrective surgery.[34] Although, as Stoller, Young, and Moore in different ways point out,[35] Foucault himself did not analyze the materialization of racialized bodies, his argument that biopower invests sexuality through "race and its relation to the discourses of health, progeny, the future of the species, and the vitality of the social body" opens such possibility.[36] As Naomi Zack argues, this Foucauldian assumption enables genealogical research on "the sexualization of black race."[37] By drawing on Fanon's discussion of the racial epidermal schema in the context of Foucault's work, Darrell Moore argues, however, that the formation of racialized male sexuality occurs not through discourse but through the visibility of difference ultimately "located in the Black man's penis and his color."[38] In fact, Moore's discussion of the construction of racialized bodies against the norm of whiteness suggests another modality of materialization, where racialized sexuality is produced through "visualization" and the technology of the white gaze rather than through the incitement to speech.[39]

Yet, although power relations in democratic regimes are not external to bodies, this does not mean that the materialization of bodies is a uniform process, coextensive with "discursive intelligibility." What I would like to suggest, therefore, is that resistance and transformation of power is enabled by different modalities of materialization—a problem Butler herself poses but does not pursue in terms of Foucault's work: "We need to ask," Butler writes, "whether there are *modalities* of materialization—as Aristotle suggests, and Althusser is quick to cite."[40] By juxtaposing *Discipline and Punish* and *The History of Sexuality*, vol. I, I propose two such modalities, implied by the difference between visible and discursive bodies, corresponding, however imperfectly, to the deployment of disciplines and the deployment of sexuality. In contrast to the discourse-sex-power alignment in the first volume of

*The History of Sexuality*, an alignment that culminates in the intensification of pleasure and in the incitement to discourse, Foucault makes clear that the disciplinary regime acting on the body is not concerned with the signification of the body but rather with its form of visibility—with "anatomo-chronological schema of behavior": "It was not or no longer *the signifying elements* of behavior or the language of the body, but the economy, the efficiency of movements . . . ; constrain bears upon *the forces rather than upon the signs*" (*DP*, 137, emphasis added).

The comparison of *The History of Sexuality* and *Discipline and Punish* suggests, therefore, that within the regime of biopower the process of materialization, which is nonviolent and yet "remains of a physical order," proceeds in different but interrelated ways: through disciplinary forms of visibility, aiming at the control of the productive forces of the body, and through putting sex into discourse, enabling the organization of power over life. In *The History of Sexuality*, Foucault remarks on the difference between these two different technologies of power in the following way:

Starting in the seventeenth century, this power over life evolved in two basic forms. . . . One of these poles . . . centered on the body as machine: its disciplining . . . all this was ensured by the procedures of power that characterized the *disciplines*: an *anatomo-politics of the human body*. The second, formed somewhat later, focused on the species body, the body imbued with the mechanics of life and serving as the basis of biological process. . . . Their supervision was effected through an entire series of interventions and *regulatory controls; a biopolitics of the population*. (*HS*, I:139)

What this passage implies is not only the contrast between individual and collective bodies but also a disjunction between two types of materialization: between the docile and disciplined body, on the one hand, and the discursive sexed body, on the other. Rather than functioning as "an incitement to discourse" and intensification of pleasure, the specific forms of visibility Foucault describes—the isolated bodies fixed in cellular space and subjected to continuous observation and evaluation of their performance—invest the productivity of the body. In contrast to the eroticization of the apparatus of power, which, as Judith Butler suggests, might constitute the possibility of resistance, the reification of bodily forces into socially useful capacities dissociates the body from its political power and eventually "reverses" its active forces into reactive forces of submission.

By stressing different modalities of materialization, I argue that feminist ethics aims not only to diagnose the disciplining of racial and sexed bodies but also to approach the body as "the locus of the dissociation" of the subject, as "the volume in perpetual disintegration" (*NGH*, 148). Furthermore, the fracture between different modalities of materialization makes it possible to link the materiality of the body invested with the different types of power to the notion of event, which Foucault defines as a reversal of forces or the emergence of the new configuration of power. In "The Discourse on Language" Foucault associates the event with a dispersion of matter:

An event is neither substance, nor accident, nor quality nor process; events are not corporeal. And yet, an event is certainly not immaterial; it takes effect, becomes effect, always on the level of materiality. Events have their place . . . it occurs as an effect of, and in, material dispersion. Let us say that the philosophy of event should advance in the direction of . . . an incorporeal materialism. (DL, 231)

As the paradoxical formulation of "incorporeal materialism" suggests, "matter" is figured here as the actualization of the specific relation between forces. Such an event of materialization precedes the distinctions between matter and form, and thus is irreducible to the corporeal as a permanently formed substance. Consequently, what is at stake in a redefinition of materialization is the possibility that bodies can undergo "the reversal of a relationship of forces" (NGH, 154). This notion of the event seems at first at odds with the materialization of bodies, described in *Discipline and Punish* and *The History of Sexuality*, where, as Grosz claims, the body seems to be merely a medium "on which power operates and through which it functions."[41] However, if power is actualized in bodies according to multiple modalities, which, despite numerous interconnections, do not constitute a unified bodily form, then the process of materialization is never complete or uniform. Because of this structural incompletion and heterogeneity, the formation of matter is open to the reversal of forces. This is what Foucault underscores when he defines bodies as "volumes in disintegration." When considered in the context of the event, the dispersion of matter does not entail a violent destruction of the body but rather opens a possibility of yet another reversal of forces, so that the intensification of pleasure or the increased productivity no longer, and not always, results in "the strict political subjection" we came to associate with docility.

Let me add that only by taking into account bodies as surfaces of events, can we make sense of what otherwise might appear as the incomprehensible contrast between docile bodies produced by the disciplinary apparatus and the body in the state of revolt, evoked in Foucault's description of prison revolts. It is important to recall at this point that the brief evocation of the prison revolts frames the entire historical project of *Discipline and Punish*: "In recent years, prison revolts have occurred throughout the world. . . . In fact, they were revolts, at the level of the body, against the very body of the prison" (*DP*, 30). As this passage suggests, Foucault is not only tracing the historical processes enabling us to understand the modes of subjection but also a possibility of resistance, understood as the reversal of forces, at the level of the bodies. I argue that this notion of resistance articulated through the body—a resistance that "divides our emotions, dramatizes our instincts, multiplies our body and sets it against itself"—is crucial for the feminist ethics of dissensus and democratic politics.

The possibility of such an ethics is disregarded, however, when feminist criticism ignores the multiple modalities of materialization in contemporary culture and focuses exclusively on the production of docile bodies. As Hilary Radner suggests, a more productive approach to resistance would focus on the disjunctions and contradictions in the production of the feminine body: "Neither a model of cultural production formulated in terms of penology ( . . . docile body), nor in terms of sexuality (the culture of the self ), is adequate to the formulation of . . . the feminine body. The feminine body is perhaps best understood as a terrain in which these two modes of cultural production both contradict and support each other."[42] This mode of analysis not only foregrounds ambiguities between agency and subjugation but also "offers a model of resistance that does not fall back on some form of repressive hypothesis."[43]

## The Genealogical Critique of the Modern Soul: Radical Finitude, Subjectivity, and Resistance

How can we reconcile the "revolts at the level of bodies" that I want to reclaim for the feminist ethics of dissensus with another assertion of Foucault, namely, that disciplinary power reverses "the political axis of individualization"? This reversal means that in modernity individuality is no longer associated with sovereignty but instead with subjection and docility (*DP*, 193). In his conception of descending individuation, Foucault develops Nietzsche's diagnosis that the individuals presupposed by contract theory are in fact produced through disciplinary training: "The right to make promises evidently embraces and presupposes as a preparatory task that one first *makes* men to a certain degree necessary, uniform, like among like, regular, and consequently *calculable*."[44] Since in modern culture individuality ceases to be synonymous with exceptional subjects and becomes associated instead with calculability, classification, and subjection, resistance can no longer be based on the liberation of identity, self-knowledge, or the claims for recognition. Consequently, to articulate an alternative model of resistance for feminist ethics, we have to radicalize the finitude and the dispersion of the subject: as Foucault puts it, the aim of resistance is "not to discover the roots of our identity but to commit itself to its dissipation" (NGH, 162).

As a way of reconciling the incompatible claims about revolt and subjection, I would like to suggest that the thesis of individualizing subjection is a genealogical reworking of Foucault's earlier analysis of finitude in *The Order of Things*. The crucial topos of finitude emerging in the nineteenth century postulates that the subject is determined by the historical forces of labor, life, and language. Since these determinations appear to be not only exterior but also anterior to the birth of the subject, they cannot be recovered in the analysis of experience or self-knowledge. Thus, the historicity of labor, life, and language separates the modern subject from her origin, which remains inaccessible and alien. For Foucault, the Marxist notion of alienation or the psychoanalytic theory of the unconscious are two different ways to thematize the radicality of this separation. No longer contemporaneous with what determines her, the modern subject is split between being and language, the unthought and the thought, the same and the other. Yet, this modern thought of finitude and the historicity of life, labor, and language is not radical enough because it is still governed by the reclaiming of origin as the site of the lost truth of the subject. Motivated by the telos of recognition, modern historicism is grounded in the figure of the self-reflective subject aiming to recover the always already lost truth of its past. Unlike the thought of the outside, the historical will to knowledge aims at the impossible conversion of "the unthought" into "the same": "More fundamentally, modern thought is advancing toward that region where man's Other must become the Same as himself."[45]

For Foucault the critique of the origin and self-reflexivity goes hand in hand with the critique of the soul animating historical knowledge. As he writes, "The historian's history finds its support outside of time and pretends to base its judgments on an apocalyptic objectivity. This is only possible, however, because of its belief in eternal truth, *the immortality of the soul*" (NGH, 152). Despite the discovery of the "radical spatiality of the body," history motivated by the ethos of recognition and the search for origin in fact resembles a project of a metaphysician that "would seek its soul in the distant ideality of the origin" (NGH, 145). No longer seeking the lost truth of the subject in the ever-receding origin, Foucault's historical genealogy of disciplinary biopower (in place of the historicity of labor and life) radicalizes the finitude of the subject and, in so doing, liberates "divergence" within its fictional identity: "Where the soul pretends unification or self fabricates the coherent identity" (NGH, 145), genealogical research "introduces discontinuity into our very being as it divides our emotions, dramatizes our instincts, multiplies our body and sets it against itself" (NGH, 154).

Perhaps now we are in a better position to understand why the ethos of resistance has to engage a genealogical critique of the modern soul. In a very Nietzschean passage, Foucault argues that the appearance of the moral conscience (soul) as a new object of punishment at the beginning of the nineteenth century is but an effect produced by the new disciplinary technologies of the body: "It would be wrong to say that the soul is an illusion, or an ideological effect. On the contrary, it exists, it has a reality, it is produced permanently around, on, within the body by the functioning of power that is exercised on those punished" (*DP*, 29). No other passage has produced more misunderstanding in Foucault feminist criticism than the one I just cited. Lois McNay, for instance, reads this passage as a "problematic inversion of Cartesian body/soul dualism," substituting the concept of the body for the concept of the person.[46] Even Judith Butler, who most rigorously defends the possibility of agency in Foucault's work, argues in *The Psychic Life of Power* that Foucault "appears to treat the subject as if it received unilaterally the effect of the Lacanian symbolic."[47] Yet, what is at stake in the critique of the soul is not the evacuation of the psyche but, as I will argue in my interpretation of Kristeva and Irigaray, a mode of intervention equivalent to the traversal of fantasy consolidating the imaginary and the symbolic identifications of the subject. In both cases, such an intervention foregrounds the finitude and dispersion of the subject—what Kristeva calls the negativization of the narcissistic ego. Indeed, as Foucault writes, genealogy "makes one 'happy, unlike the metaphysicians, to possess in oneself not an immortal soul but many mortal ones.' And in . . . these souls, history will not discover a forgotten identity eager to be reborn, but a complex system of distinct and multiple elements, unable to be mastered by the powers of synthesis" (NGH, 161).

Like the political function of fantasy, the soul not only unifies multiple fissures within modern subjectivity but also sustains the misrecognition of subjection as freedom. By diagnosing the appearance of the soul in terms of a confusion of causes and effects, Nietzsche, as Grosz points out, presents the soul as "the inwardly inflected, thwarted will to power that . . . has sought to subdue itself"[48]: "The subject (or to use a more popular expression, the *soul*) has perhaps been believed in hitherto more firmly than anything else on earth because it makes possible to the majority of mortals . . . the sublime self-deception that interprets weakness as freedom."[49] Although Foucault fails to analyze the relation between fantasy and power relations, he comes closest to indicate the political function of fantasy when, after the discussion of the eroticization of power, he compares the noncorporal soul with the speculative character of sex: "over the centuries it [sex] has become more important than our soul, more important almost than our life" (*HS*, I:156). I will discuss the relation between fantasy and power at great length in Chapters 4 and 6; for now I want to point out that fantasy, like the speculative character of sex, not only coordinates the desire of the subject but also compensates for the instability of its imaginary and symbolic identifications.[50] Insofar as it is constructed as a fictitious unity of anatomy, sensation, instinct, and meaning, or as a principle of our existence, the phantasmatic character of sex makes it possible to link together knowledge, liberation, and pleasure.

Similarly to the speculative function of sex, the soul imprinted on delinquency privatizes and separates illegality from social and political struggles with which it was still potentially linked at the end of the eighteenth century. In so doing, the soul, like sex, becomes the effective instrument of the management of collectivity. As Foucault writes, "On the horizon of these illegal practices . . . there emerged struggles of a strictly political kind . . . a good many of them were able to turn themselves to account in overall political struggles and sometimes even to lead directly to them" (DP, 273–74). As a principle of subjection of individuals, the phantasmatic soul disarms the transgression of the law, separates it from social and political struggles, and turns it into a secret in need of confession or a case of the privatized pathology in need of moral reformation.

For Nietzsche, the soul is the principle of subjection in yet another sense: by sustaining the fiction of the transcendent subject behind the relations of forces, it subjects the individuals to the condemning judgment of good and evil.[51] Foucault examines the complicity between subjection and moral valuation in his diagnosis of the mutation of liberal rights discourse into norms. Because of this mutation, liberal rights, as Wendy Brown suggests, become for Foucault a site of disciplinary regulation: "Contemporary discourses of rights converge with the disciplinary production of identities seeking them" so that rights claims become "a method of administering" modern individuals.[52] Representing a strange "mixture of legality and nature, prescription and constitution," norms refer not only to the legal set of rules and rights but also to the ideal moral nature of the individual or to the prescribed level of the aptitudes of the body. This "double juridico-natural reference" of the norm translates the knowledge of the character and the aptitudes of the body into the domain of moral valuation of individuals. Since for Foucault the normalizing judgment is itself an expression of disciplinary power, it cannot be deployed to evaluate this power, to distinguish between its legitimate and illegitimate uses. Thus, the feminist scholars, who, like Nancy Fraser, claim that Foucault fails to elaborate alternative normative criteria, miss the main point of Foucault's genealogical critique: for Foucault normative criteria themselves need to be interrogated in terms of power relations.[53]

As we have seen, the critique of the soul reveals a complicity between the historical will to knowledge, fantasy consolidating identity, and the disciplinary formation of moral conscience. The trope of the soul, and by extension, the speculative (phantasmatic) character of sex, functions as both the principle of subjugation of individuals and the unacknowledged ascetic ideal animating the historical will to truth (NGH, 158). These parallels among modern historicism grounded in the figure of the self-reflective subject, the formation of moral conscience, and the soul are likewise an effect of a certain reflective turn of the reactive forces of punishment upon the subject.[54] In her reading of Hegel, Nietzsche, and Freud, Judith Butler has identified the figure of self-reflective recoil as the main trope of subjugation. In commenting on this paradoxical figure that makes it impossible to distinguish between the inward turn of will and the interiorization of the external forces of punishment, Butler points out that "a will that takes itself as its own object and, through the formation of that kind of reflexivity, binds itself to itself, acquires its own identity through reflexivity" remains in fact in the service of disciplinary regulation.[55] What is at stake, therefore, in the critique of the soul is a possibility of resistance, that is, an overcoming of this subjugating reflexivity operating in both morality and history. By radicalizing the topos of finitude, by dissociating genealogy from the search for lost origins and "the consoling play of recognition," this ethos of resistance gives the figure of self-recoil one more turn so that it initiates its own overcoming. This is yet another sense in which his critique of the soul follows Nietzsche: "All great things bring about their own destruction through an act of self-overcoming."[56]

The possibility of overcoming the subjugating self-reflexivity emerges from the intensification of the divergence within the subject. What Foucault stresses in *Discipline and Punish* is not only a dissociation within the subject but also the internal antagonism among different subject positions "superimposed" one upon the other: "The correlative of penal justice may well be the offender, but the correlative of the penitentiary apparatus is *someone other*; this is a delinquent . . . representing a type of anomaly. . . . This penitentiary element introduced in turn *a third character* between the individual who is condemned by the law and the individual who carries out this law" (*DP*, 254, emphasis added). If we compare this passage to the mechanism of interpellation, then we have to notice that the critique of the soul (or what I will discuss in Chapter 4 as the traversal of fantasy) exposes an essential failure of interpellation, namely, the failure to institute a coherent position of an addressee.[57] This is the case because the inverted law "hails" at least two incompatible "characters" at once: the juridical subject and the pathological individual. Unlike a juridical subject abstracted from any particularity and defined only in reference to general rights and obligations, this other character, the delinquent, constitutes a particular, pathological life-form—"a pathological gap in human species" (*DP*, 254). In Foucault's discussion there is no continuity between the juridical abstraction and the sequence of the particulars, a stuttering proliferation of "this" ("this anomaly, this deviation, this potential danger, this illness, this form of existence" [*DP*, 255]) characteristic of delinquency. Because of this noncoincidence, the "hailed individual" is always "elsewhere," in an eccentric relation to a position he or she occupies.[58]

This eccentric relation to a subject position one assumes means that the effect of the Foucauldian interpellation cannot be described in terms of the specular (mis)recognition Althusser deploys. One implication of such an ec-centric relation is, therefore, that the discursive constitution of subjects can-not be reduced to an imaginary relation of recognition—and this might be the most important consequence of the rift between visibility and articula-tion. In place of the imaginary recognition of individual subjects in the ab-solute Subject, Foucault deploys the trope of the parasite to indicate the de-centered and conflicting subjectivity behind the unifying function of the phantasmatic soul. Not only the two incompatible forms of subjectivity (the juridical subject and the delinquent) coexist as the parasite and its host, but this parasitical symbiosis reveals retrospectively a prior split within the ju-ridical subject (*DP*, 256). Rather than reducing the problematic of modern subjectivity to ego formation or to a passive receptacle of power, the Foucauldian notion of resistance substantiates the Nietzschean "hypothesis," namely that "the assumption of one single subject is . . . unnecessary; per-haps it is just as permissible to assume a multiplicity of subjects, whose in-teraction and struggle is the basis of our thought and our consciousness in general?"[59]

I have consistently linked the disjunction between the forms of visibility and articulation, a disjunction I have been tracing both in the context of the materialization of bodies and the historical constitution of subjects, to the al-ternative notion of resistance, separated from the theme of self-recognition, truth, or liberation of the suppressed identities. Although it seems, as many feminist scholars point out, that *Discipline and Punish* precludes resistance, Foucault makes explicit that what motivates his project are prison revolts taking place in France in the early seventies. In the course of his study, he cites several other historical cases in which the contradictions in the struc-ture of interpellation and the modes of materialization, mobilized for the sake of resistance, politicize the crime. In the chapter "Illegalities and Delinquency" Foucault explicitly discusses the growing peasants' and work-ers' illegalities from the end of the eighteenth century to the Revolution of 1848 and the development of the complex political dimension of these ille-galities, which opposed law as an instrument of class domination: "A whole series of illegalities was inscribed in struggles in which those struggling knew that they were confronting both the law and the class that had imposed it" (*DP*, 274). In this context Foucault cites a rather minor and isolated case from August 1840 involving a thirteen-year-old delinquent. This incident was picked up and discussed extensively by *La Phalange* journal associated with the Fourierists, who in their antipenal polemics attempted to give the crime a positive political value:

He would have certainly passed without trace, had he not opposed to the discourse of the law that made him delinquent (in the name of the disciplines, even more than in the terms of the code) the discourse of an illegality that remained resistant to these coercions and which revealed indiscipline in a systematically ambiguous manner as the disordered order of society and as the affirmation of inalienable rights. . . . Confronted with discipline on the face of the law, there is illegality, which puts itself forward as a right; it is indiscipline, rather than the criminal offence, that causes the rupture. (*DP*, 290–91)

This anonymous delinquent, conjured by Foucault from the pages of the workers' press, exploits so skillfully the contradictions within the structure of disciplinary interpellation precisely at a point where law is inverted into counterlaw, and the juridical into the natural. He pits the delinquency against the law and the law against delinquency, by affirming "indiscipline," through the discredited language of the law, as a political right.

The fact that the workers' press picked up such a minor affair is for Foucault indicative of the possibilities of resistance against the disciplinary regime. The commentaries that followed in *La Phalange*, and which Foucault cites extensively, seized upon the double "juridical-natural" reference of disciplinary interpellation and gave it one more twist. In these antipenal polemics, immorality and pathology are removed from the discourse of nature and placed on the side of enslaving and normalizing civilization whereas nature and the "instinctive development," and not law, are affirmed as "immediate liberty" and inalienable right. In referring to these polemics, Foucault is obviously not interested in the Fourierist utopia proclaiming the abolition of the social restraints for the sake of instinctual gratification; what he finds in this, for him, rather atypical historical example is an inventive political strategy that manipulates and explodes fissures in modern subjectivities and in the structures of rights for the sake of resistance. For Foucault, *La Phalange* manages to politicize the polemics around the crime, to represent the problem of punishment as a political struggle rather than as a dilemma for a "humanitarian" reform. In repeating the tone of these polemics in his own study, Foucault finishes *Discipline and Punish* with a similar injunction: in the carceral city "we must hear the distant roar of the battle."

Given Foucault's account of the way liberal rights, mutated into norms, become a site of disciplinary regulation and a mode of administering of modern individuals, it might seem strange that the main example of resistance in *Discipline and Punish* is in fact mobilized by the rhetoric of rights. Is Foucault illustrating here a temptation, which he calls a "blind alley," of resisting the disciplinary power through the return to the liberal rights organized around the principle of sovereignty and the autonomy of the subject? Or is he providing here a concrete historical example of what he alluded to briefly at the end of "Two Lectures" as a "new form of right" mobilized in the struggle against the disciplinary power: "If one wants to look for a nondisciplinary form of power, or rather, to struggle against disciplines . . . it is not toward the ancient right of sovereignty that one should turn, but towards a possibility of a new form of right, one which must indeed be anti-disciplinarian, but at the same time liberated from the principle of sovereignty."[60] Elsewhere, Foucault not only affirms the importance of sexual rights for the gay movement but defines them as a new "relational rights" rather than "individual rights."[61] Since Foucault himself does not further elaborate this form of resistance associated with antidisciplinary rights separated from the liberal autonomous subject, I will pursue this possibility in the subsequent chapters by developing the performative politics of rights in the context of Claude Lefort's, Patricia Williams's, Emmanuel Levinas's, and Luce Irigaray's work. Let me suggest at this point that the separation of rights from the principle of sovereignty, subjective autonomy, and disciplinary power confronts us, as Lefort suggests, with a rethinking of rights and resistance in the context of the limits of the historical constitution of subjects.[62]

## Toward an Ethos of Becoming:
## An Aesthetic of Existence, Eroticism, and the
## Invention of the New Modes of Life

To articulate an ethics of dissensus it is not sufficient to diagnose the modalities of modern biopower and to theorize a new basis of resistance. As bell hooks reminds us, "Opposition is not enough. In that vacant space after one has resisted there is still the necessity to become—to make oneself anew. . . . That process emerges as one comes to understand how structures of domination work in one's life, as one develops critical thinking and critical consciousness, *as one invents new, alternative habits of being.*"[63] As bell hooks, Cornel West, Foucault, and Irigaray in different ways argue, the negative task of resistance has to be reconfigured into an experimental ethos of becoming, that is, into a creation of new modes of life, being, and eroticism.[64] This ethos of becoming is crucial, I argue, not only for a redefinition of ethics beyond the respect for the moral law but also for the conception of democratic struggles beyond the liberation of the repressed identities. Thus, what Foucault opposes to the ideology of liberation is not only resistance but also the experimental praxis emphasizing the creation of new ways of life:[65] "To be 'gay,'" he argues, "is not to identify with the psychological traits and the visible masks of the homosexual but to try to define and develop a way of life."[66] That is why Foucault links both the ethos of becoming and the democratic struggles with an aesthetics of existence, which approaches the relation to oneself not as a suppressed identity to be liberated or the secret truth of sex to be deciphered but as a refusal to "accept oneself as one is."

To elaborate the ethos of becoming, we have to adopt Foucault's dis-

tinction between morality, associated with the history of different moral systems and institutions that enforce them, and "ethics" referring to the work
of self-transformation subjects perform on themselves (*UP*, 29).[67] I argue
that this shift from moral law to the practices of the self allows us to rethink
the category of the performative in the context of the ethical rather than the
juridical model. In the juridical model, let us recall, the practices of the self
would aim at the approximation and the repetition of the sexual norm and,
in so doing, constitute the very identity of the subject and the moral law. In
her critique of this model of performativity, Butler brings together
Foucault's theory of power and the linguistic theory of the performative—a
theory that, as Derrida suggests, belongs more appropriately to a general
analysis of action rather than hermeneutics.[68] By connecting speech act theory with Foucault's analysis of power, Butler reformulates sexual and political identities as a performative effect of power relations and, in so doing,
contests both the stability of these identities and permanence of the law.[69]
Although Butler's theory provides a perceptive critique of the juridical
model of morality and its complicity with the hermeneutics of desire, this
critique does not take into account the Foucauldian alternative to the juridical model developed in his conceptions of sexual ethics. What we have
to ask, therefore, is how the category of the performative itself is complicated by the Foucauldian ethos of becoming. In a formulation that recalls
Nietzsche's perspectivism and Aristotle's *phronesis* (practical wisdom irreducible to theoretical knowledge since it deals with an ethical action whose
end cannot be determined in advance[70]), Foucault argues that in "ethics-ori-
ented moralities" the practices of the self are not so much concerned with
the approximation of the moral law as with the project of self-invention and
becoming. As he writes in a different context, the ethical self-relation implies that one does not "accept oneself as one is . . . ," but that one "take[s]
oneself as object of a complex and difficult elaboration" (WE, 41).[71] In contrast to the juridical model of subjectivation, Foucault refers to these ethical
practices as an aesthetic mode of existence: "What I mean by ['arts of existence'] . . . are those intentional and voluntary actions by which men not
only set themselves rules of conduct, but also seek to transform themselves,
to change themselves in their singular being, and to make their life into an
*oeuvre* that carries certain aesthetic values and meets certain stylistic criteria"
(*UP*, 10–11).

The distinction between juridical and ethical modes of subjectivation
does not imply, as Richard Wolin argues,[72] a replacement of normativity
based on rational principles by voluntarism or "decisionism" but is meant to
illustrate a mode of the regulation of acts based on a kind of a savoir-faire,
or what the Greeks call *phronesis*. Foucault illustrates this mode of regulation
in his analysis of Greek ethics. Obviously, Foucault does not intend to res-

urrect Greek ethics—certainly, not its ideal of the domination of oneself and others. As he emphatically claims, "The Greek ethics of pleasure is linked to a virile society, to dissymmetry, exclusion of the other, an obsession with penetration, and a kind of threat of being dispossessed of your own energy. . . . All that is quite disgusting!"[73] Nonetheless, if he is interested in the genealogy of sexual ethics in antiquity it is because he finds there an explicit formulation of the aesthetic regulation of ethical practice that is homologous, rather than opposed, to political praxis. Instead of the rigorous codification of forbidden acts, instead of the distinction between heterosexual and homosexual desires and the classification of individuals on the basis of their object choice, ancient ethics, Foucault argues, calls for an aesthetic regulation of action, where aesthetics enables the individual to regulate the use of pleasure (*chrēsis aphrodisiōn*) according to the variable circumstances such as needs, appropriateness of the moment, the social status of an individual, the health regimen of the body, and even climatic considerations. With its emphasis on the individuating and unforeseen elements of praxis, the Foucauldian "aesthetic regulation" of acts sounds like a certain recasting of the notion of *phronesis*, which is likewise irreducible to theoretical knowledge. Within a context of very few general principles, sexual acts and the diverse uses of pleasure in antiquity were guided by the "adjustment" of behavior—and we can hear in this term the echo of Heidegger's *Stimmung* (attunement)—to the variable circumstances rather than by the approximation to the norm or obedience to the universal law:[74] "The principle according to which this activity was meant to be regulated, 'the mode of subjection,' was not defined by a universal legislation determining permitted and forbidden acts; but rather by a *savoir-faire*, an art that prescribed the modalities of a use that depended on different variables" (*UP*, 91).

If the reiteration of the law through its repetitive approximations both aims and fails to universalize the principles of action, then the ethical use of pleasure, regulated according to *phronesis* in changing circumstances, calls for a certain individuation of the act: "In this form of morality, the individual did not make himself into an ethical subject by universalizing the principles that informed his action; on the contrary, he did so by means of an attitude and a quest that individualized his action, modulated it, and perhaps even gave him a special brilliance by virtue of the rational and deliberate structure his action manifested" (*UP*, 62). In the context of Foucault's analysis, the "quest" for an individualized action does not mean a pure expenditure of the subject's will transcending power relations; on the contrary, it implies a unique contextualization of action, a singular negotiation with the historically determined circumstances. Thus, in place of the subsumption of particular acts under the universal law—a subsumption that would fix or immobilize the range of perspectives or power relations—sexual acts, Foucault argues, are submitted to "complex stylizations of existence" within dietetics, economics, and courtship.

As neither the internalization of the moral codes nor the liberation of one's identity,[75] the ethical practice I would like to develop on the basis of Foucault's work establishes a new mode of relating to oneself—a new figure of reflexivity that would no longer perform the work of subjection to the disciplinary regime. In order to separate the ethical self-relation from the kind of subjugating reflexivity associated with the hermeneutics of desire, the knowledge of sexual identity, and the search for the ever-receding origin in the historicity of life, labor, and language, Foucault stresses not a liberation of identity but getting "free of oneself": "The relations we have to have with ourselves are not ones of identity, rather, they must be relationships of differentiation, of creation, of innovation."[76]

Yet, how can a relation to oneself that is derivative from the social framework nonetheless exceed this framework and achieve a certain irreducible singularity? According to Deleuze's interpretation of Foucault, what enables the surpassing of the socially constructed identities is the relation to the outside—to the limit of power/knowledge:

This is what the Greeks did: they folded force, even though it still remained force. They made it relate back to itself. Far from ignoring interiority, individuality or subjectivity they invented the subject, but only as a derivative or the product of a 'subjectivation.' . . . Foucault's fundamental idea is that of a dimension of subjectivity derived from power and knowledge without being dependent on them. (*F*, 101)

Similarly to Grosz's claim that the passage between the outside and the inside has to be reconfigured as "a kind of twisting or inversion,"[77] Deleuze interprets the relation to the self as the folded double of the outside. He asks, "Is there *an inside that lies deeper than any internal world,* just as the outside is farther away than any external world?" (*F*, 96). This question means that the relation to oneself is not just an interiorization of different forms of power/knowledge but also an inscription of the outside as their limit. "The outside" in question is thus what is excluded in the very process of actualization of power, namely, the not-yet-realized force. In his study of Blanchot, Foucault makes it clear that the outside is neither a position a subject can occupy nor the historically constituted positivity defining and limiting the subject from without but the void of the limit, "the ambiguous hollowness of undoing" and the new beginning (MB, 22, 25). It is through the relation to the outside as the limit of the historical formation, a limit that at the same time is a condition of possibility of the emergence of a new configuration of force, that the derivative character of self-relation achieves an irreducible singularity: "It is as if the relations of the outside folded back to create a doubling, allow a relation to oneself to emerge, and to constitute an inside which is hollowed out and develops its own unique dimension" (*F*, 100). Evocative of what Luce Irigaray describes as taking the negative upon oneself, this inscription of the outside within interiority is made possible by the dissociation between discourse and visibility, later radicalized by Foucault as the changing variables of the historical context.

The advantage of the Deleuzian reading of Foucault for feminist and queer studies is that it neither confuses the practices of the self with aesthetic voluntarism nor posits a continuous derivation between exteriority and interiority. What Deleuze disregards, however, is the significance of aesthetics, embodiment, and eroticism in Foucault's discussion of becoming. To develop a model of transformative praxis that engages both embodiment and aesthetics, I would like to juxtapose Foucault's dispersed reflections on art with Heidegger's interpretation of Nietzsche. What emerges from a fairly diffuse network of Foucault's repeated references to specific artists—Artaud, Baudelaire, Beckett, Blanchot, Borges, Cervantes, and Goya, among others[78]—is a certain affinity with the Nietzschean privileging of art as a counterforce to the decadent forms of religion, morality, and knowledge. Deleuze himself admits that "there is a final rediscovery of Heidegger" in late Foucault (*F*, 107). Foucault suggests, however, that the importance of Heidegger for his work can be dated much earlier: "It is possible that if I had not read Heidegger, I would have not read Nietzsche. I had tried to read Nietzsche in the fifties but Nietzsche alone did not appeal to me—whereas Nietzsche and Heidegger: that was a philosophical shock!"[79] There are at least three important aspects of Heidegger's interpretation of Nietzsche relevant for Foucault's reconfiguration of ethics as the aesthetics of existence. First, Heidegger interprets Nietzsche's aesthetics as the most familiar configuration of the will to power. For both Nietzsche and Foucault aesthetics in its larger sense would refer, then, not to a creation or a contemplation of the aesthetic object but to the contestation and invention of the modes of life, to "the basic occurrence of being." Second, the "aesthetics of existence" articulates a mode of self-relation that Heidegger defines as the rupture of identity manifesting itself as the feeling of rapture: "Rapture as a state of feeling explodes the very subjectivity of the subject . . . subject has already come out of himself; he is no longer subjective, no longer a subject."[80] I would like to suggest that this sense of rupture as a capacity to extend beyond oneself captures particularly well what Foucault means by the "attraction of the outside." As Foucault's literary analyses make clear, an aesthetic mode of "relatedness" does not suppress forces of dispersion, rupture, and conflict (the way the subjugating reflexivity of the soul does) but enables us to think a relation to oneself as the surpassing of the limit of the historically sedimented positionality and identity. Finally, as Nietzsche's emphasis on physiology suggests, aesthetic self-relation manifesting itself in the feeling of rapture is grounded in sexuality and embodiment. This does not mean, however, that rapture can be confused with either a blind biological state, or a frenzy of intoxication. As an aesthetic state, rapture provides a minimum of mediation between "explosion" and articulation, between the ecstatic pleasure and the invention of new forms. Evocative of the psychoanalytic concept of *jouissance*, rapture enables becoming at the edge of the disappearance of the identity of the subject.

A certain proximity between Foucault's experience of the outside and Heidegger's aesthetics of rapture can be seen already in Foucault's early essay on Blanchot, where he contrasts the dispersion of the subject with the self-reflexivity of knowledge. Inseparable from the function of a certain style, and thus from articulation, the experience of "the outside" is not limited to Blanchot's texts but is characteristic of the whole range of artistic practices frequently analyzed in Foucault's work: it is associated with Nietzsche's discovery of force, Mallarmé's staging of the subject's disappearance, Artaud's undoing of discourse through "the violence of the body," Bataille's transgression, or the experience of the double in the work of Klossowski and Roussel (MB, 17–18). Although Foucault refers here to the rather predictable modern experimental thinkers, he could have engaged a postcolonial writer like Frantz Fanon, who likewise associates political action with the invention of the new modes of life, with the introduction of "the real leap" into existence, with making "the impossible" possible: "In the world through which I travel, I am endlessly creating myself. I am part of Being to the degree that I go beyond it."[81] As both Fanon and Foucault in different ways argue, the aesthetic self-relation does not close the circle of self-reflexivity of the knowing subject but intensifies the force of dispersion and discordance within the subject—what Heidegger calls the surpassing of "the very subjectivity of the subject."

Referring neither to the interiority of the self nor even to the being of language, the aesthetic modality of relation opens the passage to pure exteriority—to the limit of history and signification:

> The event that gave rise to what we call "literature" in the strict sense is only superficially an interiorization; *it is far more a question of a passage to the "outside"*. . . . Literature is not language approaching itself until it reaches the point of its fiery manifestation; it is rather language getting as far from itself as possible. And if, in this setting "outside of itself," it unveils its own being, the sudden clarity reveals not a folding back but a gap, not a turning back of signs upon themselves but a dispersion. (MB, 11–12, emphasis added)

In Foucault's reading of Blanchot, the relation to the outside creates a "tear" within the most intimate interiority of the subject, so that the self-relation is at the same time an interruption of all relatedness. As an alternative to the subjugating self-reflexivity associated with knowledge and morality, the folding of the "I" back upon itself in Blanchot's texts does not refer to the speaking subject but paradoxically reveals "a language without an assignable subject," "a personal pronoun without a person." Like Nietzsche's state of rapture, the attraction of the outside—what the Lacanian psychoanalysis in a different register analyzes as the "real"—draws the subject out of itself. Both an infinite distance and unbearable nearness, the experience of the outside marks the continuous separation of the speaking I from its "spoken being": it "divests the interiority of its identity, hollows it out, divides it into non-coincident twin figures" (MB, 47). This intimate disjunction between the speaking and the spoken I, "this hollowness that is perhaps nothing more than the inexorable erosion of the person who speaks," opens a passage to the limit of language and experience. As Foucault writes, "The straight line separating the speaking *I* from the *he* he is in his spoken being . . . unfolds a placeless place that is outside all speech and writing" (MB, 52). Yet, it is this tear, or the separation of the self from its sedimented identity, that enables a redefinition of becoming and freedom from the liberation of identity to the continuous "surpassing" of oneself.[82]

How can we redefine the notion of praxis on the basis of this aesthetic modality of relatedness? In the well-known essay, "What is Enlightenment?," Foucault links the force of interruption associated with the experience of the outside with a critical ethos of modernity, where ethos is understood as "a mode of relating to contemporary reality . . . that at one and the same time marks a relation of belonging and presents itself as a task. A bit, no doubt, like what the Greeks called an *ethos*" (WE, 39). Through the juxtaposition of Baudelaire and Kant, the juxtaposition that interrogates the limitations of their respective positions, Foucault transforms the critical ethos of modernity into an experimental attitude enabling the practice of "freedom": "Baudelairean modernity is an exercise in which extreme attention to what is real is confronted with the practice of a liberty that simultaneously respects this reality and violates it" (WE, 41). I argue that such an experimental ethos is crucial for feminist ethics because it problematizes our belonging to the present, interrupts it, presents it as a task of transformation.

The possibility of such a recasting of the experience of the outside into an experimental praxis emerges from the critical negotiation with the limitation of philosophical and literary modernity, exemplified in the essay by the juxtaposition of Kant and Baudelaire. What Foucault wants to retrieve from Kant's philosophy is not his conception of the moral law but the negative attitude to the present, which understands "today" not in terms of the reiteration of history but in terms of the difference, or exit [*Ausgang*], from the past. Furthermore, Foucault wants to preserve the connection between this negative attitude and the public ethos of freedom. Yet, Kant's critical philosophy, which Foucault situates "at the crossroads of critical reflection and reflection on history," comes short of the ethos of freedom by drawing the necessary limitations of reason in order to assure its free and public use. By contrast, Baudelaire's ironic attitude to the present violates these limits and initiates a practice of transgression. In place of the liberation of being, such a practice imposes the task of becoming: "This modernity does not 'liberate man in his own being'; it compels him to face the task of producing himself" (WE, 42). However, unlike Kant's insistence on public freedom, Baudelaire's practice of transgression remains limited only to the separate sphere of aesthetics and private existence and thus cannot have a transfiguring effect on public and political life[83]: "This transfiguring play of freedom with reality, this ascetic elaboration of the self—Baudelaire does not imagine that these have any place in society itself, or in the body politic. They can only be produced in another, a different place, which Baudelaire calls art" (WE, 42). By playing Kant and Baudelaire against each other, Foucault wants to articulate a public ethos of freedom, a practice of transgression no longer limited to the separate sphere of art but aiming to transfigure "the body politic."

This traversal of the chiasmus of modern philosophy and aesthetics displaces the aesthetic relation to the outside—"this transfiguring play of freedom with reality"—into a practice of "possible transgression." Such a displacement entails, first, a transformation of the transcendental critique of knowledge into a practical critique of the historical conditions of experience and, second, a transformation of the critical ethos itself into an experimental attitude. For feminist ethics, the practical critique enables a "patiently documentary" reconstruction of the power/knowledge shaping subjectivity, while at the same time it problematizes the very notion of the historical conditions in the context of the "thought of the outside." This attention to the limits of the historical formation of knowledge and experience allows us to "separate out, from the contingency that made us what we are . . . the possibility of no longer being, doing, or thinking what we are, do, or think." Foucault writes:

Criticism indeed consists of analyzing and reflecting upon limits. But if the Kantian question was that of knowing what limits knowledge has to renounce transgressing, it seems to me that the critical question today has to be turned back into a positive one: in what is given to us as universal, necessary, obligatory, what place is occupied by whatever is singular, contingent, and the product of arbitrary constraints? The point, in brief, is to transform the critique conducted in the form of necessary limitation into a practical critique that takes the form of a possible transgression. (WE, 45)

Because of its relationship with aesthetics, the ethical problematization of experience does not stop with a critique of its historical conditions but also involves an experimental "attitude" aiming to surpass these historical determinations. As David Halperin suggests, it is "a capacity to 'realize oneself' by becoming other than what one is."[84]

Evoking "the mode of being at the frontiers" (WE, 45), the notion of praxis I develop is informed by both the critical ethos of genealogy and the experimental attitude of aesthetics. Based on the productive tension between genealogical critique of the historical limits of subjectivity and the aesthetics of existence aiming at their transgression, such an experimental praxis exceeds theoretical knowledge. As Cornel West similarly argues in his conception of prophetic criticism, in addition to historical diagnosis of domination, the political praxis also calls for "improvisational and flexible sensibilities that sidestep mere opportunism and mindless eclecticism."[85] It renounces, therefore, theoretical programs or global visions of the future but proceeds locally, by trial and error, to determine where change is possible and desirable:

The critical ontology of ourselves has to be considered not, certainly, as a theory, a doctrine, nor even as a permanent body of knowledge that is accumulating; it has to be conceived as an attitude, an ethos, a philosophical life in which the critique of what we are is at one and the same time the historical analysis of the limits that are imposed on us and *an experiment* with the possibility of going beyond them. (WE, 50, emphasis added)

Because it bears a relation to the outside, which is the experience of the limit of social regulation and thus of the historical constitution of subject, the experimental praxis cannot be simply reduced to a goal-oriented activity. On the contrary, the outcome of such an experimental praxis aiming to surpass the historical limits of bodies, language, and sexuality cannot be predicted in advance because it opens up a relation to a future that can longer be thought on the basis of the present. Similarly to Irigaray's politics of the impossible, Foucault's invention of the improbable stresses the radical futural dimension of praxis beyond the anticipation of the subject. "It's up to us to advance into a homosexual ascesis that would make us work on ourselves and invent—I do not say discover—a manner of being that is still improbable."[86] Thus, despite his emphasis on agency inherent in the practices of self, Foucault equally strongly argues that "no one is responsible for an emergence; no one can glory in it, since it always occurs in the interstice" (NGH, 150). This does not mean, however, that the question of agency is immaterial for Foucault but that it has to be rethought in the context of the futural aspect of the event, that is, the emergence of a different configuration of forces. The experimental ethos I propose is thus marked by the unresolvable tension between the agency and the notion of the event, which, understood as rupture, exceeds not only the current configurations of power but also the intentionality of the subject. It is this tension that enables the creation of the new forms of life—new modalities of pleasure, new modes of relations, new ways of being—beyond the present limitations.

Such an experimental praxis is crucial for a redefinition of contemporary democratic struggles beyond the liberation of the repressed identities. As both Leo Bersani and David Halperin argue, for Foucault the ideology of liberation, in particular, the ideology of sexual liberation, is complicitous with the regime of disciplinary power.[87] That is why Foucault argues that he distrusts "the tendency to relate the question of homosexuality to the problem of 'Who am I?' and 'What is the secret of my desire?' Perhaps it would be better to ask oneself, 'What relations, through homosexuality, can be established, invented, multiplied, and modulated?' The problem is not to discover in oneself the truth of one's sex. . . . Therefore we have to work at becoming homosexuals and not be obstinate in recognizing that we are."[88] Foucault extends this distrust to all forms of identity politics and argues that democratic struggles should be organized around the ethos of becoming and the invention of new modes of life instead of calling for the recognition or "liberation" of the sedimented identities complicitous with modern power. This emphasis on the overcoming of historically constituted identities and on the creation of new modes of life beyond their present limitations makes it possible to redefine the notion of freedom presupposed in democratic struggles. In this context, freedom no longer means the attribute or the possession of the subject but instead signifies an experimental praxis aiming to invent the still improbable modes of being: "I emphasize practices of freedom over processes of liberation. . . . This ethical problem of the definition of practices of freedom, it seems to me, is much more important than the rather repetitive affirmation that sexuality or desire must be liberated."[89]

As a crucial aspect of the feminist ethics of dissensus, the experimental ethos can be separated neither from political praxis nor from eroticism, embodiment, and pleasure. Indeed, if ethics is to intervene in modern power relations that operate on the level of the *bios*, it also has to be conceptualized on that level. As Foucault writes, "The idea of the *bios* as a material for an aesthetic piece of art is something that fascinates me. The idea also that ethics can be a very strong structure of existence, without any relation with the juridical per se" (GE, 260). That is why he finds the Nietzschean "extreme" formulation of aesthetics, based on the intensification and cultivation of the body and pleasure rather than soul or spirituality, particularly suggestive. As he writes in a tone surprising for him, sexuality is "a part of our world freedom. Sexuality is something that we ourselves create—it is our own creation."[90] In a similar way, Heidegger writes that "Nietzsche's mediation on art is 'aesthetics' because it examines the state of creation and enjoyment. It is the 'extreme' aesthetics inasmuch as that state is pursued to the farthest remove from the spirit, from the spirituality of what is created, and from the formalistic lawfulness."[91] As Nietzsche's emphasis on the physiology of aesthetics suggests, rapture is intertwined, on the one hand, with the intensification of the bodily pleasure and, on the other, with form, creation, and articulation. In *Twilight of Idols* (a fragment that Heidegger cites and extensively comments upon), Nietzsche writes that aesthetic self-relation depends on the intensification of bodily pleasure and, specifically, on "the rapture of sexual arousal, the oldest and the most original form of rapture."[92]

As a mode of self-relation grounded in embodiment, the aesthetics of rapture not only opens an alternative to the subjugating reflexivity associated with the fabrication of the soul, the speculative character of sex, and the search for origins but also reformulates "the attraction of the outside" in the context of eroticism. Although Foucault does not distinguish between pleasure and *jouissance*, this erotic "attraction of the outside," manifesting itself as "the explosion" of the identity of the subject, is much closer to what Leo Bersani calls the "self-shattering" gay *jouissance*, or "homo-ness,"[93] than to ego-consolidating pleasure. Both Bersani's gay *jouissance* and Foucault's erotic experience of the outside "make the subject unfindable as an object of discipline."[94] For Foucault, however, "the self-shattering" intensity of gay *jouissance* not only interrupts the disciplinary power's hold on the body but also opens a possibility of an invention of the alternative, unpredictable forms of existence: "One could perhaps say that there is a 'gay style' or at least that there is an ongoing attempt to recreate a certain style of existence, a form of existence or an art of living which might be called gay" (SC, 292). Like Nietzsche's dual emphasis on ecstatic rapture and articulation, the Foucauldian experimental ethos of queer eroticism—what he calls "a whole new art of sexual practice" (SC, 298)—involves both rupture and improvisation. Just as political practice is characterized by the creative tension between the event and agency, so too "sexual experimentation" leads not only to the disruption of the subject but also to reconfiguration of subjective and social forms of life. Tim Dean makes a similar point when he stresses the restructuring moment following the ego-shattering experience of gay *jouissance*.[95] We can see this tension between rupture, improvisation, and reconstruction in Foucault's description of the practices of S/M:[96]

What interests the practitioners of S&M is that the relationship is at the same time regulated and open. It resembles a chess game in the sense that one can win and the other lose. . . . This mixture of rules and openness has the effect of intensifying sexual relations by introducing a perpetual novelty, a perpetual tension and a perpetual uncertainty which the simple consummation of the act lacks. (SC, 299)

When considered in the light of the historical materialization of power relations in bodies, this experimentation—"the mixture of rules and . . . uncertainty"—not only aims at the intensification of pleasure but also at the reversal of forces on the level of the body. As an experience of the limit and an interruption of the historical determination of the body and sexual identity, sexual ethics not only dissociates eroticism from political subjection but also opens "a possibility for creative life."[97] What is thus at stake in the shift from the speculative character of sex to the experimental character of gay eroticism is not only a pure experience of rupture but an invention of "a manner of being that is still improbable" (FWL, 137).

Foucault associates this experimental ethics in a strong way with gayness not only because he is concerned with the specificity of gay eroticism and the invention of the gay lifestyles on its basis but also because such an invention challenges both the marginalized position of homosexuality and larger network of social relations: "Homosexuality is a historic occasion to reopen affective and relational virtualities, not so much through the intrinsic qualities of the homosexual but because the 'slantwise' position of the latter, as it were, the diagonal lines he can lay out in the social fabric allow these virtualities to come to light" (FWL, 138). This project to bring out new affective and relational possibilities, to invent modes of life that are still improbable, is not limited therefore to "private" erotic relations but, as we have seen, is an integral part of gay politics: "What a gay movement needs now is much more the art of life than a science . . . of what sexuality is."[98] By stressing the importance of experimental eroticism in imagining "the world differently from what it is at present," Darrell Moore extends the Foucauldian insight and claims that "the reconceptualization of sexuality is necessary to practices of antiracism; especially given the importance of sexuality in the practice of racism."[99] In anticipation of Irigaray's "politics of the impossible," Kristeva's discussion of "new imaginary," and bell hooks's emphasis on the improvisational qualities of multiracial democratic politics, I would extend this insight even further and argue that connection between eroticism and the experimental practice is also a crucial part of feminist, antiracist politics.

I would like to end my reflections on the sexual ethos of becoming with "what is most 'difficult' in the work of . . . Foucault: the least resolved, the most open"[100]—namely, the problematic of friendship. This problematic shifts the emphasis from the transformation of the historical forms of life to the ethical relations with others. Foucault not only consistently argues that the development of the alternative ways of gay life is intertwined with the invention of the "polymorphic" erotic and social relations but in fact claims that what makes homosexuality most disturbing to the homophobic culture is not the sexual act itself but the possibility of the new modalities of friendships and love. By asking the ethical question about "what relations, through homosexuality, can be established, invented, multiplied and modulated,"

Foucault suggests that gay ethics tends toward the problematic of friendship. In so doing, he contests the separation of friendship from erotic relations in Greek ethics and the sexual solitude in Christian ethics. As he points out, "It's very significant that when Plato tries to integrate love for boys and friendship, he is obliged to put aside sexual relation. . . . If you look at Plato, reciprocity is very important in a friendship, but you can't find it on the physical level; one of the reasons why they [the Greeks] needed a philosophical elaboration in order to justify this kind of love was that they could not accept a physical reciprocity" (GE, 257–58). In order to integrate friendship and eroticism, Foucault argues that gay sexual ethics would have to address not only the alterity of the other but, more specifically, "the pleasure of the other": "Is the pleasure of the other something that can be integrated in our pleasure, without a reference either to law, to marriage, to I don't know what?" (GE, 258). Although Foucault never develops the explicit ethical model of the sexual relations, his attempt to bring together eroticism and friendship does suggest that the nonappropriative encounter with the Other cannot be theorized apart from embodiment, sexuality, and pleasure.

This shift of emphasis from the becoming of the subject to the pleasure of the Other raises a host of provocative questions about the possible connections between "the attraction to outside" and the attraction to the Other, between the ecstatic rupture of the subjective identity and the traumatizing impact of alterity, between the practices of the self and the responsibility for the Other. Foucault never answers these questions because to do so would require him to renegotiate the ethos of becoming in the context of the ethics of alterity. To follow these questions further, and thus to move beyond a certain limitation of the Foucauldian ethics, I will pursue intersections between the ethos of becoming and the ethos of responsibility in the context of Lyotard's, Irigaray's, and hooks's work.

. . .

In this chapter I have articulated the ethos of becoming as a crucial aspect of the ethics of dissensus. I have elaborated this ethos first as the negative but necessary task of resistance to modern forms of disciplinary power and, second, as the positive project of the transformation of subjective identities and social forms of life. I have argued that this ethos not only intervenes in the existing power relations but also provides a new basis for democratic struggles and liberation movements. Whether it is seen as resistance or experimental praxis, this ethos shifts the ethical problematic from the obedience to universal law or moral codes to the disruptive temporality of becoming manifesting itself in the creation of the yet "improbable" modes of being. By stressing the fact that this transformation is inseparable from eroticism and pleasure, the ethics of dissensus contests the disembodied ethical subject transcending sexual and racial differences. Foucault once said that Breton "remoralized writing, as it were, by demoralizing it completely"[101]—in a paraphrase of this statement, I would say that the ethics of dissensus remoralizes bodies, practices, and eroticism, by "demoralizing completely" the traditional domain of ethics.

## CHAPTER 2

# Ethical Responsibility, Eros, and the Politics of Race and Rights

IN THE PREVIOUS CHAPTER I argued that the ethos of becoming—understood as the double task of resistance and the creation of the yet "improbable" modes of being—is an indispensable element of the feminist ethics of dissensus. Yet, although this ethos allows us to intervene in the existing power relations and articulate a new basis for democratic struggles, it reaches its limit in the context of the nonappropriative relations to the Other: it cannot account for what Foucault describes as the problematic of friendship and the ethical concern with the pleasure of the Other. To move beyond this limitation, the feminist ethics of dissensus has, therefore, to renegotiate the ethos of becoming in the context of the ethics of alterity. At stake here is a productive tension between the transformative political praxis and ethical obligation, between the disruptive temporality of invention and the anarchic signification of otherness, and, finally, between political and ethical significance of embodiment.

To explore this tension, I turn now to the radical reformulation of ethical responsibility proposed by Emmanuel Levinas—a responsibility that does not presuppose the autonomous subject, transcendental law, or universal moral judgment but rather rests on the asymmetrical "relation without relation" with the Other. Articulated within the context of Continental philosophy, Levinas's ethics has recently begun to influence numerous fields in the humanities ranging from religion and literature to the current debates on multiculturalism.[1] As Lawrence Buell observes, Levinas has become "the most central theorist for the poststructuralist dispensation of turn-of-the-century . . . ethical inquiry."[2] Yet, despite the influential work of Drucilla Cornell, Robert Bernasconi, Jacques Derrida, Tina Chanter, and Luce Irigaray, among others, most of the poststructuralist interpretations of Levinas fail to engage the political implications of his thought in the context of sexual and racial difference. To overcome the shortcomings of this reception, I reread Levinas's ethics in context of Luce Irigaray's and Patricia Williams's work in order to elaborate the significance of the asymmetrical relation to the Other for the feminist ethics of dissensus and the politics of radical democracy. Such an encounter among Levinas's ethics, feminist theory of sexual difference, and race theory is motivated by two main concerns. First, I want to rearticulate Levinas's concept of "anarchic" ethical passions in the context of the feminist articulations of sexuality and embodiment. If in the previous chapter I discussed bodies as the site of the materialization of power and resistance, in this chapter I develop the ethical structure of embodiment, which, although inscribed within power relations, is nonetheless irreducible to them. By disrupting the oppositions between matter and form, nature and culture, passivity and activity, this notion of embodiment might allow us to move beyond the impasse created by the sex/gender distinction. Second, I articulate the significance of the ethical respect for the Other in the context of the proliferating democratic struggles against racial, sexist, and class oppression. In so doing, I redefine Levinas's concept of the political in the context of the performative politics of race and rights and, conversely, rethink the performative in the context of ethical obligation. By bringing these concerns together in the light of Levinas's central question— "what meaning can community take on in difference without reducing difference?" (*OB*, 154)[3]—I develop the importance of ethical responsibility and anarchic passions for the politics of radical democracy.

## The Ethical Passions of Emmanuel Levinas

To elaborate the feminist ethics of dissensus, I turn to Levinas's later work in which he shifts the discussion of responsibility from the obedience to moral law to the paradoxical experience of sensibility, embodiment, and passion verging on delirium. Thus, if Foucault allows us to contest the disembodied subject of democratic politics, Levinas calls into question the disembodied subject of ethics. As Simon Critchley writes, "The entire phenomenological thrust in *Otherwise than Being* is to 'ground' ethical subjectivity in sensibility and to describe sensibility as proximity to the Other, a proximity whose basis is found in substitution."[4] Indeed, Levinas argues that the aim of the book is to "disengage the subjectivity of the subject from reflections on truth, time and being . . . borne by the said; it will then present the subject, in saying, as a sensibility" (*OB*, 19). This achievement of Levinas's ethics, which makes the question of passion and corporeality central to ethical experience, is at odds, however, with the parallel development in *Otherwise than Being*, namely, with what Tina Chanter calls "an eclipse of Eros and femininity" and the corresponding privilege given to maternity purified of sexuality. Chanter asks, "Why is it that the only aspect of eros responsible enough to gain admission in *Totality and Infinity* is that of fecundity? And by 1974, in *Otherwise than Being*, why does maternity occlude paternity, while eros is abandoned altogether?"[5] By exploring the tensions between these two mutually incompatible developments in Levinas's work, I elaborate in this section the relation between the ethical structure of embodiment and language. Second, on the basis of Levinas's reformulation of responsibility as passion, I not only rethink his earlier formulations of eros and femininity in *Totality and Infinity* but also examine a possibility of a sexual ethics.

What is remarkable in Levinas's later work is that the possibility of ethical responsibility is located not in consciousness or free will but specifically in incarnation, defined as "the extreme way of being exposed." For Levinas the philosophical privilege granted to reflection and consciousness, that is, to the "for itself," signifies freedom and the coincidence of the self with itself at the price of the negation of both alterity and the body. As Levinas writes, the for itself of consciousness "is always a self-possession, sovereignty, *arche*" (*BPW*, 80). Associated with will, spontaneity, and mastery, consciousness can grasp responsibility only in terms of its own freedom. By contrast, Levinas's ethics posits responsibility prior to the will and the intentionality of consciousness—a responsibility that befalls or summons the ego before any initiative or choice of the subject: "Irreducible to consciousness, even if this relation overturns consciousness and manifests itself there—obsession traverses consciousness contrariwise inscribing itself there as something foreign, as disequilibrium, as delirium undoing thematization, eluding *principle*, origin, and will. . . . This movement is, in the original sense of the term, anarchic" (*BPW*, 81). As an exposure to radical exteriority, responsibility is experienced as something foreign to the subject rather than as a commitment the subject assumes freely for herself: "It is *already* a summons of extreme exigency, an obligation which is *anachronistically* prior to every engagement" (*BPW*, 81). As such, obligation signifies a breakdown of intentionality, or, as Lyotard puts it, a displacement of the I from the position of enunciation to the position of the addressee.

In answering the question of how an ethical responsibility can be reflected in consciousness, Levinas argues that consciousness—the for itself— does not exhaust the meaning of the subject. What persists alongside consciousness, and yet is not encompassed by it, is the "living flesh," the embodied ego, or what Levinas calls the "ipseity." Thus, for Levinas the initial instance of the displacement of consciousness from the position of enunciation is to be found in the body itself. In a movement evocative of Merleau-Ponty's critique of the primacy of the negativity and transcendence of consciousness (for itself) over the inertia of the body (in itself), Levinas rethinks embodiment not only as the condition of relations to objects but also as a prototype of an ethical experience. In contrast to the transcendence of the body in self-reflection, "oneself," or ipseity, signifies for Levinas an embodied self—a prelogical, presynthetic entwinement of thought and carnality, or what Levinas calls "being in one's skin."

If, following Susan Handelman, we might describe "being in one's skin" as " 'the materialist' interruption"[6] of traditional ethics, this designation confronts us with the task of working out the relation between the materiality of the body and language. The emphasis on embodiment makes it impossible to limit Levinas's theory of discourse to the familiar contrast between the saying and the said. For Levinas, the said represents the unity and systematicity of propositional discourse, aiming at synchronizing and establishing relations between different terms. On the philosophical level, the said, with its correlation of the subject and object, structures the discourse of knowledge. On the linguistic level, the said can be approximated to the symbolic order, to the provenance of the signifier and the abstractness of the linguistic code. The saying, by contrast, reveals a unique ethical dimension of signification that is a precondition of every communicative situation. To disclose the signification of the saying, one needs to shift the analysis of language not only from the notion of the system to what speech act theorists call the "linguistic act," but also from the spontaneity of enunciation to the originary receptivity of the speaking subject. As a condition of "a relation without relation," the saying signifies an exposure to the Other, a possibility of being addressed by the Other prior to any intention, need, or demand of the subject. It is a modality of address and contact, a turning toward the Other that produces an inversion of the I prior to the narcissistic identification with one's own image. The saying reveals that the original position of the subject qua subject is in the accusative "me" rather than the nominative "I" of enunciation. Although the saying is always already mediated by the said, it nonetheless interrupts and transcends the symbolic order, preserving in this withdrawal the trace of the ethical relation to alterity, the nonthematizable exposure of the subject to the Other. It marks a rupture not only of philosophical reason but also of discursive power relations.

In order to understand Levinas's claim that language is already incarnation, the disjunction between the saying and the said has to be reworked in the context of embodiment and sensibility. Although the incarnation of language exposes for Levinas the structuring role of the said in sense perception, the saying allows him to redefine sensibility beyond vision and sight. In its "pre-ontological weight," the said is not merely a system of signs representing reality but has a constitutive role in perception—"it already bears sensible life" (OB, 35). In its double function of verbalization and nominalization, the order of the said both structures and resolves the ambiguity of sense perception—the ambiguity of the sensed and the sensing, identity and duration. Verbalization allows the sensible qualities of the perceived things to be transformed into the time of consciousness whereas nominalization constitutes in this temporal flow the identities of the perceived qualities and endows them with meaning. Although the said reveals the ambiguity of sense perception, at the same time, it synchronizes perception, time, meaning, and consciousness and thus designates the sensible as always already intelligible.

The saying, by contrast, reveals a different sense of sensibility and describes it as the capacity for being affected by the Other: "To be in one's skin is an extreme way of being exposed" (*OB*, 89). By situating the act of enunciation in the context of a response to the Other, the saying contests not only the spontaneity but also the disembodied character of enunciation. As Levinas repeatedly argues, the saying, in its corporeal form, is the very signification of sensibility. In contrast to the epistemological significance of sense perception, the saying reveals an ethical sense of embodiment as exposure and vulnerability: "In *the form of corporeality*, whose movements are fatigue and whose duration is aging, the passivity of signification, of the one-for-the-other is not an act, but patience, that is, *of itself sensibility*" (*OB*, 55, emphasis added). It is a prereflective sensibility characterized by touch rather than by vision: "In starting with *touching*, interpreted not as palpation but as caress, and *language*, interpreted not as the traffic of information but as contact, we have tried to describe *proximity* as irreducible to consciousness" (*BPW*, 80). Influenced by the late work of Merleau-Ponty, the figure of the touch signifies, as Elizabeth Grosz argues, not the mastering spontaneity of vision but contiguity, contact, and exposure to the outside.[7] Given the fact that the significance of touch has been elaborated in *Totality and Infinity* almost exclusively in the context of erotic love, the recurrence of this figure to describe the ethical structure of sensibility implies that the ethical passions cannot be separated from eros and sexuality as Levinas seems to suggest.

By elaborating the ethical import of the sensible, Levinas departs from his earlier insistence in *Totality and Infinity* that the ethical experience transcends sensible life, although it should be stressed that even in that text he already contests the primacy of vision in order to redefine sensibility as enjoyment (*jouissance*): "Sensibility is not a fumbling objectification. Enjoyment, by essence satisfied, characterizes all sensations whose representational content dissolves into their affective content" (*TI*, 187). And yet, as Levinas argues in *Totality and Infinity*, since perception reduces the Other to the order of knowledge, whereas the complacency of enjoyment reduces the world to the consumption and possession of the subject, ethical relation with the Other has to transcend both of these forms of sensibility: "The relation with the Other alone introduces a dimension of transcendence, and leads us to a relation totally different from experience in the sensible sense of the term, relative and egoist" (*TI*, 193). It is precisely this separation of ethical responsibility from the sensible life that Levinas contests in *Otherwise than*

*Being.* In so doing, Levinas overcomes, as Tina Chanter suggests, a certain formalism of the ethical relation that still persists in *Totality and Infinity*.[8] This new development in Levinas's ethics means not only that the disjunction of the said and the saying does not transcend the order of the sensible but also that it creates a similar noncoincidence between the epistemological and the ethical forms of sensibility.[9] I will argue that this noncoincidence allows us to redefine enjoyment itself as anarchic delirium—as the *jouissance* of the sexed body.

It is this inseparability of body and language, of expression and sensibility, that is crucial for the feminist ethics of dissensus. Like much contemporary feminist theory, Levinas's ethics contests the disembodied subject of enunciation and the corresponding reduction of language to formalism. In particular, we can see here parallels between Levinas and Irigaray, who likewise rejects those accounts of the linguistic constitution of the subject that ignore the function of embodiment. As she writes in *An Ethics of Sexual Difference*, "The subject who enunciates the law is, they tell us, irrelevant, bodiless, morphologically undetermined . . . the net of a language which he believes he controls but which controls him, imprisons him in a bodiless body, in a fleshless other, in laws whose cause, source, and physical living reason he has lost."[10] Yet, for both Levinas and Irigaray, the intersection of embodiment and language does not entail a reduction of the body to the passive surface of inscription and the corresponding abstraction of language from the body but, on the contrary, exposes the ambiguity inherent in the linguistic constitution of the body.

For Levinas this ambiguity of constitution emerges already in the phenomenological reduction of the body. In an attempt to constitute the flesh as the objective body, consciousness finds itself already dependent on incarnation: "Flesh then, as objective body, is thus constituted for consciousness out of 'powers' that are already tributary to this body. Consciousness turns out to have already called upon what it is only just supposed to be constituting" (*OS*, 97). For Levinas, as for Merleau-Ponty, this anachronism does not disclose a vicious circle but reveals "the original incarnation of thought" (*OS*, 97).[11] Although it can be belatedly grasped by consciousness as the objective body, embodiment reveals a prior "intimate" exteriority upon which consciousness and language themselves depend[12]: "The irreducible circumscribed here does not come from a non-interiorizable outside, an absolute transcendence. In constituting consciousness itself . . . , a paradoxical ambiguity appears: the texture of *constituting* is stitched with threads coming also from the *constituted*, without that provenance having had to answer to any 'intentional aim'" (*OS*, 108). The chiasmic ambiguity of the constituted and the constituting character of the "living flesh" means that embodiment cannot be confused with either the biological body or the passive receptivity of matter: "The fundamental concept of ipseity, while tied to incarnation, is not a biological concept" (*BPW*, 87). Furthermore, this ambiguity means that the significance of embodiment cannot be reduced to its historical constitution—it is not "a uniqueness of natural or historical conjuncture" (*BPW*, 84). As Levinas argues, embodiment is always already "the inaugural event of culture": "Culture does not come along and add extra axiological attributes, which are already secondary and grounded, onto a prior, grounding representation of the thing. The cultural is essentially embodied thought expressing itself, the very life of flesh manifesting . . . original significance of the meaningful or the intelligible" (*OS*, 110). Thus, the ambiguity of incarnation—the anachronism of the constituted and the constituting—cannot be resolved into the classical oppositions of nature and history, body and language, passivity and activity, and, to anticipate the terms of feminist discussions, sex and gender, but makes both sides of these oppositions undecidable. Instead of privileging one side of these oppositions over the other, Levinas elaborates the chiasmic reversibility of the body and language: the obverse side of the linguistic constitution of the body is the incarnation of language, which renders this constitution incomplete and indeterminate. If we rearticulate this insight in terms of sex/gender, we could say that these chiasmic reversals of the cultural constitution of gender into sexualization of language, and vice versa, make the very distinction of sex/gender insufficient. Consequently, the constituting/constituted ambiguity of embodiment contests not only the desexualization of the body in Levinas's ethics but also its "sexualization" according to sex/gender divide. As I will argue below in my discussion of Irigaray, this ambiguity reveals instead the irreducible mark of sexual difference. By exposing the failure of sense and the limit of the discursive *constitution* of bodies, sexual difference epitomizes par excellence the disruptive, *constituting* character of embodiment.

The most original engagement between Levinas's ethics and feminism can occur, however, in the context of the ethical interpretation of the constituted/constituting ambiguity of embodiment. The ethical significance of the sexed body that I want to elaborate in my theory of the ethics of dissensus does not deny the fact that the materialization of the body occurs, as the work of Michel Foucault and Judith Butler has showed us, in the matrix of discursive power relations. This insight is consonant not only with a mediation of embodiment through the order of the said but also with Levinas's critique of the internal relation between discourse and domination. Exposing the inherent connection between knowledge and power, Levinas claims that "it is in the association of philosophy with the State and with medicine that the break-up of discourse is surmounted. The interlocutor that does not yield to logic is threatened with prison or the asylum or undergoes the prestige of the master and the medication of the doctor" (*OB*, 170). By extending Levinas's claims about power and language to the constitution of the bodies, we can say that this constitution reveals the *"political character of all logical rationalism,* the alliance of logic with politics" (*OB,* 171, emphasis added). And yet, the very ambiguity of the bodily constitution also means that the linguistic materialization of the body in Levinas's philosophy cannot be limited exclusively to its political determination. If for Foucault the constituted/constituting ambiguity of embodiment is linked to the possibility of the reversal of power relations on the level of the bodies, for Levinas this ambiguity implies an anarchic ethical saying, which interrupts and retreats from the discursive power relations. Thus, perhaps the most original contribution of Levinas's work to the contemporary debates on the body lies in the fact that it enables the elaboration of the ethical significance of flesh and, by extension, opens a possibility of an ethics of sex, understood as the "anarchic" interruption of the discursive determination of gender. Even though this possibility is never realized in Levinas's own work, and even though his own conception of eros and femininity remains entangled in patriarchal, metaphysical tradition, the necessary interdependence of responsibility and incarnation paves the way to the feminist ethics of sexuality.

The ethical significance of the body is, indeed, what is at stake in Levinas's redefinition of corporeal schematism. Given the chiasmic structure of body and language, it is not surprising that Levinas argues in *Otherwise than Being* that "the concept of the incarnate subject is not a biological concept. The schema that corporeality outlines submits the biological itself to a higher structure" (*OB,* 109). What is this schema that makes embodiment a "condition" of an ethical experience of unconditional responsibility? In what way does the corporeal schematism make the lived body already an effect of substitution, of one being for the other? Levinas redefines here the notion of corporeal schematism elaborated by Merleau-Ponty in *The Primacy of Perception,* where the body schema, modeled on Lacan's notion of the mirror stage, guarantees both the coherence of the embodied ego and provides a map of the possible relations to objects and to others: "A 'corporeal or postural schema' gives us at every moment a global, practical, and implicit notion of the relation between our body and things, of our hold on them."[13] More evocative of Merleau-Ponty's later work on the dehiscence of the flesh and the chiasmic "crisscrossing" between the embodiment and the world, sensing and the sensed,[14] Levinas's schematism does not stress the unification of the embodied ego but exposes disproportion or constriction characteristic of the flesh. One can see here a certain parallel between Levinas's revision of schematism and Irigaray's redefinition of the psychoanalytic concept of the embodiment, also inspired by Merleau-Ponty's analysis of the touch in *The Visible and the Invisible.* Since for Levinas the constitution of the body is already dependent on the exposure to the outside, the schematism of the body is no longer a precondition of the subjective mastery over things but rather describes the "hold" of exteriority on the subject. Preceding the identification with the visual schema, which, indeed, guarantees the mastery of the ego and the unification of the body, the bodily schematism Levinas outlines has the structure of constriction rather than that of the visual container: "The body is not merely an image or a figure; above all, it is the in-oneself and contraction of ipseity" (*BPW*, 87).

Understood as exposure and constriction, the schematism of embodiment unhinges the classical relation between matter and form. Unlike the materiality of matter, which is defined in terms of the unity with its form, the materiality of embodiment is characterized by a disproportion or noncoincidence with form, which, nonetheless, does not imply a disjunction between different terms. It is the movement of contraction, or the spasm of matter, that traces the knot of ipseity: "The ego is *in itself* not like matter is in itself, which perfectly wedded to its form, is what it is. The ego is in itself like one is in one's skin, that is to say, cramped, ill at ease in one's skin, as though the identity of matter weighing on itself concealed a dimension allowing a withdrawal this side of immediate coincidence, as though it concealed a materiality more material than all matter" (*BPW*, 86). This schematism of embodiment does not unify the ego but, on the contrary, inscribes the noncoincidence with oneself within the lived body and makes it the basis of the ethical relations to others.

Enabling and preceding the movement of loss and recovery characteristic of the identification of consciousness with itself, the paradoxical structure of embodiment exhibits a disjunction between two opposite yet inseparable moments: between an irremissible attachment to oneself and the radical exposure to the outside. If one can still use the term "identity" for such a knot in which exposure to exteriority constitutes what is most intimately one's own, it is an identity of nonessence, evocative of Lacan's term of "extimacy" or Derrida's "transcendence within immanence."[15] As Levinas writes in an extremely suggestive passage, evocative of Luce Irigaray's phenomenological analysis of mucous and elemental passions, "that this unity be a torsion and a restlessness, irreducible to the function that the oneself exercises in the ontology . . . presents a problem. It is as though the atomic unity of the subject were exposed outside by breathing, by divesting its ultimate substance even to the mucous membrane of the lungs, *continually splitting up*" (*OB*, 107, emphasis added). The decisive difference between Irigaray and Levinas lies, however, in the fact that for Irigaray such a schematism of embodiment discloses an ethical significance of eros and the female body—her being neither one nor two—whereas for Levinas it is tied to the anguish of the unsexed subject.

The negativity of constriction marks the singularity of the lived body in contradictory terms of the withdrawal from consciousness and the impossibility of slipping away from one's body. Similarly, this negativity reveals the anarchic withdrawal of the body from the order of the said while at the same time maintaining the impossibility of abstracting language from the body. The materiality of embodiment, its paradoxical identity without essence, signifies, therefore, the impossibility of taking distance from one's body, the impossibility of transcending one's skin: "Unlike consciousness, which loses itself so as to find itself again in the retentions and protensions of its time, the oneself does not slacken the knot attaching it to the self only to tie it once more. . . . The oneself is the irremissible identity that has no need to prove or thematize this identity" (*BPW*, 85). This is another sense in which the materiality of embodiment is more "material" than matter because the opacity of the body—what Lyotard calls the "unthought" of the body and what psychoanalysis designates as sex—withdraws from the coincidence with consciousness, form, and language. Always already mediated and yet withdrawn from the said, incarnation indicates a paradoxical exile, or even the splitting of the subject, without, however, being a cause of alienation of the subject from itself. As Levinas writes, "It is . . . a withdrawal *in itself*, an exile *in itself*, without foundation in anything else, a noncondition. It is a withdrawal without spontaneity, and thus always already over, always already past" (*BPW*, 85).

The inability of the ego to flee from one's own skin, despite the fact that the body is always already withdrawn from the ego, becomes for Levinas a paradigm of ethical responsibility that befalls the subject prior to any initiative. Interpreted in ethical terms, being in one's skin signifies an exposure to accusation, the impossibility of fleeing responsibility. If in this chapter I have indicated the way this ethical structure of embodiment complicates sex/gender distinction, in the subsequent chapters I will develop the racial significance of "being in one's skin" in the context of Frantz Fanon's work.[16] For now I want to say that even though Fanon focuses his discussion of skin primarily on the "epidermalization" of racial oppression, he nonetheless argues that even this profoundly allergic reaction to the black body attests to what racism wants to erase: the ethical significance of embodiment. That is why Fanon ends *Black Skin, White Masks* with the final "prayer" of the body: "O my body, make of me always a man who questions!"[17] According to Fanon, the embodiment is the condition not only of questioning and resistance but also of the ethical relation to the Other. For Fanon, like for Levinas and Irigaray, this ethical significance of the body is crystallized in the figure of touch and sensibility, in "the quite simple attempt to touch the other, to feel the other."[18]

In a similar way, for Levinas the constriction of embodiment does not signify a mere limitation of being but is an effect of a prior ethical relation to the Other—an effect of "having-the-other-in-one's-skin" (*OB*, 115). Drawing on the Latin etymology of the word "anguish" (*angustia*), which means "narrowness," or "constriction," Levinas writes that "this anguish is not the existential 'being toward death' but the constriction of an 'entry within,' which is not a flight into the void but a passage into the fullness of the anxiety of contraction" (*BPW*, 86). By dissociating the movement of constriction from the Heideggerian "being toward death," he describes it instead as the exposure to the Other, a passage into responsibility up to the point of substitution for another. As Susan Handelman suggests, the inspiration for this redefinition of constriction might come from the Jewish kabbalistic tradition of *tzimtzum*: "There is an interesting analogy here to the kabbalistic idea of God's creation through God's self-contraction—*tzimtzum*—rather than expansion. . . . For Levinas, the emptying out or contraction of the subject is what opens it to the positivity of the ethical relation, not the negativity of the abyss."[19]

I would like to suggest another analogy between the contraction of the subject and Irigaray's definition of sexual difference as taking the negative upon oneself. In her reading of Levinas, Luce Irigaray redefines this ethical relation to the Other in terms of sexual desire and the *jouissance* of the body. As a mark of sexual difference, the constriction of embodiment creates an interval between matter and form as the place of erotic desire: "*Desire* . . . occupies the place of the *interval*. . . . Desire demands a sense of attraction: a change in the interval, the displacement of the subject or of the object in their relations of nearness" (*ESD*, 8). This reading is enabled by Levinas's re-thinking of responsibility in terms of anarchic passion: "All the transfers of sentiment . . . could not take root in the ego were it not, in its entire being, or rather its entire nonbeing, subjected not to a category, as in the case of matter, but to an unlimited accusative" (*BPW*, 91). An ethical body is, in other words, a passionate body. Such a passionate body is a condition of being in the accusative, of responsibility, and substitution. For Levinas, carnality and passion are in fact the only analogues capable of conveying the anteriority of responsibility to freedom. He writes, "This formulation expresses a way of being affected that can in no way be invested by spontaneity: the subject is affected without the source of the affection becoming a theme of re-presentation" (*BPW*, 81). Evocative of the *jouissance* of the body, the ethical passion verging on delirium captures the inversion of intentionality and the disturbance of consciousness without converting this disturbance into representation (*BPW*, 82).

What is crucial for the feminist ethics of dissensus is that this emphasis on the ethical significance of passion, sensibility, and embodiment enables a departure from the Kantian legacy: Levinas contests not only the symmetry between responsibility and freedom, which means that responsibilities cannot be freely chosen or assumed by the ethical subject, but also the purification of ethical imperatives from all "pathological passions." In his *Critique of Practical Reason* Kant attempts to curtail the anarchic force of the categorical obligation by maintaining the interchangeability between obligation and freedom, on the one hand, and obligation and the law, on the other. The reversed deduction of the categorical imperative—the moral law taken as a premise for the negative deduction of freedom—aims to establish the equivalence between a specific obligation ("act in such a way") and the universal norm ("so that the maxim of your will can always be valid as the principle of a universal legislation also"). By rewriting obligation as the universal principle, Kant, as Lyotard points out, reduces prescriptives to the descriptive metalanguage of norms.[20] Yet, as Levinas's ethics implies, another consequence of this reduction of responsibility to the metalanguage of law lies in the separation of duty from embodiment. This intervention not only destroys the equivalence between obligation, law, and freedom but also contests the purification of the ethical imperative from "pathological" passion. For Levinas the scandal of these equivalences not only betrays "the ego's infatuation with knowledge" but also reveals the suppression of the body and passion. As Alphonso Lingis suggests, Levinas "reverses the Kantian position; for him responsibility, sensitivity to others, does not conflict with, mortify, sensibility for mundane beings, but makes it possible."[21]

This radical potential of Levinas's work is undercut, however, at the moment it confronts sexuality. Levinas's fidelity in *Otherwise than Being or Beyond Essence* to the ethical significance of incarnation, sensibility, and passion should have led him to discuss what Luce Irigaray calls an ethical encounter "in embodied love." Yet, although Levinas admits passions into the realm of ethics, he repeats the classical Kantian gesture of purification and dissociates those passions from any association with sex. I would argue that such a purification assumes in Levinas's work two forms: ethical masochism and sublimation. In a Kantian manner, Levinas maintains the separation of ethics from sexuality at the price of reducing the ethical significance of passion to pain and anguish. In so doing, Levinas's work remains vulnerable to the critique of Kantian ethics advanced by Lacanian psychoanalysis. As Slavoj Žižek observes, for Lacan Kant's "very renunciation of 'pathological' enjoyment (the wiping out of all 'pathological' content) brings about a certain surplus-enjoyment" in pain itself.[22] And if in Kant's case, this surplus of obscene enjoyment in the very stringency of the law can be compared to the sadism of the superego, what guarantees that in Levinas's work the anguish of the ethical subject does not collapse into a secret enjoyment of the pain itself, into an original ethical masochism? Does not this possibility suggest that it is necessary to elaborate an ethics of sex rather than to exclude eroticism from the domain of ethics?

The other way Levinas avoids an ethics of eros is through the process of sublimation associated in his work with the idea of divine creation and paternal love. According to Simon Critchley, sublimation allows for a necessary recovery from the traumatism of responsibility: "The radical *separation* of trauma that defines the ethical subject requires *reparation*" through the work of sublimation.[23] Although I do not disagree with this function of sublimation in general, I do contest the specific form of sublimation in Levinas's texts, namely, the desexualization of Eros expressed in God's creation and paternal love: "Does not this thought, in its absolute diachrony, in the noninstant of creation, where the self called to being is not there to hear the call which it obeys, conceive an unlimited and anarchic passivity of the creature?" (*BPW*, 89). This turn to divine creativity, and to its earthly counterparts, paternal love and asexual motherhood, suggests not so much a suppression of sexuality but precisely its idealizing sublimation, which exists side by side with a certain hostility (in Levinas's terms, "violation" and "disrespect" [*TI*, 260, 262]) to the nonsublimated form of eros represented by feminine sexuality. As the obverse side of sublimated love, expressed for instance in the association of femininity and welcome, female sexuality in Levinas's work is relegated to animality, profanation, shame, indecency, and irresponsible infancy, and is thus associated with all the terms that evoke and justify the Kantian exclusion of "pathological passions" from the domain of ethics.

In her critique of Levinas, Irigaray is particularly attentive to this oscillation between sublimation and the exclusion of eros from ethics. Unable to imagine an ethics of sexuality, Levinas's male lover eventually turns toward the transcendent God while the woman is plunged back into the abyss of the nonhuman—"the not yet of the infant" or no longer that of the animal: "The loved one would be relegated to the abyss so that the lover might be sent back to the heights. The act of love would amount to contact with the irrationality of discourse, in order to send the loved one back to the position of fallen animal" and man to the ecstasy in God.[24] As Irigaray claims, this masculine sublimation of eroticism obliterates an expression of divinity in woman's sensibility and in the act of love itself. Yet, if the turn to God justifies, like an alibi, the exclusion of eros and femininity from ethics, then, Irigaray asks, how can this conception of divinity constitute an ethical relation? According to Irigaray, "If some God obliterates respect for the other as other, this God stands as the guarantee of a deadly infinity."[25] That is why Irigaray rewrites Levinas's *à-Dieu*, which according to Derrida, "bear(s) witness to the surplus of an infinity of meaning," as the erotic relation of *j'aime à toi*.[26]

To exit this circle of sublimation and debasement, and to prevent the disjunction between the spiritual creation and the eroticism of the flesh (in Irigaray's terms, the split between the Angel and the mucous), Irigaray argues that ethical relation has to be inscribed in the very gap between à-Dieu and à toi. By linking Levinas's discussion of sensibility with sexuality, Irigaray redefines ethical passion as erotic wonder:

This feeling of surprise, astonishment, and wonder in the face of the unknowable ought to be returned to its locus: that of sexual difference. The passions have either been repressed, stifled, or reduced, or reserved for God. . . . But it is never found to reside in this locus: Between man and woman. Into this place came attraction, greed, possession, consummation, disgust, and so on. But not the wonder which beholds what it sees as if for the first time, never taking hold of the other as its object. (ESD, 13)

For Irigaray, the redefinition of wonder as an erotic passion escapes the pitfalls of both masochism and sublimation. In her reading of Descartes, Irigaray argues that wonder, the astonishment in the face of the totally Other, is the ethical passion par excellence. Her point is that wonder, as the first passion, precedes the opposition of pleasure and unpleasure, and by implication, Levinas's distinction between narcissistic enjoyment and ethical anguish. Consequently, despite its privileged position in Levinas's and Kant's ethics, pain for Irigaray is a secondary sensation, already dependent on a judgment whether the encounter with the Other is agreeable or not to the subject. When returned to the locus of sexual relation, wonder not only does not compromise the ethical alterity of the lover but, on the contrary, registers the fact that this erotic encounter is wholly different from all expectations, demands, or knowledge. Rather than being an expression of egoism, eroticism, Irigaray argues, suspends our schemas and definitions, enabling us to encounter "the other not transformable into discourse, fantasms, or dreams, the other for whom it is impossible that I substitute any other, any thing, any god."[27] The eroticization of passion prevents, therefore, the reduction of sexuality either to "the complacent pleasure of dual egoism" (TI, 266) or to the sublime "coveting" of the son.

Based on Levinas's concept of embodiment, Irigaray's ethical significance of eroticism revises and extends his discussion of passivity and temporality. For Irigaray, the ethics of eros restores to sexual pleasure its status of creation, reserved in Levinas's work for God.[28] This creativity of erotic pleasure complicates Levinas's claim that ethical passions reveal the anarchic passivity of the body. We have to remember that Levinas's paradoxical formulation of anarchic passivity not only inverts the imperialism of consciousness but also contests the opposition between passivity and activity. As we have already seen, for Levinas the ambiguity of the constituting and the constituted character of embodiment makes the classical opposition between passive matter and active form untenable. The anarchic character of passivity is another example where this opposition breaks down: the ethical passivity of embodiment lies not in the submission of matter to form, or matter to discourse, but in the anarchic susceptibility to passion. For Irigaray, however, the passionate erotic body is anarchic not only in its susceptibility to passion but also in its creativity. As she insists, erotic passion, prior to any procreation or "coveting" of the child, is already a creation in itself: "having to create, give birth to, engender, the mystery that she bears—prior to any conception of a child."[29] Rather than transcending the sexed body, the erotic creation consists in the transformation of the flesh, in the rebirth of the lovers bestowing on each other life.

In such an act of creation, lovers give each other time and future. This emphasis on future in erotic pleasure further complicates Levinas's discussion of the temporal structure of embodiment. For Irigaray, the radical achievement of Levinas's work lies in the shift from the spatial discussion of embodiment as the location of perspective to the temporality of the body. However, the time of flesh cannot be limited exclusively to "the diachrony of aging,"[30] but, as Levinas's own discussion of the constituted/constituting ambiguity suggests, it has to be linked with the disruptive, futural aspect of history. No doubt, Levinas focuses on aging in order to suggest a correspondence between the temporality of the body and the diachrony of the trace of the Other. As aging, the temporality of the body presents itself as a passive synthesis, as the very lapse of time irretrievable by memory. In a similar way, the trace of the Other signifies for Levinas "an immemorial past," which nonetheless troubles the present (TO, 355). Although in "The Trace of the Other" Levinas argues that such an immemorial past can only be experienced in the encounter with the Other, in "Substitution" he locates such temporality already in the withdrawal of the body from the time of consciousness. Just as the trace of the Other is incommensurate with the order of the said, so too the recurrence of the flesh, the passive synthesis of aging, evades the time of consciousness.

Yet, this limitation of the recurrence of flesh to what Levinas calls "the dead time" of aging is already a symptom of the exclusion of sexual difference from ethics. The darker side of this exclusion lies in the fact that the male lover invariably seeks to recover from the passive synthesis of aging through the procreation of the son. According to Levinas in *Totality and Infinity*, "The relation with the child . . . establishes a relationship with the absolute future, or infinite time. . . . In fecundity the tedium of . . . repetition ceases; the I is other and young. . . . Fecundity continues history without producing old age" (*TI*, 268).[31] The juxtaposition of *Totality and Infinity* with *Otherwise and Being* demonstrates that aging and the futurity of procreation are structural counterparts, and one cannot revise one without challenging the other. That is why Irigaray's emphasis on the time of sexual *jouissance* is decisive because it opens another ethical dimension of temporality, irreducible either to the "dead time" of aging or to the future announced by procreation. What lovers create is a future that is not dependent on the procreation of the child: "A future coming, which is not measured by the transcendence of death but by the call to birth of the self and the other. . . . Searching for what has not yet come into being, for himself, he invites me to become what I have not yet become."[32] This relation with the future is not transformed into a power, anticipation, or project of the subject but closely resembles the Levinasian idea of infinity. By disrupting the oppositions between the futurity of becoming and the diachrony of responsibility, between creativity and passivity, sexuality makes it impossible to dissociate the ethos of alterity from the ethos of becoming.

In the end I would like to suggest that Levinas fails to elaborate an ethics of eros because he lacks a radical theory of sexual difference. Despite this lack, his analysis of embodiment in fact does reconfigure the traditional notion of white masculinity. As he himself puts it, his work suspends the "virile and heroic" conception of masculinity in the Western philosophical tradition, by exposing the masculine subject to the constriction of embodiment, passivity of aging, vulnerability, and passion. How can we rethink female sexuality and racial differences in the light of Levinas's insights about the ethical structure of embodiment? The answer to this question is still very much a matter of invention. I will argue in Chapters 4, 5, and 6 that to pursue the possibility of such an invention, we will have to renegotiate the ethics of alterity in the context of the feminist theories of sexual and racial differences.

## Ethics, Race, and Rights: Reflections on the Politics of Radical Democracy

Having suggested that sexuality makes the dissociation between becoming and obligation impossible, I want now to renegotiate the disjunction between the ethos of alterity and the ethos of becoming in the context of political praxis. Feminist ethics of dissensus raises an important question concerning the relevance of Levinas's ethics for contemporary democratic politics. Levinas himself has addressed this question throughout his career: not only in his two major books, *Totality and Infinity* and *Otherwise than Being or Beyond Essence*, but also in a variety of interviews and essays dealing with the issues of human rights, ideology, nationality, revolution, and the historical mission of the state of Israel.[33] Drawing on Levinas's political reflections, I would like to examine the relation between ethics, race, and the politics of radical democracy. Although the importance of Levinas's ethics for democracy has been recently acknowledged by a variety of authors, such as Jacques Derrida, Drucilla Cornell, Robert Bernasconi, Simon Critchley, and Iris Young, the specificity of Levinas's political discourse—the distinct political genre of the said—has yet to be developed.[34] In this chapter I attempt to reconstruct such a political genre in the context of Levinas's and Patricia Williams's reformulation of human rights. Despite their differences,[35] both Levinas's and Williams's provocative revisions of rights, motivated by the history of racism, anti-Semitism, and exploitation, call for a "more nuanced" sense of responsibility in democratic politics. By reformulating political discourse based on the struggle for human rights rather than on the philosophical model of the said, I not only revise Levinas's initial oppositions between totality and infinity, war and peace, the said and the saying, but also raise the question about the role of ethical responsibility in racial conflicts and the antagonistic relations of modern democracy. As Robert Bernasconi suggests, it is indeed a question about the possibility of an "ethical culture."[36]

In the aftermath of the ideological critiques of morality as the system of law legitimating class exploitation—critiques, which extend to the denunciation of the discourse of rights as yet another expression of bourgeois ideology—Levinas and Williams pose the question whether the deepening of the democratic process requires a renewal of ethics.[37] A similar question has been asked in different ways by various critics of liberal democracy, ranging from Marxists and communitarians to poststructuralist theorists of radical democracy. While affirming the separation of morality from politics, which in modern political language is expressed in terms of the priority of rights over the common good, Chantal Mouffe, for instance, posits the task of articulating "the ethics proper to politics"[38]—an ethics that would express a community compatible with the respect for difference. What is at stake in this often oblique turn to ethics is a critique of liberal individualism, which, by asserting the primacy of private interests, is incapable of thinking democratic community beyond its instrumental function (for example, in terms of the promotion of self-interest) and has a hard time legitimating social justice on this ground.[39] To articulate Levinas's and Williams's contributions to this debate, I will discuss their redefinition of human rights in the context of the theories of radical democracy developed by Ernesto Laclau and Chantal Mouffe. In contrast to Levinas's separation of war and obligation, Laclau and Mouffe affirm irreducible antagonism as a horizon of democracy and thus implicitly raise the question about the relation between antagonism and ethics. I hope that this confrontation between Levinas's ethics, Williams's race theory, and the politics of radical democracy will allow us to address central issues in postmodern and feminist theories: What can an ethics of respect for the Other mean in the context of the proliferating democratic struggles mobilized in the name of the differences of race, gender, class, sexuality, and ethnicity?[40] And conversely, what kind of an ethics is necessary in order to assure us, in Seyla Benhabib's words, that "the agon of . . . politics, or the contest of pluralisms that cannot be adjudicated at the higher levels, will all be instances of good and just democratic politics as opposed to being instances of fascism, xenophobic nationalism, right-wing populism?"[41]

Echoing Horkheimer's and Adorno's analysis of the entanglement of domination and the Enlightenment, Williams's and Levinas's critique of liberalism focuses on the contradiction between the political philosophy of the Enlightenment, based on the correlation between rationality, freedom, and equality, and the racist legacy of European imperialism culminating in the experience of slavery and the Holocaust.[42] As Patricia Williams writes in *The Alchemy of Race and Rights*, her inquiry into "the ethics of law and the meaning of rights" has been inspired by her family history of the enslaved great-great-grandmother and her white owner: "I see her shape and his hand in the vast networking of our society, and in the evils and oversights that plague our lives and laws. The control he had over her body . . . the power he exercised in the choice to breed her or not . . . in his attempt to own what no man can own, the habit of his power and the absence of her choice."[43] In a similar vein, Levinas argues in the 1984 essay, "Peace and Proximity," that "this history [of freedom] does not recognize itself in its millennia of . . . imperialism, of human hatred and exploitation, up to our century of world wars, genocides, the Holocaust, and terrorism; of unemployment, the continuing poverty of the Third World; of the pitiless doctrines and cruelties of fascism . . . up to the supreme paradox where the defense of the human and its rights is inverted into Stalinism" (*BPW*, 163). Confronted with the history of domination, anti-Semitism, and racial terror, democratic theory and praxis have to envision a new conception of justice that would reflect multicultural society without reducing it to the war of particular interests.

For both Levinas and Williams, this new conception of justice in a democratic society cannot be divorced from what Williams calls "a more nuanced sense of legal and social responsibility" (*ARR*, 11). By exposing the complicity between liberalism and the history of racism, Williams offers a devastating critique of justice limited to the protection of property rights, which leads to the increasing privatized ownership of the public goods and to the rationalization of "public unaccountability and, ultimately, irresponsibility" for racial oppression (*ARR*, 47).[44] What is at stake in Williams's critique is a recovery of "agency and responsibility" obscured by, on the one hand, the reduction of justice to the authority of the " 'impersonal' rules and 'neutral' principles" (*ARR*, 11–12) and, on the other, by the "rhetoric of increased privatization" of human rights (*ARR*, 47). Without this accountability, we continue to live in the world, where "some I's are defined as 'your servant,' some as 'your master' . . . and almost everyone hides from the fact of this vernacular domination by clinging to the legally official definition of an I meaning 'your equal'" (ARR, 63). In an ongoing critique of Hobbes, Levinas similarly criticizes the reduction of justice to the protection of private interests and regulation of hostile freedoms. It makes a difference, he writes, whether justice in democracy proceeds "from a war of all against all or from the irreducible responsibility of the one for the other" (BPW, 169). Rather than being a limitation of hostile freedoms, justice for Levinas reveals a necessary co-implication between ethical responsibility for the singular Other and the principle of equality for all: "It is very important to know whether the political order defines man's responsibility or merely restricts his bestiality" (LR, 247–48). Yet, despite this critique of liberalism neither Williams nor Levinas want to ground justice in the priority of the common good—the shared moral values of the community—as the communitarian critics of liberalism (for instance, Michel Sandel, Charles Taylor, and to a certain extent, Alasdair MacIntyre) propose. On the contrary, it is a question of relating egalitarian justice to the irreducible responsibility for the Other and the accountability for the history of oppression.

Although the function of justice in Levinas's work has been frequently interpreted in terms of the incessant interruption of totalizing politics by the infinity of ethics,[45] I think it is a limited and, ultimately, misleading way to read his contribution to political theory. The interpretation of politics as a totality is no doubt informed by Levinas's "Preface" to Totality and Infinity, where he systematically opposes politics, history, war, and totality to ethics, infinity, peace, and transcendence: "Morality will oppose politics in history . . . when the eschatology of messianic peace will come to superpose itself upon the ontology of war" (TI, 22). I argue, however, that once Levinas poses the question of justice irreducible to the application of the law, he is compelled to revise, term by term, the initial opposition so that neither the import of ethics is exclusively associated with infinity nor democratic politics is reducible to totality. Indeed, as Derrida writes, the relationship between ethics and politics in Levinas's work forms "deliberately contradictory, aporetic, . . . dialectical (in the sense of transcendental dialectic)" structure,[46] which he describes as "beyond-in: transcendence in immanence, beyond the political, but in the political."[47] In fact, Levinas himself warns us against the temptation to interpret justice in democracy as "a degradation of obsession, a degeneration of the for-the-other, a diminution, a limitation of anarchic responsibility" (OB, 159). Already in Totality and Infinity he claims that the question of political justice is not simply superimposed or added to the asymmetrical relation to the Other because the ethical subject is from the start answerable to all others: "The third party looks at me in the eyes of the

Other. . . . It is not that there first would be the face, and then the being it manifests . . . would concern himself with justice; the epiphany of face qua face opens humanity" (*TI*, 213).[48] Yet, if the responsibility for the Other always already bears a relation to all others, if the ethical relation is "from the start" doubled into political discourse, then, the signification of alterity becomes more complex than the initial formulation given by Levinas: alterity is not just "infinitely transcendent" and "infinitely foreign" but both incomparable and comparable, transcendent and inscribed in immanence (*OB*, 158). Recently, Iris Young has suggested the term "asymmetrical reciprocity" for this paradoxical doubling of the political and ethical signification of otherness.[49] Since the signification of alterity entails "from the first" a political dimension, which in the democratic regime is expressed in terms of justice for all, then it does not make sense to speak about the interruption of democratic politics by ethical transcendence. Rather, it would be more appropriate to analyze the relation between the disruptive temporality of democratic politics and the anarchic ethics in terms of the difference/deferral operating between the two sides of chiasmus: just as the asymmetrical relation to the Other from the start opens the question of politics, so too the proliferation of differences characteristic of democratic politics retains a reference to anarchic responsibility, which situates the subjects participating in a democratic process as accountable to others.

Yet, to articulate such a complex relation between ethics and democratic politics, the ethics of dissensus has to depart from Levinas's definition of political discourse on the basis of the philosophical system still predominant in *Otherwise than Being*. As we have seen, Levinas's theory of discourse in *Otherwise than Being* is based on the crucial distinction between the philosophical said and the ethical saying. Whereas the saying expresses the unique ethical dimension of every communicative situation and signifies a traumatizing and disruptive exposure to the Other prior to the enunciation or intention of the subject, the said represents both philosophical and political discourse, based on unity, systematicity, totality, and synchrony between different terms. Because in *Otherwise than Being* Levinas does not distinguish between different "genres" of the said (to use Lyotard's phrase), he treats political discourse as analogous to philosophical system. However, in the context of the postmodern theories advanced by Lyotard, Foucault, Derrida, Laclau, and Mouffe, among others, the analogy between the philosophical and the political discourse is hardly sufficient since it fails to account for the modernization of power operating through the proliferation of differences rather than through the totalization of the political or semantic field. Furthermore, the philosophical emphasis on the contemporaneity and systematicity does not reflect the futural and disjunctive temporality characteristic of transformative praxis and democratic politics. Consequently, the

ethics of dissensus has to elaborate a distinct political genre of "the said" irreducible to the philosophical system still predominant in *Totality and
Infinity* and *Otherwise than Being*.

I would like to develop such a model of the responsible political discourse, irreducible to totality, synchrony, and systematicity, on the basis of
Levinas's and Williams's redefinition of human rights. In my discussion of
Foucault, I have mentioned his speculation on the possibility of the antidisciplinary formulation of human rights, no longer predicated on the principle of sovereignty. I would like to propose that we can find an example of
antidisciplinary rights in Levinas's and Williams's work. By criticizing the
liberal interpretation of human rights as the protection of individual freedoms against the interference of others and the state, they concur with Marx
that the problem with the liberal interpretation is that it reduces the
significance of rights to "the guarantee of egoism" of the isolated "monad"
withdrawn into itself and separated from political community.[50] The liberal
politics of rights all too frequently assumes, as Habermas reminds us, "the
form of compromises between competing interests"—the regulation of
conflict throughout the institution of the value-neutral procedures of the
state.[51] Even though human rights protect individual freedom against government intervention and against the coercion by the majority, Levinas argues that the politics of compromise formation among conflicting right
claims and competing interests subordinates human rights to the regulation
by the state—to "necessities constituting a determinism as rigorous as that of
nature indifferent to man even though justice . . . may have served as an end
or pretext for political necessities" (*OS*, 123). In her critique of John Stuart
Mill, Williams similarly argues against the reduction of freedom and obligation to private property: "Freedom becomes contractual and therefore obligated . . . and obligation is paired not with duty but with debt" (*ARR*, 43).
Confined to the resolution of conflict through the protection of private
property and the reciprocal limitations of the individual wills, the idea of justice in liberal theory becomes an expression of "pure measure," "assimilat-
ing the relation between members of the human race to the relation between individuals of logical extension, signifying between one another
nothing but negation, additions or indifference" (*OB*, 124). This notion of
justice not only prevents a positive articulation of democratic community
and freedom but also implies their increasing commodification so that equality becomes a function of exchange and calculation. As Williams writes,
"We use money to express our valuation of things. We express equivalen-
cies through money and in the process of laying claim we introduce a powerful leveling device . . . we also dispense with the necessity of valuing or
considering . . . whatever is outside the market" (*ARR*, 29–30).

By exposing the complicity of liberalism, Western rationality, commodification, and racism, both Williams and Levinas argue for the ethical re-definition of rights based on the notion of responsibility irreducible to the market values of exchange, calculation, and "turf wars" (*ARR*, 67).[52] For Williams the critical unmasking of the liberal mythology of rights is a nec-essary but insufficient critical gesture—the mask itself has to be put to new "good ends" (*ARR*, 164). Consequently, she argues that the task of critical legal studies "is not to discard rights" but to transform them from the per-spective of those racialized others who were deprived of them. For Williams the conferral of rights for the historically disempowered—slaves, the home-less, mental patients—first of all symbolizes "all the denied aspects of their humanity: rights imply a respect that places one in the referential range of self and others, that elevates one's status from human body to social being" (*ARR*, 153). The conferral of rights changes, therefore, a location of these subjects in the pragmatics of the political discourse: instead of being only a referent—the "it"—they can assume the positions of the addressee and ad-dressor. Yet, this revision of the pragmatics of the rights discourse ultimately leads to the radical transformation of the fundamental premise of human rights so they no longer protect the property or the negative freedom of iso-lated individuals but express an original sociality and "collective responsibil-ity" (*ARR*, 153). What is at stake in this reformulation is not only an attempt to release rights from "the dry process of reification" (*ARR*, 163) but "a larger definition of privacy and property: so that privacy is turned from ex-clusion based on self-regard into regard for another's fragile autonomy. . . . The task is to expand private property rights into a conception of civil rights" (*ARR*, 164–65). As Mouffe and Laclau argue, the discourse of rights is not only "the marker of our citizenship" but also an expression of "our re-lation to others" (*ARR*, 164).[53] For Levinas, this relational character of human rights manifests itself concretely in the arena of democratic politics as the defense of the rights of the other person: "Their original manifestation as rights of the other person and as duty for an I . . . that is the phenome-nology of the rights of man" (*OS*, 125). Based on ethical responsibility, this commitment to the defense of the rights of others is a necessary corrective to what bell hooks frequently criticizes as the narrow understanding of re-sistance based on "self-centered longing for change": "Often . . . the long-ing is not for collective transformation of society, an end to politics of dom-ination, but rather simply for an end to what we feel is hurting us."[54]

By refusing the opposition between individual rights and collective re-sponsibility, between "moral utopianism" (*ARR*, 154) and political transfor-mation, Williams's and Levinas's reinterpretation of human rights on the basis of the "regard for another" changes the meaning of individual freedom. Neither what Isaiah Berlin calls "a negative freedom" (that is, an absence of coercion)[55] nor an economic commodity transferable through contract, the ethical understanding of freedom entails a positive engagement for the sake of the Other. As Levinas writes, "My freedom and my rights, before manifesting themselves in my opposition to the freedom and rights of the other person, will manifest itself precisely in the form of responsibility. . . . An inexhaustible responsibility: for with the other our accounts are never settled" (*OS*, 125). Opposed not only to the liberal pursuit of private interests but also to the communitarian concept of the common good, freedom grounded in responsibility implies a nontransferable, noninterchangeable commitment to justice. Consequently, Williams's redefinition of rights based on "the regard for another" and Levinas's defense of the rights of others offer an alternative to both the liberal model of citizenship based on self-interest and to the communitarian model of the common good.

In a manner evocative of Claude Lefort's argument that the mobilization of democratic struggles in the name of human rights implicitly challenges the limits of legality, Levinas and Williams affirm a certain eccentricity of rights with respect to the law. Similarly to Lefort's claim about "the irreducibility of the awareness of right to all legal objectification, which would signify its petrification in a corpus of laws,"[56] Williams argues against the "rigid" systematization and legal reification of rights, in "which life is drained . . . as the cement of conceptual determinism hardens round" (*ARR*, 163). For Levinas, too, the significance of human rights cannot be limited to their expression in concrete laws because they are "the measure of all law and, no doubt, of its ethics" (*OS*, 116). Because they are eccentric to the law, the appeal to human rights is the basis for an ethical interrogation of the existing legality.[57] Enabling an ongoing expansion of the rights' "frame of reference," which as Williams argues, gives "voice to those people or things that, by virtue of their object relation to a contract, historically have had no voice" (*ARR*, 160), this eccentricity is concretely expressed, according to Levinas, in "the right to fight for the full rights of man, and the right to ensure the necessary political conditions for that struggle" (*OS*, 120). By challenging the limits of the existing legality, the ongoing expansion of the rights' "frame" of reference (*ARR*, 161) assures that the politics of human rights is not an apologetics for existing democracies but rather an incessant obligation to strife for what Derrida calls "an infinite 'idea of justice'" (*FL*, 25). In contrast to Wendy Brown's trenchant critique of liberal rights as a mode of subjection to state regulation,[58] Levinas argues that the right to fight for the rights of others opens "in a political society a kind of extra-territoriality," a certain outside of the state and the law. In an even more paradoxical formulation, he claims that it is the task of democracy to guarantee not only a respect for human rights but also this "extra-territoriality" of rights vis-à-vis the regulation of the state.[59] The regime of democracy is, then, not simply coextensive with the exercise of rights but has to insure a certain excess of rights—in Williams's words, their generous extension (*ARR*, 161)—beyond the limits of the existing law. As Levinas puts it, "The capacity to guarantee that extra-territoriality and that independence defines the liberal state and describes the modality according to which the conjunction of politics and ethics is intrinsically possible" (*OS*, 123).

Based on an intrinsic "conjunction" of politics and ethics, this extraterritoriality of rights with respect to the law reveals the performative character of the rights discourse, encapsulated in Lefort's claim that "rights go beyond any particular formulation that has been given of them; and this means that their formulation contains the demand for their reformulation" (*PFMS*, 258). It is precisely this performativity, manifesting itself in the gaps, "double-voiced" rhetoric and "multilingual semantics" of rights (*ARR*, 149), that is at stake in Williams's call for the "alchemical transformation" of rights:

> It is true that the constitutional foreground of rights was shaped by whites, parceled out to blacks in pieces, ordained from on high in small favors, random insulting gratuities. Perhaps the predominance of that imbalance obscures the fact that the recursive insistence of those rights is also defined by black desire for them. . . . "Rights" feels new in the mouths of most black people. (*ARR*, 164)

I argue that Williams's insistence on the performative character of rights allows us to redefine the political discourse in democracy beyond the philosophical model of totality and contemporaneity offered by Levinas in *Otherwise than Being*. The continuing struggle for rights—for instance, reproductive rights, gay and lesbian rights, minority rights, rights of the homeless, "rights to food, shelter and medical care" (*ARR*, 26)—can be understood as the reiteration of the law, which instead of totalizing its meaning, opens the possibility of its revision.[60] To recall Butler's well-known formulation, we can say that the demand for the reformulation of rights produces a certain "dissonance" within the law.[61] The performative effect of the declaration of rights depends, therefore, not only on the preservation of the law but also, as Derrida reminds us, on the force of rupture separating the new formulation from its original legal context.[62] Although the performative declaration of rights by disenfranchised groups always refers to the existing laws, it also maintains within itself "irruptive violence" enabling the repeatable break from the existing legality. According to Derrida, although "a performative cannot be just, in the sense of justice, except by founding itself on conventions . . . it always maintains within itself some irruptive violence" (FL, 27).

I stress the performative character of the political "said" in democracy because I want to make clear that Levinas's and William's attempts to revise the meaning of human rights do not intend to legitimate the existing liberal democracies but rather to define democratic politics as an ongoing task of transformation.[63] Consequently, the performative aspect of human rights allows us to formulate the futural structure of democracy, which for Levinas constitutes an irreducible utopian, messianic element of democratic politics,[64] and for Williams—"moral utopianism" and "a fiercely motivational, almost religious, source of hope" (*ARR*, 163). Making a similar argument in secular terms, Judith Butler claims that "the subjection of every ideological formation to *re*articulation . . . constitutes the temporal order of democracy as an incalculable future, leaving open the production of new subject-positions, new political signifiers."[65] By enabling the production of new political signifiers, the reiteration of rights not only stresses the historicity of the political form of democracy but also opens its "incalculable" future.

In "Force of Law," Derrida sees in the performative futurity of democracy the condition of both justice and political transformation: "Perhaps it is for this reason that justice, insofar as it is not only a juridical or political concept, opens up for *l'avenir* the transformation, the recasting or refounding of law and politics. . . . There is no justice except to the degree that some event is possible which, as event, exceeds calculation, rules, programs, anticipations and so forth" (FL, 27). Such a concept of justice is excessive with respect to the law, although the law remains necessary for its operation: justice is irreducible to the "anonymous legality governing the human masses, from which is derived a technique of social equilibrium, placing in harmony the antagonistic and blind forces throughout transitory cruelties and violence" (*BPW*, 169). As Patricia Williams similarly claims, justice is irreducible to "principles like baseballs waiting on dry land for us to crawl up out of the mud and claim them" (*ARR*, 11–12).[66] Consequently, justice motivating the struggle for human rights demands not only a "jurisprudence of generosity" (*ARR*, 8) but also the claiming of responsibility for its continuous reinterpretation.

This futural character of race and rights enables us to renegotiate the disjunction between the ethos of becoming and the ethos of responsibility. As Claude Lefort writes, "A politics of human rights and a democratic politics are thus two ways of responding to the same need: to exploit the resources of freedom and creativity . . . ; to resist the temptation to exchange the present for the future; to make an effort, on the contrary, to discern in the present the signs of possible change which are suggested by the defense of acquired rights and the demand for new rights" (*PFMS*, 272). In the context of Levinas's work, however, the futurity of democracy, which I have discussed thus far in terms of the performative dimension of human rights, needs to be articulated in relation to the diachrony of responsibility—the ethical saying—that incessantly troubles the present without being reflected in it.[67] This means that the notion of the performative itself is redefined with respect to the ethical obligation. Thus, the future of democracy is not only an effect of unresolvable antagonism, as Mouffe and Laclau argue, but also a mark of creativity and inexhaustible responsibility. According to Drucilla Cornell, "this ethical insistence . . . protects the possibility of radical trans-formation within the existing legal system."[68] It is this incompletion of the present, which for Levinas is tied with the diachrony of responsibility, that opens the future of democracy as an ongoing task. Furthermore, the di-achrony of responsibility poses the problem of egalitarian justice not as a principle but as a question open to conflicting interpretations. Thus, the in-scription of the diachrony of responsibility into the futural politics of human rights preserves a noncoincidence at the core of democracy as the possibil-ity of the plural interpretations of justice.

Emerging from the negotiation between the ethos of responsibility and the ethos of transformation, the performative politics of race and rights I have been developing in this chapter challenge not only the concept of to-tality but also the opposition between ethical peace and the politics of war. In *Totality and Infinity* Levinas argues that "the moral consciousness can sus-tain the mocking gaze of the political man only if the certitude of peace dominates the evidence of war" (*TI*, 22).[69] Levinas's critique of violence is directed primarily against the Hobbsian and the Hegelian concepts of war legitimating the power of the state and its monopoly on the legitimate use of violence.[70] Furthermore, Levinas exposes the complicity between war and the philosophical concept of totality, which he defines as the complic-ity between power and knowledge: "The visage of being that shows itself in war is fixed in the concept of totality, which dominates Western philoso-phy" (*TI*, 21). This critique of war as the paradigm of totalizing politics can-not be applied, however, to the postmodern theories of power and lan-guage, advanced by Lyotard, Foucault, Derrida, Laclau, and Mouffe, among others, which associate antagonism with the proliferation of differences rather than with totalization. Furthermore, Levinas's rejection of agonistic politics is undermined by his own emphasis on "the right to fight for rights." Williams argues, "Rights contain images of power, and manipulating those images, either visually or linguistically, is central in the making and mainte-nance of rights" (*ARR*, 234).

By manifesting the internal relation between force and signification, the performative character of human rights contests the opposition between peace and war, ethics and politics.[71] Without the irruptive violence, the dis-course of rights could not maintain its extraterritorial status, could not chal-lenge the limits of legality in the name of the ethical responsibility for the Other. Derrida was one of the first critics to articulate this incompatibility between Levinas's ideal of eschatological peace and the requirements of speech addressed to the Other: "Language can only indefinitely tend toward justice by acknowledging and practicing violence within it. Violence against violence. . . . This *vigilance* is a violence chosen as the least violence. . . ."[72] If we think through the performative force of discourse, both in its dimension of obligation and the proclamation of rights, then a certain kind of violence can be said to characterize language itself: "Discourse . . . if it is originally violent, can only *do itself violence*, can only negate itself in order to affirm itself . . . without ever *being able* to reappropriate this negativity" (VM, 130). This predicament of violence practiced against violence allows us to theorize obligation—what Levinas calls a "subversion of essence"—as performative force in its own right. As Jill Robbins points out, "It is possible to understand the force of Levinas's ethical language to be its irreducibly performative dimension."[73] Thus, in place of the dichotomy between peace and war, we might want to ask how the performative force of obligation can mobilize the struggles for human rights against the unjust power relations based on racist, economic, and sexist oppression.

In his essay, "Ideology and Idealism," Levinas himself acknowledges this complex predicament of discourse where the performative force of obligation is mobilized against the violence of domination. In his affirmation of revolution as an ethical act,[74] Levinas begins to elaborate a notion of resistance against domination, the suppression of difference, and, as Lyotard points out in *Differend*, the erasure of the wrong suffered by victims. According to Levinas, the conjunction of ethics and politics authorizes a "rebellion" against unjust political and economic systems "even if in its injustice . . . [society] is stable, ruled by law, submissive to a power and forming an order, a state, a city, a country, or a professional organization" (*LR*, 242). In *Difficult Freedom*, he similarly claims that the passivity of obligation does not entail a "sense of resignation in the face of revolutionary spirit but . . . connects the spirit of patience to true revolution. This revolution comes from great pity" (*DF*, 155). And in the most stunning reversal of his own initial presuppositions, Levinas not only affirms rebellion against the unjust society as "the spirit of our age" but also describes the anarchic subversion of essence experienced in responsibility as "disorder or permanent revolution" (*LR*, 242). This acknowledgment of permanent revolution as the condition of democratic society and ethics does not subordinate responsibility to the calculation of power but, on the contrary, in Derrida's words, suggests that violence and war "*still* presuppose, and thus *always* manifest" transcendence of the Other, separation, and hospitality.[75]

By drawing on the work of Williams, Derrida, and Levinas, the ethics of dissensus I develop not only places obligation in the context of antagonisms constitutive of language and social identities but also complicates Chantal Mouffe's understanding of conflict, which she defines, after Carl Schmitt, as the friend/enemy relation: "In the domain of collective identifications, where what is in question is the creation of a 'we' by the delimitation of a

'them,' the possibility always exists that we/them relation will turn into a relation of the friend/enemy type. . . . This can happen when the other, who
was until then considered only under the mode of difference, begins to be
perceived as negating our identity" (*RP*, 2–3). Mouffe claims that this hostility in democracy can be defused by converting the category of the enemy
into the adversary, "whose existence is legitimate and must be tolerated"
(*RP*, 4). Yet, the distinction between the enemy and the adversary is
insufficient for several reasons. First, by reifying the multiple relations of
race, gender, sexual orientation, and class into the anthropocentric conflict
of "us versus them," Mouffe presents a rather narrow view of hegemonic
politics—that is, the articulation of the network of equivalences among diverse democratic struggles—based on sameness. As hooks argues, the politics
of us versus them amounts to the construction of "false frontiers—the idea
that *you* make or construct someone as an enemy who you have to oppose,
but who in fact may have more in common with you than you realize.
However, in this society it is easier for us to build our sense of 'community'
around sameness."[76] Second, the concept of the adversary reduces the
signification of alterity to a dialectical opposite—to the negative against
which the subjective or collective identity is constituted. Since the notion of
the adversary obliterates the singularity of the Other and turns alterity into
a type delineated from the common ground through the opposition to
"our" subjective or collective identity, it perpetuates the notion of the
Other as the imaginary site of our alienation and, as the psychoanalytic theory of the imaginary teaches us, cannot help but perpetuate hatred and ambivalence. In this sense, the concept of the adversary might still be complicitous with what Patricia Williams describes as the displacement of the
internal conflicts in a democratic regime on the imaginary figure of a racial
enemy. As Williams argues, "Whites must take into account how much this
history has projected onto blacks all criminality and all of society's ills. It has
become the means for keeping white criminality invisible" (*ARR*, 61). And
finally, as Williams fears, this reduction of otherness to the adversary reflects
the commodification of differences: " 'Black,' 'female,' 'male,' and 'white'
are every bit as much properties as the buses, private clubs, neighborhoods,
and schools that provide the extracorporeal battlegrounds of their expression" (*ARR*, 124).

Consequently, the question that Levinas and Williams pose for the politics and ethics of radical democracy is whether the struggle for human rights
can be mobilized without the sense of responsibility for the Other's oppression, and whether the diffusion of hatred does not require a different sense
of alterity irreducible to the constitution of oppositional identities entangled
in the network of power/knowledge. Although I agree with Mouffe that
democratic politics occurs already on the level of the constitution of identi-

ties, I argue that the ethical signification of alterity is what exceeds such a constitution. In other words, the differentiation of multiple identities in the oppositional network of power/knowledge represents, in the light of Levinas's work, only one aspect of politics—its "said." For Levinas, however, justice, solidarity, and the desire for "a better society" are inconceivable without the ethical saying—that is, without the respect for an infinite alterity irreducible to oppositional identity. Levinas clarifies this tension between cultural/political and ethical signification of the Other in the following way: "The other is present in a cultural whole and is illuminated by this whole, like a text by its context. . . . His cultural signification is revealed and reveals as it were *horizontally*, on the basis of the historical world to which it belongs. . . . But this mundane signification is found to be disturbed and shaken by another presence, abstract, not integrated into the world. . . . His presence consists in *divesting* himself of the forms which, however, manifest him" (TO, 351). Neither an imaginary site of alienation nor the dialectical opposite of identity, the ethical signification of alterity in the Levinasian sense can only be expressed in terms of responsibility, which, by creating irremissible disturbance in the order of knowledge (both self-knowledge and the knowledge of the other), disrupts the individual and collective forms of identification. This formulation of infinite alterity preserves the excess of justice over knowledge and the priority of the ethical nonindifference to others over the determination and contestation of their identities. As Levinas and Williams suggest, the contestation of universality in the name of difference is not a sufficient political response to the impasses of modernity if this critique is not motivated by the anxiety of responsibility, which situates political agents as being accountable to others, as answerable for the multiple forms of domination.

## The Question of the Community/Community in Question: Difference, Fraternity, and Affect

In the previous section I elaborated the performative politics of race and rights based on the irreducible social and ethical responsibility for the existing forms of domination. Yet, as I argued in the first part of this chapter, ethical responsibility is inseparable for Levinas from sensibility, affect, and passion. How can these two insights redefine a democratic community in the light of this passionate respect for difference? In Williams's words, how can we imagine a "dizzyingly diverse" community (*ARR*, 234) that will cease to "divide public from private, black from white, dispossessed from legitimate" (*ARR*, 7)? Indeed, if I can rephrase Levinas's famous question, "what meaning can community take on in difference without reducing" either difference or passion? (*OB*, 154). By pursuing these questions, I will argue that the feminist ethics of dissensus will have to problematize the issue of community not only in the context of agonistic politics of gender, race, and class differences but also in the context of ethical responsibility and sexual passion.

The issue of community evokes the numerous critiques of liberalism, ranging from communitarianism to the theories of deliberative democracy. In her critical response to these debates, Chantal Mouffe argues for a type of democratic community that moves beyond the false dichotomies of individual rights versus common good, negative liberty versus participation: "Our choice is not only one between an aggregate of individuals without common public concern and a premodern community organized around a single substantive idea of the common good. To envisage the modern community outside this dichotomy is the crucial challenge" (*RP*, 65). By rejecting the liberal notion of the instrumental community formed to promote the pursuit of private interests and the communitarian vision of the substantive community determined by the shared moral vision (the common good), Mouffe articulates the ethico-political bond of the democratic community in terms of symbolic identification with the fundamental values of democratic revolution—liberty and equality: "what we are looking for is a way to accommodate the distinctions between public and private, morality and politics . . . without renouncing the ethical nature of political association" (*RP*, 66). In contrast to an imaginary community of the common good, Mouffe proposes a symbolic community of shared language, of a common "grammar of conduct" (*RP*, 67–69). Because Mouffe's and Laclau's conception of radical democracy allows for the conflicting interpretations of these democratic values, the community they argue for is "without a definite shape or a definite identity and in continuous re-enactment" (*RP*, 67). Since the ethico-political bond is formed through the identification with democratic values and the conflicting interpretation of these values from the positions of racial, sexual, and class differences, Laclau's and Mouffe's concept of community is characterized by the constitutive contradiction between diversity and equivalence, particularity and universality, equality and difference, antagonism and consensus. Instead of resolving these contradictions, the politics of democracy has to maintain them as the condition of its possibility and its future.

The democratic community implied in the performative politics of race and rights also moves beyond the dichotomy of liberalism and communitarianism. Based on a double movement of mediation and subversion of unity, synchronization and diachrony, comparison and preservation of the irreducible difference, this kind of community, according to Derrida, inscribes an "essential disproportion . . . that strives to denounce not only theoretical limits but also concrete injustices" (FL, 20). What is crucial for my theory of the feminist ethics of dissensus is that this double movement of mediation and the dissemination of difference neither converts the anarchic and asymmetrical relation to the Other into the synoptic vision of social totality nor institutes a new principle of justice based on the communitarian ideal of the shared moral values. On the contrary, as Iris Young suggests, Levinas's work allows us to theorize a pluralist community on the basis of the "asymmetrical reciprocity"—that is, the acknowledgment of differences as irreversible. The asymmetrical reciprocity mandates not only the inclusion of diverse perspectives into a decision-making process but, as Patricia Williams argues, requires "listening at a very deep level, to the uncensored voices of others" (*ARR*, 150) rather than imagining their point of view. According to Young, "while comparing the situation . . . of agents according to some standard of equality is ultimately necessary for theorizing justice, prior to such comparison there is a moment of respect for the particular embodied sensitivity of the person."[77]

This model of mediation and dissemination of differences is, however, irreducible to a purely symbolic community, separated from embodiment, passions, and sensibility. Although Levinas elaborates a symbolic model of political community "instituted by language" (*TI*, 214) and consisting of "the absolutely separated" interlocutors interrogating the question of justice, he also supplements it with the notions of fraternity and paternal love, which inscribe the passionate dimension of responsibility in public life. The unresolved tension between these two heterogeneous concepts of community suggests that Levinas attempts to account for the constitutive role of passion in the structure of the democratic politics without engaging the questions of desire and sexuality. As I argued in the first part of this chapter, Levinas's definition of the ethical saying in terms of passion, sensibility, and embodiment is at odds with his desire to exclude eros and female sexuality from ethics. If we read paternal love as a socially acceptable sublimation of the "indecent" and private ("clandestine" is Levinas's term) sexual passion, then the ideal of fraternity allows Levinas to admit passionate responsibility into political life while dissociating it from femininity and sexuality.

Although the idea of paternity is obviously problematic for feminism, it is even more so for the race theory. In the context of the performative politics of race and rights, this familial ideal of paternal love sounds bitterly ironic: it recalls more likely the horror of the rape of black women by white masters and the dispossession of their children rather than promoting interracial solidarity. As Patricia Williams writes, "Slaves were not treated 'as though' they were part of the family. . . . Too often the unspoken power of white masters over slaves was the covert cohesion of family. Those who were, in fact and for all purposes, family were held at a distance as strangers and commodities. . . . They could be sold down the river with no more consideration than the bales of cotton they accompanied" (*ARR*, 161–62). By exploring these contradictions between the notion of fraternity and the democratic community of difference, I want to preserve Levinas's insight that the public discourse in democracy is inseparable from affect, sensibility, and love while contesting the patriarchal interpretation of these affective affinities.

Let us look at these heterogeneous formulations of community more closely. Evocative of Lefort's analysis of the symbolic form of democracy characterized by the institution of the empty place of power and the inde-terminacy of social relations, democratic community emerges, according to Levinas, with the question of justice: "What do I have to do with justice?" (*OB*, 157). What opens this collective space of questioning is responsibility, which positions the interlocutors as being answerable to others and ac-countable for the existing systems of domination. Neither a liberal instru-mental community formed to promote the pursuit of private interests nor the communitarian substantive community determined by the shared moral vision, Levinas's minimal community of question does not even entail an identification with the common democratic values, which, according to Chantal Mouffe constitute the ethico-political bond of democracy. As Simon Critchley, following Hannah Arendt, suggests, the community emerging out of the politics of human rights is associated with questioning the legitimacy of political order rather than with a search for epistemologi-cal foundations (*ED*, 237). It is a groundless and, in Derrida's words, "threatened" community emerging "within that fragile moment when the question is not yet determined enough for the hypocrisy of an answer to have already initiated itself beneath the mask of the question" (VM, 80). That is why it is easier to characterize this community in a negative way. As "a multiplicity of non-additive" (*OS*, 118), such a community cannot be constituted either by resemblance or by a common cause, or a common task, or "the unity of genus" (*TI*, 214). By allowing for diverse interpretations of justice and rights in the context of racial, gender, and class inequalities, such a democratic community has an irreducible performative dimension—that is, it is a community, to borrow Chantal Mouffe's apt phrase, "in continuous re-enactment" (*RP*, 67). One can indeed argue that Levinas's and Williams's performative politics of race and rights is a fine example of "the constitution of the political community, not something that takes inside the political community" (*RP*, 69).

If the performative politics of race and rights can correspond to Lefort's notion of the empty place of power and the indeterminacy of social rela-tions, then Levinas's theme of fraternity and paternal love complicates the purely symbolic articulation of the communal bond. Although Levinas rightly contests the separation of affect from democratic politics, unfortunately, his reduction of the affective intensities of discourse to the imaginary ideal of paternal love transforms the political space of questioning into "immutable significance": "Should not the fraternity that is in the motto of the republic be discerned in the prior non-indifference of one for the other . . . and in which the justice of the rights of man takes on the immutable significance and stability, better that those guaranteed by the state?" (OS, 125). Although Levinas opposes fraternity to the idea of resemblance or causality because it involves an aspect of incomparable difference "whose logical status is not reducible to the status of ultimate difference in a genus" (TI, 214), the commonality of the community now precedes the political process rather than emerging from it: the fraternal community "involves the commonness of the father, as though the commonness of a race would not bring together enough" (TI, 214). Evocative of Kristeva's discussion of the imaginary father as the seed of the ego ideal, paternal love constitutes each son as both unique and equal, "as a brother among brothers" (TI, 279). In such a community, the future is no longer associated with the performative politics of human rights but with the paternal gift of love: "Paternity is produced as an innumerable future" (TI, 279). And yet, in the context of the history of racism and slavery, evoked inadvertently by Levinas's appeal to "the commonness of the father, as though the commonness of a race would not bring together enough" (TI, 214), the ideal of paternal love is turned into its opposite—as Williams argues, for the "black race" the "careless reality of white fatherhood" is associated with rape, dispossession, and the threat to survival rather than with the gift of the future. The story of Williams's great-great-grandmother who was owned by the white master illustrates how this perverse "gift" of white fatherhood threatens to erase the selfhood of the black children: "Her children were the exclusive property of their father (though that's not what they called him). . . . Her children grew up reverent of and obedient to this white man—my great-great-grandfather—and his other children, to whom they were taught they owed the debt of their survival" (ARR, 18, emphasis added). Thus, in contrast to the asymmetrical and heterogeneous political community enacted around the respect for difference, the politics of homosocial fraternity is established through the double erasure of racial and sexual difference. It is a dangerous politics that deteriorates into the order of the same.

As Kelly Oliver has noted, Levinas's discussion of paternity as an ethico-political bond of community is nonetheless unusual insofar as it is associated with the gift of love rather than with the symbolic law.[78] In the context of feminist critiques exposing the correlation between masculine subjectivity and the contractual/legal notion of liberal citizenship, Levinas's split articulation of community between rights and love represents a strange case. Levinas's distrust of the contractual community, his politicization of the seemingly "private" virtues, such as love, patience, and relations to others, might be associated in an uncanny way with certain feminist alternatives to liberal citizenship based on the feminine "ethics of care." Influenced by Nancy Chodorow and Carol Gilligan, this type of feminism, according to Mary Dietz, seeks to enrich public politics "by the virtues of the private realm, and a personhood committed to relational capacities, love, and caring for others."[79] By noting this similarity between Levinas and certain feminist critiques of liberalism, I do not mean to suggest that it would be sufficient for feminist democratic politics to enlarge the concept of passionate fraternity by including sisterhood and maternal love as the models of political solidarity. On the contrary, as the history of feminism shows, the ideal of sisterhood has been all too frequently implicated in a similar erasure of racial and class differences among women.[80] Nonetheless, Mouffe's and Dietz's alternative based on the conflicting interpretations of the egalitarian principles of justice is also inadequate insofar as it excludes the questions of affect, passion, and sexuality from the public realm and thus perpetuates the split between the agonistic political communities and the intimate communities of passion, between the ethics of rights and the ethics of love. As hooks points out, "Our desire for radical social change is intimately linked with the desire to experience pleasure, erotic fulfillment, and a host of other passions. . . . The shared space and feeling of yearning opens up the possibility of common ground where all these differences might meet and engage one another."[81] Thus, rather than choosing between the symbolic community of justice and the more intimate community of love, between performative politics and ethical obligation, the feminist ethics of dissensus has to contest these dual oppositions and to renegotiate the politics of cultural differences in the context of sexuality, on the one hand, and passionate obligation, on the other. What emerges from this renegotiation is the heterogeneous model of solidarity based on the necessary interrelation between antagonism, obligation, and affect.

The alliance between feminist democratic politics and Levinas's ethics I imagine and advocate in this book would embrace the anarchic responsibility based on the asymmetrical relation to the Other and solidarity based on the performative politics of race and rights while supplementing both of these crucial concepts with a desublimated version of passion and sexuality. As Drucilla Cornell, Luce Irigaray, and bell hooks in different ways argue, such an alliance challenges the division between the ethics of sex and the politics of rights.[82] Consequently, by contesting not only the disembodied but also desexualized subject of ethics, the feminist rearticulation of obligation I propose in this chapter opens a possibility for a feminist ethics of sex, understood as the "anarchic" rupture of the discursive determinations of race and gender. As I will argue in Chapter 5, such a negotiation between feminism and Levinas's work preserves the model of democratic community based on the double work of the mediation and the dissimulation of differences while replacing the structural role of paternity with sexual difference, understood not as filiation but as the labor of disappropriation. On the one hand, this inscription of sexual difference into the performative politics of race and rights disrupts the dichotomies that structure Levinas's work: the oppositions between war and peace, justice and desire, responsibility and erotic passion, the anarchic signification of alterity and transformative political praxis. On the other hand, the question of sexuality and obligation redefines the very notion of the performative politics in the context of the anarchic alterity and the constituted/constituting ambiguity of embodiment. Although it disrupts the established boundaries of discourse, this encounter between Levinas's ethics, race theory, and feminist politics is productive: it allows us to articulate a feminist ethics of dissensus that is not limited to the struggle against gender inequality but instead reflects what bell hooks calls "our capacity to care about the oppression and exploitation of others."[83] Such vision of ethics promotes solidarity across differences of race, gender, sexual orientation, and class, without divorcing it from either passionate dissent or conflicting desires. In the second part of this book, I will discuss in greater detail the models of such solidarity suggested by Irigaray's ethics of sexual difference, Kristeva's third generation of feminism, and hooks's reworking of Martin Luther King's "beloved community."

## CHAPTER 3

# Toward an Ethics of Dissensus
## Lyotard's Agonistic Politics
## and the Pursuit of Justice

JUXTAPOSING LEVINAS'S ETHICS, feminism, and critical race theory has allowed us not only to disrupt the binary oppositions between ethics and politics, obligation and becoming, peace and war, but also to redefine political discourse in democracy. I have suggested that such a discourse, based on the dissemination and mediation of differences, should be articulated in the gap between the ethos of becoming and the ethos of alterity, between the futural temporality of political praxis and the anarchic diachrony of obligation. And, since Levinas's concept of obligation is inseparable from passion and sensibility, I have argued that the political discourse of radical democracy would have to address the constituted/constituting ambiguity of embodiment and sexuality. By turning now to Lyotard's work, I want to rearticulate the political "said" in terms of the dispersal of antagonisms and their partial reconsolidation in hegemonic formations. This redefinition will not dispense with ethics but rather will allow us to encounter it in the context of the extreme case of antagonism—what Lyotard calls the "differend"—which lacks the means of articulation but which nonetheless imposes an obligation to respond to the obliterated wrongs.

In his concern with the differend, Lyotard, like Michel Foucault, underscores the limits of the juridical concept of power and the necessity of thinking the event within the historical formations of discourse. The crisis of the juridical manifesting itself as the differend is characterized by the radical disjunction between the "legitimate" operation of power and the demands of justice. Signaled by the lack of judgment applicable to both parties, the differend represents the extreme case of the social conflict that cannot be resolved because the wrong is not signifiable in the idiom in which the articulation and regulation of the conflict takes place. By stressing the obligation to bear witness and redress such a wrong, Lyotard foregrounds the predicament of ethical judgment proceeding without the criteria of justice.

Consequently, the limits of the juridical dramatize not only the modernization of disciplinary power but also the necessity of obligation and judgment
in political life.

I propose to read the differend as an "agitated passage"—that is, in
Kantian words, as "the rapid succession of repulsion and attraction"—between the postmodern rephrasing of the political and the question of ethics.
If in the previous chapter I reinscribed the Levinasian concept of responsibility, which for Levinas remains exterior to politics and war, within the
*polemos*, in this chapter I argue for the necessity of rethinking antagonism in
the context of ethical obligation and judgment. Since in the case of the
differend the antagonism is not a part of the political discourse (the said) but
rather is its very limit—that which is nonsignifiable within the political vocabulary—ethical obligation will allow us to respond and judge these limits
of political articulation. The question of the differend complicates, therefore, the relationship between the political "said" (which I will redefine in
this chapter as hegemonic formation) and the ethical saying, between antagonism and obligation: instead of being mediated by the said, the saying responds to the *polemos*, which cannot be articulated within the hegemonic
formation. As a result of this displacement, the eschatological dimension of
the Levinasian ethics crosses the path with the "pagan" historicity of the
differend. Conversely, the recurring threat of the differend opens a different
concept of politics, no longer reducible to "the art of foreseeing the war and
of winning it by every means."[1] I will argue that such a passage between
politics and ethics, between *polemos* and obligation, opens a space for an
elaboration of a feminist ethics of dissensus that neither renounces the intervention into multiple structures of oppression nor forgets the burden of ethical responsibility.

## Lyotard's Pragmatics of Radical Democracy: Antagonism, Hegemony, Differend

To articulate the role of dissensus in my theory of feminist ethics, I would
like to compare Lyotard's work with Laclau and Mouffe's theory of radical
democracy. Through this comparison, I will argue for the necessity of supplementing hegemonic politics with ethics while contesting the normative
discourse as an effect of hegemonic articulation. Like many other political
theorists—Foucault, Lacoue-Labarthe, and Derrida, to name only a few—
Lyotard protests the reduction of the political into theories of democracy
premised on the elimination of conflict as the goal of social justice. As
Chantal Mouffe eloquently puts it, both communicative and liberal conceptions of democracy presuppose that "the more democratic a society is,
the less power would be constitutive of social relations"; thus, they are in-

capable of coming to terms either with the nature of the political or the notion of justice. Even if conceived only as utopian possibilities, such conceptions of justice preclude contestation, dispute, or conflict over the constitution of political identities or over the demands of justice itself. By stressing dissensus, the conception of ethics I advocate does not promise such utopian resolution of conflict. This means that the question of justice in democracy not only arises out of conflict but also is itself submitted to dispute. As David Carroll eloquently puts it, at stake here is "the pursuit of an Idea (in the Kantian sense) of justice that . . . does not put an end to disputes and differences, that is continually in search of its rules and laws rather than presupposing and simply applying them to each case."[2]

This predicament of justice resonates with the theory of radical democracy proposed by Ernesto Laclau and Chantal Mouffe in *Hegemony and Socialist Strategy*. The politics of radical democracy is based on three fundamental premises: first, it affirms the radical contingency, ambiguity, and proliferation of the antagonisms and the dispersal of the social as the effect of the democratic revolution; second, it points to the irreducible operations of power and antagonism in the formation of all social relations and identities; and third, it argues that resistance to the existing forms of oppression requires a partial hegemonic consolidation, or convergence, of the proliferating democratic struggles. For Laclau and Mouffe antagonism stems from the relational character of language where signs acquire meaning through their differentiation from other signs and from the unavoidable suppression of this relation—what Laclau and Mouffe call, after Derrida, an exclusion of a "constitutive outside." Since antagonism does not take place between actors with already established identities but rather constitutes both social identities and the positions of actors themselves, it cannot be dismissed as an external relation but has to be seen as an internal, constitutive difference of all social relations and identities. Because of the absence of the transcendental foundations, the proliferation of democratic struggles and radical contingency of social relations in the democratic regime, the constitution of political identities, the formation of coalitions, and even the specific forms of antagonism can only be a matter of hegemonic articulations, which remain unstable and subject to further contestation. Indispensable for democratic politics, such hegemonic formations—for instance, the coalition among the antisexist, anticapitalist, and antiracist forces—is established by creating the chains of equivalence among diverse democratic struggles against manifold forms of oppression. If the dispersed antagonisms are "floating signifiers," hegemonic articulations establish contingent relations and connections among them.[3] Since it is based on comparison and equivalence, the concept of hegemonic formation allows us to redefine more precisely the Levinasian notion of the political "said" in the context of the constitutive role of antagonism and the dispersal of power in a democratic regime. Expressing the precarious equilibrium between equivalence and difference, or, as Mouffe puts it, the dialectic between decentering and recentering, hegemonic formation poses thus a political problem of creating contingent links between divergent subject positions and democratic struggles against multiple forms of oppression.[4]

Laclau and Mouffe argue that precisely this concept of hegemony is missing in Lyotard's one-sided focus on the dispersal of meaning and the proliferation of antagonisms. Yet, by adopting Lyotard's notion of dissensus, I do not want to dispense with the necessity of articulating the constitutive contradictions between diversity and equivalence, equality and difference, antagonism and consensus, but to stress the limit cases of articulation—the differends, or the antagonisms that lack the means of expression within hegemonic arrangements. As I will show, hegemonic formations and differends have to be seen as two correlative sides of democratic politics. Thus, I will argue that the hegemonic articulation of the intersecting links among diverse democratic struggles is a necessary but insufficient element of feminist ethics of dissensus because it cannot respond to the limit cases of the *polemos*, where victims cannot signify their wrongs. The differends are not "floating signifiers" that can be connected through the chain of equivalence with other struggles; they are the obliterated wrongs that cannot be signified within a hegemonic discourse. What is, therefore, at stake in the differend is not a postmodern celebration of the fragmentation of meaning but rather the obligation to redress an injustice that lacks the means of expression. Consequently, I will argue that to intervene in the situation of the differend, feminist ethics of dissensus has to supplement hegemonic politics of articulation with a notion of an indeterminate ethical judgment proceeding without a concept.

Although Lyotard stresses the irreducible role of an ethical judgment in political life, his work allows us to complicate Levinas's theory of ethics in the light of the antagonism constitutive of language. Like Foucault, Laclau, and Mouffe, Lyotard argues that antagonism is already inscribed in the possibility of language: conflict is open simultaneously with the linguistic universe, since it is implicated in the mode of linkages between heterogeneous phrases. Consequently, he treats the pragmatics of discourse under the rubric of "general agonistics" rather than communication or structure: "To speak is to fight, in the sense of playing, and speech acts fall within the domain of a general agonistics" (*PC*, 10).[5] Yet, Lyotard is concerned with the problematic of linking the incompatible phrases/genres of discourse—that is, in Laclau and Mouffe's terms, with the necessity of creating hegemonic formations—and argues that these links are not based simply on the equivalence but are themselves effects of contestation and suppression of the alternative modes of connection.[6] The multiplicity of stakes and genres of discourse transforms every hegemonic linking into a victory over alternative possibilities. Just as the "nothingness" between phrases—that is, the absence of the preexisting connections—opens the possibility of antagonism, so too the unavoidable necessity of connecting phrases, of creating hegemonic arrangements, carries with it the possibility of injustice.[7] It is precisely the unpredictability of democratic struggles and the worry about the perpetuation of injustice that makes indeterminate ethical judgment a crucial part of democratic politics.

What turns the necessity of linking into a political question par excellence is the occurrence of the phrase understood as an event. Such an event does not merely reveal a new signification but also dramatizes an "occurrence before the signification." Like Foucault, Lyotard draws a distinction between the occurrence of the event—"it happens"—and its meaning or content—"what happens."[8] As Stephen Watson suggests, this disjunction means that " 'one never knows what *Ereignis* is.' This event involves rather an abyss which no 'pre-ontological comprehension' might reconquer, forcing instead an interpretation whose articulation would need to take place beyond hope of immanence and determinateness."[9] By exceeding the structure of representation, the event brings an always unexpected interruption of the existing hegemonic arrangements and thus renews the possibility of conflict and the necessity of judging the linkages. As a rupture of the historical determination and an opening toward the unknown future, the occurrence sustains the conflict over connections, finality, and stakes of discourse. The possibility of the event is thus what politicizes the necessity of linking and raises the problem of hegemonic formations: rather than being predetermined, linguistic and social relations become an object of contestation and dispute.

By foregrounding heterogeneity and conflict in the political life, the theory of ethics I am proposing has to address what Lyotard diagnoses as the dispersal of the social in the democratic regime. In response to criticisms that he "fails to reconcile his insistence that the differend is the product of a purely linguistic incommensurability . . . with his claim that the differend is shaped by struggle, frustration, and suffering,"[10] Lyotard argues that social relations in democracy exist as the plurality of "I," "you," "us," and "them" instances. An effect of the institution of the empty place of power in democracy, the dispersal and complexity of the social means that its origin cannot be derived from any foundational discourse. Thus, although the social is always already presupposed in every phrase, its nature and identity is not. As David Carroll suggests, this impossibility to determine the nature of the social in advance poses "the social as a question to be determined."[11] Consequently, the social bond in democracy has to move beyond the two dominant modern conceptions of sociality Lyotard diagnoses in *The Postmodern Condition*: (1) society as the functional whole whether of organic (romanticism), communicational (Habermas), or functional (Luhmann) variety; and (2) the dialectical, Marxist notion of the social divided along the lines of class struggle. Instead, social relations have to be reconceived on the model of the heterogeneous language games, "which accepts agonistics as a founding principle" (*PC*, 16). Since both the social subject and the dialectical notion of struggle is diffused along the heterogeneous and plural network of language games or phrases, collective identity cannot be finalized by a determined judgment or hegemonic articulation without leaving a remainder of antagonism. A striking consequence of the constitutive role of conflict in the determination of collective identities is a temporal deferral of these identities because the recurring threat of the differend can put them back into question. As Lyotard writes, "The nature of the social . . . is immediately deferred. For, since it is given along with the universe of a phrase, since the finality . . . of this universe depends upon the phrase by which one links onto the preceding one, and since this linking is a matter of differends . . . the social is the referent . . . of a judgment to be always done over again" (*D*, 140). Despite their partial hegemonic consolidations, collective identities—for instance, women—remain a referent of an indeterminate judgment. Consequently, this impossibility of the final determination of the social not only reveals the contingent character of hegemonic articulations but also opens a horizon of justice as the incessant necessity of judging without fixed criteria or law, where the outcome of this judgment provokes further contestation.

   This relation between the irreducible dimension of conflict in social life and the indeterminate ethical judgment allows us to articulate a more complex diagnosis of the reduction of the political: what endangers democratic politics in postindustrial capitalist societies is not only the elimination of antagonism for the sake of justice but also the erasure of justice for the sake of antagonism or efficiency. As Lyotard's polemics with Niklas Luhmann's system theory and Habermas's communicative rationality suggests, there is a double decline of political praxis under the conditions of postmodernity, manifesting itself either as the replacement of justice by the technological criteria of efficiency or by the transcendence of the *polemos* by the normative criteria of justice. In Luhmann's "system theory" the instabilities and exclusions characteristic of social complexity serve the function of the system's self-reproduction and thus generate social stability, even though the specific social changes are unplanned and unpredictable. In this framework, legitimation, or for that matter any prescriptive function, becomes obsolete. One of the most startling symptoms of this obsolescence is Luhmann's charge of "victimology" in Lyotard's thinking: "From Marx to Lyotard this has happened under the aspect of a victimology. The excluded is determined as a class or in some other way observed as human, mourned, and reclaimed for society."[12] The obsolescence of justice means that judgment, desire, and agency are subordinated to the technological/administrative criterion of efficiency: "Luhmann replies ... that it is possible to guide individual aspirations ... in order to make them compatible with the system's decisions. . . . Administrative procedures should make the individuals 'want' what the system needs in order to perform well" (PC, 62). For Lyotard, this erasure of justice is a symptom of the reversal of democratic politics into technocratic terror.[13]

Paradoxically, the second reduction of the political lies in the attempt to reclaim justice as the normative basis for social praxis. In order to contest the obsolescence of justice, Habermas and, in a different way, Karl-Otto Apel aim to recover the normative criteria transcending antagonism: Apel through his appeal to the quasi-transcendental interpretative community; Habermas through the notion of rational communicative interaction.[14] Although Lyotard agrees with Habermas's diagnosis of the political crisis, he argues that Habermas's project to establish normative criteria of justice transcending social conflicts leads to another reduction of democratic politics: Habermas's "cause is good, but the argument is not" (PC, 66). In the light of this double erosion of political praxis, feminist ethics of dissensus has to steer between the two diametrically opposed alternatives: between the elimination of justice for the sake of either efficiency or conflict, on the one hand, and the transcendence of antagonism for the sake of justice, on the other.

Rather than adopting the normative criteria of justice, or the universalizable validity claims, purporting to transcend conflict, the kind of ethics I advocate treats normative criteria as a result of a hegemonic articulation. I have already advanced a critique of the norm in the context of Foucault's analysis of the disciplinary power, but I want to return to this question again in the context of Lyotard's analysis of genre in The Differend. "Hegemonies of genres, which are like figures of politics" (D, 141), are fixed modes of linking phrases, unifying the linguistic and social heterogeneity. Lyotard points to the hegemonies of different genres established at different moments of history: for instance, Christianity established a narrative genre; the Industrial Revolution privileged a technical genre with its subordination of judgment to efficiency; capital gave priority to the economic genre, democracy to deliberation. Yet, genres are invisible figures of hegemonic politics insofar as they aim to transform the mechanism of hegemonic articulation into the "dignity" of transcendent norms. I will argue that the consequences of this reduction are devastating not only for politics but also for ethics. That is to say, genres make consistent use of prescriptives to cover over conflict at the price of neutralizing ethics.

On the discursive level, genres function like hegemonic articulations: they prescribe certain strategies for winning, establish correlatives among different struggles and demands, and imprint "a unique finality onto a multiplicity of heterogeneous phrases by linkings that aim to procure the success proper of that genre" (*D*, 129). Despite the variety of goals prescribed by different genres—for a tragedy such a goal would be a pity and fear felt by a spectator, for the technical genre, the efficiency of performance—the mode of persuasion deployed by genre is comparable to the hypothetical obligation in Kant's *Second Critique*. In both cases, the prescriptive force of "ought" depends on the stakes to be won: if you want to achieve that, then you ought to do this (*D*, 116). This agonistic, hegemonic character of genre is covered over, however, on a metadiscursive level, where strategies for winning are transformed into normative discourse. The performative effect of this transformation neutralizes the prescriptive force of obligation while at the same constituting the political authority of the tribunal, which proclaims given strategies as norms: "The norm is what turns a prescription into a law. *You ought to carry out such and such an action* formulates the prescription. The normative adds: *It is a norm decreed by x or y*. . . . One may wonder whence *x* and *y* hold their authority. They hold it from this phrase, which situates them on the addressor instance . . ." (*D*, 142). As normative discourse, genres work in a circular and tautological fashion: they convert hegemonic articulations into norms by appealing to an authority of the tribunal, while at the same time they establish this authority by placing it in the position of the enunciation of norms. As this aporia of legitimation shows, the authority of the tribunal—for example, the people in democratic deliberation—stems form the sole fact that it is placed in the position of the addressor of these norms. Lyotard's analysis of genre not only demonstrates that the identities of political actors cannot be presupposed as given but also that the legitimation of political authority ends in aporia, which means that it cannot be derived from anything else but a performative effect of the norm. What this demystification of the normative discourse contests is not the necessity of the hegemonic articulation but its transformation into the metalanguage of norms transcending antagonism.

Among many genres—myth, narrative, techno-science—analyzed in *The Differend*, Lyotard focuses in greatest detail on deliberative democracy, which has been reclaimed, by Habermas among others, as a safeguard not only against the reversal of democracy into totalitarianism but also against the unfortunate "postmodern" dispersion of politics and culture. Directed primarily at Habermas and Apel, but also in different ways at the debate between liberals and communitarians, Lyotard's critique of deliberative democracy questions its fundamental assumptions: first, that it is possible to come to agreement on rules valid for all genres and thus reconstitute "ethical totality" (*Sittlichkeit*); second, that it is possible to reach consensus apart from hegemonic articulation; and third, that the understanding of the social bond can be derived from the theory of communication, from which agonistics is excluded.[15] At stake in this questioning is an alternative democratic politics "that would respect both the desire for justice and the desire for the unknown" (*PC*, 67).

In the light of this critique, I propose to see the process of deliberation as a contingent hegemonic formation, which leads to the emergence of new differends in the very process of reaching consensus. The emergence of the differends shows that the communicative rationality advocated by Habermas cannot be separated either from technological reification or from conflict.[16] As Lyotard points out, the pragmatics of deliberation do not present one unified genre but rather a concatenation of heterogeneous conflicting discourses—cognitive, prescriptive, and technological, among others. The unacknowledged antagonism among different forms of subjectivity implied in these discourses can be transcended only at a price of its projection outside the bounds of collectivity onto the real or imaginary opponent. Thus, the articulation of the identity, the goals, and the means of the collective practical subject is invariably established in relation to the phantasmatic figure of the enemy: "There is presupposed on the opponent's part a set of abstract and 'practical' ends, symmetrical to 'our' ends even if they are different. It is still a question of 'winning'" (*D*, 149). It is this unacknowledged reification and the projection of internal antagonisms outside the bounds of collectivity that risks being implicated in cultural imperialism. As Lyotard soberly remarks, "It is therefore not at all surprising that the representatives of the new process of legitimation by 'the people' should be at the same time actively involved in destroying the traditional knowledge of peoples, perceived from that point forward as minorities or potential separatist movements destined only to spread obscurantism" (*PC*, 30).

Although the end of deliberation brings decision and resolution, the paradoxical concatenation of genres points to the limits of consensus and to the persistence of antagonism. The unity of genres that compose the deliberative politics is supposed to be guaranteed by the answer to the initial prescriptive question: "What ought we be?"—that is, by the identity of the self-legislating subject. Yet, the answer to this question remains provisional and subject to the dialectic in the Kantian sense—a dialectic between theses and antitheses without end "since it concerns if not cosmological then anthropological" antinomies. Thus, despite consensus, deliberation puts the "transcendental illusion of enunciation" into question: it shows that collective identity is constructed, provisional, and open to contestation. The process of deliberation is therefore more fragile than narrative because the gaps between incompatible genres and the conflicts between their forms of subjectivity can be more easily perceived. In place of a community of consensus, these gaps present the social bond more like a "monster formed by the interweaving of . . . heteromorphous classes of utterances" (*PC*, 65). In so doing, deliberation exposes the differend in the social fabric even though the collective identity based on the transcendental illusion of enunciation helps to conceal it.

By exposing the process of deliberation as an unacknowledged hegemonic formation, I affirm the necessity of creating hegemonic connections among heterogeneous democratic struggles against different forms of oppression and, at the same time, call for the supplementation of hegemonic politics with an obligation to bear witness to the differend. It is important to remember in this context that the differend does not represent an instance of conflict between two articulated positions but rather a case of injustice where a wrong is not signifiable, where the very capacity to testify is threatened with destruction. To use psychoanalytic vocabulary, we can say that the differend signals the expulsion of conflict from the symbolic field of signification to the realm of the real:

> I would like to call a *differend* [*différend*] the case where the plaintiff is divested of the means to argue and becomes for that reason a victim. If the addressor, the addressee, and the sense of testimony are neutralized, everything takes place as if there were no damages. . . . A case of differend between two parties takes place when the "regulation" of the conflict that opposes them is done in the idiom of one of the parties while the wrong suffered by the other is not signified in that idiom. (*D*, 9)

What the possibility of the differend signifies, therefore, is not only the irreducible dimension of antagonism and the precariousness of hegemonic formations but also their limits. Although Lyotard's attention to the linguistic, political, and ethical crisis signaled by the differend has provoked incompatible accusations ranging from the obsession with "victimology"[17] to the infatuation with the postmodern fragmentation of meaning, the penchant for the ineffable, and the disregard for "the domination of the more powerful language games and its repressive power structure,"[18] this focus on the limits of articulation, the extreme case of which is the destruction of the capacity to testify to suffered damages, enables us to supplement hegemonic politics with a concern with justice. Based on the obligation to bear witness to the differend, such justice cannot be limited to the identification with democratic values but, as I will argue in the next section, has to be based on the indeterminate judgment proceeding without criteria. Since any articulation of conflict can be implicated in injustice, the differend reveals the endless necessity of judging while at the same time problematizing "the good faith" of critical judgment. By embracing the predicament of an ethical judgment without a law, an ethics of dissensus that I advocate in this book not only strives to create alternative hegemonic formations in order to articulate and contest the interlocking patterns of domination based on the racial, gender, and class inequalities but also bears an obligation to respond to and intervene in the erased conflicts in which victims cannot signify their damages.

This obligation becomes all the more important if we consider the disturbing possibility of the differends caused by the foundational democratic principles of equality and liberty for all. In *The Alchemy of Race and Rights*, Patricia Williams alerts us to startling cases of racial and gender injustice produced by color-blind justice in a color-conscious society. According to Williams, it is the very neutrality of justice that makes it impossible to testify to the racist and gender discrimination: "Blacks and women are the objects of a constitutional omission that has been incorporated into a theory of neutrality."[19] Among many other instances, she recounts how she could not articulate her own experience of racist discrimination—for instance, being denied entrance to a Benetton's store—in a legal discourse that did not allow her to mention either her race or the name of the store. She concludes, "The blind application of principles of neutrality, through the device of omission, acted either to make me look crazy or to make the reader participate in old habits of cultural bias."[20] Although the color-blind justice is supposed to be an antidote for racist bias, it ends up ignoring racism and recriminalizing its victims. As a paradigmatic example of this reversal, Williams cites the case of the white gunman shooting four black teenagers in a New York subway. The public response to this crime was telling: it attempted to reduce the crime of the white shooter to a "reasonable" expression of fear while accusing the black victims of "criminal propensities." By making white criminality invisible, the neutrality of justice "for all" not only obliterates the damages but in fact blames the victims themselves for the crime.

The numerous instances of such differends—from judging racism according to the rules of racial neutrality to the disregard of differences among women in feminist theory—call attention to the obliteration of wrongs in the process of hegemonic formation. Although democratic politics must establish links among different forms of inequality in order to fight the interlocking patterns of oppression, the notion of equivalence on which hegemonic formation rests risks perpetuating further injustice. Consider, for instance, the critiques of the normative heterosexuality by queer theorists or the indictment of white feminism by women of color for its failure to address racial and class oppression. These cases reveal differends within feminism, where the inequalities among women have been obliterated by the hegemonic articulation of women's oppression. It is precisely because hegemonic formations risk effacement of certain forms of injustice in the process of their articulation that democratic politics has to assume responsibility for acknowledging and responding to the limits of political discourse signaled by the differend.

The concern with bearing witness to the differends in democratic politics reveals a crucial difference between the model of agonistic politics I advocate and a certain postmodern reworking of the Nietzschean concept of power. In reversing Clausewitz's dictum that war is politics continued by other means, Foucault famously asks: "If power is properly speaking the way in which relations of forces are deployed . . . , rather than analyzing it in terms of cession, contract or alienation, should we not analyze it primarily in terms of *struggle, conflict* and *war*?"[21] Although the concept of dissensus I'm proposing here approaches power relations in a manner similar to Foucault, I nonetheless argue that a model of war alone cannot articulate a more just response to the differend. Not only can war be implicated in the narratives of legitimation and in the utopian views of the alternative tribunal, but, more importantly, it fails to explain the stakes or the necessity of a just judgment. That is why Lyotard persistently returns to the problem of justice in Kant's and Levinas's work despite his closeness to Nietzsche[22]:

> It cannot even be said that . . . war, class struggle, or revolutionary violence are more just than the tribunal because they would expose the differend instead of masking it under litigation. . . . It shows that another tribunal and other criteria of judgment . . . are possible and seem to be preferable. But, supposing the change took place, it is impossible that the judgments of the new tribunal would not create new wrongs, since they would regulate . . . differends as though they were litigations. (*D*, 140)

In my theory of an ethics of dissensus, I argue that the problem of normativity and the problem of justice cannot be solved with the deployment of the agonistic model of power, although this model is indispensable for democratic politics. Consequently, neither Levinas's separation of the totality of war from the infinity of justice nor Nietzsche's and Foucault's demystification of morality as the expression of the will to power "do justice" to the necessity of judging the unpredictable outcome of social and political conflicts. In order to prevent the reduction of justice to the juridical authority or to the technocratic requirements of efficiency, the politics of radical democracy has, therefore, to supplement the hegemonic articulation of multiple forms of antagonism with an ethical judgment without the assurance of normative criteria.

### Every Wrong Ought to Be Expressed: Signs of History, The Necessity of Judging, and the Force of Obligation

In the previous section I argued that to intervene into the situation of the differend, the feminist ethics of dissensus has to supplement hegemonic politics of articulation with a notion of an indeterminate ethical judgment proceeding without a concept. Yet, how do we judge that the differend takes place if the wrong lacks the means of expression/articulation and thus cannot be the object of cognition? How do we respond to an injustice signaled merely by the "alarm" of feeling? This is indeed the central ethico-political dilemma the differend poses for hegemonic politics: "The differend is the unstable state and instant of language wherein something which must be able to be put into phrases cannot yet be. This state includes silence, which is a negative phrase, but it also calls upon phrases which are in principle possible. This state is signaled by what one ordinarily calls a feeling: 'One cannot find words,' etc." (D, 13). As Lyotard puts it in the "Dossier," at stake here is "to find, if not what can legitimate judgment (the 'good' linkage), then at least to save the honor of thinking" (D, xii). If, as we have seen, the differend cannot be resolved by the appeal to the legal tribunal or the tribunal of history (D, 31), then what kind of judgment can do justice to this "unstable instant of language"? To articulate the structure of such a judgment I will examine Lyotard's analysis of Kant's sign of history in the context of Levinas's notion of obligation.

In the aftermath of his critique of the normative discourse, Lyotard elaborates a modality of judgment similar to what Levinas calls an "eschatological judgment"—a judgment, which calls for an evaluation of each particular case without a rule or without a reference to the totality of history. As Levinas writes in his Preface to *Totality and Infinity*, "The eschatological, as the 'beyond' of history, draws beings out of the jurisdiction of history and the future. . . . Submitting history as a whole to judgment, exterior to the very wars that mark its end, it restores to each instant its full signification in that very instant: all the causes are ready to be heard. It is not the last judgment that is decisive, but the judgment of all the instants in time. . . . "[23] In his essay, "Levinas' Logic," Lyotard cites the Levinasian analysis of the biblical story of God saving Ishmael from dying of thirst as an example of such a judgment. Despite the angels' protestations that Ishmael is not worth this divine intervention because he will later hurt Israel, God refuses to judge the instant according to the totality of history but insists on the singularity of the ethical situation. As Lyotard comments, the scandal of Levinasian eschatological judgment is that "God himself, the number one enunciator by all accounts . . . is not concerned to, nor has power to, calculate his orders as a function of situations anterior or posterior to, or independent of, the instant of giving them; and that accordingly there does not exist a tribunal (or stock exchange) of history where all acts (or shares) would be offset against one another with a view to liquidating debts" (LL, 285).

As this analysis suggests, Lyotard concurs with Levinas that the totality of history cannot be appealed to as the tribunal of ethical or political judgment. Yet, in the case of the differend, the difficulty of judging each instant without a criterion is further compounded by two additional obstacles: first, by responding to the historicity of the conflict, such a judgment cannot be situated "beyond history," although it, too, contests the notion of history as a totality; second, such a judgment has to account for the crisis of the presentation of the particular. The differend problematizes not only the linkages between the phrases always already subject to contestation but also the limits of presentation—the very ability to say "this is the case." As Lyotard writes in the Kantian idiom, the relevance of which will become apparent in a moment, "How does the critical philosopher judge that it is the case when there is no intuition to present for the case?" (SH, 164).

In response to the crisis of presentation, Lyotard reformulates the ethico-political judgment by relying rather heavily on the model of the sublime.[24] This ethical resuscitation of the sublime cannot be adequately understood, however, without taking into account the Kantian concept of the sign of history, which displaces the aesthetic judgment of the sublime to the realm of politico-historical reality. By disregarding the function of the sign of history in Lyotard's argument, his critics keep perpetuating the same argument ad nauseam about the retreat of postmodern theory from the world of needs and compensations either into the aesthetic pleasure of invention or into the "unnecessary metaphysical drama" of the ineffable: "The victim's cry that first appears to be a demand for restitution, for justice within a legal system, is in reality a protest against all systems that would presume to set standards for the adjudication of wrong."[25] From this claim it is just a short step to Terry Eagleton's remarkable conclusion that Lyotard's preoccupation with aesthetics is but a substitute for the lack of political and historical analysis.[26] In contrast to Eagleton's hasty claim, it might be worth recalling Frederic Jameson's careful examination of the persisting aesthetic categories in any articulation of history and politics, like, for instance, the residues of romance in the Marxist theory of history. In adopting the Lacanian and the Althusserian notion of history as the inaccessible Real, or the absent cause, Jameson redefines the aesthetic as the necessary and active textualization of history: "History is *not* a text, not a narrative, master or otherwise, but . . . as an absent cause, it is inaccessible to us except in textual form, and that our approach to it and to the Real itself necessarily passes through its prior textualization . . . in the political unconscious."[27]

Since Lyotard's critics often disregard his repudiation of "aesthetic politics," they miss the fact that at stake in the return to Kant's indeterminate judgment is the question of judging historical-political reality: "It is not true that one can do an aesthetic politics. . . . Aesthetic judgment allows for the discrimination of that which pleases from that which does not please. With justice, we have to do, of necessity, with the regulation of something else" (*JG*, 90). Since the differend presents the problem of judging the wrong that cannot be the referent of the cognitive/descriptive discourse, it necessitates rethinking the ways in the which "the datum of history" is given. One of the crucial ways in which Lyotard wants to restore the possibility of judging the differend is by maintaining the distinction between the historical fact, established through the procedures of verification and evidence, and the Kantian "sign of history."[28] Historical fact, for Lyotard, "is not what is 'given'" (D, 4), but a result of hegemonic articulation. In contrast, the sign of history, often announced through affect, functions as the negative presentation of what is not presentable under the hegemonic regimen of verification.

The difference between the historical fact and the sign of history is all the more crucial since the appeal to "historical evidence" has been used by "revisionist" historians, such as Faurisson, to deny the historical reality of the Holocaust and to silence the survivors' testimony. For Lyotard, the Holocaust is the event that in the most singular way points to the political and moral crises of modernity and thus necessitates the revision of the claim of history. The specific question that frames *The Differend* is how one listens to the testimonies of the inhumanity of Auschwitz, how one responds and bears witness to the destruction of reality and speech signified by this most catastrophic event of "our time." As Lyotard writes,

The 'revisionist' historians understand as applicable to [the name of Auschwitz] . . . only the cognitive rules for the establishment of historical reality and for validation of its sense. If justice consisted solely in respecting these rules, and if history gave rise only to historical inquiry, they could not be accused of a denial of justice. . . . But, with Auschwitz, something new has happened in history (which can only be a sign and not a fact), which is that the facts, the testimonies which bore the traces of *here's* and *now's*, the documents which indicated the sense . . . of the facts, and . . . finally the possibility of various kinds of phrases whose conjunction makes reality, all of this has been destroyed as much as possible. (D, 57)

For Lyotard, the expression of the "sign of history" not only encapsulates Kant's historical-political writing but also enables "a reconsideration of the historico-political reality of our time" (SH, 162). After Auschwitz, such a reconsideration has to take into account "not only reality but also the meta-reality that is the destruction of reality" (D, 57). Because the sign of history saves the possibility of judging the destruction of reality, Lyotard reclaims Kant as "our contemporary," as a philosopher who, despite his failure to write a critique of "the philosophical reason," still marks "a prologue to postmodernity" (SH, 163).

For Kant, the difference between the empirical evidence and the sign of history illustrates two incompatible modes of judging historical/political reality. In cognitive discourse, judgment treats the object as an example validating cognition. If we reconfigure the Kantian descriptive discourse as a hegemonic articulation, then the process of judging would treat the particular case as a validation of established links, but it would be still a matter of a determined judgment subsuming a particular under a concept. Yet, in the dialectical discourse dealing with Ideas, which include the ideas of historical progress, such a presentation of the object corresponding to the idea is by definition not possible.[29] In that case, judgment can proceed only analogically, presenting merely "as if referent"—that is, an analogical object "which would be its referent if the phrase were cognitive," but which can never function as an example. This analogical substitution saves the possibility of "judging a phrase, even when there is no empirical case directly presentable for its validation" (SH, 165).

Rather than being an exception, the sign of history dramatizes for Lyotard the predicament of the political/historical discourse as such:

> The same thing [de-realization of the object] holds, perhaps even more radically, for the historico-political object, which as such has no reality, and for any political faculty of knowing, which must remain inexistent. The only things that *are* real . . . are phenomena. . . . The series of these phenomena, which makes up the history of humanity, . . . is never itself given. This series is not given but is the object of an Idea. (SH, 168)

By saving the possibility of judging a "de-realized" historico-political object, the sign of history suggests a response to the predicament of the different, which likewise presents us with the necessity of judging the political discourse in the absence of the empirical evidence for its validation. Unlike empirical evidence, which is restricted to the presentation of the phenomena validating cognitive discourse, the sign of history points to the formless and "figureless" event "refractory to all functions of presentation." Yet, in contrast to the transcendental illusion, which claims to see beyond the limits of sensibility and experience, the Kantian enthusiasm "sees nothing, or rather sees *the* nothing and refers it to the unpresentable" (SH, 173). Whereas the transcendental illusion treats ideas as if they referred to phenomena, and while the analogical judgment refers to "as if phenomena" (analoga) (D, 131), the sign of history problematizes the analogy on the basis of analogical judgment.

In Lyotard's reading of Kant, the sign of history presents us with an object "refractory to all functions of presentation—even by analoga." This interpretation takes Kant's writings on history in the direction opposite to Hannah Arendt's argument, which, by stressing public communicability, aligns the sign of history with the judgment of the beautiful.[30] Although for both Arendt and Lyotard the ethico-political judgment is based on affect,[31] Lyotard focuses on the feeling of pain rather than pleasure. What functions for Kant as a sign of history—the spectators' enthusiasm for the French Revolution—is the extreme version of the sublime feeling, which underscores the failure of the presentation of an object that could possibly correspond to the Idea of the cosmopolitan Republic or to the Idea of progress. In my reading of Kristeva in chapter 4, I will articulate the affective paradox of the aesthetic judgment in the context of the heterogeneous subject split between desire and drive, signifier and affect. Based on the feeling of pain, such a judgment remains entirely negative, without the support of analoga or symbols: "The *dementia* of enthusiasm . . . bears witness to the extreme tension felt by spectating mankind—a tension between the 'nullity' of what is presented to it and the Ideas of reason" (SH, 174). This redefinition of the sign of history as the presentation of the unpresentable on the basis of affect destroys the false dichotomy set up by the descriptive historical discourse: "The alternative is not: either the signification that learning . . . establishes, or absurdity" (D, 58).

Lyotard retrieves the Kantian "sign of history" in order to respond to the "de-realization of objects" corresponding to the "proper names" of our cat- astrophic history, which, like Auschwitz, throw the historical and political knowledge into a crisis (SH, 162). Yet, what functions for us as a sign is no longer a painful enthusiasm for the great historical upheavals like the French Revolution but rather the overwhelming silence surrounding the suspension of the historical/political commentary in the aftermath of the Holocaust:

The scholar claims to know nothing about it, but the common person has a com- plex feeling, the one aroused by the negative presentation of the indeterminate . . . the silence that the crime of Auschwitz imposes upon the historian is a sign for a common person. Signs . . . are not referents to which are attached significations val- idatable under the cognitive regimen, they indicate that something which should be able to be put into phrases cannot be phrased in the acceptable idioms. . . . This feel- ing does not arise from an experience felt by a subject. . . . The silence that surrounds the phrase, *Auschwitz was the extermination camp* is not a state of mind, . . . it is the sign that something remains to be phrased which is not. . . . (D, 56–57)

By judging the silence surrounding the unpresentable as a sign of the vic- tim's wrong, the critical subject at the same time testifies that "every wrong ought to be able to be put into phrases" even though it cannot be phrased in the available "idiom" (D, 13).[32] Through the silence and the feeling of pain that accompanies it, the differend confronts the subject with an oblig- ation not only to testify and redress the wrong but also to institute a new sense of addressee, addressor, and testimony.

What is striking in Lyotard's discussion of the sign of history is that the limits of hegemonic articulation lead to the explicitly ethical formulations like "every wrong ought to be able to be put into phrases, . . . a new com- petence (or 'prudence') must be found" (D, 13), or "something which must be able to be put into phrases cannot yet be." The recurrence of such pre- scriptive phrases in the context of Lyotard's discussion of social injustices re- quires a reflection on the place of ethical obligation in the politics of democracy. Unlike frequent efforts to demystify ethics as a mode of privatized, apolitical experience, which reduce social antagonism to the privatized experience of the good and evil, I contest the reduction of ethics to normative criteria. By opposing the conservative political work performed by privatized moral discourse, the kind of ethics I propose elaborates a radical sense of responsibility in political life without grounding politics in a normative discourse.

Yet, to consider the effects of such responsibility, which obliges one to find the means of expression and compensation for the obliterated wrongs, we can no longer remain within orbit of the Kantian thought but instead have to return to Levinas's ethics. It is only in the context of Levinas's work that ethical obligation can be emancipated from the universality of moral law and thus considered in the situation of the differend. However, one of the startling effects of this "emancipation" is the dislocation of the critical subject from the role of the autonomous spectator/legislator. Paradoxically, in order to judge the sign of history, the subject can no longer maintain the position of the critical judge but also has to undergo a displacement into an addressee of ethical prescription. Thus, if the sign of history saves the possibility of judging the unpresentable, and restores "the honor of thinking," then the ethical obligation assumed in such a judgment interrogates the infatuation of the judging subject with the priority of thought and honor.

Unlike the Kantian enthusiasm, which verges on the pathological pathos and thus remains ethically suspect, judging the differend subjects the political subject to the burden of ethical obligation. This recourse to obligation does not aim to restore moral validity to political judgment; on the contrary, it even undermines its aesthetical validity insofar as this validity is based on the subreption of the disjunction between the subject and the object for the play of the subjective faculties. To underscore the anarchic force of such obligation, Lyotard consistently deploys Levinas's ethics with and against Kant's moral law. As is the case with Levinas, for Kant, too, morality is irreducible to theoretical cognition. In contrast to the hypothetical obligations, which are like strategies leading toward a goal and thus depend on the clearly prescribed stakes and conditions, the categorical obligation remains for Kant unconditional and unlegitimated. The impossibility of deducing the moral law (or its reversed deduction—the moral law taken as a premise for the negative deduction of freedom) in Kant's *Critique of Practical Reason* shows that the prescriptive force of categorical obligation cannot be deduced from cognition or from the political calculation of stakes. As this failure of deduction, which is concomitant with the failure of theoretical discourse, suggests, obligation happens like an event—it is impossible to speculate on its origin or destination. It precedes commentary and cognition and thus remains anarchic and unlegitimated.[33]

Kant, however, curtails the anarchic force of the categorical obligation by maintaining the interchangeability between obligation and freedom, on the one hand, and obligation and norm, on the other. In order to expose the assimilation of responsibility to knowledge, Lyotard submits Kant's formulation of the categorical imperative to a logical and pragmatic critique.[34] This double critique of the Kantian moral law underscores the decisive character of the Levinasian intervention, which precisely destroys the series of equivalences set up by the categorical imperative: between the descriptives and prescriptives, obligation and norm, obligation and freedom, and, finally, between the addressee of prescriptives and the subject of enunciation. For Levinas the scandal of these equivalences merely betrays "the ego's infatuation with knowledge" and with the free spontaneity of speech. Following Levinas, Lyotard argues that neither the symmetry between the self and the Other nor the free assumption of the obligation can be maintained. In particular, the pragmatics of prescriptive phrases disrupts the continuity between the obligated self and the subject of enunciation. As Lyotard claims, "To find oneself placed in the pragmatic position of being obliged is incommensurable with the position of enunciation, even of enunciating prescriptives" (LL, 308). Unlike the joy of "the destination of the subject" (D, 166) discovered in the judgment of the sublime, obligation marks a dispossession of the ethical subject. The violence of obligation lies precisely in the deprivation of the free use of oneself, in the dispossession not only of one's narcissistic image and enjoyment but also of the power of enunciation and judgment. Lyotard writes, it "happens unforeseeably as the scrambling of the phrase universe in which *I* is *I*" (D, 112). Or, to evoke Derrida's argument in "The Force of Law," we can say that obligation can be experienced only as an aporia of experience, as that which is not given to experience.

Confronted with the performative force of obligation, with the prescriptive that every wrong ought to be expressed, the judging "I" foregoes the spontaneity of enunciation and becomes displaced instead onto the addressee of a prescription, onto a "you" as in the phrase "you ought to." Unlike Kant's interchangeability between obligation and free will, Lyotard concurs with Levinas that such displacement puts the judging subject into the position of a hostage. By blocking the passage from "you ought to" to "I am able to," the figure of the hostage displays the aporia, or the contradiction, in the position of the judging subject:

This incommensurability is the same as that of freedom with the condition of being a hostage. If there is freedom, it always and necessarily plays itself out on the enunciative instance. But the ethical and political question does not begin with that of the freedom enjoyed by the "*I*"; it begins with the obligation by which the *Thou* is seized. Not with the power to *announce* . . . , but with the other power, . . . that of being *bound to*. . . . (LL, 308)

To describe the aporia of the obligated subject in the antithetical terms of being a hostage and a host is certainly shocking if not scandalous, especially since this rhetoric might suggest an analogy between the victim of persecution and the recipient of obligation. Far from suggesting such an analogy, the Levinasian rhetoric of being a hostage aims to displace the Hegelian discourse of persecution in order to underscore the immeasurable abyss between the dialectical and the ethical formulation of alterity. Unlike the transcendence of the Other, the dialectical discourse of persecution posits alterity only in terms of the negation of the same:

> So the persecutor reasons thus: only alterity is just, the unjust is always the other of the just, and so all that is unjust is just. . . . For if the premise states that the rule is alterity, then it necessarily authorizes . . . the same to be drawn from the other and the other from the same. . . . Such is the mechanism of the Hegelian description; this phenomenology is ironic by means of its "I understand you." (LL, 276)

In the ethical encounter, however, the Other who both is a source of generosity and keeps the subject a hostage is not the enemy, not the dialectical opposite, or a moment of alienation that could possibly be overcome in the odyssey of homecoming. The Levinasian formulation of infinite alterity is not reducible to "the other of the same" nor is obligation equivalent to "I understand you." The aporetic condition of being both a hostage and a host of the Other dramatizes not only the displacement of the subject from the position of the enunciation but also the entwinement of responsibility with the anarchic obsession and passion that befalls the ego prior to its will. Consequently, just as the significance of the Other has to be distinguished from the authority of the tribunal proclaiming norms, so too the condition of the obligated subject has to be differentiated from the subjectivation to power relations: if the process of subjectivation consolidates subjective identity, the paradox of anarchic obligation disrupts this identity and calls it into question.

By displacing the judging subject into a position of an addressee, the performative effect of obligation also restores a paradoxical possibility of an address for a victim. A victim who, in the situation of the differend, lacks the means of expression for the suffered wrong becomes, in the ethical encounter, an interlocutor who demands a response. In other words, to be situated as an obligated subject is an asymmetrical correlative of the Other who calls the subject to responsibility for the social wrongs. Unlike the erosion of the testimony, the pragmatics of the ethical situation posits obligation as an ethical response to the call of the Other, even though this call does not amount to the fullness of speech but manifests itself as a trace of the disruption of discourse.

We can compare the call of the Other with the ethical responsibility experienced in the situation of the differend:

In the differend, something "asks" to be put into phrases, and suffers from the wrong of not being able to be put into phrases right away. This is when the human beings who thought they could use language as an instrument of communication learn through the feeling of pain which accompanies silence . . . that they are summoned by language . . . to recognize that what remains to be phrased exceeds what they can presently phrase, and that they must be allowed to institute idioms which do not yet exist. (D, 13)

This comparison between the differend and ethical obligation returns us to the question of responsibility in political life. Such responsibility confronts us with the following paradox: the Other, whose infinite alterity is refractory to thematization, obligates the subject to testify to the obliterated damages and to restore the capacity to signify them. Clearly such responsibility to find the means of expression and compensation for the obliterated wrongs cannot be limited to hypothetical obligations, or juridical justice. It is a minimal but categorical responsibility to testify to the differends and to find the (impossible) idiom for phrasing them.

In *The Differend*, there is no direct passage between the notices about obligation and the notices about the sign of history. In fact, they are separated both logically and topographically in the choreography of diverse arguments. And yet, the "guiding thread" of these notifications, which I have tried to reconstruct here, is nonetheless crucial for the ethical supplementation of agonistic politics: it uncovers a peculiar "de-realization" of the critical subject in the process of judging a "de-realized" historical object. If we wish to preserve for this de-realization the ethical name of obligation, we risk contaminating what Levinas calls the eschatological dimension of ethics by the "pagan" historicity of the *polemos*. Yet, this risk is worth taking; indeed, to use Levinas's words, it is "a very fine risk," which enables us to exit the philosophical discussion of the history of war, aptly characterized by Levinas as "the ontology of totality," and to confront instead the differends of history. As I have argued, Levinas himself undertakes such a risk in his writings on human rights when he redefines obligation as a struggle for the rights of others. In a more radical way, Lyotard allows us to displace and reinscribe the opposition between history as the totality of war and the eschatological infinity of ethics. In place of the opposition between the historicity of war and the eschatological dimension of ethics beyond conflict, deployed in different ways not only in Levinas's ethics but also in Laclau and Mouffe's radical democracy and in the feminist politics of difference, my theory of the ethics of dissensus stresses the necessity of assuming the responsibility for a just judgment within agonistic politics. It is this difficult negotiation between ethical obligation and political conflict that I see as the crucial task for feminist theory today.

## Toward a Feminist Ethics of Dissensus:
## The Sexed Body as an Analogon of Justice

Partly because of the pivotal role his work *The Postmodern Condition* has played in the debates about postmodernity, Lyotard has had the bad (or good) luck to be interrogated within feminist theory as a representative of postmodernism. As a result of this "exemplary role," his work has frequently been read in terms of the cautionary tale about the possible misuses or dangers of postmodernism for feminism. Thus, the question posed most frequently to Lyotard is whether his work can be "compatible with the normative content of feminism, not just a theoretical position but as a theory of women's struggle for emancipation."[35] What is symptomatic about this type of reading is that it usually focuses on Lyotard's critique of metanarratives but ignores the critique's aftermath, the search for an alternative justice. This omission is perhaps a symptom of a reluctance to question "the normative content" of feminism itself. In contrast to this reception, I argue that a more productive rapprochement between Lyotard's work and feminist theories would occur in the context of the complex negotiations between the agonistic politics of difference and the ethical judgment grounded in embodiment. To pursue these negotiations, I will juxtapose feminist readings of Lyotard with Lyotard's interpretation of feminism and close with Mae Gwendolyn Henderson's influential essay, "Speaking in Tongues: Dialogics, Dialectics, and the Black Woman Writer's Literary Tradition."

From the outset, feminist critiques of Lyotard are split according to different conceptions of feminism defined either as a continuation of the emancipatory promise of modernity or as the political project of postmodernity. Seyla Benhabib's works, namely, "Epistemologies of Postmodernism: A Rejoinder to Jean-François Lyotard" and her *Gender, Community, and Postmodernism in Contemporary Ethics*, are powerful examples of the first position; whereas Nancy Fraser and Linda Nicholson's essay, "Social Criticism without Philosophy: An Encounter between Feminism and Postmodernism," is a compelling instance of the second. Reformulating Habermas's project of communicative ethics, Benhabib's criticism of Lyotard seeks to advance the emancipatory potential of feminist critical philosophy by preserving universalizable validity claims. In contrast, Fraser and Nicholson's critique is motivated by a vision of feminist social criticism "without philosophy," and thus without a need for a global theory of justice to validate a politics of difference. What emerges from these somewhat missed encounters is a crucial question for the project of feminist ethics, namely, how to reformulate the relation between justice and embodiment in the context of agonistic politics.

Warning that a feminist alliance with Lyotard's "strong" version of postmodernism entails the "risk of incoherence,"[36] Benhabib claims that

Lyotard's critique of metanarratives, autonomy, and philosophy fails to distinguish between operations of power and the normative criteria of justice and thus "is not only incompatible with but would undermine the very possibility of feminism as the theoretical articulation of the emancipatory aspirations of women."[37] According to Benhabib, "agonistic" politics can lead to two contradictory outcomes: either to the polytheism of values, which does not allow for a "practical-moral" critique of social inequalities, or to some unacknowledged criterion of justice, which creates an internal contradiction and blindness to validity claims in his work. The ambiguity Benhabib sees in Lyotard stems, however, from her exclusive focus on one side of his thought—on the agonistic conception of language, which perpetuates the legacy of Nietzsche—to the glaring disregard of his work on justice and reflective judgment, which continues the legacy of Kant, Buber, Derrida, and Levinas, among others. This disregard is evident even in Benhabib's more mitigated recent work, in which she admits that "the task of philosophical politics today is the conceptualization of new forms of association which will let the 'differend' appear in their midst."[38] In place of the either/or choice she places before feminism—between the indifferent struggle of heterogeneous forces or the normative criteria of justice— Lyotard poses a different task of thinking justice within conflict, that is, the task of pursuing a just judgment in face of the contestation over the criteria of such judgment.

The force of Benhabib's critique is to pose the question of justice as a central issue for the feminist political project, its weakness is to reduce this question to universalizable validity claims. By contrast, Fraser and Nicholson reject universal validity for the sake of difference and, in so doing, disregard the problem of justice in their conception of postmodern feminism. As a consequence, their negotiation between feminist theories and Lyotard's work is reduced to the mutual correction of the global/local perspective of social criticism. They argue that Lyotard's project of social criticism is too localized and thus is incapable of diagnosing systemic inequalities of race, class, and gender. Because of its limited scope, it would fail to diagnose the oppression of women, which, as Gayle Rubin aptly puts it, presents "endless variety and monotonous similarity."[39] Yet, to claim that Lyotard confines us only to local, nontheoretical criticism is to confuse metanarratives of legitimation with the denotative statements. Although the critique of legitimation examines the constitution of norms and political authority, the denotative level of analysis deals with descriptive statements, which might include the "large-scale historical narrative and social-theoretical analyses of pervasive relations of dominance" Fraser and Nicholson advocate.[40] Thus, the dissolution of metanarratives Lyotard describes entails neither an abandonment of larger social analysis of systemic inequalities nor a rejection of the normative problematic but rather a delegitimation of both the collective practical subject and the notion of justice based on universal judgment and the autonomy of will. Rather than confining us to myopic local criticism, Lyotard's critique of metanarratives calls for a pursuit of the social justice based on dissensus. As I have argued in the first part of this chapter, this means that the validity claims of any description of women's oppression are based on the hegemonic articulation that is partial and contingent and therefore open to contestation.

If, as Nicholson and Fraser claim, the dissolution of metanarratives in postmodernism seems to rule out the possibility of "a critical analysis of large scale institutions and social structures,"[41] the persistence of these metanarratives within feminism forecloses the analysis of gender, race, and class inequalities among women. The feminist critiques of metanarratives is evident not only in the increasing contestations within feminism but also in the explicit attempts to fashion feminist theory in the nineties on the model of dissensus, suggested for instance, in such different works as bell hooks's *Yearning* and *Outlaw Culture*, Jane Flax's *Disputed Subjects*, Diane Elam and Robyn Wiegman's *Feminism Beside Itself*, or Patricia Hill Collins's *Fighting Words: Black Women and Search for Justice*. Bell hooks, for instance, has repeatedly criticized white feminism not only for its incapacity to address the differences of race, class, or heterosexual bias but also for its appropriation of the discussion of race to further marginalize the theoretical contributions made by the women of color:

An example which readily comes to mind from the feminist movement centers on efforts made by women of color to call attention to white racism in the struggle as well as talking about racial identity from a standpoint which deconstructs the category of "woman." Such discussions were part of the struggle by women of color to come to voice and also to assert new and different feminist narratives. Many white feminists responded by hearing only what was said about race and most specifically about racism. . . . White feminists could now centralize themselves by engaging in a discourse on race, "the Other," in a manner which further marginalized women of color, whose works were often relegated to the realm of experiential. In actuality the theoretical groundwork for all reconsiderations of the category "woman" which consider race . . . was laid by women of color.[42]

As hooks's argument makes clear, working-class women, African-American women, women of different ethnic backgrounds and sexual orientations have been placed in the position of the differend within feminist theory even when their voices have supposedly been heard—they have been deprived of the means of signifying their oppression by the hegemonic discourse that claims to struggle for the emancipation of all women.

For Fraser and Nicholson the appropriate response to the accusations of white feminist theory is a project of postmodern feminism based on the cultural/historical determination of the ever-increasing number of differences:

not only of gender, class, and race but also of ethnicity, age, sexual orientation—by definition, the list has to be open-ended: "Postmodern-feminist
theory . . . would replace unitary notions of woman and feminine gender
identity with . . . complexly structured . . . social identity, treating gender as
one relevant strand among others, attending also to class, race, ethnicity, age,
and sexual orientation."[43] In one respect, this vision of postmodern feminist
theory mirrors closely Lyotard's analysis of the complexity of the social bond
dispersed along the heterogeneous network of language games. Unfortunately, this similarity is restricted only to the historical analysis of differences
because Fraser and Nicholson disregard the fact that the heterogeneity of the
social calls for the partial hegemonic consolidation, on the one hand, and for
ethical judgment, on the other. Thus, what is missing in this formulation of
postmodern feminism is a concept of justice that would correspond to a
delegitimation of the collective subject.

   The fact that Lyotard's work can be criticized simultaneously on the contradictory grounds of universality and difference, philosophical and an-
tiphilosophical social criticism, normative justice and antagonistic politics,
suggests that his work does not fit easily within either of these alternatives.
Furthermore, I would argue that these either/or oppositions are too con-
strictive for feminism itself: in fact, neither the local, nontheoretical politics
of difference without ethics nor the grand theory of normative justice transcending conflict are viable options for feminist theory today. By moving
beyond these oppositions, the feminist ethics of dissensus I propose reformulates the project of the feminist politics of difference. Such an ethical reformulation of the agonistic politics is based on three crucial interventions.
First, it takes into account the limit cases of the antagonism that lack the
means of expression and resolution; second, it supplements the hegemonic
articulation of struggle and resistance with the necessity of justice based on
anarchic obligation and indeterminate judgment; and third, it reconceptualizes ethical judgment in the context of embodiment and sexuality.

   I will articulate the effects of these interventions more fully in my interpretations of Kristeva, Irigaray, and bell hooks in the second part of this
book. For now I want to stress that to redress differends within feminism requires not only a critique of unwarranted generalizations, which could be
corrected by a better knowledge of historical and cultural differences, but
also an elaboration of ethics in the aftermath of a delegitimation of the practical collective subject—women—and its claim to speak for all women in the
name of the common goal of emancipation. As bell hooks argues, without
claiming responsibility for racial and class oppression, the knowledge of
differences risks the denial of racial and economic injustices, perpetuated this
time by feminism itself. According to hooks, "Postmodern theory that is not
seeking to simply appropriate the experience of 'Otherness' to enhance dis-

course or to be radically chic should not separate the 'politics of difference' from the politics of racism."[44] For hooks, the recognition of the injustice of racism and the commitment to political transformation contest the neutrality of knowledge and require, in addition to historical specificity, persistent self-critique and a "fundamental attitude of vigilance rather than denial."[45] Similarly, for Lyotard, the description of cultural differences, no matter how precise, cannot respond to the demand of justice: "There is nothing to prove that if a statement describing a real situation is true, it follows that a prescriptive statement based upon it (the effect of which will necessarily be a modification of that reality) will be just" (*PC*, 40).

If feminist readings of postmodernism pose the question of justice as a central but unresolved issue in feminist politics, Lyotard's reading of feminism credits feminist theory for diagnosing the erasure of the sexed and racial bodies in the legitimations of patriarchal power. Written at the same time as *The Postmodern Condition*, Lyotard's essay, entitled "One of the Things at Stake in Women's Struggles," provides an important supplement to his analysis of legitimation—a supplement in which Lyotard returns to the problem of the sexed and racial bodies in order to outline "a politics that would respect both the desire for justice and the desire for the unknown" (*PC*, 67). Lyotard's turn to the problematics of the sexed and racial bodies in feminism is at the same time a return to his earlier interest in reworking the phenomenological problematic of the sensible and intelligible in the Freudian perspective of the unconscious, which dramatizes the abyss between the libidinal intensities of the body and the intentionality of consciousness. Although Lyotard abandons this line of research in the middle of his career because he suspects that libidinal politics alone cannot come to terms with the problem of injustice and thus risks indifference or even "violence and terror,"[46] in his engagements with feminism he argues that the question of justice cannot be adequately posed without rethinking the embodiment.[47]

In both of his essays, "One of the Things at Stake in Women's Struggles" and "Can Thought Go on without a Body?," Lyotard contests the erasure of the body from different modes of sociopolitical legitimation. Contrary to Fraser and Nicholson's worry that Lyotard is primarily concerned with the status of philosophy, his critique of metanarratives in fact raises the opposite problem, namely, the question of embodiment:

[A human] is equipped with a symbolic system that's both arbitrary . . . , letting it be less dependent on an immediate environment, and also "recursive," . . . allowing it to take into account (above and beyond raw data) the way it has of processing such data. . . . It can even abstract itself from itself and take into account only its rules of processing, as in logic and mathematics. The opposite limit of this symbolic recursiveness resides in the necessity by which it is bound . . . to maintain regulations that guarantee its survival. (CTGWB, 12–13)

As Lyotard points out, the metadiscourse of norms aims to transcend not only the agonistic relations but also the body and its relations with the world. The only limit to the recursiveness of the symbolic—its necessary rootedness in immanence—that techno-science or philosophy recognize is the concern with the survival of the body. Yet, to pose the limit to abstraction exclusively in terms of needs suggests that a certain unacknowledged abstraction of the body from sexual difference has already taken place.

The abstraction of language from the sexed and racial bodies posits language as the active principle constituting the meaning of objects and reduces bodies to the passive surface of inscription. This critique of metalanguage is similar to the recent feminist attempts to rethink the significance of the body apart from the sex/gender distinction, which, as Elizabeth Grosz points out, associates gender with the process of socialization operating on the level of cultural consciousness/discourse and treats the sexed body as the material ground of social inscription. Like Luce Irigaray, Lyotard argues that the disembodied character of language manifests itself in the persistent relation between sexuality, death, and political authority in the Western philosophical tradition running from Socrates to the contemporary scientific dream of artificial intelligence without a body: "What is pertinent for distinguishing the sexes is the relation to death: a body that can die, whatever its sexual anatomy, is masculine; a body that does not know that it must disappear is feminine. Men teach women of death, the impossible, the presence of absence" (TSWS, 112).

The dual determination of metalanguage as the abstraction from the sexed and racial bodies and the active principle of meaning is crucial, Lyotard argues, to the patriarchal model of legitimation of political authority, the origins of which he sees in the conception of Greek democracy. For Lyotard, the formation of patriarchal authority exposes a certain analogy between the symbolic agency of language constituting the meaning of the body and the power of the normative discourse constituting the order of the social corpus: in both cases the transcendent metalanguage, abstracted from embodiment and antagonism, claims to form the "corpus in its entirety." Reduced to the passive surface of inscription, the corpus is no longer legible as the locus where the struggle over meaning takes place. The complicity "between political phallocracy and philosophical metalanguage" depends, therefore, on "the line of demarcation," which is at the same time the line of sexual and racial division, "between an empirical given, women, the great unknown and a transcendent or transcendental order that would give them meaning" (TSWS, 119). Unlike the constituted/constituting ambiguity of embodiment I analyzed in the previous chapter, both political phallocracy and philosophical metalanguage are based on the principle of active determination of meaning—that is, on the power of unlimited initiative and decision.

As Lyotard's critique of the metadiscourse of norm in *The Differend* makes clear, the principle of the active determination of meaning—the power of initiative and decision—is localized in the position of enunciation, that is, in the performative authority of the tribunal proclaiming norms. Lyotard makes a similar argument in his earlier analysis of the patriarchal power: "The activity men reserve for themselves arbitrarily as *fact* is posited legally as the *right* to decide meaning" (TSWS, 119). Together with the right to constitute meaning, groups of free men in ancient Greece claim the political right to constitute the whole social order—they "allocate the responsibilities of the *corpus socians* for themselves." In contrast, women, foreigners, and slaves, relegated to the place of the constituent, are identified with those parts of the social body that remain to be formed and governed. Influenced by Irigaray, Lyotard associates disembodied philosophical metalanguage with the emergence of the homosocial order in which women and racialized others are either figured as objects of exchange or expelled beyond the borders of intelligibility:

An empty center where the Voice is heard (God's, the People's—the difference is not important, just the Capital letters), the circle of homosexual warriors in dialogue around the center, the feminine (women, children, foreigners, slaves) banished outside the confines of the *corpus socians* and attributed only those properties this *corpus* will have nothing to do with: savagery, sensitivity, matter . . . hysteria, silence. . . . (TSWS, 114)

This intrinsic relation between disembodied language and political authority inscribes sexed body in the network of other differences constitutive of the polis, in particular, racial differences: in the Greek *polis*, the differences between men and women are determined in the context of the relations of citizens and its others—barbarians, foreigners, children, and slaves.

In his analysis of contemporary global capitalism and techno-science, Lyotard diagnoses a different modality of abstraction evident, for instance, in the leveling of differences in the process of commodification ("women disappear into the male cycle, integrated either as workers into the production of commodities, as mothers into the reproduction of labour power, or again, as commodities" [TSWS, 116]) or in their subordination to the criterion of technological efficiency. Under these conditions, women's struggle might be seen as an attempt to safeguard sexual difference and to use it as a weapon against both capital and patriarchy. As Fraser and Nicholson have eloquently pointed out, this indeed was the goal of feminist theories in the eighties. By situating the women's movement in the context of the struggles for decolonization, Lyotard, however, sees another, more radical, potential in feminist practice and theory—an attempt to rethink sexed and racial bodies by destroying the transcendent normative discourse.

What this early essay "One Thing at Stake in Women's Struggle" adds to the critique of the normative discourse in *The Differend* is an important insight that the transformation of the particular strategies of winning into norms transcending political conflict occurs at the price of effacing embodiment as the site of historical struggles. Consequently, the "normative we" is a "disembodied we" and those who occupy that position and thus claim its performative power know how, in good Hegelian fashion, to make use of death, how to risk life in order gain mastery, the ultimate expression of which is the capacity of thinking death itself. As Lyotard writes, "Thought without a body is the prerequisite for thinking of the death of all bodies . . . and of the death of thoughts that are inseparable from those bodies" (CTGWB, 14). Given this analysis, what is at stake in the women's movement and in the struggles for decolonization, is not just an attempt, as Seyla Benhabib suggests, to close the gap between the normative and the declarative we, between those who enunciate the norms and those who are subjected to them. More fundamentally, it is the contestation of the disembodied character of the normative discourse from the embattled position of the sexed and racial bodies. As Lyotard writes, "If the women's movement has an immense impact equal to that of slaves, colonized peoples, and other 'under-developed' groups, it is that this movement solicits and destroys the (masculine) belief in meta-statements independent of ordinary statements," sensibility, and perception (TSWS, 119–20). Ultimately, I would argue, at stake in women's struggles is a search for a different model of justice and citizenship, no longer predicated on the universalizable norms transcending conflict and embodiment.

If we reject the normative discourse transcending embodiment and struggle, then how can we imagine the relation between the body and the "justice of multiplicities"? In Lyotard's essay "Can Thought Go on Without a Body?," a feminist philosopher, in the figure of which I am tempted to see Luce Irigaray, argues that sexuality functions as the limit to both abstraction and the language of constitution. In contrast to the normative discourse that posits metalanguage as the transcendence of power relations inscribed in the body and in contrast to the techno-science that produces the phantasm of the artificial intelligence without a body, Lyotard's feminist philosopher approaches sexuality as the model of the fundamental incompleteness of thinking, as the suspension of determination manifesting itself in the receptivity to what is not yet. By rejecting the paradigm of metalanguage that treats the body as the passive surface and language as the active constitution of sexuality, this rethinking of embodiment not only builds on a Foucauldian notion of the body as the materialization of power relations but also recovers sexuality as the unthought, or the unconscious of thought. Conceived as the limit of separability of language from embodiment, sexuality also obstructs the complete determination of race and gender norms in the symbolic. This means that sexual difference is itself marked by incompleteness, or as Lacan suggests, by the failure of sense[48] and thus cannot be determined by the symbolic without a remainder. Exceeding symbolic/political determination and regulation of bodies, this remainder of sex "makes thought go on endlessly and won't allow itself to be thought" (CTGWB, 23). By indicating the failure and incompleteness of sense, such a remainder disseminates sexuality beyond the binary opposition of femininity and masculinity. For Lyotard the growing attention to homosexuality, bisexuality, and transvesticism opens a possibility of alternative sexual relations, no longer dominated by compulsory heterosexuality. Rather than grouping men and women into two mutually exclusive subject positions, the withdrawal of sex from meaning opens multiple "erotic potentialities" comparable to what "Freud calls . . . *polymorphous perversion* in the child" (TSWS, 117).

In contrast to the abstraction of thought from the body characteristic of the language of constitution and determination, the withdrawal of sex from the realm of sense marks a certain transcendence in immanence. In other words, Lyotard's contestation of the disembodied metalanguage allows not only for a discussion of bodies as the sites of regulation and materialization of power but also for the analysis of sexuality as the limit, or the remainder, of that regulation. One consequence of such a formulation of sex in excess of the symbolic constitution/regulation of sexed and racialized bodies is the implicit relation between the embodiment and the process of judging the differend. In a manner evocative of Levinas's discussion of the chiasmic ambiguity of the constituted and the constituting character of "the original incarnation of thought,"[49] where thought, in an attempt to constitute the body, finds itself always already dependent on embodiment, Lyotard calls our attention to the other side of this paradox: thought (and language) is inseparable from the phenomenological body, but sex is always already irretrievably withdrawn from thought. Like Irigaray, Lyotard links therefore the constituted/constituting ambiguity of embodiment with sexuality. To expose this paradoxical logic of the bodily remainder beyond the limitations of Levinas's thought, Lyotard refers to the discontinuous temporality of Freud's deferred action: "It inscribes effects without the inscription being 'memorized' in the form of recollection" (CTGWB, 21).[50]

This paradox situates the remainder of sex not only as the limit of thinking but also as analogon of ethical judgment. Rather than being entirely constituted by language, sexuality "is what initially sets up fields of perception and thought as functions of waiting, of equivocation" (CTGWB, 21). Like a historical sign indicating a de-realized historical object, sexuality can be approached as a sign of radical exteriority enabling the negative presentation of the unpresentable and the unthought:

We think in a world of inscriptions already there. Call this culture if you like. And if we think, this is because there's still something missing in this plenitude and room has to be made for this lack by making the mind a blank, which allows the something else remaining to be thought to happen. But this can only "emerge" as already "inscribed" in its turn. . . . The unthought hurts because we're comfortable in what's already thought. (CTGWB, 20)

By marking the limit of the linguistic constitution of objects, the withdrawal of sex allows us to register, therefore, what is missing, what is still unthought, not only in the sphere of sense perception but also in culture at large. Through the overlapping of thinking, suffering, and *jouissance*, this carnal receptivity to what is lacking in the world of available articulations bears a striking resemblance to the process of judging the differend, which is also characterized by the painful attentiveness to the limits of the presentable. Let us recall that the necessity of judging the differend entails responding to what is not signifiable in the idiom of the tribunal in which the regulation of conflict takes place. Such a judgment is often based on "the alarm of feeling," or the affect of pain, which Levinas defines as the capacity for being affected, and Lyotard—as the patient awaiting what is not yet. Because it is based on sensibility and affect, the very possibility of an ethical judgment depends on the often unthematized "debt" to embodiment, to what Levinas calls the irreducible condition of "being in one's skin." Both the embodied thinking and the process of judging are thus characterized by a certain attentiveness to the limits of the presentable. However, for Lyotard embodied thinking is inseparable from sexuality. Can we therefore extend Lyotard's analogy and say that sexuality is the only *analogon* of the complexity of justice occluded by the metanarratives of legitimation? If this analogy is right, then embodied thinking contests not only the principle of metalanguage but also the normative conception of justice.

How can this analogy between embodied thinking and "the justice of multiplicities" be articulated in the context of racial and gender oppression? Although Lyotard analyzes the sexed body in the context of both the women's movement and decolonization struggles, we have to turn elsewhere in order to find out what the "justice of multiplicities" can signify in the context of the agonistic politics of race, sexuality, and gender. I would like to suggest that one of the most compelling articulations of such justice can be found in Mae Gwendolyn Henderson's influential essay, "Speaking in Tongues: Dialogics, Dialectics, and the Black Woman Writer's Literary Tradition." Although Henderson's essay is primarily concerned with literary tradition, her account of the ways race, sex, and gender structure black female subjectivities suggests a model of justice that disregards neither the reality of political struggle nor the dimensions of embodied thinking. This model of justice is implied in Henderson's paradigm of speaking in tongues, which signifies both the crucial role of embodiment and the complexity of sociolinguistic relations in the situation of racial and sexual oppression. Although, like Chantal Mouffe, Henderson stresses the agonistic relations of race and gender constitutive of black female subjectivities, she at the same time analyzes the "testimonial" relations based on identification, affirmation, listening, and desire:

> Through the multiple voices that enunciate her complex subjectivity, the black woman writer not only speaks familiarly in the discourse of the other(s), but as Other she is in the contestatorial dialogue with the hegemonic dominant and subdominant or "ambiguously (non)hegemonic" discourses. . . . As such, black women writers enter into testimonial discourse with black men as blacks, with white women as women, and with black women as black women. At the same time, they enter into a competitive discourse with black men as women, with white women as blacks, and with white men as black women.[51]

Henderson's emphasis on the intertwined agonistic and testimonial speech acts of black women writers refuses the either/or thinking that so frequently characterizes postmodern ethics and politics: either contestation or testimony, resistance or obligation, freedom or responsibility to others. Black women's discourse, Henderson suggests, bridges both sides of this divide while maintaining their incompatibility.

To theorize the simultaneous occurrence of testimonial and antagonistic speech acts, characteristic of black women's subjectivity, Henderson not only supplements Bakhtin's contestatory model of heteroglossia with Gadamer's hermeneutical model of listening but also exposes the limitations of both of these theories by drawing on the resources from black women's literary tradition. Although Henderson embraces the Bakhtinian notion of antagonism, she points out his inability to articulate the significance of silence: "In their works, black women writers have encoded oppression as a discursive dilemma, that is, their works have consistently raised the problem of the black woman's relationship to power and discourse. Silence is an important element of this code" (*ST,* 151). Henderson discusses crucial scenes in Zora Neale Hurston's *Their Eyes Were Watching God* and in Sherley Anne Williams's *Dessa Rose* in which the main female characters experience the impossibility of signifying their oppression within the hegemonic idiom of white justice. Evocative of Lyotard's discussion of the differend, the testimony of black women before the white tribunal puts them in danger of self-betrayal. The impossibility of testifying to the suffered wrongs cannot be adequately expressed by the Bakhtinian heteroglossia because the voices of black women are not heard as an "opposing view." Without contesting and reconfiguring the limits of expression imposed on them, they cannot enter into discursive confrontation with the white hegemony. Thus, the notion of hegemonic articulation needs to be supplemented by taking into account si-

lence indicating the obliteration of voices in the very process of setting up
the confrontation between the opposing points of view.

In order to work out the range of affirmative and testimonial relations to
the Other, Henderson submits the Gadamerian hermeneutics to an equally
radical revision. In this case, Henderson exploits the ambiguity within the
hermeneutical model of noncontestatory communication, in which the emphasis can be placed either on consensus mediated by the common tradition
or on listening to a wholly other "Thou." Although she stresses the importance of the shared history and literary tradition among black women writers, Henderson explores the limits of consensus by evoking the "foreign-
ness" of the Other and the opacity of the sexed body. In the first powerful
example of these limits, Henderson evokes the ecstatic tradition of speaking
in tongues in the black Pentecostal Holiness Church: "In the Holiness
church, . . . speaking unknown tongues (tongues known only to God) . . .
emphasizes the particular, private, closed, and privileged communication between the congregant and the divinity. Inaccessible to the general congre-
gation, this mode of communication is outside the realm of public discourse
and *foreign* to the known tongues of humankind" (ST, 149, emphasis added).
By disrupting the bounds of familiar communication, the foreign tongue
preserves the opacity of language and the otherness of the divinity.
Significantly, for Henderson the ecstatic mode of speaking in tongues represents an instance of embodied speech, which she explores by referring to
Kristeva's notion of the semiotic. For Henderson the religious practice of
ecstatic glossolalia, associated with the church of her mother, revives and
evokes the mother/child semiotic relation where language is still steeped in
rhythm, gesture, and drive and not yet reduced to symbolic abstraction. A
similar limit of abstraction and intelligibility is reached in sexual *jouissance*.
By interpreting Toni Morrison's *Sula* in the context of Kristeva's semiotic,
Henderson reads sexual *jouissance* as a rupture and a "precondition" for re-
vising discursive determinations.

The juxtaposition of Henderson's and Lyotard's work raises a crucial
question for the project of feminist ethics, namely, how to reformulate the
relation between justice and embodiment in the context of agonistic politics.
Both Henderson's interpretation of Sula's *jouissance* and Lyotard's analysis of
the sexed body approach embodied thinking as the presentation of the unpresentable, as the analogue of justice irreducible to abstract normative criteria. By marking what is missing in the antagonistic articulations of racial
and gender differences, this bodily sign enables not only an attentiveness to
silenced voices but also a transformation of the dominant speech. Indeed, by
reading such a sign as a figure for speaking in tongues, Henderson treats sexuality not only as a limit of language but also as a "precondition" for the revision and contestation of the existing power relations. Exposing the limita-

tions of both the agonistic and the testimonial speech acts, Henderson's analysis of embodied speech in the black women's literary tradition opens a space for a feminist ethics of dissensus, which places the questions of justice and embodiment at the center of the antagonistic relations.

In this chapter, I have argued that the possibility of a feminist ethics of dissensus can emerge only from a complex negotiation between the hegemonic articulation of the multiple forms of antagonism and the ethical responsibility grounded in embodiment. The outcome of this negotiation is neither nontheoretical politics of difference without ethics—that is, a politics reduced to the indifferent struggle of the heterogeneous forces—nor a utopian theory of justice transcending conflict. Rather, at stake in the feminist ethics of dissensus is a decisive reformulation of the politics of difference, so that it not only strives to create alternative hegemonic formations in order to contest the interlocking patterns of domination based on the racial, gender, and class inequalities but also bears an obligation to redress the differend—the erased conflicts in which victims cannot signify their damages. Finally, I have suggested that such a politics bears a necessary relation to embodiment, conceived not only as a site of struggle but also as a condition of ethical judgment. By exposing what is missing in the antagonistic articulations of racial and gender differences, sexuality marks, therefore, a point where the feminist politics of difference crosses the path with a feminist ethics of dissensus in an infinite pursuit of justice.

## CHAPTER 4

# The Libidinal Economy of Power, Democracy, and the Ethics of Psychoanalysis

IN THE FIRST PART of this book, I elaborated two main aspects of the ethics of dissensus—the ethos of becoming and the responsibility for the Other—in the context of *polemos*, hegemonic politics, and the modern forms of power constitutive of democracy. I argued that the ethics of dissensus does not aspire to the neutral position transcending power, provided for instance by normative criteria, but rather articulates the difficult role of responsibility and freedom in democratic struggles against racist and sexist oppression. In place of obedience to moral law or reassuring normative criteria enabling us to judge the outcome of these struggles in advance, such an ethics supplements hegemonic politics with an infinite responsibility for the Other, a responsibility that never ceases to obligate us to find the means of expression and compensation for the obliterated wrongs. I argued that such an ethics is crucial for feminism because it provides an alternative to both the indifferent struggle of heterogeneous forces, on the one hand, and to the utopian vision of justice transcending the antagonisms of race, class, sexuality, and gender, on the other.

By turning to Kristeva's work on psychoanalysis, I want to articulate two new aspects of the feminist ethics of dissensus: what I call, in a reference to Judith Butler's recent project, the libidinal economy of power and "the psychic life" of ethics. In contrast to most discussions of power focused exclusively on external struggle, I examine the subject's conflicting relation to "the Other within" and ask under what conditions it can function either as a condition of responsibility or as an exacerbation of social antagonism. To answer this question, I examine first the relevance of feminist psychoanalysis for the theories of democracy by rethinking constitutive antagonisms, the instability of social relations in democracy, and their hegemonic articulations in the context of the libidinal economy of drive subtending the sociosymbolic order. By stressing the inseparability of the sociosymbolic from the libidinal economy of the drive, I move the analysis of the "psychic life of power" beyond the problem of identifications, predominant in both Judith Butler's, Ernesto Laclau's, and Chantal Mouffe's political theories, toward the question of fantasy, *jouissance*, and the irreducible negativity within the subject at odds with its social positionality. This rethinking of the constitutive antagonism in democracy in the context of Kristeva's heterogeneous and conflicted subject, split between desire and drive, signifier and affect, foregrounds the political function of fantasy in hegemonic politics and, in so doing, contests the disembodied and desexualized character of citizenship separated from the affective and libidinal dimension of intersubjectivity.

The relation between the negativity of the drive and the constitutive antagonism in democracy provides a context of my second topic in this chapter—the "psychic life" of ethics. Through the juxtaposition of Levinas's ethics of responsibility and Kristeva's ethics of "the irreconcilable," I develop a psychoanalytic model of the ethical relation to the Other, irreducible either to the narcissistic reflection of the ego Ideal or to the fetishistic embodiment of the abject in social relations. By pushing Kristeva's and Levinas's ethics toward their limits, I define such a model as the interplay of three movements: the traversal of fantasy; the sublimation of the death drive; and the confrontation with the abject as one's own most intimate yet inassimilable alterity. By rethinking the conditions of ethical responsibility in the context of the libidinal economy of the drive, I contest the separation of ethics not only from embodiment and sensibility but also from conflict and sexuality.

## Racist Fantasies:
## The Libidinal Politics of Nationalism and Fascism

I would like to begin the discussion of the libidinal economy of power in the context of Kristeva's work on fascism and nationalism in order to foreground two elements missing in Judith Butler's analysis of "the psychic life" of power[1]: the political mobilization of destructive *jouissance* and the ideological function of racist fantasy. As Slavoj Žižek argues, fantasy structuring enjoyment indicates a political dimension of power "beyond interpellation," that is, beyond the symbolic and imaginary identifications.[2] The unconscious hold of fantasy depends on its double function as a defensive screen, protecting the subject against direct intrusion of the real, on the one hand, and as an obscene invisible supplement of power, covering over the instability of the symbolic and the sociopolitical antagonism, on the other. In this sense, fantasy not only situates the subject in relation to its object cause of desire but also compensates for the instability of its imaginary and symbolic identifications. The paradox of fantasy lies, therefore, in the fact that by coordinating the desire of the subject, it at the same time functions as "a screen concealing the gap . . . the abyss of the desire of the Other," that is, "the 'death drive' in its pure form" (*SO*, 118).[3] Because, according to Žižek, fantasy plays a crucial role in hegemonic formations—a role often at odds with the explicit political program—democratic politics needs both to articulate the equivalence among diverse struggles against oppression and to traverse fantasies that might underlie such articulations.

Kristeva examines this libidinal dimension of power beyond identification in her work on the reversal of democracy into fascism. By focusing on destructive *jouissance* and fantasy in political life, Kristeva investigates, on the one hand, the uses of abjection in fascism and, on the other, the function of the Freudian "logic" of the uncanny in xenophobia and racism. In both of these cases, she aims to diagnose "the drive foundations" and the "libidinal surplus value" of racism: "For this indeed is the economy, one of horror and suffering in their libidinal surplus-value, which has been tapped, rationalized, and made operative by Nazism and Fascism" (*PH*, 155).[4] To examine the political function of racist fantasies, I would like to situate Kristeva's discussion of fascism in the context of Claude Lefort's theory of totalitarianism. As programmatically antidemocratic political forms, fascism and Stalinism emerge, Lefort argues, as countermeasures to the fragility of democracy, manifesting itself in the disincorporation of power and the indeterminacy of social relations. What totalitarianism first of all negates is the symbolic character of the empty place of power instituted in democracy: it aims to restore the connection between power and the body by mobilizing the fantasy of social unity grounded in social substance and ultimately embodied in the figure of the leader. In the totalitarian regime, the notion of immanent power leads to the fusion of the state and civil society, of political and administrative power, and to the subordination of the political apparatus to the central relation between the leader and the ruled. The negation of the division between the state and society is intertwined, according to Lefort, with the negation of the internal antagonisms within society—in their place, fascism sets up the fantasy of the unified, self-sufficient, and transparent society in control of its organization and destiny. As Lefort points out, these two images of "the People-as-One" and "the Power-as-One" embodied by the leader are two sides of the same fantasy—the fantasy of the corporeality of power grounded in the substance of the social body: "Power ceases to designate an empty place: it is materialized in an organ . . . which is supposed to be capable of concentrating in itself all the forces of society."[5] As both Foucault and Lefort in different ways argue, the totalitarian demand for unconditional loyalty, and its promise of the restoration of social wholeness, whether based on the purity of race, as is the case in fascism, or proletariat class, as in Stalinism, cancels the symbolic function of power as an empty place and reintroduces into modernity the premodern logic of identification based on the substance of the social body. Thus, the ideological coherence of totalitarianism is intimately bound with the phantasmatic revitalization of the social body.

For Lefort the phantasmatic reincorporation of power can be assured of its consistency by the invention and expulsion of the enemies that threaten to pollute the social body. As he argues, "The constitution of the People-as-One requires the incessant production of enemies. It is not only necessary to convert, at the level of phantasy, real adversaries of the regime or real opponents into the figures of the evil Other: it is also necessary to invent them. . . . The campaigns of exclusion, persecution and, for quite a while, terror reveal a new image of the social body. The enemy of the people is regarded as a parasite or a waste product to be eliminated" (*PFMS*, 298). This reification and displacement of what Chantal Mouffe calls the constitutive antagonisms of democracy into a figure of the imaginary enemy replaces the unstable sociosymbolic order with the phantasmatic integrity of the social body: "The pursuit of the enemies of the people is carried out in the name of an ideal of social prophylaxis. . . . What is at stake is always the integrity of the body. It is as if the body had to assure itself of its own identity by expelling its waste matter, or as if it had to close in upon itself by withdrawing from the outside, by averting the threat of intrusion by alien elements" (*PFMS*, 298). For Lefort the expulsion of enemies is but one of the symptoms that the phantasmatic revitalization of the body coincides with its opposite, with the unleashing of the death drive into social relations and with the eventual dissolution of the subject (*PFMS*, 306).

To diagnose this phantasmatic logic of the reincorporation of power mobilized by the fascist and racist ideologies, I would like to compare Kristeva's and Fanon's analysis of phobia. A complex elaboration of aggressivity and want demonstrating the weakness of the symbolic order, phobia reveals a correlation between the fantasy of incorporation and the projection of internal antagonism within the subject on the hallucinatory object. As Kristeva argues in *Powers of Horror*, the phobic fear of an object is a defensive screen for the fear of the void constitutive of symbolic order, subjectivity, and social relations.[6] The status of the phobic object, then, is a hallucinatory metaphor that points to the objectless state of the death drive—a metaphor that no longer operates in signifiers but finds the signifying material in drive and perception (hallucination): "Phobia is a metaphor that has mistaken its place, forsaking language for drive and sight" (*PH*, 35). To offset fear associated with the void constitutive of signification, the phobic subject regresses to the narcissistic fantasy of the cannibalistic and murderous incorporation of the maternal breast; yet, this fusion with the maternal body, which promises *jouissance*, is threatening in its own right because the subject is always already located in the symbolic order governed by the prohibition of incest. In response to the symbolic threat of the superego, the subject inverts the fantasy and puts itself in place of the object—instead of devouring the mother, it is being devoured: "In phobia, fear and aggressivity . . . come back to me from the outside. The fantasy of incorporation by means of which I attempt to escape fear . . . threatens me nonetheless, for a symbolic, paternal prohibition already dwells in me. . . . In the face of this second threat . . . I attempt another procedure: I am not the one that devours, I am being devoured by him" (*PH*, 39). What this phobic structure reveals is the paranoid projection of the incestuous *jouissance* and the murderous aggressivity of the death drive onto the Other. In the phobic fantasy, the imaginary others, for instance, the racist and misogynist constructions of Jews, blacks, and women, become a metaphor of a subject's own aggression, of its "empty and incorporating mouth."

Once mobilized by the political regime in paranoid fashion—that is, through the repudiation of want—the phobic regression to the narcissistic mechanisms of incorporation and projection allows the collectivity to ground the symbolic in the social body and to displace instabilities, negativity, and aggression on the imaginary other who seems to threaten its purity from without. As Kristeva writes, when "that imaginary machinery is transformed into a social institution . . . what you get is the infamy of fascism" (*PH*, 25). It is important to stress that for both Kristeva and Fanon any deflection of phobia into the social is mediated through the internalized social judgment of the superego (*PH*, 15). For Fanon, the choice of the phobic object evoking anxiety and revulsion is always culturally, economically, and politically overdetermined.[7] This means that the phantasmatic construction of the imaginary other as the "maleficient," polluting, or threatening agent is culturally and historically specific, reflecting and supporting gender, race, and class power relations. At the same time, fantasy reveals, in Kristeva's words, the libidinal "surplus value" of enjoyment that fills a void in these antagonistic relations.

I would like to focus for a moment on two paradigmatic examples of the racist mobilization of phobia in modernity: on Frantz Fanon's analysis of "psychopathology" of colonialism and Kristeva's discussion of anti-Semitism and xenophobia. In his pioneering analysis in *Black Skin, White Masks*, Fanon diagnoses the psychosexual mechanism of racism crystallized in the phantasmatic construction of the black subject as "a phobogenic object" (*BSWM*, 151). In an ironic rewriting of the little Hans story, Fanon describes his encounter with the little white boy who at his sight throws himself into his mother's arms with a cry "Mama, the nigger's going to eat me up" (*BSWM*, 114). As a "foundational fantasy" supporting the racist structure of interpellation, the little boy's fear exemplifies "Negrophobia" as the expression of white aggressivity, indeed, as the metaphor of the white boy's "empty and devouring mouth" longing for the fusion with the lost maternal body. In this fantasy frame, both the incestuous desire for the lost *jouissance*—for the union of meaning and being, for the impossible reincorporation of power—and the punishing aggressivity of the superego are externalized in the black body. Fanon writes, "The civilized white man retains an irrational longing for the unusual eras of sexual license, of orgiastic scenes, of unpunished rapes, of unrepressed incest. . . . Projecting his own desires onto the Negro, the white man behaves 'as if' the Negro really had them" (*BSWM*, 165). According to Fanon the distinguishing feature of the racist fantasy is that this conflict between the reincorporation of power and the aggressivity of the superego is inscribed on the black body. Because of this "epidermalization" of the fantasy, the black body is experienced in racist imaginary as a "biological" threat to the imaginary integrity of the white body. Fanon writes in reference to Lacan's mirror stage, "The Negro, because of his body, impedes the closing of the postural schema of the white man" (*BSWM*, 160). Such a phobic construction of the black body as the repository of what is "the inassimilable" (*BSWM*, 161)—the abject, phallic *jouissance*, and the aggressivity of the death drive—consolidates the false unity of the symbolic order and the ideological coherence of whiteness.

Although Fanon writes that, unlike the Negro, the Jew signifies "the intellectual danger" (*BSWM*, 165), Kristeva's analysis of the fascist mobilization of anti-Semitism reveals a similar mechanism of fantasy, aggression, and *jouissance*. In her analysis of anti-Semitism, Kristeva focuses on Louis-Ferdinand Céline, whose "style represents the height of twentieth-century French literature and whose anti-Semitic and para-Nazi pamphlets reveal one of the blackest aspects of contemporary history" (*PP*, 314).[8] As the author of experimental literary texts, Céline was admired by a number of leftist intellectuals, including Sartre, and condemned by nationalist critics for the decomposition of national language; as the writer of the most virulent anti-Semitic pamphlets, he was enthusiastically praised by the fascist cultural critics such as Lucien Rebatet.[9] As Alice Kaplan and David Carroll acknowledge (although not without criticism), Kristeva refuses to separate Céline's innovative style from his reactionary pamphlets but focuses on the point where his avant-garde performance of abjection collapses into anti-Semitic fascist propaganda.[10] On the basis of Céline's writing, Kristeva diagnoses a double gesture of racist fantasy supporting fascist ideology: "the rage" against the unstable symbolic order and a call for a "counterweight," for another law "seen as mystic positivity" (*PH*, 178). The instability of the symbolic leading to the anarchy and nihilism of Céline's texts—"the horror of hell without God"—is ultimately reversed into a delirious yearning for the "absolute, full, and reassuring" law: "[Céline's] adhering to Nazism . . . becomes integrated as an internal, an inherent counterweight, as a massive need for identity, a group, project, meaning" (*PH*, 136–37).

Céline's "massive need" for identity based on the positivity of the law is a manifestation of the delirious racist fantasy of the reincorporation of power, promising the union of meaning and *jouissance*: this "*material positivity*" of the law, "a full, tangible, reassuring, and happy substance, will be embodied in the Family, the Nation, the Race, and the Body" (*PH*, 178). As Kristeva argues, Céline's anti-Semitic writings transform the experience of abjection into the phallic ambition to name the unnameable, to create the ultimate totality of the substance and law, meaning and Being. Céline's anti-Semitism and fascism can be seen, therefore, as a reversal of the secular logic of democracy into "a kind of parareligious formation," into a fantasy of "the immanence of substance and meaning, of the natural/racial/familial, of the feminine and the masculine, of life and death—a glorification of the Phallus that does not speak its name" (*PH*, 179).[11] By becoming the Phallus, the delirious subject merges with the abject, experiencing both the phallic *jouissance* and the paranoid rage to exterminate any obstacle exemplifying its impossibility. This phantasmatic fusion with the archaic mother forecloses the symbolic function and destroys all forms of exteriority.

In Céline's anti-Semitic fantasies, the obstacle to the delirious fusion with the abject is embodied in the figure of the "Jewish brother," who is associated with both the paternal master hoarding *jouissance* and with the feminized abject excrement:

The abject is then embodied in the figure of a maleficent agent, both feminine and phallic, miserable and all-powerful. . . . What once defied discourse now becomes the ultimate object of one and only one interpretation, the source and acme of a polymorphous *jouissance* in which interpreter, this time in his delirium, is finally reunited with what denies, exceeds, and, excites him. . . . This interpretative delirium . . . found in Céline the Jew as its privileged object in the context of Hitlerism. (*PP*, 318)

As both Kristeva's analysis of Céline's misogynist and anti-Semitic fantasies and Fanon's discussion of the psychopathology of racism show, the impossibility of *jouissance* and the paranoid rage is displaced in the racist imaginary onto the figure of the envied and despised racialized other: "The fantasy of a Jewish threat, weighing against the Aryan world . . . in a period when, on the contrary, persecutions against the Jews are beginning, cannot be explained in any other way; it emanates directly out of that vision of the Jew as a being of having, as issuing from the All in which he joys, and especially from the immediate sexualization of that jouissance" (*PH*, 183). Symptomatic of the deflection of the abject into the social realm, the racist and misogynist fantasies display the "drive economy" always already rationalized and mediated by the social judgment. As such, these fantasies support and consolidate the long history of anti-Semitic and racist discourse, in which "the Jew" or "the Negro" increasingly represent a "metaphysical source of evil," the source of every destruction.

The function of the racist fantasies is not limited, however, to the fascist ideology of the immanence of law and substance but also has to be interrogated in the context of democratic politics. In 1989 *Etrangers à nous-mêmes*, translated into English as *Strangers to Ourselves*, Kristeva diagnoses the phantasmatic logic of the democratic nation-state by focusing on the function of the foreigner as a symptom of what Chantal Mouffe calls "irreducible social antagonisms." In order to preserve the unity of national community, the intrinsic contradictions of the democratic state are reified and projected onto the external figure of the foreigner—the trope, which, as David Carroll demonstrates, has often been synonymous in anti-Semitic nationalist literature with the image of the Jew.[12] As a symptom of the internal contradictions in the democratic nation-state and the impasses of political rationality, the foreigner both enables and confounds the clear separation between myth and reason, the archaic and the modern, the man and citizen, *jouissance* and law, same and other: "The difficulty engendered by the matter of foreigners would be completely contained in the deadlock caused by the distinction that sets the *citizen* apart from *man*. . . . The process means . . . that one can be more or less a man to the extent that one is more or less a citizen, that he who is not a citizen is not fully a man. Between the man and a citizen there is a scar: the foreigner" (*ST*, 97–98). Permeated with hatred and *jouissance*, this symptom, however, does not display merely the impasses of the political rationality or logical contradictions but crystallizes "the prickly passions aroused by the intrusion of the *other* in the homogeneity of a group" (*ST*, 41).[13]

In *Strangers to Ourselves*, Kristeva analyzes the logic of the social symptom according to the Freudian logic of the uncanny, which describes an unsettling return of the repressed *jouissance* and irreducible excess of the drive within the symbolic register.[14] As Mladen Dolar points out, the Freudian uncanny belongs to the historical formation of the Enlightenment, emerging as a counterpart of the disintegration of the religious communities and the subsequent formation of modern nation-states. If in the premodern political affiliations the dimension of the uncanny—the threatening proximity of *jouissance*—was covered over by the sacred and assigned to the place of sovereignty,[15] the institution of the empty place of power in modern democracies turns the uncanny into the "unplaceable" surplus of negativity eroding national identifications. This uncanny image of the foreigner "comes in the place and stead of the death of God and, with those who are believers, the foreigner is there to bring him back to life" (*ST*, 40).[16]

Addressing the contemporary crisis of European identity generated by the

opposite tendencies of economic consolidation and the spread of ethnic particularisms, the rise of anti-Semitism, and postcolonial conflicts,[17] Kristeva
diagnoses the violence of xenophobia as a defensive response to a double
negation of the national attachment that the figure of the foreigner represents. On the one hand, the foreigner's ethnic and racial difference—"the
face that is *so other* bears the mark of a crossed threshold" (*ST*, 4)—undermines the imaginary likeness on which the ego and the group model their
identity. Being always in excess, the figure of foreigner condenses all
differences and antagonisms, which negate the illusory commonality of ordinary life and language (*ST*, 23). This mechanism of projection covers over
the negativity and the antagonisms within the group by presenting them as
a threat emanating from without: the foreigner becomes "the image of a
malevolent double" into which the group "expels the share of destruction it
cannot contain" (*ST*, 183). By contrast, the uniqueness of the foreigner
functions as a promise of *jouissance* that is always already lost in collective
life.[18] In the xenophobic fantasy, the catastrophic happiness of the foreigner—"happiness seems to prevail, *in spite of everything*, because something
has definitely been exceeded . . . the space of a promised infinite"—signifies
the destructive *jouissance* and by the same token manifests its traumatic loss
in the collective life (*ST*, 4). As a figure of the lost *jouissance*, the foreigner,
or the racialized Other, functions in national fantasies as what Lacan calls
"the imaginary agent of deprivation," who threatens to deprive us of our
good. By blaming the Other for the theft of enjoyment, the group conceals
"the traumatic fact that [it] . . . never possessed what was allegedly stolen."
As both Žižek and Kristeva argue, national affiliation cannot be sustained by
merely symbolic and imaginary identifications; it requires a supplementary
function of phantasmatic enjoyment, transforming the emptiness of the symbolic into the substance of national community. According to Žižek,
"Nation *exists* only as long as its specific *enjoyment* continues to be materialized in a set of social practices and transmitted through national myths that
structure these practices."[19] As a function of collective belief, *jouissance*
promises to fill the symbolic void on several levels: on the political level, the
empty place of power instituted by democracy; on the moral level, the void
of the Supreme Good created by Kant's formal conception of the categorical imperative; and on the linguistic level, the void created by the arbitrary
character of the sign.[20] Yet, as Kristeva argues, the phantasmatic enjoyment
that "invalidate[s] the arbitrariness of signs" and fills the empty place of
power in democracy is inseparable from a threatening experience of strangeness (*ST*, 186). This recurrence of anxiety projected on the figure of the foreigner points to the paradoxes of *jouissance* commemorated in national
myths—always already lost, such a *jouissance* is still barred by a prohibition.
By supplementing the "weakness of language as a symbolic barrier" to *jouis-*

*sance*, the imagined national community finds itself threatened by both the loss and the proximity of prohibited *jouissance*.

Kristeva's diagnosis of racist fantasies and her emphasis on the ambivalence of national identifications provides an important counterweight to Benedict Anderson's influential study, *Imagined Communities: Reflections on the Origins and Spread of Nationalism*. By the end of his discussion of the institutions and social processes that enable the rise and spread of nationalism, in particular, the appearance of the modern conception of "empty" historical time, the arbitrary language, the convergence of capitalism with print technology, and, we can add after Lefort, the institution of the empty place of power, Anderson admits that the analysis of identifications fails to explain the affective "surplus value" characteristic of group formation: "It is doubtful whether either social change or transformed consciousness, in themselves, do much to explain the *attachment* that peoples feel for the inventions of their imaginations."[21] By explaining this libidinal "attachment" in terms of fantasy, I want to argue that the political function of fantasy not only underlies national affiliations but also is at work in different ways in most group formations. That is why democratic politics cannot be limited to hegemonic coalitions but has to interrogate the political mobilization of destructive *jouissance*, the obverse side of which is all too often constituted by ethnic violence, anti-Semitism, and xenophobia.

## Kristeva's Ethics: The Negativization of Narcissism and the Respect for the Irreconcilable

Kristeva's diagnosis of the libidinal economy of racism, fascism, and xenophobia motivates her search for a new ethics of psychoanalysis in the wake of the crisis of Western rationality.[22] Yet, despite the numerous references to ethics throughout her career, the reconstruction of the specific meaning of "ethics" in Kristeva's project is not an easy undertaking. This is so not only because the ethics of psychoanalysis, like other postmodern ethical reflections considered in this book, does not offer a positive program or a set of rules for a new morality, but also because the meaning of ethics changes at different stages in Kristeva's work. Working through the Hegelian tradition of *Sittlichkeit* in *Revolution in Poetic Language*, Kristeva starts her ethical inquiry with the question of freedom realized through social change. In *Tales of Love* she is more concerned with the transcendence of narcissism through the ethical relation to the Other revealed in love. In *Strangers to Ourselves* the task of ethics is to traverse the hatred and the fear experienced in the face of Other by acknowledging the dis-ease with "the other scene" within the subject. For Kristeva all these different modalities of ethics of psychoanalysis inhere in what she calls "the negativization of narcissism"[23]—that is, in the acknowledgment of the internal alterity and antagonism within the subject. Kristeva analyzes many instances of the subject's own unsettling heterogeneity—the abject, the uncanny, the death drive, sex, and the aporia of primary narcissism—all of which point not only to different modalities of "the strange within the familiar" (ST, 183) but also to the possible projection of this discovery onto the Other.

The changing emphasis in Kristeva's work raises a crucial question for an ethics of dissensus: namely, in what sense can the acknowledgment of the internal alterity and antagonism within the subject be a condition of responsibility in intersubjective relations. Although an increasing number of feminist critics, among them Drucilla Cornell, Alice Jardine, Jaqueline Rose, Kelly Oliver, Jean Graybeal, and Marilyn Edelstein, have stressed the importance of ethics in Kristeva's project,[24] this question has not been sufficiently addressed. In order to find the means of mediating between "the irreconcilable" within the subject and the responsibility for the Other, I reconsider Kristeva's ethics of psychoanalysis in the context of Levinas's work.[25] Before I address some of the difficulties inherent in such an engagement, let me suggest briefly why the juxtaposition of Levinas and Kristeva is crucial for the notion of the ethics I develop in this book and for the contemporary debates on ethics more generally. First of all, despite all their differences, both Kristeva's and Levinas's ethical projects are fundamentally opposed to the totalitarian ideologies grounded in the unity of social body, the narcissistic fantasies of completeness, or the idealized imaginary community without difference, conflict, or division. Second, the psychoanalytic account of the antagonism, alterity, and heterogeneity within the subject complicates significantly Levinas's account of the ethical experience; in turn, Levinas's work poses a challenge for psychoanalysis to work out an ethical model of responsibility based on the radical heteronomy of the other person. Furthermore, the juxtaposition of Levinas and Kristeva allows us to reconsider the relation between ethics and social conflicts in the context of the negativity and antagonism within the subject represented by the libidinal economy of the drives. Such an emphasis on the division and conflict within the subject makes the Levinasian separation of ethics from all forms of violence rather untenable—on the contrary, it forces us to accept vigilance and elaborate responsibility for violence. And finally, by pushing Kristeva's and Levinas's ethics toward their limits, the ethics of dissensus I develop contests the separation of responsibility from embodiment, love, and sexuality.

Recently, a number of scholars have investigated the possibility of the critical rapprochement between Levinas and psychoanalysis in the context of Lacan's work.[26] Yet, despite some striking similarities in Lacan's and Levinas's texts regarding the extraordinary importance of alterity, temporality, trauma, desire, and the asymmetrical relation to the Other (to the Other sex in Lacan, or to the face of the Other in Levinas), any sustained negotiation between these two projects sooner or later confronts two obstacles: first, the irreducible difference in their formulations of otherness; and second, the difficulty of working out the ethical responsibility for the Other in psychoanalytic terms. Regarding the first obstacle, Hans-Dieter Gondek writes that "a fundamental difference between Lacan and Levinas on the question of the Other needs to be brought out. While 'Levinas's thought remains in play—a play of difference and of analogy—between the face of God and the face of my neighbor . . . ,' the Other for Lacan is first of all faceless; the Other is *a site* . . . that is required so that the play of signifiers does not remain an empty play."[27] We can confront this obstacle, however, if we focus not only on the contrast between the alterity of the face and the otherness of the symbolic order but also on the radical exteriority (Lacan's *das Ding*, Levinas's trace, Kristeva's abject) manifesting itself at the limits of language. For someone not familiar with Levinas's ethics the term "face" might be misleading since for Levinas it does not connote a presence or an appearance of the Other but, rather, an exorbitant trace transcending the order of representation. To underscore the withdrawal of alterity from the order of appearance, Levinas describes the trace of the Other in temporal terms as an immemorial past that has never been present but, like the traumatic event, can only be experienced retrospectively. It is this anarchical and traumatizing relation to the Other that calls the subject to responsibility prior to any initiative or freedom of the ego. In the Levinasian ethics, the encounter with the Other is irreducible to the imaginary order of intersubjective identifications but, in a manner evocative of Kristeva's negativization of narcissism, involves a profound displacement of the narcissistic ego, an insurmountable disturbance of the domestic economy, a disruption of propriation and property—a calling into question of everything one wishes to claim as one's own: "The heteronomous experience we seek would be an attitude that cannot be converted into a category, and whose movement unto the other is not recuperated in identification."[28]

Before I discuss Kristeva's account of otherness, I would like to consider for a moment a passage where Lacan comes closest to Levinas's sense of alterity as the paradoxical epiphany of the face, which withdraws itself from the order of appearance and displaces the subject from the nominative "I" to the accusative "me." For Lacan as for Kristeva, this sense of alterity manifests itself in the encounter with the foreigner—*Fremde:*[29]

I believe that one finds in that word [you] the temptation to tame the Other, that prehistoric. . . . Other, which suddenly threatens to surprise us and to cast us down from the height of its appearance. "You" [*Toi*] contains a form of defense and . . . it is entirely in this "You," and nowhere else, that one finds what I evoked today concerning *das Ding*. (*SVII*, 56)

The address to the Other in terms of a "you"—a pronoun that implies intersubjective reciprocity—is a defensive attempt to master the strangeness of the Other and reduce it to the imaginary order of identification. If we take seriously Lacan's claim that one finds *das Ding* "entirely in this 'You' and nowhere else," then we can say that the figure of the stranger represents the encounter with the Other in the Levinasian sense and at the same time provokes a mode of defense in the form of the domesticating "you." Nonetheless, even this defensive response displaces the ego from its position of mastery. As Lacan continues, what corresponds to this defensive "you" is not the nominative "I" but the accusative " 'Me!' of apology, a 'Me!' of refusal, a 'Me!' that is simply not for me [*un Moi d'excuse, un Moi de reject, un Moi de très peu pour moi*]" (SVII, 56).[30]

Although in both Lacan's and Levinas's work the traumatizing encounter with the stranger/neighbor functions as the primal scene of ethics, the crucial difference lies in the fact that for Lacan the heteronomous experience of "the fundamental strangeness" illustrates the paradox of *jouissance* whereas for Levinas it commands the subject, beyond the experience of anxiety or fright, to ethical responsibility. Consequently, if psychoanalytical theory is to clear the ground for ethics, it has to negotiate the passage from fright—what Levinas calls "a horror of the other that remains other"—to responsibility. By turning to Kristeva's work,[31] I propose to define such a passage as the negativization of narcissism followed by the sublimation of the death drive. More specifically, I argue that the psychoanalytic model of ethical relation to the Other can be characterized as the interplay of three movements: the traversal of fantasy; the encounter with the abject as one's own most intimate yet inassimilable alterity; and the sublimation of the death drive. This interplay confronts the subject with the inassimilable otherness within herself and the exorbitant alterity of the Other while deflecting the violence of the death drive from the murderous destruction of the Other toward the restructuring of the symbolic order.

In order to understand the ethical relation to the Other as the negativization of narcissism rather than what Kaja Silverman calls the "active idealization" of the loved object,[32] we have to go through the detour of Kristeva's discussion of the aporia of the primary narcissism—the aporia negated by the ideal ego and the "Edenic image" of narcissism elaborated in a defensive way by "the neurotic subject when he sets himself under the aegis of the father" (PH, 63). If the ubiquity of narcissism in psychic life, from the formation of the ego Ideal to sexual relations, shows, according to Freud, the reduction of the Other to an imaginary reflection of an ideal image of the ego, Kristeva argues that the aporetic structure of primary narcissism also reveals the opposite economy—namely, the fact that emergence of the archaic form of the ego is already an effect of the inscription of the void in the psyche and the presymbolic relations to alterity. Preceding the specular identification in the mirror stage, primary narcissism is not an original state of autoeroticism but an effect of a new "psychic action"—which Kristeva describes as the movements of metaphoricity and rejection constituting the ego through the archaic relations to otherness.

In *Tales of Love*, Kristeva argues that the presymbolic ternary structure of primary narcissism is a kind of knot formed by two very different modalities of otherness—the violent rejection of the abject mother and the primary idealizing identification with the imaginary father: "Narcissism would be that correlation (with the imaginary father and the 'ab-jetted' mother) enacted around the central emptiness of that transference" (*TL*, 41–42). Understood as a metaphorical shifting, primary identification functions as an originary "intrasymbolic" transference of the not yet ego into the place of maternal desire. Associated with the incorporation characteristic of the oral phase, primary identification is not, however, a cannibalistic introjection of a partial object but rather an assimilation of the Other's words, which provide a model for the future subject.

Despite Kristeva's frequent disclaimers about its theoretical inappropriateness, the gendering of primary identification as paternal appears problematic and has been criticized on numerous occasions by feminist critics.[33] Rather than entering this debate directly, I want to point out that primary narcissism is not gendered in itself but retroactively: such gendering is always already an effect of the mediation of fantasy and secondary narcissism reflecting social judgment. Only by exposing this retroactive constitution of primary narcissism, can Kristeva submit it to critical "negativization," for instance, when she points out that the magnet of primary identification represents in fact the qualities of both parents—"a nourishing-mother-and-ideal-father, in short a conglomeration that already condenses two into one" (*TL*, 222). Furthermore, she not only uncovers the complicity between social judgment and heterosexual fantasy but also frequently points to the alternative, homosexual female fantasy of "the reunion of a woman–mother with the body of *her* mother"—the body desired all the more passionately because "it lacks a penis: that body cannot penetrate her as can a man" (*DL*, 239). Kristeva underscores a mediation of homosexual fantasy even in the normative heterosexual female desire that allows a woman "to secure once and for all . . . possession of the nourishing mother" in the figure of the husband (*TL*, 226). It is, of course, deeply problematic that in Kristeva's work lesbian desire manifests itself more frequently through normative heterosexual displacements like motherhood or artistic practice, which indeed suggests, as Judith Butler has argued, that "lesbian sexuality is intrinsically unintelligible."[34] However, by arguing that primary identification does not just reinforce "the fully ideological division" between maternal and paternal[35] but, because of its instability, opens a possibility of homosexual identification for both sexes, I want to point out a place where the heterosexual privilege in Kristeva's work is at odds with the presuppositions of her theory.

Since primary identification both preserves the emptiness within the psychic space and constitutes the first mode of defense against the death drive, it presupposes the other pole of primary narcissism—the rejection of the abject mother. In a manner evocative of Melanie Klein's splitting of the object, the opposition between primary identification and the rejection of the abject in *Tales of Love* splits the pre-Oedipal mother into the "loving," "nourishing" mother and "clinging" mother, into the maternal desire supporting primary identification and the "maternal container," a receptacle for the inassimilable negativity of the drives. How can we interpret this splitting of the pre-Oedipal mother into what Kelly Oliver calls the sublime and the abject?[36] If the nourishing mother, together with the primal father, functions as the magnet of the primary identification and thus constitutes the minimum of idealization, the seed of the ego Ideal and the subsequent idealizations of the Other as the reflection of that Ideal, the abject mother signifies what is excluded from the pleasure principle and narcissistic identifications— the negativity of the drive and the signification of the primordial "unnameable otherness" (*PH*, 59). Repudiated within the narcissistic economy and covered over by the structure of fantasy, the abject signifies "the horror of the other that remains other."

I would like to suggest that, in the context of Levinas's work, the abject can be interpreted as the primordial constriction constituting the ipseity of ego—a condition of possibility of the heteronomous relation to alterity within the symbolic. Since it signifies the expulsion of what is inassimilable to the subject, Kristeva's abject, like Lacan's *das Ding*, carves out the first outside of the subject—a nonsymbolizable "beyond" of representation and signification registered in the quest of desire only as something missed and not as the subject's correlative—from its most intimate interiority. As Lacan writes, "*das Ding* is at the center only in the sense that it is excluded. That is to say, in reality *das Ding* has to be posited as exterior, as the prehistoric Other that it is impossible to forget—the Other whose primacy of position Freud affirms in the form of something . . . strange to me" (SVII, 71).[37] Although worked out in a very different idiom, Kristeva's psychoanalytic account of the abject is parallel to Levinas's phenomenological argument that the archaic dimension of the embodied ego—"the oneself" preceding the intentional consciousness—is an effect of the exposure to the Other. As we have seen, for Levinas this dimension of ipseity is coextensive with the "originary" receptivity to the Other, with "having-the-other-in-one's-skin."[38] In both Levinas's and Kristeva's work, the aporetic identity of "oneself" (an identity of nonessence, as Levinas puts it) forms a knot, where the exposure to exteriority both constitutes what is most intimately one's own and enables an ethical relation to the Other.

The detour through Kristeva's theory of primary narcissism reveals the knot of the intimate exposure to the Other—what Lacan calls in Seminar VII "extimacy"—as a condition of possibility of ethics. This extimate structure of ipseity allows us to define the psychoanalytic model of the ethical relation to the Other as the interplay of two opposing movements: as "the minimum of idealization" and the traversal of fantasy, as the sublimation of the death drive and the impossible transfer to the place of the abject as one's own most intimate yet inassimilable alterity. We can interpret these two sides of the ethical relation as the drive-based rearticulation of the Levinasian distinction of the saying (the nonthematizable exposure to the Other) and the said (the return to the economy of discourse). By stressing both sides of the relation to the Other—the traversal of fantasy and the encounter with the abject, on the one hand, and the sublimation of the death drive, on the other—this model ceaselessly confronts the subject with the inassimilable otherness within himself and the exorbitant alterity of the Other while deflecting the violence of the death drive toward the destruction of the narcissistic unity of the ego and toward the restructuring of the symbolic order.

Let us look at each side of the ethical relation—the traversal of fantasy and sublimation—in turn. As we have seen, unconscious fantasies support the political framework of power by covering over the constitutive void in the symbolic order. In this sense, fantasy not only structures the subject's desire but also compensates for the instability of its imaginary and symbolic identifications. As Kristeva's work on anti-Semitism and Fanon's analysis of racism shows, what consolidates the ideological coherence of the social order is this phantasmatic constitution of the sexualized and racialized Other as the fetishistic embodiment of the subjective and social antagonism. Unlike the psychotic repudiation of the symbolic or the projection of the irreconcilable negativity of the drive on others, the traversal of fantasy confronts the subject with abjection as its own most intimate exteriority. Such an encounter with the abject—with what is intolerable and irreconcilable with not only imaginary but also symbolic identifications of the subject—enables the negativization of narcissistic ego and the interruption of narcissistic economies in love and social relations. Consequently, the traversal of fantasy and the transfer to the place of abjection allows the subject to abandon the idea of the Other either as the reflection of the ego-Ideal or as the hostile negation of its identity and to approach her instead as the irreducible "finite being" (*TL*, 120).

As I have suggested earlier, the other aspect of the ethical relation is constituted by sublimation. Yet, even though the minimum of sublimation (understood as the change in the aim of the drive) is indispensable to sustain a traumatizing encounter with the Other, the ethical function of sublimation is irreducible either to the paradoxical fashioning of the representation of the nonrepresentable or to the idealization of the object (raising the object to the dignity of *das Ding*).[39] As Lacan reminds us in Seminar VII, both of these forms of sublimation represent yet another mode of defense against "whatever is open, lacking, or gaping at the center of our desire"—indeed, a way of covering over this very "dam-age" (SVII, 84). Consequently, we need a different account of sublimation, where the main emphasis is neither on what Simon Critchley describes as the aesthetic veiling and unveiling *das Ding*[40] nor on the defense against the trauma but rather on the concern with the violence of the death drive in intersubjective relations. In Levinas's language, it is a concern with the temptation to kill that the appearance of radical alterity invariably provokes. In the aftermath of the traversal of fantasy, which precisely exposes idealization as a defensive mechanism covering over the inconsistencies in the symbolic and the subject, this ethical function of sublimation can be understood as the deflection of the aggressivity of the death drive for the destruction of the narcissistic unity of the ego and for the possible restructuring of language. To refer to Joan Copjec's argument, this form of sublimation allows the drive to find satisfaction elsewhere than where its aim is—not in death or the murderous destruction of the Other but in creativity and life.[41]

We can define the ethical function of sublimation by referring to what Kristeva calls in *Revolution in Poetic Language* the return of the negativity of the death drive within the symbolic function. By deflecting the violence and negativity of the death drive from the murderous destruction of the Other toward the symbolic, sublimation enables not only a nonviolent response to the Other but also a reconstruction of the sociosymbolic relations. Understood as a form of sublimation, the return of rejection within the symbolic function differs from the psychotic repudiation of the symbolic (it is not a regression to the "inarticulable instinctuality" [*RPL*, 148]), from the hatred of the Other, and from the curbing of that aggressivity through the formation of the superego—it "defies both the verbal symbolization and the formation of a superego" (*RPL*, 152). It is also distinct from the intellectual sublation of the death drive in the symbol of negation, which Freud describes as the "intellectual acceptance" of what is repressed. As the third degree of negativity, the deflection of the death drive toward the symbolic disrupts the logical and ideological constraints of the subject's position, opening in this way both a nonviolent relation to the Other and a possibility of symbolic transformation (*RPL*, 170).

I would like to analyze briefly how the ethical relation to the Other functions in transference and in erotic and social relations. For Kristeva, transference—"the major dynamics of otherness, of love/hatred for the other"—

reveals the fact that the psyche is not a fixed narcissistic entity but an open and heterogeneous system dependent on the Other (*TL*, 15). By stressing the fact that "the systems operating in transference are open" (*TL*, 15), Kristeva does not see transference the way Lacan does, as the process that separates the demand for love from the economy of drive but rather as "the opening up of each system [semiotic and the symbolic] into its heterogeneous elements," that is, as the destabilization and the infusion of the symbolic with *jouissance*. Yet, if transference is to function as "permanent stabilization-destabilization between the *symbolic* . . . and the *semiotic*," then the analyst, Kristeva suggests, has to occupy a double position of the ego Ideal and the abject subject of desire (*TL*, 16). On the one hand, by keeping the ego Ideal separate from the superego, and by maintaining a certain rift within the paternal function, the analyst sustains the analysand's capacity for the symbolic identification, idealization, imagination, and metaphoricity in the midst of hatred, thus allowing for a deflection of the death drive and its sublimation within the symbolic. Yet, although the analyst temporarily embodies the fantasy of the loving Father/Mother in order to support the analysand's symbolic identification and restore the psychic space, she also occupies the position of "abject subject of desire" (*TL*, 31)—a position, which enables the analysand to traverse the fantasy masking the inconsistency of the symbolic order and to experience the irreducible negativity of the drive: "He will then trigger within the psychic space his love has allowed to exist the tragicomedy of life drives and death drives" (*TL*, 31). Only by occupying this double position of the ideal and the abject, the analyst, Kristeva argues, can avoid being an idealized Great Other, or even a loathed *Führer* from *Group Psychology*. The analyst's position as the "abject subject of desire" recalls Lacan's argument in Seminar XI that the analyst's fall from the idealization enables the subject to "cross the plane of narcissistic identifications" and to confront the experience of the drive behind the fundamental fantasy. Thus, despite their different understanding of transference, Lacan and Kristeva agree that what is at stake in the analytic process is the negativization of narcissism, that is, the crossing of the imaginary and symbolic identifications, the traversal of the fantasy, and the confrontation with the inassimilable negativity of the drive.

Kristeva's analysis of transference provides a model for the ethical relation in love. The main ethical question Kristeva poses in *Tales of Love* concerns the problem of a nonnarcissistic love of the Other, irreducible to the reflection of the ego-Ideal. Far from idealizing love, Kristeva, as Jacqueline Rose observes, exposes ambivalence and contradictions in Western amorous discourse—the contradictions between death and regeneration, hate and idealization, being for the Other and the aggrandizement of narcissism[42]: "A hymn to total giving to the other, such a love is also, and almost as explicitly, a hymn to the narcissistic power to which I may even sacrifice it, sacrifice myself" (*TL*, 1–2). For Kristeva the difficulty of the ethical relation in love is illustrated by the two central Freudian insights, namely, that the foundation of love is narcissistic and that for the pleasure ego hate represents an older, if not the first, relation to exteriority. This correlation between the narcissistic ego, pleasure, and love, on the one hand, and externality, pain, and hate, on the other, creates a vicious circle where the only relation to the radical exteriority occurs through hatred, whereas "the blending-love with the One is elimination of otherness" (*TL*, 120). What enables the subject to break this circle and to transcend the sway of the pleasure principle is the negativization of narcissism accomplished through the confrontation with the negativity of the drive embodied in the abject. Although Kristeva focuses her analysis primarily on the mechanisms of idealization, her definition of love as a knot of the symbolic, imaginary, and the real suggests that the narcissistic idealization of the Other in love is a defensive attempt to cover over the subject's own essential incompleteness and heterogeneity. What thus opens a possibility of a nonnarcissistic love is the undoing of the idealization of the Other, accompanied by another form of sublimation, by the divergence of the death drive toward the restructuring of the symbolic order. I will describe this form of love in greater detail in the context of Luce Irigaray's work; for now I want to say that the ethical relation in this case is no longer predicated, as Žižek suggests, on filling the void in the Other and in oneself by offering oneself as an object of the Other's desire but on what Lacan describes in Seminar XI as the "infinite" love outside the limits of the law. Such an infinitization of love through the negativization of narcissism and the subsequent sublimation of the death drive enables an erotic relation to the infinitely Other, irreducible to the ego Ideal.

In *Strangers to Ourselves* Kristeva extends her exploration of the ethical signification of alterity from amorous discourse to the encounter with the stranger in social relations. If the main ethical problem in love lies in the idealization of the Other to cover over the subject's own essential incompleteness, in social relations it is the constitution of the Other—in particular, the sexual or racial Other—as the phobic object. As we have seen, for Kristeva the uncanny signification of the stranger in social relations most frequently functions "as a psychotic *symptom*" that is, as the fetishistic or the paranoid embodiment of the internal negativity of the subject or the social group. As Kristeva's analysis of anti-Semitism and Fanon's discussion of racism have demonstrated, the racialized and sexualized Other functions in the social fantasy as the impediment toward the achievement of *jouissance* and full social identity. Consequently, what is at stake in ethical social relations is not just the undoing of idealizations but, as Žižek and Kristeva in different ways suggest, the identification with the symptom. According to Žižek, the psychoanalytic interpretation of the symptom consists of two stages. First, it involves the critical diagnosis of the ideological overdetermination of the symptom—in the context of Kristeva's and Fanon's work, this would entail the cultural, economic, and political analysis of racial and sexual oppression. In the second stage, the identification with the symptom involves the traversal of fantasy that fills the void of the sociosymbolic and promises *jouissance* by externalizing the negativity and lack in the other. The identification with a symptom in this context leads to a recognition that the abjection, negativity, and disruption of identity attributed to the Other are in fact projections of the social or subjective antagonism. Such an identification with the symptom is a correlative of the "crumbling" of the defenses of the ego (*ST*, 188) and the acknowledgment of the irreconcilable traumatizing alterity within the subject. Consequently, if fear and the violent rejection of the Other are to be surmounted, then both the subject and the collectivity has to give up the mirage of full identity, which can be maintained only at the cost of projecting the internal division, anguish, and conflict on the stranger.

By deflecting the negativity of the death drive toward the reconstruction of the symbolic and the disruption of the narcissistic identity of the ego, Kristeva's ethics not only enables an ethical relation to the Other but also implies a certain subjective freedom. In this respect, Kristeva agrees with bell hooks and Frantz Fanon that liberation struggles must coincide with the liberation of the subject from the narcissistic ego. From an early *Revolution in Poetic Language* to more recent *Sens et non-sens de la révolte: Pouvoirs et limites de la psychoanalyse* (Paris: Fayard, 1996), Kristeva has consistently explored the possibility of becoming, social practice, and freedom. As I have stressed in my discussion of sublimation, she locates this possibility in the postsymbolic return of the negativity of the death drive, which she interprets as a materialist recasting of the Hegelian concept of Force. Although productive of the symbolic function, this return of negativity cannot be subordinated either to the Hegelian closure of the One or to the signifying unity of the symbolic. In contrast to Hegel's repulsion, Kristeva calls the rejection of the death drive "a-mediating" rupture of all unity, including the unity of the narcissistic ego.

Jacqueline Rose argues that Kristeva's ethics of negativity "describes a subjective position which avoids conformity . . . and esoterism and marginality."[43] Indeed, by decentering the ego and putting it in conflict with its social position, the postsymbolic return of rejection implies a notion of freedom, which is irreducible either to the agency of the ego or to its opposite, anarchy. Although for Kristeva subjectivity is always already constituted by the symbolic, the return of the negativity of the death drive means that the subject is never coextensive with its social position. By "reactivating" the ideological contradictions within the subject's position, the traversal of fantasy and the return of the death drive opens a possibility of transgression of the sociosymbolic positionality: "The subject never is. The *subject* is only *the signifying process* and he appears only as a *signifying practice*, that is, only when he is absent *within the position* out of which social, historical, and signifying activity unfolds" (*RPL*, 215).[44] This relation between ethics and negativity allows us to move beyond respect for the law toward the transformation of social relations and subjective identities.

By rethinking Kristeva's psychoanalytic ethics in the context of Levinas's work I have developed a model of ethical responsibility that allows us to negotiate between the becoming of the subject-in-process and the respect for the irreconcilable, the negativity of the drive and social antagonism, social practice and the responsibility for the Other. Based on the traversal of the political function of fantasy and the sublimation of the death drive, this model of ethical relations does not aim to transcend subjective and political conflicts but intervenes into social antagonisms by acknowledging the unsettling negativity of the drive and its externalization in the phobic constructions of the racialized and sexualized Others. This reconsideration of the ethics of dissensus in the context of the libidinal economy of the death drive not only promotes vigilance against violence but, in so doing, also makes responsibility inseparable from embodiment, affect, and sexuality. As I will argue in the next section, such an ethics of dissensus is productive for feminist politics of radical democracy not only because it enables what Judith Butler calls a transformation of the symbolic "under the pressure of social practices"[45] but also because it links the question of practice to affectivity and the ethical responsibility for violence.

## Women's Time and the Politics of Radical Democracy

What are the implications of the libidinal economy of power and "the psychic life" of ethics for the politics of radical democracy? By extending Kristeva's critique of the purity of the Kantian formalist ethics, which underlies many contemporary discussions of the public sphere, citizenship, and communicative rationality, including Lefort's discussion of disincorporation of power, I argue that the ethics of dissensus provides an alternative to both the politics of democracy purged of all "pathological" passions and to its reversal into the substantiality of power in fascism. By foregrounding the libidinal surplus value of the constitutive antagonism of democracy and the role of fantasy in hegemonic formations, I want not only to radicalize the notion of conflict in political and subjective life but also to stress the increased role of ethical judgment in democratic struggles. Rearticulated in the context of the heterogeneous logic of drive and affect, such a judgment calls for the traversal of fantasy in order to unravel the defensive externalizations of the death drive in the phobic constructions of women and racialized Others. To elaborate the role fantasy, libidinal economy of the drive, and ethical judgment in democratic politics, I will focus on Kristeva's discussion of the catharsis of abjection in *Powers of Horror*, her analysis of democratic community in *Strangers to Ourselves*, and on the function of sexual difference in group formation.

The importance of psychoanalysis for the theories of democracy has been acknowledged by theorists as diverse as Claude Lefort, Chantal Mouffe, Slavoj Žižek, Drucilla Cornell, and Joan Copjec, all of whom turn to psychoanalysis in order to extricate the political subject from the liberal legacy of the unitary nature endowed with natural rights prior to its social or historical determination. As an alternative to the liberal tradition, Mouffe, for instance, proposes a psychoanalytic understanding of the subject who "does not have an original identity . . . but is primarily a subject of a lack. As a result, whatever identity s/he has can be constituted only through acts of *identification*."[46] For Laclau and Mouffe, the split subject of psychoanalysis reflects the constitutive contradictions of democracy between equality and conflict, diversity and equivalence, particularity and universality, antagonism and consensus. As we have seen, Kristeva, like Slavoj Žižek and Rey Chow, radicalizes this thesis by emphasizing the limits of sociosymbolic identifications represented by the internal impossibility and antagonism with the subject—by the traumatic real and the negativity of the drive.[47]

In this section, I turn to Kristeva's heterogeneous subject, split between desire and drive, signifier and affect, the symbolic and the semiotic, not only to radicalize the notion of antagonism but also to contest Lefort's and Mouffe's thesis of the disincorporation of power in a democratic regime. It is this thesis of disincorporation that prevents them from interrogating the role of fantasy and libidinal investments underlying hegemonic formations in democratic politics. In response to Marx's criticism of human of rights as an egotistical monad based on the ideological fiction of a man without sociohistorical determination,[48] Lefort proposes to rethink the discourse of rights in the context of the political mutation of power, which, in the democratic regime, belongs to everybody and nobody and thus can be represented only as an empty place. Unlike the ancien régime, where the political power and the unity of the community is incarnated in the double body of the king, and unlike the totalitarian fantasy of the reincorporation of power in the immediacy of the social body, the secular democracy dissolves the corporeality of power and, in so doing, exposes both the indetermination of the subject and the antagonistic character of social relations: "The modern democratic revolution can be best recognized in this mutation: there is no power linked to a body. Power appears as an empty place. . . . There is no law that can be fixed, whose article cannot be contested. . . . Lastly, there is no representation of a center and of the contours of the society: unity cannot now efface social division" (*PFMS*, 303). What corresponds to the institution of the empty place of power in democracy, Lefort argues, is not the liberal ideology of the unitary human nature without social determination but, as Joan Copjec suggests, the symbolic idea of the *indeterminable* subject, that is, the desiring subject that exceeds its historical determination, and for that very reason can claim the agency of reformulating the already established rights.[49]

Although Mouffe's and Lefort's reformulations of the subject of democracy provide powerful critiques of both essentialism and the reductive notion of social construction, they have little to say about the role of embodiment and sexuality in democratic citizenship. Lefort diagnoses with great precision the ideological function of the body in the totalitarian regime; yet, he fails to investigate an alternative relation between the body and democracy—in a way, his thesis about disincorporation of power leaves little room for such a discussion. For similar reasons, Chantal Mouffe postulates that the truly democratic citizenship should be abstracted from sexual difference: "The fact that sexual difference has been central to the structure of modern citizenship, and that it has had negative consequences for women, can also be redressed by constructing a new conception of citizenship where such a difference becomes truly irrelevant."[50] Ironically, these critiques of the "rights of man," and its contemporary opposite, the social construction of historicism, perpetuate not only the disembodied character of citizenship but also what William Connolly calls the "thin" conception of the public sphere separated from the "visceral" dimension of intersubjectivity.[51]

Although Kristeva also stresses the indeterminacy of the law in democratic regimes, she underscores the impossibility of the complete disincorporation of power and the symbolic order. If Michel Foucault interprets this impossibility in terms of the disciplinary training of citizens' bodies and Frantz Fanon in terms of the epidermalization of oppression, Kristeva focuses on the failure of the total separation of the sociosymbolic from the heterogeneous logic of drive and affect. According to Kristeva, the instability of the democratic regime can be more appropriately described as the impurity of the law rather than a complete separation of the body, *jouissance*, and power. Even though in all her works Kristeva associates the indetermination of the law with different modalities of the semioticization of the symbolic, I want to rethink here the indeterminacy and antagonism of democracy in the context of the most troubling case represented as abjection in order to work out the model of a just judgment responsive to the irreducible heterogeneity of democratic community.

Like Lefort, Kristeva argues that abjection dramatizes two diametrically opposed outcomes of the dissolution of certainty in modernity—one of them, discussed at greater length in *Strangers to Ourselves*, lies in the institution of the democratic regime, the other one, discussed primarily in the context of Céline in *Powers of Horror*, lies in the reversal of democracy into fascism. Linked to the condition of the possibility of democracy, abjection at the same time reveals the threat of totalitarianism. Although in *Powers of Horror* Kristeva concentrates primarily on the premodern religious formations, which provide different modes of the prohibition of abjection, and on the fascist ideology, which covers over the instability of the abject by the fantasy of the "material positivity" of the law incarnated in the racial purity of the nation, she also allows us to thematize the "secular ordeal" of abjection, corresponding to the antagonism and contingency of the democratic regime.

Considered in the context of democracy, the secular ordeal of the abject challenges both the totalitarian fantasy of power grounded in the immanence of the unified social body and the modern fantasy of the complete separation of power from *jouissance*. In contrast to both of these fantasies, abjection reveals a precarious condition of in-between—between the symbolic and the semiotic, delirium and perversion, symptom and sublimation. When considered in the context of democratic politics, abjection can be said to describe the subjective experience of the loss of the substantial ground of power: "The abjection of self would be the culminating form of that experience of the subject to which it is revealed that all its objects are based merely on the inaugural *loss* that laid the foundations of its own being" (*PH*, 5). In this sense, the instability of the symbolic order manifesting itself in abjection—the permeability of the inside and the outside boundaries, the weakness of cultural prohibitions, the crisis of the symbolic identity, and the emergence of the disruptive temporality—dramatizes what Lefort describes as "the experience of the ungraspable society, uncontrollable society, initiated by democratic revolution" (*PFMS*, 304). According to Kristeva, "It is thus not lack of cleanliness or health that causes abjection but what disturbs identity, system, order" (*PH*, 4).[52] This fragility of the law exposed in abjection is linked specifically to a crisis of authority and its psychic representation—the typology of the superego. What abjection reveals is the lack of the guarantee for the law institutionalized in the secular regime of democracy as the empty place of power. As Lacan argues in Seminar VII, the constitutive default of the superego "generates ever more powerful aggression in the self" because the guarantor of the law "is lacking, the guarantor who provides its warranty, namely, God himself" (*SVII*, 194). It is precisely this lack of guarantee that produces the infusion of the perverse enjoyment into the operations of the law, language, and judgment: "Hence a jouissance in which the subject is swallowed up but in which the Other, in return, keeps the subject from foundering by making it repugnant" (*PH*, 9). What we see in abjection is, therefore, a paradoxical function of that law, which does not exclude what it prohibits but, on the contrary, "shatters the wall of repression" and takes the subject back to the crisis of primary narcissism and to its "origin in drive." By tearing the "veil of oblivion," the abject is a form of commemoralization proper to drive, a memory of the oblivion that causes the reappearance of the prohibited *jouissance* in the perverse enjoyment of repugnance.

If Kristeva's analysis of the abject reveals a profound ambiguity of the instability of the law, which can either lead to the radicalization of democratic struggles or to the reversal of democracy into totalitarianism, then what is a political response to this ambiguity? The answer to this question lies neither in the secularized version of religious prohibitions—which Kristeva describes as "the sacrificial, compulsive, and paranoid side of religions"—nor in a discourse of science, which Kristeva associates with the sadistic control of the object—but in a new model of judgment implied by the ethics of psychoanalysis. In what sense can this judgment counteract a regression to the phobic narcissism and delirium, which Kristeva sees at work in fascistic fantasies and Fanon in the psychopathology of racism? Based on the traversal of the ideological function of fantasy consolidating hegemonic formations and on the confrontation with the death drive, such a judgment ceaselessly presents the subject with "a heterogeneous, corporeal, and verbal ordeal of fundamental incompleteness" (*PH*, 27) and, in so doing, unravels the defensive projections of this ordeal onto racialized and sexualized others. As Kristeva writes, we should never stop "harking back to symbolization mechanisms, within language itself, in order to find in a *process* of eternal return, and not in the *object* . . . the hollowing out of anguish in the face of nothing" (*PH*, 42–43).

Working "with and against abjection," this notion of judgment is based on the catharsis of the abject within the symbolic order: "Catharsis seems to be a concern that is intrinsic to philosophy insofar as the latter is an ethics" (*PH*, 28). Although catharsis dissolves the fantasy of the incorporation of law, it is not equivalent to a religious or philosophical purification. In particular, it is irreducible to the Kantian separation of the law from pathological passions or to a contemporary cult of "the unadulterated treasure of the 'pure signifier'" (*PH*, 27). Defined as "an impure process that protects from abject only by . . . being immersed in it," analytical catharsis acknowledges and repeats the logic of affect, rejection, and *jouissance* in signifying practice and, in so doing, enables the sublimation of the death drive: "The abject, mimed through sound and meaning, is *repeated*. Getting rid of it is out of the question. . . . One can, however, bring it into being a *second time*, and differently from the original impurity. It is a repetition through rhythm and song, therefore through what is not yet, or no longer is 'meaning'" (*PH*, 28, second emphasis added).

By drawing on Kristeva's formulation of the abject as a synthesis of judgment and affect and her references to the Kantian sublime, I would like to compare the function of catharsis with the Kantian reflective judgment. When Kristeva compares the abject to the sublime, she points out that although both phenomena present us with the limits of presentation, in the case of the sublime there is "*something added*" to abjection (*PH*, 12). I propose to interpret this "*something added*" as the problematic of an indeterminate judgment. In so doing, I would like to rearticulate what Lyotard describes as the predicament of a just judgment in democracy, namely, the irreducible necessity of judging social struggles even if the criteria of such a judgment are themselves an object of contestation, in the context of the heterogeneous logic of the drive. Consequently, such a judgment in search of the criteria of justice has to be defined not only in the light of Kant's reflective judgment grounded in pleasure and pain but also in light of the Freudian negative judgment derived from the drive. In her analysis of Freud's negative judgment, Kristeva points out that although symbolic negation allows for the intellectual acceptance of the repressed, it maintains the essential aspect of repression by separating the intellectual from the affective process, that is, from the drive's "corporeal foundations stemming from the concrete history of the concrete . . . subject" (*RPL*, 162). Based on the intellectual sublation of the drive, Freud's judgment can be compared to a determinate judgment based on concept. Kristeva asks, however, whether it is possible to articulate the affective process of drive in such a way that it is neither arrested in terms of full symbolization nor subsumed by the superego. What mode of judgment would correspond to this articulation? In *Revolution in Poetic Language*, Kristeva associates this type of judgment with the semioticization of the symbolic, which reflects indeterminable articulation of the drives. I would like to suggest that in *Powers of Horror* the indeterminable articulation of the drives is analogous to Kant's reflective judgment, which, likewise, does not involve a mediation of a concept but rather is based solely on the subjective affect of pleasure or pain (affect reflecting harmony or conflict of mental faculties).[53] Needless to say, this rapprochement between the Freudian and the Kantian judgment redefines the discord of the mental faculties as the irreducible conflict between drive and desire, signifier and affect, meaning and *jouissance*, and, in so doing, ruins the purity and disinterestedness of the aesthetic judgment, risking what Kant would call a "pathological" or "barbaric" reduction of taste.

The interconnections between catharsis, judgment, and the traversal of fantasy allow us to see the difference between the two forms of recurrence of abjection in Kristeva's text: between the pathological regression to phobic narcissism, which is intertwined with the defensive projection of internal negativity onto the Other, and the reflective judgment based on the subject's own internal division, negativity and impurity. To underscore this difference, I would like to recall Dominick LaCapra's suggestive reformulation of the Freudian distinction between "acting out" and "working through." Significantly for my analysis, LaCapra associates "working through"—what I have articulated as the traversal of fantasy—with ethico-political judgment: "Working-through implies the possibility of judgment that is not apodictic or ad hominem but . . . self-questioning, and related in mediated ways to action."[54] The implications of this kind of judgment are not limited solely to the therapeutic dimension of the psychoanalytic cure, aesthetics, or historical interpretation but have important relevance for democratic politics. I would like to claim that it is the reflective judgment based on the subject's own internal heterogeneity, conflict, and impurity that can bear witness to the nonidentical—to what has been excluded by the racist of homophobic superego "beyond the scope of the possible, the tolerable, the thinkable" (PH, 1). To articulate the political function of catharsis, I would like to compare it with Arendt's and Lyotard's theory of democratic politics based on Kant's reflective judgment—that is, the mode of thinking the particular when the universality is not given but merely implied through the appeal of the agreement of others.[55] Concerned with the erosion of judgment in contemporary political life, Arendt finds more radical implications for democracy in Kant's Critique of Aesthetic Judgement rather than in the purity of the moral law, the legacy of which reverberates in many formulations of the liberal notion of democracy and social contract, including Rawls's theory of justice.[56] In Lectures on Kant's Political Philosophy, Arendt sees in the judgments of taste a model for political judgments in diverse democratic communities insofar as the latter also involve the appeal to the judgments of others—that is, publicity and a hope of the intersubjective agreement—without the mediation of the universal law or a determinate collective identity. Although Arendt does not think through the implications of affect for her otherwise formal conception of citizenship, she indirectly grants the feelings of pleasure and pain a key importance in the cultivation of representative political thinking and in the reconstruction of a democratic community based on "putting oneself in place of everybody else."[57] In her work on deliberative democracy, Seyla Benhabib interprets Arendt's publicity of judgment as an outcome of the reversibility of perspectives among the participants in a democratic process.

In her recent work on Arendt, Kristeva approvingly refers to Arendt's political interpretation of the Kantian aesthetic judgment, anticipated in her earlier work by the notion of phronesis (the singular, practical wisdom irreducible to theoretical knowledge): "Sophia (theoretical knowledge) cannot be applied to human affairs in their fragility. . . . Human affairs demand an aptitude that is at once intellectual, affective and moral. This aptitude [*phronesis*] develops in the plural deliberation internal to the space of appearance that is politics."[58] Similarly to her own interpretation of catharsis, Kristeva argues that for Arendt this singular judgment manifests itself in an exemplary way in tragedy where it sets itself in opposition not only to the theoretical knowledge but also to the authoritative judgment of the master: "*Phronesis* forbids anyone from placing themselves in the position of the master or from imposing systematic points of view. Tragic representation is in this way indispensable to a life in common, to a *bios politikos* in which speech produces conflicts."[59]

Although Kristeva's interpretation of catharsis also replaces the authoritative judgment of the master with the indeterminate judgment as a mode of thinking the particular and the nonidentical, her heterogeneous, split subject of psychoanalysis foregrounds the impure judgment of the sublime (which similarly foregrounds the irreducible conflict within the subject) rather than the disinterested judgment of the beautiful. What corresponds to such a judgment is not the *sensus communis* manifesting itself in the identification with others but a heterogeneous community shaped by conflict, division, and difference—a community closer to Lyotard's differend than to Arendt's representative thinking or Benhabib's reversibility of perspectives. Specifically, the acknowledgment of the economy of drive in the intersubjective field not only foregrounds the passionate, ambivalent, and unconscious aspect of communication, usually ignored by the ethics of communicative rationality, but also, as Lacan points out, opposes the reciprocity of identification grounded in narcissistic economy. In place of identification, the disjunction between the outward and the inward movement of the drive dramatizes not only the heterogeneity of the subject but also the asymmetry in the subject's relation to the Other. That is why Kristeva argues in *Strangers to Ourselves* that the democratic community postulated by psychoanalysis has to preserve the irreducible difference within and between the subjects. As she points out, the subjective or collective identity "no longer exists ever since Freud and shows itself to be a strange land of borders and othernesses ceaselessly constructed and deconstructed" (*ST*, 191). What the psychoanalytic concept of the heterogeneous subject implies is "a paradoxical community," "made up of foreigners who are reconciled with themselves to the extent they recognize themselves as foreigners" (*ST*, 195). Such a disintegrated community might appear, to refer to Jean-Luc Nancy's argument, "inoperative"[60] insofar as it fails to produce a common essence or identity, but it is the only mode of solidarity with others that reflects the democratic ideas of pluralism, antagonism, and diversity.

The only adequate articulation of collectivity in such democratic community, which takes into account the antagonistic differences between and within subjects rather than seeking consensus based on the uniformity of values or a common identity, can only be a matter of reflective judgment.[61] Since collective identity in democratic community is fractured and contested, and thus cannot be determined by a concept, it can be merely implied by the reflective judgment as a regulative idea of democracy. By supplementing the law with the question of affect and drive, the notion of reflective judgment criticizes both the imaginary organic community, which assumes in the fascist ideology the phantasmatic phallic unity of the social body, and the symbolic community of contract, which subsumes differences into a system of formal equivalences. As Kristeva writes in "Women's Time," the democratic community of difference points to the limits of the symbolic as a system of exchange—a system, which sets equivalences among diverse elements: "It seems to me that the role of what is usually called 'aesthetic practices' must increase not only to counterbalance the storage and uniformity of information by present mass-media . . . but also to demystify the identity of the symbolic bond itself, to demystify, therefore, the *community* of language as a universal and unifying tool, one which totalizes and equates" (WT, 210).

I would like to argue that the demystification of the sociosymbolic bond, the traversal of racist and homophobic fantasies, and the inscription of the libidinal economy of the drive into democratic politics is crucial for feminism because it enables us to reconceive the theory of democracy in the light of race and sexual difference. Like most other feminist critics of Kristeva, I have little patience for her often reductive and simplistic remarks about feminism as a monolithic "power-seeking ideology."[62] Nonetheless, I believe there are more interesting implications in her work regarding the importance of sexual difference for democratic politics. For instance, although she does not discuss it directly, the question of sexual difference is implied in Kristeva's redefinition of democratic community beyond the notion of brotherhood and "paternal authority":

> We are far removed from a call to brotherhood, about which one has already ironically pointed out its debt to paternal and divine authority—"in order to have brothers there must be a father." . . . On the basis of an erotic, death bearing unconscious, the uncanny strangeness—a projection as well as a first working out of death drive— . . . sets the difference within us . . . and presents it as the ultimate condition of our being *with* others. (*ST*, 192)

To think through the implications of this passage, I propose to take seriously Kristeva's claim in "Women's Time" that the history and future of feminism, like that of psychoanalysis, is tied to the democratic tradition. By contesting the disembodied subject of liberalism and the sexual neutrality of the political authority, which tends to reproduce what Juliet MacCannell has called the regime of the brother,[63] both feminism and psychoanalysis raise the question about the significance of sexuality and sexual difference for democratic politics.

As Kristeva points out, the dilemmas of feminism are inherited from the impasses of the liberal democracy. Defined by the logic of identification with the values of the democratic state, that is, with universal equality and liberty, the first generation of liberal feminism has been dominated by the goal of extending the "rights of men" and by securing "equal access" to power for women. Within this political program, the issue of sexual difference could be raised only negatively, that is, as "the rejection, when necessary, of the attributes traditionally considered feminine insofar as they are deemed incompatible with the insertion in that history" (WT, 193–94).[64] Distrustful of the universalizing and homogenizing discourse of equal rights, the second generation emerging in Europe after May 1968 has pursued the politics of "sociocultural recognition" of sexual difference and women's identity. By exploring the "dynamic of the signs," this feminism of difference not only seeks to rearticulate the specificity of women's bodies and subjective experiences, such as sexuality, motherhood, and work, but also raises the question of the sacrificial character of the social contract separated from embodiment and sexuality. The risk of this generation, as Kristeva sees it, lies either in a renunciation of political praxis for the sake of aesthetic or religious expression of women's experience, or in the reduction of politics to the utopian vision of the countersociety, "imagined as harmonious, without prohibitions, free and fulfilling," where "fantasized possibilities of jouissance take refuge" (WT, 202). Calling for a critical traversal of this fantasy of the archaic fulfillment underlying the mobilization of the counterpower, Kristeva argues that the denial of antagonism and negativity in the utopian vision of the immanence of the sexed body and power based on the quasi-religious belief in the archaic phallic mother risks the reversal of democratic regime into totalitarianism (WT, 204).

The third generation of feminism, defined by Kristeva as "*insertion* into history and the radical *refusal* of the subjective limitations imposed by this history's time on an experiment carried out in the name of the irreducible difference" (WT, 195) inherits, then, a dilemma similar to the one confronted by the psychoanalytic revisions of democracy: namely, how to contest the abstract and formal character of the liberal citizenship, which relegates all the substantial differences to the private sphere, without falling into a trap of the utopian mirage of the immanence of the power and the body. Kristeva's tentative solution to this dilemma lies in deepening both the problematic of equality and difference through the reconfiguration of socialism and Freudianism—a rather different task than Nancy Fraser's call for the supplementation of the politics of recognition with the politics of redistribution.[65] Like those theoreticians of radical democracy who want to extricate the democratic ideals of freedom from the capitalist mode of production, Kristeva argues that the alliance between feminism and democracy has "to extend the zone of egalitarianism to include the distributions of goods as well as access to culture" (WT, 195).[66] The turn to Freudianism within this radicalized democratic vision allows Kristeva to reformulate the question of sexual difference as well as the libidinal economy of other differences leveled down by both the discourse of liberalism and socialism—Kristeva mentions religious and ethnic differences but, clearly, the question of race, which figures more explicitly in her critique of xenophobia and anti-Semitism, is the unspoken that haunts the entire essay and exposes its limitations.

Although Kristeva is rather cryptic about the third generation of feminism, I would like to mention four contributions raised by this "new signifying space, both corporeal and desiring" to the theory of democracy. First, Kristeva takes seriously the contestation of the sacrificial character of the sociosymbolic contract by the third generation, even though, as Judith Butler points out, she does not diagnose adequately the modernization of the patriarchal power and its ambiguous relation to psychoanalysis (the way psychoanalysis has been seen as both perpetuation of this power and its radical critique).[67] Yet, despite these limitations, I find Kristeva's call for an alternative political "discourse closer to the body and emotions, to the unnameable repressed by the social contract" (WT, 200) still an important goal for feminist democratic politics.[68] As I have shown in this chapter, such a discourse allows us to diagnose the libidinal economy of power and the ideological function of racist fantasies supplementing and consolidating hegemonic formations.

Second, Kristeva associates this "more flexible and free discourse" with the new feminist imaginary, which is irreducible either to imaginary identifications or to fetishization of language (WT, 207). Rather, this new imaginary is tied to "rebellious potentialities," to the possibility of invention inherent not only in aesthetic practices but also in any political action aiming to transform the status quo.[69] Based on the return of rejection within the symbolic, this "new imaginary" encapsulates Kristeva's own analysis of the semioticization of the symbolic, evident in her theories of the metaphor, imagination, sensation, and catharsis, and thus expresses her own desire for "a more flexible" discourse of psychoanalysis. In the next chapter, I will explore further the implications of this concept for political praxis in the context of Irigaray's sexual imaginary and Castoriadis's "radical social imaginary." For now I want to stress that Kristeva's new imaginary underscores a double movement: the interiorization of "*the founding separation of the sociosymbolic contract*" into subjective and sexual identity, on the one hand, and the inscription of the economy of the drives into sociosymbolic order, on the other. In this way Kristeva hopes to avoid reducing femininity either to its current symbolic articulation or to a utopian position outside language and politics. Only by combining separation inherent in language with the demystification of the symbolic purity and the stability of the social contract, can women contest the patriarchal hierarchies of gender, depart from the binary model of sexual difference, and express both their singularity and the multiplicity of their identifications "beyond horizon, beyond sight, beyond faith."

The third point I want to make is that Kristeva's concepts of the new imaginary and the indeterminate judgment allows us to conceive a collectivity and solidarity among women, without appealing to a notion of a common identity based on a determinate concept, such as a common oppression, or common gender identity. Since, as Kristeva's emphasis on the temporality of the future perfect suggests, this collectivity is indeterminate, that is, it exceeds its past determinations and is open to future reformulations and contestations, its paradoxical identity can only be an object of an indeterminate judgment operating without a concept.[70] This notion of collectivity acknowledges the contestation and dissimulation of the category of "women" in the context of the differences of class, race, and sexual orientation (as Kristeva puts it, "the apparent coherence which the terms 'woman' assumes . . . essentially has the negative effect of effacing the differences among the diverse functions or structures which operate beneath this word" [WT, 193]) while allowing for women's solidarity across differences. Although the inscription of asymmetrical sexual difference within citizenship dramatizes the fact that the collectivity of women cannot be encapsulated by a concept without a remainder or without contestation, the solidarity of women remains a regulative idea of feminism just as justice and community remain regulative ideas of democracy. I will develop further this notion of solidarity in the context of bell hooks's idea of coalition building in the multiracial democracy.

This notion of collectivity does not entail the abandoning of the discourse of rights embraced by the first generation of feminism but rather permits its reformulation. As Lefort points out, the indeterminable social identity (which, as I argued, insofar as it is indeterminable, can only be an object of reflective judgment) enables new articulations or contestation of the existing rights and thus indirectly tests the limits of legality. The emergence of new political movements, such as the struggle for women's, gay and lesbian, and minority rights, shows that the question of justice in democracy cannot be simply reduced to the extension of the existing rights for new groups. Rather, as Lefort and Williams brilliantly argue, the extension of democratic struggles around the axis of racial, sexual, and ethnic differences shows that the very formulation of rights in democracy "contains the demand for their reformulation." In the next chapter, I will examine more closely another instance of such reformulation by thinking through Irigaray's concept of "sexuate rights." Remaining within the orbit of Kristeva's work for now, I want to stress that the reformulation of rights corresponds to the futural structure of the new imaginary and to an endless necessity of judging without fixed criteria. By linking the discourse of human rights with reflective judgment, invention, and imagination, the feminist reformulations of human rights has to deploy the resources of "freedom and creativity" in order to resist what Lefort calls "the temptation to exchange the present for the future" (*PFMS*, 272). Oriented toward the future, the feminist struggle for human rights I advocate through my reading of Williams, Lefort, and Kristeva represents a transformative politics of "cultural *re*volt" and "permanent conflict."[71]

Many critics of Kristeva worry that such a dispersion of sexual identities and the sites of democratic struggle entails an extreme privatization of sexual difference and a reduction of politics, as Paul Smith argues, to "liberal humanism which defends art and dissidence over other social practice."[72] According to Nancy Fraser, Kristeva's focus on "*intra*subjective tensions" surrenders the "ability to understand *inter*subjective phenomena, including affiliation . . . and struggle."[73] Similarly, Jacqueline Rose wonders about the difficulty, if not impossibility, of constructing "a political identity out of processes heralded as the flight of identity itself."[74] Yet, what these criticisms have consistently missed are the most interesting implications of Kristeva's work: the ideological function of fantasy underlying hegemonic formations, the libidinal economy of power, and the political significance of her ethics. By stressing "the potentialities of *victim/executioner* which characterize each identity," the Kristevan ethics of psychoanalysis not only radicalizes, as Slavoj Žižek and Rey Chow in different ways argue,[75] the antagonisms within the subjective identities and group affiliations but also emphasizes responsibility for violence that accompanies the contestation of social relations—"the *responsibility* which all will immediately face of putting this fluidity into play against the threats of death which are unavoidable whenever an inside and outside, a self and other, one group and another, are constituted" (*WT*, 210).

By turning to psychoanalysis and feminism, I have articulated in this chapter two new aspects of the ethics of dissensus: the libidinal economy of power and the psychoanalytic model of ethical responsibility. Such an inscription of the economy of drives into intersubjectivity not only stresses the heterogeneous sites of conflict within democracy and within feminism itself but also supplements Mouffe's friend/enemy model of political conflict with the analysis of negativity and aggression within the subject—with what Kristeva calls the internal modalities of "*victim/executioner*." This emphasis on the libidinal surplus value of the constitutive antagonism of democracy not only radicalizes the dispersal of antagonisms in democratic regimes but also

shows the role of fantasy in the consolidation of hegemonic formations, political identities, and affiliations. It is because fantasy plays a crucial role in
hegemonic formations—a role often at odds with the explicit political program—that democratic politics needs not only to articulate the equivalence
among diverse struggles against oppression but also to traverse fantasies that
might underlie such articulations. By rethinking the "psychic life of power"
in the context of fantasy, *jouissance*, and the negativity of the death drive, I
not only complicate hegemonic politics but also stress the increased role of
ethical responsibility and judgment in democratic struggles. Based on the
traversal of fantasy and the sublimation of the death drive, the psychoanalytic
model of ethical responsibility that I have proposed in this chapter unravels
the defensive externalizations of the death drive in the phobic constructions
of women and racialized Others and, in so doing, allows the subject to "respect the irreconcilable" in intersubjective relations: its own unsettling heterogeneity and the exorbitant alterity of the Other.

## CHAPTER 5

# Labor of the Negative
## The Impossible Ethics of Sexual Difference
and the Politics of Radical Democracy

AFTER ELABORATING the ethical relation in the context of the libidinal economy of power, I would like to examine more closely the significance of sexual difference for the ethics of dissensus and its role in the theory of radical democracy. For this reason I turn to Luce Irigaray, who provides one of the strongest and most controversial articulations of an ethics of sexual difference in the context of democratic politics. If for Kristeva the possibility of ethics lies in the acknowledgment of the alterity and negativity within the subject, for Irigaray it is the respect for sexual difference that is a condition of ethical relations with others,[1] heterogeneous democratic culture, and the invention of the new modes of life.

By reconsidering sexual difference in the context of the ethics of dissensus, I want to propose a theory of sexual difference that still has a political future and ethical relevance for feminism. Although it has been an effective tool of the feminist critique of phallocentrism in the 1980s and of the sex/gender divide in the 1990s,[2] the theory of sexual difference has been increasingly questioned by such diverse feminist theorists as Hortense J. Spillers, bell hooks, Deborah E. McDowell, Evelynn Hammonds, Valerie Smith, Elizabeth V. Spelman, Judith Butler, Gayle Rubin, and Ellen T. Armour, among others, for its implication in heterosexism and its disregard of the differences among women.[3] In the light of these contestations, it is not surprising that Pheng Cheah and Elizabeth Grosz, the editors of the recent special issue of *Diacritics* devoted to Irigaray's work, open their introduction with the following question: "What political future(s), if any, does sexual difference have?"[4] As a rejoinder to this fundamental question I would like to pose several of my own: Can we think about sexual difference in futural terms as a condition of becoming? What is the relation between the political future of sexual difference and the future of radical democracy? Can a theory of sexual difference develop an ethical model of erotic relations without reinscribing heterosexuality? And finally, can a theory of sexual difference contest the erasure of race in white feminism without repeating the gesture, diagnosed by Ann DuCille, bell hooks, Valerie Smith, and Deborah E. McDowell, among others, of appropriation or commodification of black feminist thought?[5] How can we rethink the relation between sexual difference and racial differences among women without collapsing them into the same type of difference?

The most compelling defense of sexual difference has been articulated by the psychoanalytic critics and feminist philosophers ranging from Joan Copjec, Slavoj Žižek, Jacqueline Rose, Elizabeth Abel, and Elizabeth Weed to Drucilla Cornell, Rosi Braidotti, and Tina Chanter.[6] And despite their trenchant critiques of the shortcomings of psychoanalysis, African-American feminist theorists such as Hortense J. Spillers, Evelynn Hammonds, and Claudia Tate have offered provocative reformulations of sexual difference in the context of race.[7] As the persistence of this debate suggests, feminism still needs a theory of sexual difference, but a theory that is more dynamic, more democratic, and more ethical—a theory capable of foregrounding not only the futurity of democracy and the antagonistic differences among women but also the ethical respect for alterity in all its forms. In order to develop such a theory, I would like to engage and radicalize three crucial concepts in Irigaray's work: the labor of the negative; the impossible; and the work of "disappropriation." The trajectory of my argument is as follows: first, I theorize how the impossible and the negative of sexual difference can be linked to the affirmation of becoming, disjunctive temporality of history and the possibility of social transformation. Second, I elaborate the labor of the negative actualized through sexual difference in the context of the ethical responsibility in erotic relations. Finally, I reconsider sexual difference in the context of democratic politics in order to contest the disembodied notion of democratic citizenship, on the one hand, and in order to criticize Irigaray's inability to address the antagonistic differences among women, in particular, the differences of race, on the other. I argue that the rethinking of the theory of sexual difference in a double context of ethics and politics enables us to radicalize all three of these areas of feminist inquiry.

## The Negative and the Impossible:
## The Disjunctive Temporality of Sexual Difference[8]

I would like to begin the discussion of the future of sexual difference with one of the most important and most enigmatic of Irigaray's terms—the labor of the negative, which I read as the impossibility to define sexual difference in positive terms. Evoking and redefining both the Freudian castration and the Hegelian determinate negation beyond their phallic economies, Irigaray argues that sexual difference is the condition of the actualization of the negative in the subject—what she calls "taking the negative upon oneself" (*ESD*, 120).[9] In a manner evocative of Lacan's discussion of separation as the superimposition of two lacks, the labor of the negative accomplished through sexual difference reveals the internal division and self-limitation of the sexed subject. By marking a passage from the negative in-itself to the negative for-itself, sexual difference can be read as a negation of any particularity positing itself as the universal. Based on the labor of the negative and a work of "disappropriation," the assumption of sexual difference reveals the limits of the symbolic positions rather than an identification with a positive identity. Like Joan Copjec's emphasis on the antinomies of sexual difference,[10] this notion of sexual difference foregrounds the internal splitting, disappropriation, and alterity of the subject. Irigaray writes:

The *mine* of the subject is always already marked by disappropriation [*désappropriation*]: gender [*le genre*]. Being a man or a woman means not being the whole of the subject or of the community or of spirit, as well as not being entirely one's self. The famous *I* is another, the cause of which is sometimes attributed to the unconscious, can be understood in a different way. *I* is never simply *mine* in that it belongs to a gender. Therefore, I am not the whole [*je ne suis pas tout*]. (*ILTY*, 106; *JA*, 166)

Yet, as I will argue in this chapter, this negative characterization of sexual difference will have to be radicalized to contest what bell hooks, Valerie Smith, Elizabeth Spelman, and Ellen Armour diagnose as the white solipsism, that is, the persistence of whiteness as the invisible mark of universality and the corresponding association of race with nonwhiteness.[11] According to bell hooks, "Race is always an issue of Otherness that is not white; it is black, brown, yellow, red, purple even. Yet only a persistent, rigorous, and informed critique of whiteness could really determine what forces of denial, fear, and competition are responsible for creating fundamental gaps between professed political commitment to eradicating racism and the participation in the construction of a discourse on race that perpetuates racial domination."[12] Consequently, if, as Irigaray argues, the labor of the negative undermines any identity—individual or collective—based on wholeness, it will also have to negate whiteness as the symptom of the "double erasure" of race in white feminism.[13] Even more so, it has to contest the unspoken "presumption of whiteness" in Irigaray's own texts.

Because it stresses the limits of identity and positionality, this radicalized negativity of sexual difference cannot be conflated with the social gender identities produced through the imaginary and symbolic identifications. On the contrary, by foregrounding "the impossible"—contradictions, conflicts, incompletion—in the formation of all identities, the labor of the negative in sexual difference prevents the reification of the existing gender and racial stereotypes into political or "natural" norms, thus opening the possibility of their refiguration. In the psychoanalytic context, this formulation of sexual difference as the impossible suggests a relation to the register of the real—that is, to what is excluded from the domain of symbolization. As Slavoj Žižek writes, "The claim that sexual difference is 'real' equals claim that it is 'impossible'—impossible to symbolize, to formulate as a symbolic norm."[14] Consequently, if Irigaray, like Copjec or Rose,[15] seems to distinguish sexual difference from other kinds of difference it is because this difference implies not a stable position but its disappropriation, not a normative identity but its impossibility, not the unity of the subject but its internal heterogeneity and incompleteness, not a positive identity but the negativity "in the self and for the self [ce négatif en soi et pour soi]" (ILTY, 106; JA, 166).

Yet, "the impossible" of sexual difference not only reveals a "groundless ground" of all sexual relations—that is, a ground that ungrounds the normative impositions of sexuality—but also stresses the openness to the future: "The relation between man and woman, men and women, takes place on the grounds of a groundless ground [sur fond d'un fond sans fond]. It is without definite resolution or assumption, always becoming [en devenir] . . . between one and the other, the ones and the others, with no end or final reckoning" (ILTY, 107; JA, 169). Paradoxically, the impossible of the sexual difference is fundamentally linked to the possibility of becoming, to the affirmation of the future transcending present limitations. By negating the currently existing cultural sexual norms, the negativity of sexual difference enables the ongoing transformation of sexual relations—what Irigaray calls the invention of "a new age of thought, art, poetry, and language" (ESD, 5). In this context I read Irigaray's claim that sexual difference exists not merely as the diagnosis of its erasure in the homosocial culture but, more fundamentally, as the indication of its irreducibly temporal character, its potential to negate the status quo and create new modes of life. This emphasis on the disjunctive temporality of sexual difference allows us to "temporalize" Lacan's thesis that the Woman does not exist and to reinterpret it as the affirmation of becoming. By linking the "impossible" status of sexual difference to the possibility of social transformation I agree with Judith Butler's argument that "the hetero-pathos that pervades the legacy of Lacanian psychoanalysis and some of its feminist reformulations can be countered only by rendering the symbolic increasingly dynamic, that is, by considering the conditions and limits of representation and representability as open to significant rearticulations and transformations under the pressure of social practices."[16] Given a certain persistence of "the hetero-pathos" in some of Irigaray's formulations of sexual difference, it is perhaps ironic that her emphasis on the invention of the impossible reverberates most closely with the work of one of the most influential gay theorists—with Michel Foucault's call for the invention of the modes of life that are still "improbable."[17]

To provide a theory of sexual difference that is more dynamic and open to transformation, I would like to rearticulate Irigaray's notion of the impossible in the context of Cornelius Castoriadis's concept of the radical social imaginary.[18] As Margaret Whitford suggests, the juxtaposition of Irigaray and Castoriadis situates the discussion of sexual difference not only in the framework of the existing social institutions, for instance, law, religion, or the modes of economic exchange, but also in the context of the disjunctive temporality of history.[19] What is characteristic of Castoriadis's work is the tension between the social imaginary and the radical imaginary—a tension reflecting the ambiguity between the constituted and the constituting character of society, between the determination and rupture in history. For Castoriadis, the rupture of such discontinuous becoming escapes the very opposition between the specular order of imaginary (mis)recognition and the symbolic order of language. Situating the theory of sexual difference in this context makes it possible, I argue, to stress its dynamic character and thus to displace the discussion of "the language of essence" to "the language of historicity."[20]

To articulate the relation between the "impossible" status of sexual difference and the discontinuous temporality of history it is important to distinguish the radical imaginary from the more familiar Lacanian concept of the imaginary associated with the formation of the ego in the "mirror stage." Rather than offering a straightforward critique of Lacan, Irigaray recalls his well-known diagnosis of the contradictory function of the bodily image—or more precisely, the spatial captation of the image—in the formation of the ego. As Lacan argues, the corporeal image provides the first schema enabling the integration of the body and the first organization of drives: through the mediation of the *Gestalt*, the fragmented and disorganized body of the infant acquires its first form. Yet, the function of this *Gestalt* remains contradictory. On the one hand, the anticipation of the mastery of one's body in the future enables the unification of the embodied ego and, thus, initiates a certain process of becoming; on the other hand, the mirror stage is characterized by the inertia that blocks all further becoming (the phrases Lacan uses are "formal fixation" or "spatial captation"). As Lacan writes, "Everything turns on what . . . [is] paradoxical, contradictory in the *ego's* function: if too developed, it stops all development, but in developing, it reopens the door to reality" (*SVII*, 74). Lacan interprets this "essential resistance to the elusive process of Becoming"[21] as an impasse created by the narcissistic fixation on the corporeal image and the pulverizing aggression of the death drive. For Lacan, the negativity of alienation reveals the aggressivity of the death drive as the correlative of the narcissistic identification with the image: "The notion of an aggressivity linked to the narcissistic relation and to the structures of systematic *méconnaissance* and objectification . . . characterize[s] the formation of the ego."[22] According to Richard Boothby, the death drive signifies in this context "the disruptive return" of the real of the fragmented body "against the limited form of the imaginary ego."[23]

Although it aims to critique Lacan's notion of the imaginary, Castoriadis's account of the social imaginary in *The Imaginary Institution of Society* is quite in keeping not only with Lacan's emphasis on the alienation inherent in the constitution of the imaginary identity but also with Slavoj Žižek's diagnosis of the political function of fantasy filling the lack in the symbolic order. In Castoriadis's political theory, the constituted/constituting ambiguity of history is reflected in the two versions of the imaginary—social and radical. For Castoriadis the social imaginary reveals the always already instituted world-disclosure, embodied in historically specific institutions. In this sense, the social imaginary determines the functionality of social institutions, anchoring and limiting the infinity of possible symbolic structures by providing them with a signified content, which offsets the arbitrary and temporal character of the sign: "This element—which gives a specific orientation to every institutional system, which overdetermines the choice and the connections of the symbolic networks, . . . the basis for articulating what does matter and what does not . . . —is nothing other than the *imaginary* of the society or of the period considered."[24] By fixing the range of possible identifications, values, and socially significant objects, the social imaginary, a principle of historical overdetermination and unification, evokes the political function of fantasy—what Žižek articulates as "the fantasy-space within which community organizes its way of life."[25] As I argue in my discussion of Kristeva, sexual and racial fantasies structuring enjoyment not only coordinate desire but also fix the instability of the imaginary and symbolic identifications and conceal the irreducible dimension of antagonism in social life.[26] Their unconscious hold depends, therefore, on their double function as a defensive screen protecting the subject against direct intrusion of the real and as an invisible supplement of power. Yet, Castoriadis's analysis of the social imaginary adds to the discussion of fantasy an emphasis upon the foreclosure of historical transformation. By fixing social identity, the historically specific institution of the social imaginary negates the disruptive temporality of history:

> Everything occurs as if society had to negate itself as society, conceal its being as society by negating the temporality . . . that it brings into existence . . . the denial of time displays a necessity inherent in the institution as such. Born in, through, and as the rupture of time . . . the institution in the profound sense of the term can exist only by posing itself as outside of time. (*IIS*, 213–14)

Thus, although Lacan and Castoriadis work on two different levels (identifications and fantasy on the one hand, and social institutions on the other), they both stress the fact that the institution of the imaginary identity blocks further becomings.

Where Castoriadis and Irigaray differ from the early work of Lacan is in their dynamic interpretation of the disjunctive temporality of history and the constituting character of society. Escaping the usual opposition between the imaginary and the symbolic, the disruptive temporality of the radical imaginary, is a "common root" of changes in both the symbolic and the imaginary registers. Associated with productive imagination and the creation ex nihilo, this "radical" imaginary would correspond in Lacan's later work to the traversal of fantasy and the confrontation with the real. Evocative of Kristeva's "new imaginary," the radical social imaginary is thus not only a source of alienation and the autonomization of institutional life but also a condition of emancipatory change: "The social-historical present gives us a blinding and paroxystic illustration of this present each time instituting society irrupts within instituted society, each time society as instituted is self-destructed by society as instituting, that is to say each time another instituted society is self-created" (*IIS*, 201). Even though Castoriadis aims to recover the revolutionary socialist project, he makes clear that the disruptive temporality of radical imaginary is not confined merely to the moment of revolution but is at work, in various degrees, in every social reproduction: "Even when, in appearance, a society is merely 'preserving itself,' it never ceases to alter itself" (*IIS*, 201).

It is on the level of the radical imaginary that I would like to situate the "impossible" of sexual difference. Such a theory of sexual difference prevents its conflations with the existing symbolic and imaginary structures and links it instead with the disruptive temporality of history. When interpreted in the light of the radical imaginary, the impossible of sexual difference dramatizes the tension between the instituted and instituting character of social life, between identity and rupture, between historical determination of racial and gender identities and the possibility of their transformation. Future-oriented and linked to the emergence of the new modes of life and institutional arrangements, sexual difference, like the radical imaginary, announces a possibility of a break from the intertwined historical determinations of race, gender, and class, acknowledging in this way both the indetermination of history and the lack of closure in the social systems of signification.

By situating sexual difference in the context of the inaugural, disruptive temporality of history rather than conflating it with the constituted gender identity, I want not only to stress the larger institutional ramification of Irigaray's work, evident for instance, in her discussion of the law, rights, religion, economic justice, and the culture of difference but also to interpret

the "utopianism" of her work as an expression of the discontinuous temporality characteristic of historical change.[27] As Christine Holmlund, among
others, points out, where Irigaray's work seems problematic is not in its critique of phallocentrism but in the "visionary re-creations of an undefinable,
non-unitary female identity based on difference."[28] Although Drucilla
Cornell has powerfully defended "the unerasable trace of utopianism" as the
expression of the fact that we are never simply "hostage" of our surround-
ings, most of Irigaray's readers find this utopian articulation of sexual
difference as essentialist at best, or imperialist, at worst.[29] To address these
criticisms, I propose to read the "utopianism" of Irigaray's work in terms of
the radical sexual imaginary, that is, not as a positive recovery of the truth of
sexual difference but as an articulation of the disjunctive temporality characteristic of the emergence of the new modes of life.

   This emphasis on the disjunctive temporality of sexual difference complicates the symbolic solution to the fixity of the imaginary identity.
Although Irigaray agrees with Lacan's analysis of the blockage of becoming
inherent in the spatial captation of the bodily ego, she extends this diagnosis by arguing that the visual imaginary, characterized by the unity of form,
expresses the masculine economy of sameness (SVII, 28), which makes
woman and her sex appear as a "horror of nothing to see." Yet, Irigaray's
own critique of sameness is equally insufficient because it fails to take into
account what race theorists from Du Bois and Frantz Fanon to Hortense
Spillers, Patricia Williams, Evelynn Hammonds, and bell hooks diagnose as
the specular economy of race organized around the white look.[30] In the
context of Fanon's critique of the racist imaginary, the "horror of nothing
to see" would be primarily associated with the abjected black body, a body
that is made to stand for everything that "impedes the closing of the postural
schema of the white man."[31] Furthermore, what this specular economy of
racism reenacts is not only what Michele Wallace and Charles Mills describe
as the trope of racial invisibility and nonexistence of blackness[32] but also the
hypervisibility of the black women's sexuality.[33] As Hortense Spillers,
Patricia Hill Collins, and Valerie Smith argue, the racist associations of the
black women with excessive sexuality is the obverse side of the asexuality ascribed to white women.[34] According to Smith, it is precisely the phantasmatic constructions of black women as "sexually voracious" that makes
them "the most vulnerable and least visible victims of rape."[35] Ironically, as
Evelynn Hammonds points out, "The construction of the black female as
the embodiment of sex" is correlative of the "invisibility of black women as
the unvoiced, unseen everything that is not white."[36] In the light of this discussion, in Lacan's early work the symbolic solution to the impasses of the
specular economies of race and gender is insufficient: it neither takes into account the violence that the symbolic homosocial order, supported by sexist

and racist fantasies, inflicts on sexualized and racialized others[37] nor links the instability of the imaginary and symbolic identifications with the possibility of change. By contrast, the emphasis on the disruptive temporality of sexual difference, in particular, when it is linked to what Fanon describes in his polemics with Hegel as "the possibility of the impossible,"[38] could enable the traversal of the ideological function of the racist and sexist fantasies and the reworking of both the imaginary and symbolic structures beyond the objectifying economy of "solids."

Drawing on the variety of sources—Merleau-Ponty, Levinas, Lacan, and Castoriadis—Irigaray attempts to recover the temporal "'mechanics' of fluids" obfuscated on the imaginary level by the structure of the specular image and on the symbolic level by the privilege given to closed sets and to the "*symbol of universality*" (*TS*, 108). This dynamic character of the imaginary and the symbolic allows us to rearticulate the ethos of becoming elaborated in different parts of this book in the context of the temporal structure of embodiment. Irigaray illustrates this temporalized economy in the figure of the two sets of lips: "Two sets of lips that, moreover, cross over each other like the arms of the cross, the prototype of the crossroads *between*. The mouth lips and the genital lips do not point in the same direction" (*ESD*, 18). The chiasmus formed by two pairs of lips implies not only the inseparability of the embodiment and speech, of the female imaginary and the symbolic, but also the temporal and spatial between [*entre*], the locus of the event, where "*time must redeploy space* [*le temps devrait redéployer l'espace*]" (*ESD*, 18; *ÉDS*, 24). By stressing the homology between the temporal pulsation of the unconscious and embodiment elaborated by Lacan, Irigaray insists that the sexed body has to be seen as "an in-finite, un-finished flesh"  (*ESD*, 186). No longer modeled on the perception of space, the time of the sexual imaginary constitutes a radically different form of embodiment "without closing . . . [the world] off or closing off the self" (*ESD*, 141). Liberated from the spatial "geometrism" (*TS*, 112), the radical sexual imaginary, and the libidinal economy that subtends it, posits the incompleteness and "non-suture" of embodiment as a function of the intensity of becoming rather than as an expression of the "property" of the body. Unlike the temporality of anticipation in the mirror stage where future mastery contrasts sharply with present immaturity and eventually leads to a paralysis blocking all further development, the future opened by the radical imaginary is predicated neither on the anticipation nor on the mastery of the ego. It is an unforeseeable future beyond the possible, "that which cannot be anticipated because it is other . . . Beyond the limits of its 'I can'" (*ESD*, 211). Thus, the dynamic character of the sexual imaginary opposes the idea of "one universe" (*TS*, 30), not because it inscribes the essential fluidity of the female body but because it reflects the discontinuous temporality, negativity, and the limit of the body marked by sexual difference. It is the conjunction of the temporality and sexual difference and not the essence of the female body that questions both identity thinking and, as Castoriadis has taught us, the concept of the identitary time.

Although many of Irigaray's readers stress the porosity and the fluidity of the female embodiment, most consider this fluidity as either a "literal" or "figurative" attribute of the sexed body rather than as an effect of the temporal structure of becoming. The most significant consequence of this disregard for temporality is, as Drucilla Cornell has argued, the charge of essentialism that has dominated the reception of Irigaray's work.[39] What the discussion of essentialism, whether it is perceived as "strategic" or not, cannot account for is, first, Irigaray's emphasis on the temporality of the body and, second, her critique of immediacy. It might be worthwhile to recall at this point that Irigaray consistently criticizes the lure of immediacy on many levels ranging from the mystification of the pre-Oedipal sexuality ("extolling the pre-Oedipal as a liberation from the norm of genital sexuality entails all the caprice and immaturity of desire" [*ILTY*, 27]) to intuitive knowledge of experience, from the empiricism of history to the utopian dream of the immediate community among women. Consequently, an ethics of sexual difference cannot be confused with a recovery of "immediate affect, with self-certainty, mimetic or recapitulative intuitive truth, with historical narrative, etc." (*ILTY*, 62). In response to these lures, she flatly proclaims that "there is no . . . 'natural immediacy'" (*ILTY*, 107).

By stressing Irigaray's critique of the natural immediacy, I move the discussion of female embodiment beyond the opposition between essentialism and its opposite, the *figurations* of flesh,[40] and focus instead on the constituted/constituting ambiguity of history. Like the constituted/constituting ambiguity of flesh in Levinas's work, all the strategic tropes Irigaray deploys—touch, mucous, two lips, the threshold—do not merely indicate the constitution of the female body beyond the scopic economy of the image but, precisely, link embodiment with temporality. Not merely an alternative morphology of women's bodies, the radical sexual imaginary articulates a temporal structure of "a *morphe* in continual gestation" (*ESD*, 193). The figure of the touch, for instance, can signify for Irigaray a porosity of the female body and the fluidity of the inside and the outside boundaries only because the touch "metabolizes itself in the constitution of time" (*ESD*, 191). It is "the temporalization of touch" that signifies the threshold, the opening to the future, and the passage between. By emphasizing the temporality and the intensity of bodily becomings, an ethics of sexual difference contests the confinement of time to the interiority of the male subject and the corresponding association of the female body with the exteriority of space—a set of distinctions, as Irigaray's work on Aristotle and Plato shows, deeply entrenched in the Western philosophical tradition.[41] The temporal structure of embodiment challenges the phantasmatic construction of the female body as the negative space, abyss, the obverse of God, as "a horror of nothing to see," or as a nostalgic reminder of the first and ultimate dwelling associated with the maternal body (ESD, 7).

As Foucault, Lyotard, and Kristeva in different ways argue, this emphasis on the constituted/constituting temporality of history enables us to analyze sexed bodies not only as the materialization of the specific relations of power but also as the productive condition of becoming, as the surpassing of the historical limits of power, knowledge and discourse. This emphasis on the unfinished, temporal structure of embodiment does not negate the Foucauldian analysis of modern bodies as the materialization of disciplinary power but, very much in line with his interpretation, contests the notion of the body as a permanently formed substance.[42] In fact, as I argue in the first chapter, Foucault himself has posited and investigated with great historical precision the productive tension between the constituted and the constituting character of society, between determination and rupture in history. Thus, although they proceed by different paths—Foucault by analyzing heterogeneous modalities of the materialization of disciplinary biopower, Irigaray by stressing temporality in the psychoanalytic account of embodiment—both of them link the materiality of the body invested with different types of power with the discontinuous temporality of the event, which Foucault describes as the reversal or shift in the configuration of forces. Because for both Irigaray and Foucault the materialization of bodies has an incomplete temporal structure, it is open to change and transformation.

For Irigaray, the disruptive temporality manifests itself on the level of the body as the first passion, the status of which she discusses in the context of Freud's theory of the drives (ESD, 80) and Descartes's reflection on wonder [l'admiration]. As this psychoanalytic framework suggests, Irigaray reinterprets the rupture of wonder as a figure of jouissance. For Irigaray both jouissance and the passion of wonder originate on the threshold between the materiality of the body and language—it is "a passion that maintains the path between physics and metaphysics, corporeal impressions and movements toward an object" (ESD, 80). And yet, Irigaray suggests, wonder is an affect Freud forgot. What is this "forgotten" dimension of drive revealed in wonder? Irigaray's reading of wonder in Descartes suggests that she wants to stress the eventlike structure of jouissance and thus to indicate the disruptive temporality of the drive emerging beyond, or perhaps through, the compulsion to repeat. Like Castoriadis's radical imaginary, wonder, the passion of jouissance, enables us to think of the present as a break from the past rather than as an actualization of the predetermined conditions: "Outside of repetition. It is the passion of the first encounter" (ESD, 82). It is not by coincidence that Irigaray consistently defines wonder as an opening of a "new space-time" (*ESD*, 75). Similarly to Foucault's reading of the Nietzschean "rapture," Irigaray's interpretation of wonder stresses "what has not yet found a setting" (*ESD*, 186). It is precisely in these terms that Castoriadis describes the time of the radical imaginary: "The *present*, the *nun* is here explosion, split, rupture—the rupture of what is as such" (*IIS*, 201). Evocative of Heidegger's concept of the event,[43] this emphasis on rupture posits the present as a suspension of the past determinations. By destroying the linear concept of history, such a suspension opens the past itself to retrospective, futural determinations.[44] In this sense wonder reveals the indeterminacy of both history and the body—it "corresponds to time, to space time before and after that which can delimit. . . . It constitutes an *opening* prior to and following that which surrounds, enlaces" (*ESD*, 81–82). Although the disruptive time of the radical imaginary can be covered over by the desire for presence (which, according to Castoriadis, corresponds to the reduction of the radical imaginary to the evolutionary time) or by the nostalgia for origins, the passage it opens between no longer and not yet is, for Irigaray, a condition of possibility of both desire and freedom: "Is wonder the time that is always covered over by the *present*. . . . Where I am no longer in the past and not yet in the future. The point of passage between two closed words, two definite universes, two space-times. . . . In a way, wonder and desire remain the spaces of freedom . . ." (*ESD*, 75–76).

By radicalizing the impossible of sexual difference in the context of the disjunctive temporality, I move beyond the impasse created in the reception of Irigaray's work by the opposition between essentialism and social construction and foreground in its place the productive ambiguity of the constituted/constituting character of history. This interpretation of sexual difference allows us not only to interrogate the symbolic and imaginary identifications of race, gender, and class in the context of power reflecting the *constituted* character of history but also to link the incompleteness of these identifications to the possibility of becoming, to the transformation of the institutional structures, to the *constituting*/creative aspect of the radical imaginary.[45] Yet, what I also want to stress is that the disruptive and transformative potential of sexual difference can be actualized and assessed only in the context of the specific historical determinations of what the sociologists Patricia Hill Collins and Margaret L. Andersen call "the interactive systems" of race, class, and gender relation.[46] In fact, I argue that when we reduce sexual difference to only one side of the determination/disruption divide, we neutralize its critical potential. By attending to sexual difference in light of *both* the constituting/constituted character of history, we can not only study "race, class, and gender from the perspective of the matrix of domination" but also take into account, as Collins and Andersen themselves note, the "creative and visionary"[47] aspects of political praxis. In many ways, this kind of double analysis is yet to take place.

## Labor of Love, Labor of the Negative: An Ethical Model of Erotic Relations

The ethics of dissensus I propose in this book contests the opposition between ethical obligations and the becoming of the subject as mutually exclusive ethical trajectories. The question that I would like to pose now is whether we can come up with a theory of sexual difference that can enable a certain negotiation between two different lines of ethical inquiry discussed in this book: between the ethos of becoming represented by the work of Nietzsche, Deleuze, Foucault, and discussed in this chapter in the context of Castoriadis, and the ethos of responsibility represented by Levinas, Derrida, and Lyotard.[48] The importance of Irigaray's work for my project lies in the fact that it refuses to align itself with either side of this divide. Although Irigaray, like Castoriadis, links the temporality of becoming with an incessant emergence of otherness, she refuses to confine the concept of alterity merely to self-alteration but stresses "the advent or the event of the other" (*ESD*, 75). In fact, Irigaray argues that the Other encountered in love is not a hostile freedom blocking my own but the very source of my becoming: "*Who are thou? I am* and *I become* thanks to this question" (*ESD*, 74). Consequently, she maintains neither the rigid separation between becoming and obligation, as is the case in Levinas's work, nor their symmetrical reversibility as is the case in Kant's ethics.

Yet, how can these seemingly contradictory claims—the affirmation of becoming and the respect for the nonthematizable alterity of the Other—be negotiated without evoking the Kantian reversibility of freedom and obligation? The answer to this question lies in the theory of sexual difference as an enabling condition of both the becoming of the subject and the ethical relation to the Other. The question that we have to ask, therefore, is in what sense the negativity and the impossibility of sexual difference can be a condition of the ethical respect for the Other? Because sexual difference negates any attempt to posit the particular as the universal or to consolidate it into a universal norm, it both affirms the futurity of becoming and fosters respect for "differences everywhere: differences between the other races, differences between the generations, and so on" (JLI, 110). By stressing the ethical respect for differences, I want to dissociate the labor of the negative accomplished through sexual difference from the Hegelian alienation in the master/slave dialectic. Instead, I argue that the identification with sexual difference is a movement toward the internal division and limitation of the subject for the sake of Other's becoming: "The ascetism of the negative thus seemed necessary to me but more out of consideration for the other and from collective good sense than as a process of consciousness that would lead to a more accomplished spirituality. . . . Hegel knew nothing of a negative like that" (*ILTY*, 13). In this context, "taking the negative upon oneself" has to be understood as the negation of the negation, that is, as the negation of the externalized negativity of the subject in the Other. Yet, in a manner similar to Adorno's negative dialectic, such a negation of the externalizing activity of thought leads to anti–Hegelian outcome: to the preservation of the nonidentical. Because it annuls the externalization of the internal limitation of the subject, "taking the negative upon oneself" (*ESD*, 120) prevents the construction of the Other either as the alienating opposite or as the compensatory complement of the subject. Consequently, the internalization of the negative does not sublate the Other into the same but, by placing "a limit on my horizon, on my power" (JLI, 110), preserves her irreducible alterity. It is in this sense that the negativity of sexual difference is a condition of the ethical respect for the asymmetrical otherness.

In psychoanalytic terms, the labor of the negative is a correlative of what Kristeva analyzes as the negativization of narcissism: in both cases, the confrontation with the internal splitting of the subject facilitates the unraveling of the defensive projections of that negativity onto the Other. Taking the negative upon oneself reveals the fact that it is not the antagonistic relationship with the Other that prevents the accomplishment of the full identity but the internal negativity within the subject—what psychoanalysis designates as the death drive. In this sense, the labor of the negative can be seen as a sublimation of the death drive. As I suggest in my reading of Kristeva, an ethical act of sublimation deflects the aggressivity of the death drive from the destruction of the Other toward the transformation of the imaginary and symbolic structures. Such a rethinking of the labor of the negative in the context of psychoanalysis makes it possible to alter the Hegelian desire for recognition into an ethical acknowledgment of the transcendence of the Other. As Irigaray writes, "I recognize you means I cannot know you in thought or in flesh. The power of the negative prevails between us. I recognize you goes hand in hand with: you are irreducible to me. . . . Between us there is always transcendence" (*ILTY*, 103–4).

Although Irigaray claims that acknowledgment of sexual difference fosters the ethical respect for "differences everywhere" (JLI, 110), I want to focus in greater detail in this section on the ethical model of erotic relations. To avoid the reinscription of the heterosexual paradigm that sometimes characterizes the discussions of sexual difference, I want to stress the distinction between sexual difference, which foregrounds the disappropriation, limitation, and incompleteness of any sexual identity, and sexual relation, which can refer to either homosexual or heterosexual eroticism. Although

Irigaray herself argues that "it's important not to confuse sexual choice with sexual difference" (JLI, 112), she often does precisely that, especially when she refers to the heterosexual couple as a model of both sexual difference and the ethical paradigm of sexual relations.[49] Responding to this confusion of sexual difference and sexual relation in Irigaray's work, Judith Butler argues that *An Ethics of Sexual Difference* makes "heterosexuality into the privileged locus of ethics, as if heterosexual relations, because they putatively crossed this alterity, which is the alterity of sexual difference, were somehow more ethical, more other-directed."[50] In order to contest the interpretation of an ethics of sexual difference as a prescription for heterosexuality, I argue that the labor of the negative accomplished through sexual difference, insofar as it negates either the externalization of the negative in the Other or the reduction of the Other to the complement of the subject, enables the respect for the alterity of the Other in both heterosexual and homosexual relations.[51] In other words, the Other in sexual relation cannot be equated with the other sex. I agree here with Elizabeth Grosz and Pheng Cheah, who in their polemics with Judith Butler and Drucilla Cornell claim that "neither *respect for* the other sex nor *fidelity to* one's sex necessarily implies an obligatory *desire for* the other sex."[52]

The ethical model of sexual relation that I elaborate in this chapter stems from a rather complex negotiation among Lacan's, Irigaray's, and Levinas's work. Although this model is indebted to Lacan's theory of the traumatic asymmetry of sexual relation, I reinterpret this asymmetry as an ethical affirmation of the irreducible alterity of the Other, emphasized by Irigaray and Levinas. I am particularly interested in the way the asymmetry of sexual relation opens a possibility of an infinite love, mentioned briefly by Lacan in Seminar XI. Irreducible to the compensatory function of the narcissistic love, which turns the Other into a complement of the self, this "limitless love," love "outside the limits of the law, where alone it may live,"[53] can be read as a mode of an ethical relation that respects the infinite alterity of the sexual partner.

Although clearly indebted to Levinas's conception of alterity, the ethical model of sexual relation I propose refuses the separation of eroticism from ethics. Despite Levinas's critique of psychoanalysis, his ambivalence about erotic love in fact supports the psychoanalytic conclusion that narcissistic love reduces the Other to the complement of the subject and thus cannot figure as the basis of ethics. Although Levinas distinguishes erotic voluptuosity from any simple complementarity between lovers, he nonetheless concludes his discussion of Eros in *Totality and Infinity*, "To love is also to love oneself in love, and thus to return to oneself. Love . . . is pleasure and dual egoism."[54] This definition of Eros as "dual egoism" mirrors very closely Lacan's diagnosis of the narcissistic function of love in *Encore*: "Analysis demonstrates that love, in its essence, is narcissistic."[55] In his critique of the narcissistic economy of love in Seminar XI, Lacan points out that the loved object is placed in the position of the ego Ideal, that is, at the point from which the ego itself appears as worthy of love. In Seminar XI, the fall from this deceptive idealization of the Other is accomplished on the basis of the object *a*—the object cause of desire, the representative of the lost *jouissance*. In *Encore*, however, the object *a* situated on the feminine side of sexual difference becomes increasingly problematized as a fetishistic semblance of being. Thus, Lacan points out that the subject approaching his partner as object *a* never encounters the Other as "Other" but merely as the fetishistic "substitute-prop": "When one is a man, one sees in one's partner what one props oneself up on, what one is propped up by narcissistically" (*E*, 87). Since the sexual relation in this case boils down to a fantasy compensating for the impossible of sexual difference, Lacan argues that the fetishistic "substitute-prop, or substitute for the Other in the form of the object of desire is *a*-sexual" (*E*, 127). Because in fantasy the object *a* "plays the role . . . of that which takes the place of the missing partner" (*E*, 63), Lacan argues that for the masculine subject "the Other as such remains a problem in Freudian theory" (*E*, 127). This is exactly the point that Irigaray raises in her critique of Levinas, namely, that his conception of Eros reduces femininity to a support of male narcissism: the beloved "would only maintain the male lover in his love of self, as he makes himself beloved" (*ESD*, 211–12).

Confronted with the impasses of narcissistic love, Levinas separates sexuality from the ethical "relation without relation." The other option of course would be to reconceptualize sexual relation apart from the narcissistic economy. What opens up this possibility and what thus prevents the confusion of Eros with "the pleasure of dual egoism" is Lacan's claim that narcissistic love is a defense mechanism making up for the asymmetry of the sexual relation rather than reflecting its actual character. Drawing on Irigaray's work, I want to reinterpret this asymmetry as a paradoxical condition of an ethical encounter in Levinas's sense.[56] In order to develop an ethical model of erotic relations, I refer briefly to the contrast between two different orders of significations, between the said and the saying (*le dit* and *le dire*), between the statement and the address to the Other, deployed in different ways in Lacan's, Levinas's, and Irigaray's work. Representing the unity and the totality of discourse, the said, for all three of these writers refer to the structure of predication reflecting the ontology of being.[57] Unlike the substantialization of being produced by the said, the saying, the effect of writing, according to Lacan, puts the subject on the path of ex-sistence, or para-being (being beside itself) (*E*, 44). In other words, Lacan reads the saying in the Heideggerian way as a mark of the event of language and the withdrawal of being: "For the property of what is said is being. . . . But the property of the act of saying is to ex-sist in relation to any statement" (*E*, 102).[58] Although Levinas concurs with Lacan that the saying is irreducible to the substantialization of being, he interprets it not only in terms of "ex-sistence" eccentric to truth but also as a paradoxical modality of address, as a traumatizing turning toward the absolutely Other that produces an inversion of the subject. Unlike the different modalities of the erasure of alterity through domination, knowledge, or narcissistic love, the nonsymmetrical relation to the Other interrupts the ego's narcissism by calling the subject to responsibility. By interrupting the said, the saying preserves the ethical signification of the Other as a trace of the "utterly bygone" past, which has never been present but which nonetheless troubles and obsesses the subject.

As we can see, the difference in these interpretations of the saying lies in the fact that Levinas stresses its ethical signification as the traumatic relation to the absolutely Other whereas Lacan seems to emphasize the ex-sistence of the subject. Nonetheless, in *Encore*, this ethical signification of the saying is implied indirectly as something that is forgotten in the Western tradition of courtly love, which, by reducing the Other to being and ontology, turns into hatred. As Lacan points out, "a hatred, a solid hatred, is addressed to being" (*E*, 99), and nothing concentrates so much hatred as the act of saying. At the end of *Encore* Lacan speaks of the test of love confronted with the impossibility of sexual relation and the inadequacy of "one's jouissance of the Other taken as a body." Can love sustain the encounter with the Other in the face of this inadequacy between alterity and being? For Lacan, love fails this test as soon as it interprets both alterity and *jouissance* in terms of being, transforming thus the contingency of the sexual encounter into necessity. Lacan reaches here a remarkably Levinasian conclusion, namely, that by approaching the Other in terms of being, love reduces her to the order of the same and, in so doing, turns into hatred: "The subject . . . shifts from the other to the being. . . . That gets us bogged down in a mirage-like apprehension. For it is love that approaches being as such in the encounter" (*E*, 145). One possible implication of this critique of love is that the ethical model of sexual relation would have to be conceptualized beyond, or "otherwise than being."

To define sexual relation as an ethical saying more explicitly than Lacan does, I would like to turn to Irigaray's *An Ethics of Sexual Difference* and *I Love to You*. In both of these texts, she analyzes the modality of the address to the Other as indirection and intransitivity—that is, as an oblique "relation without a relation" that does not reduce the Other to the narcissistic "substitute prop" of the subject.[59] In the context of Levinas's work, indirection can be described as a shift from the language of exchange and knowledge— from "the said" structured and supported by fantasy to the ethical "saying." Indeed, in her discussion of indirection, Irigaray stresses the Levinasian tropes of generosity, sensibility, and listening. Interpreted as an ethical say-ing, indirection constitutes a mode of listening that disrupts the discourse of demand for being produced by the love/hate ambivalence. By suspending knowledge and articulation, such a listening has a temporal structure of a fu-ture beyond the anticipation of the subject: "*I am listening to you* is to listen to your words as something unique, irreducible, especially to my own. . . . I am listening to you prepares the way for the not-yet-coded, for silence" (*ILTY*, 116–17).

As if responding to Lacan's suggestion that he articulates something pos-itive through negation (*E*, 58–59), Irigaray allows us to reinterpret the lack of complementarity between the sexes as a condition of an ethical encounter with the sexual partner. In order to distinguish "indirection" from either the objectification of the Other through knowledge or its reduction to the nar-cissistic support of the subject in fantasy, Irigaray proposes the neologism "I love to you" as a model of an ethical relation. Although I read "I love to you" as an instance of the erotic ethical saying Levinas could not quite imag-ine, I also want to point out that this phrase was initially invented by Lacan. As he points out in *Encore*, the neologisms "I love to you" and "I think to you" constitute "a clear objection" to the conceptualization of the Other as the object symmetrical to the subject: "I once spoke of a language in which one would say, "I love to you" (*j'aime à vous*), that language modeling itself better than others on the indirect character of . . . love" (*E*, 104). In Irigaray's rewritten version of this neologism (*j'aime à toi*) the letter "à" ("to") indicates the asymmetry of sexual relation rather than the semblance of being—the object *a*—taking the place of the missing partner. As Irigaray writes, "*à* prevents the relation of transitivity, bereft of the other's irre-ducibility. . . . The 'to' maintains intransitivity between persons, between the interpersonal question, speech or gift [*Le 'à' empêche le rapport de transi-tivité sans irréductibilité de l'autre*]" (*ILTY*, 109; *JA*, 171). As a trace of an oblique address and a radical disconnection, the proposition "*à*" marks the exposure to the Other and constitutes a barrier preventing the assimilation of the Other into an object or a semblance of being—an assimilation that turns love into an act of "cultural cannibalism" (*ILTY*, 110). It is a mark of the "nonimmediacy" and the irreversible asymmetry of the sexual relation. In the lower part of Lacan's diagram of the formulas of sexuation, the propo-sition "*à*" would occupy the place over the arrows indicating the paradoxi-cal mode of the relation without relation.

Yet, the ethical mode of sexual "relation without relation" can emerge only in the aftermath of the traversal of fantasy, which serves as a support of the subject's being. As Slavoj Žižek writes, "It is precisely this deception of the fundamental fantasy that the act of 'traversing the fantasy' serves to dispel: by traversing the fantasy, the subject accepts the void of his nonexistence."[60]

By putting the subject on the path of ex-sistence, or para-being (*E*, 44), the traversal of fantasy can be thus read a correlative of an ethical saying in the Levinasian sense: it enables us to formulate the paradoxical relation to the absolutely Other "otherwise than being." However, if we remember that it is phantasmatic object *a* that offers a semblance of being, then the traversal of fantasy opens a relation to the sexual partner irreducible to the "a-sexual" object *a*. When Žižek considers the traversal of fantasy in the context of sexual relations, he suggests that it is easier for women to accomplish this act, whereas men "come up against a condensed phantasmatic kernel, a 'fundamental symptom' . . . they are unable to renounce, so all they can do is accept it as an imposed necessity. In short, 'traversing the fantasy' is conceived as feminine, and 'the identification with the symptom' as masculine."[61] In the context of my interpretation of the traversal of fantasy as the correlative of an ethical saying, this would mean that the ethical relation can emerge only on the feminine side. Is this why Žižek is far more emphatic about the necessity of the traversal of the fantasy in political life whereas in the context of sexual relations he worries that when the "knot" of fantasy is dissolved, "subject loses his/her universal capacity to engage in sexual activity"?[62] Yet, if we refer to Žižek's earlier analysis of the symptom in *The Sublime Object of Ideology* and to Kristeva's discussion in *Strangers to Ourselves*, then "the identification with the symptom" cannot just mean the acceptance of its necessity. Rather it involves a twofold process consisting, first, in the critical interpretation of the ideological overdetermination of the symptom and, second, in the distancing from the enjoyment and the acceptance of the lack rather than seeking to fill it with the substitute-prop. Thus, if it is to function as an ethical act, the identification with a symptom on the masculine side ought to be equivalent with what Irigaray describes as "taking the negative upon oneself" for the sake of the alterity of the Other.

By staging the critical dialogue among Levinas, Lacan, and Irigaray, I want to rearticulate the contrast between the two orders of signification—the saying and the said—in the context of the erotic sensibility of the body.[63] As I argued in Chapter 3, Levinas aligns the said with the epistemological function of perception and the ethical saying with the vulnerability of the body, with its capacity for being affected by the Other: "To be in one's skin," Levinas writes, "is an extreme way of being exposed" (*OB*, 89). It is not difficult to hear the echoes of Levinas's carnal sensibility in Irigaray's description of touch and the porosity of the body. Yet, we have to remember that touch is for Irigaray a figure of the partial drive, which she adds to Lacan's list of partial drives because it dramatizes in a most striking way the disjunction between outward and inward movement of the drive. Consequently, this evocation of Levinas's insights also entails their displacement: just as she rethinks the constituted/constituting ambiguity of embodiment in the context of sexual difference, she extends Levinas's concept of ethical sensibility and "anarchic susceptibility to passion" so that it can encompass *jouissance* and erotic attraction. In her critique of a lingering masochism in Levinas's work, Irigaray refuses to reduce ethical sensibility—the capacity for being affected—to vulnerability and suffering alone but supplements it with that other *jouissance*, the *jouissance* of the speaking body.

For both Irigaray and Lacan, this reinterpretation of the ethical saying in terms of the *jouissance* of the speaking body is intertwined with the contestation of the economy of solids, that is, the substantialization of the body in the order of the said. In *Encore,* Lacan argues that the order of the said, based on the collectivization of the signifier, evident, for instance, in nouns derived from adjectives, "translates" the fragmented body of the partial drives into a substance: "To collectivize [the function of the signifier] in a way that resembles a predication, . . . adjectives made into nouns [*substantivés*] (*E*, 20). "As soon as we turn things into nouns, we presuppose a substance" (*E*, 21). Repeating the petrification of the subject in the signifier on the level of embodiment, the order of the said (*le dit*) (*E*, 21) produces the effect of substantialization "by 'corporizing' (*corporiser*) the body in a signifying way" (*E*, 23). Consequently, in the order of the said the body appears as a substance of enjoyment rather than as "a drift of jouissance." According to Bruce Fink, the French *corporiser* means giving a body to a spirit or turning fluid into a solid. This process of substantialization of the body is contrasted in *Encore* with the temporality of verbalization, which is ultimately interpreted as the saying (*le dire*): "The verb is defined as a signifier that is not as stupid . . . as the others . . . , providing as it does the movement of a subject to his own division in jouissance" (*E*, 25). We can infer from this contrast between the said and the saying that the saying might corporize the body in a different manner: not as a substance but as an affected, speaking body. The speaking body marks a certain excess with respect to what is enunciated (the said) because what it speaks is "llanguage" saturated with *jouissance*—it speaks the unconscious knowledge in the form of affects: "Llanguage affects us first of all by everything it brings with it by way of effects that are affects . . . the effects of llanguage . . . go well beyond anything the being who speaks is capable of enunciating" (*E*, 139). What the affected body speaks, then, is that other satisfaction which, by marking a "beyond" to knowledge, being, and phallus, "puts us on the path of ex-sistence" (*E*, 77). Paradoxically, the speaking body says more than can be said because it misses "what it wants to say"—it misses "its effective jouissance" (*E*, 121). Its saying, Lacan suggests, is but a cry "that's not it"—"the very cry by which the jouissance obtained is distinguished from the jouissance expected" (*E*, 111).

Irreducible to imaginary unity, the psychoanalytic concept of the speaking/affected body allows us to reinterpret the contrast between the saying and the said as the disjunction between *jouissance* and being, between drive and signifier. In the context of Irigaray's economy of fluids, ethical sensibility signifies not only as the vulnerability of the body but also as llanguage saturated with *jouissance*. Similarly, the ethical saying becomes another figuration of the sensible transcendental, bringing together the antithetical figures of the angel and the mucus, of transcendence and sensibility. Yet, my interpretation of the saying in terms of the economy of the fluids not only associates the ethical saying with *jouissance* but also complicates its temporal structure. As a marker of *jouissance*, ethical saying would be a passage between the anarchic diachrony of the past that has never been present and the infinite future of becoming. As Irigaray points out, the temporality of *jouissance* "opens on to infinity, without sending it back to an origin or a goal deprived of an access" (*ESD*, 200). By excluding *jouissance* of the speaking/ affected body from ethics, Levinas associates the emergence of the infinite future exclusively with the procreation of the child (*TI*, 269) and paternity (*TI*, 272). As the simultaneous process of "alteration and identification," paternity for Levinas constitutes the only relation to the Other that opens a possibility of becoming for the subject. It is thus a privileged moment where the respect for alterity and the future of becoming no longer contradict each other: "But the inevitable reference of the erotic to the future in fecundity reveals a radically different structure: . . . he [the subject] will be other than himself while remaining *himself*" (*TI*, 272). Irigaray argues, however, that the "inevitable reference of erotic to future" cannot be limited to the telos of procreation because this relationship to temporality is disclosed for the first time in the creation of *jouissance*. Prior to any procreation of the child (*ESD*, 201), it is the experience of *jouissance* in "the face-to-face encounter of two naked lovers" that constitutes an ethical creation of Eros. Irigaray claims, therefore, that Levinas's discussion of "fecundity" reflects the appropriation and the erasure of the temporal structure of *jouissance*.

This exclusion of Eros from ethics leads, however, not only to the reinscription of the patriarchal model of heterosexual reproduction but also to the characterization of the social bond as fraternity. By contesting such a homosocial model, Irigaray replaces Levinas's concept of paternity with sexual difference. She argues that the inscription of the undecidable ethics of sexual difference in democratic politics prevents the totalization of politics, on the one hand, and the reification of differences, on the other. As Gayatri Spivak suggests, "To learn the agency of the caress" is "to keep unlearning agency in the literal sense and allowing space for the *être-écrit(e)*, even in the pores of struggles recognizably 'political.'"[64] According to Spivak, the ethical respect for the Other challenges both the fetishization of the Other and its obverse side, "the convention of taking others as collections of selves."

For these reasons, political struggles, Spivak argues, have to risk "the intimate and inaccessible alterity" of others and ourselves.

## "Between Passion and Civility": Toward a Democratic Culture of Difference

In her later work on sexuate rights, civil identities, and the culture of difference, Irigaray examines more explicitly the relevance of sexual difference for democratic politics.[65] By focusing frequently on the ironic role of Antigone in Hegel's interpretation of the ethical community, Irigaray diagnoses contradictions in the position of contemporary women vis-à-vis the ethical order of the polis.[66] Although women have won the formal rights of citizenship in Western democracies, the liberal discourse of rights has not yet been transformed to express a culture of sexual difference. Without a culture of difference constructed within the larger horizon of economic equality, women, Irigaray argues, are caught in a double bind between "the minimum of social rights they can obtain . . . and the psychological or physical price they have to pay for that minimum."[67] As Etienne Balibar remarks, "it may indeed be significant that the discourse of 'culture,' which has always tended to multiply cultures and subcultures according to all human groupings possible in time and space . . . *never invokes* . . . the idea of a distinction *between 'men's culture' and 'women's culture'*. . . . As if *this* particular dividing line . . . could never give rise to a division of culture without overturning the very meaning of the word."[68] For Balibar this absence of a culture of sexual difference means that women, like other oppressed groups, form a paradoxical "collection under a single name of subjects whom nothing binds to one another, except their always singular way of *being an exception*." This status of an exception binds, nonetheless, "a community together in reality."[69]

In a well-known but controversial thesis, Irigaray argues that in order to transform this paradoxical role of femininity in the Western conception of the political, it is necessary to revise the concept of democratic citizenship in the light of sexual difference. Like many other readers of Irigaray, I criticize her culture of sexual difference for its inability to address differences among women, especially racial differences. Yet, before I renegotiate Irigaray's culture of difference in the context of race theories proposed by Mae Gwedolyn Henderson, bell hooks, Manning Marable, or Cornel West, I want to consider for a moment the possible political value of the radicalized notion of sexual difference I elaborated in this chapter—that is, sexual difference as the negative and the impossible. What does it mean to inscribe the labor of the negative and the impossible in the context of democratic politics? Obviously, at stake here is not the transformation of the existing gender identities—reflecting, as black and queer theorists have argued, white, heterosexual, middle-class subjectivities[70]—into political norms but, on the contrary, the emphasis on the impossible as the limit of all political positions. Consequently, the most important implication of the negativity of sexual difference is not even the recognition of women's legitimate right to construct their political identities that Irigaray advocates but, more fundamentally, the contestation of the binary opposition between the abstract concept of liberal citizenship and its opposite, the reification of proliferating differences as unmediated particulars.

Like many other feminist political theorists—Carole Pateman, Iris Young, Chantal Mouffe, Drucilla Cornell, Anna Yeatman, and Patricia Williams, among others—Irigaray claims that the liberal citizenship, based on the homosocial fraternity and property, excludes sexual difference from political identity.[71] By relegating all the differences and particularisms, such as sex, race, class, and ethnicity, to the private sphere, liberalism supports the notion of the abstract public, and the disembodied political subject separated from the body, race, and sexuality. Yet, if Irigaray argues that the political diversity of women cannot be affirmed without challenging the abstraction of the liberal citizenship, she also claims that the opposite solution, the affirmation of unmediated differences risks a complicity with the traditional positioning of women in the polis as an assembly of particulars (one + one + one) incapable of acquiring a political identity. As Pheng Cheah and Elizabeth Grosz point out, for Irigaray the uncritical affirmation of the dispersal into "atomistic singularities" is in complicity with "the logic of the one."[72] To avoid the either/or alternatives of the liberal citizenship abstracted from all differences and its opposite, the affirmation of the differences as unmediated particulars, I would like to consider the political significance of sexual difference in the context of the contradictory logic of radical democracy suspended between equivalence and difference. This interpretation of sexual difference would have to respond to two interrelated dilemmas in the discourse of radical democracy: first, it would have to rethink a relation between the particular and the universal without, on the one hand, abolishing the singularity in the universal and embracing neutral atomistic particulars, on the other. As bell hooks puts it, "Many people mistake a critique of the universalizing ethos with a rejection of commonality and common bonds. . . . I feel that it's not that we want to do away with the notion of commonality, but that we want to find the basis of commonality in something other than a notion of a shared experience or common oppression."[73] Second, it would have to negotiate between the equivalence presupposed by the democratic ethos of equality and liberty for all and the irreducible differences of race, gender, and class reflected in the plurality of the conflicting interpretations of this ethos.

Both of these dilemmas of democracy are addressed by Ernesto Laclau and Chantal Mouffe in their work on the role of hegemony and articulation in democratic politics. As Laclau points out, the uncritical "assertion of the pure particularism, independently of any content and of the appeal to a universality transcending it, is a self-defeating enterprise"[74] culminating in two incoherent political positions. If, on the one hand, we recognize that differences are the effects of subordination and affirm all of them without judging them according to some underlying democratic principles, we end up affirming reactionary and progressive differences indiscriminately. If, in contrast, we posit impartial differences divorced from antagonism, then we not only ignore the reality of domination but also posit the abstract universal as the neutral substratum of all these differences. To avoid this incoherence and to articulate the relation between difference, antagonism, and democracy, Laclau proposes the paradoxical interpretation of the universal not as the underlying principle explaining identity but as a "missing fullness" in each identity: "No particularity can be constituted except by maintaining an internal reference to universality as that which is missing."[75] Because it marks the failure of the full actualization of any political position or principle, such a universal puts all of them in question and opens the possibility of their conflicting interpretations. This interpretation of the universal as the impossibility of the full actualization of political identities, as the unattainable horizon that marks the disproportion and asymmetry between the universal and the particular, coincides closely with my reading of sexual difference as the impossible labor of the negative. Yet, in the light of sexual difference this interpretation of the missing universality not only stresses the impossibility of its realization but, in fact, splits it into two: "The particularity of this universal is that it is divided into two" (*ILTY*, 50). Such a negative and fractured notion of the universal at work in sexual difference negates any particularity positing itself as the universal. Consequently, despite Chantal Mouffe's rejection of sexual difference from democratic citizenship,[76] the negativity of sexual difference in fact supports her argument that "no limited social actor can attribute to herself the representation of the totality and claim in that way to have the 'mastery of foundations.'"[77]

By contesting Mouffe's assumption about irrelevance of sexual difference for political identities, my interpretation aims to radicalize both the theory of sexual difference and democratic politics. On the one hand, the consideration of sexual difference in the context of radical democracy will allow me to criticize Irigaray's work for its inability to address sufficiently the dimension of antagonism and differences among women. As I will show in my engagement with Henderson's theory of the black female subjectivity, the fact that sexual difference dramatizes the impossibility of achieving full gender or racial identity is inextricably linked to the contestation of these identities. The labor of the negative in this context cannot mean just an abstract expression of the respect for racial and class differences among women but has to, first of all, negate the unquestioned universality of whiteness and to articulate how these differences intersect and inscribe the dimension of antagonism within subject positions. Because the impossible of sexual difference reveals that no single woman can actualize her gender, the meaning of femininity and feminism is open to endless contestation. Furthermore, the negativity of sexual difference makes it possible to rearticulate the constitutive contradiction of democratic citizenship while contesting its disembodied and desexualized character. Mouffe explains the contradiction between equivalence and diversity in terms of the symbolic identification with the democratic "grammar of conduct"—with the ethos of equality and liberty for all—that provides an indispensable minimum of commonality and at the same time submits this ethos to conflicting interpretations, reflective of insurmountable differences: "A radical democratic conception of citizenship could . . . provide that bond created through equivalence, that form of commonality that does not erase differences. It can play such a role because . . . the commonality that is made possible by equivalence is not the expression of something positive, of a common essence, but something purely negative."[78] Yet, this explanation of the constitutive contradiction in terms of symbolic identification is insufficient: symbolic identifications by themselves do not preserve plurality and conflict of interpretations. It is only by stressing the internal limit of all political identifications revealed by the impossible of sexual difference that we can explain the constitutive contradiction of democracy and prevent the reification of this contradiction in the figure of the external enemy.[79] Furthermore, the emphasis on the political significance of sexual difference not only contests the desexualized and disembodied political bonds but also challenges a one-sided valorization of antagonism at the expense of that other side of the labor of the negative—the obligation for the Other. Thus, if Irigaray's work must be criticized for its inability to address antagonisms and differences among women, then Mouffe's disregard for sexual difference can be reproached for an equally problematic privileging of war and conflict.

The complicity between the sublation of sexual difference, disembodied universal, and the political valorization of war is most clearly demonstrated in Irigaray's critique of Hegel. As Tina Chanter shows, the political value of war for Hegel lies in the negation of the antagonistic particularisms in the civil society, which tend to isolate themselves from the ethical whole of the polis and threaten to dissolve the unity of the state.[80] War at the government's disposal is thus the means of mediation that manifests the power of the Spirit, that is, in Hegel's words, "the power of the whole, which brings these parts together again into a negative unity, giving them the feeling of their lack of independence." Hegel argues that the threat of war "violates" the independence of the individuals by making them "feel in the task laid on them their lord and master, death."[81] Evocative of Emmanuel Levinas's ethics, Irigaray's critique of war as the political model of mediation is intertwined with the rejection of totality as the basis for democratic politics. Irigaray associates both of these ideals expressed in the Hegelian concept of the ethical community (*Sittlichkeit*) with "the labor of the negative on man's terms: death as . . . the real or the symbolic dissolution of the citizen in the community, and enslavement to property or capital" (*ILTY*, 23). She further argues that the Hegelian valorization of the threat of death is a reminder that the ethical totality in polis is achieved through the renunciation of the body and the sublation of sexual difference.[82] She thus exposes a systematic complicity between the value of war as the means of forming the ethical totality of the polis and the construction of the "antinatural" universal transcending the sexed body.[83] By replacing war with the negativity of sexual difference as the political mode of mediation Irigaray contests the closed nature of the dialectic and submits the Hegelian teleology of "the end of History" to temporal unfolding: "The end of an era of history; this is . . . what Hegel did not imagine. . . . The dialectic must therefore be reapplied to the unfolding of History itself" (*ILTY*, 55–56).

I would like to suggest that this shift from war to the negative of sexual difference as the impossible mode mediation both draws upon and radicalizes the typical accounts of Lacan's formulas of sexuation. Although both Irigaray's and Lacan's formulations of sexual difference contest the fantasy of unity in the discourse of love and politics, the main difference in their positions lies precisely in the way they approach the process of mediation between the particular and the universal. As we know, in Lacan's formulas of sexuation, the inscription of the limit of castration constitutes the masculine side as the universal totality (even though this totality is a mirage), whereas the absence of such a limit on the feminine side renders woman's universality impossible: "It will not allow for any universality—it will be a not-whole" (*E*, 80). For Žižek, Lacan's formulas of sexuation mean that "the 'masculine' universe involves the universal network of causes and effects," whereas "the 'feminine' universe is the universe of boundless dispersion and divisibility which, for that very reason, can never be rounded off into a universal Whole."[84] I argue, however, that Žižek's interpretation takes into account neither the contingency of the phallic function stressed by Lacan nor the historical impact of courtly love on Lacan's formulation of sexual difference. In contrast to Žižek, Irigaray claims that the labor of the negative provides the limit and the means of mediation between the singular and the universal for both sexes: "Universal and a particular are reconciled, but they are two. Each man and each woman is a particular individual, but universal through their gender" (*ILTY*, 51). This emphasis on the mediation of the universal and the particular does not aim to eliminate the paradoxical and antinomic character of sexual difference; rather, the question Irigaray poses is how to mobilize these antinomies in order to dispel a double mirage of "Man . . . the human generic, and women . . . the one + one + one . . . of this human kind" (*ILTY*, 64). In other words, the impossible of sexual difference undermines the claim to totality on the masculine side, whereas its negativity prevents the "boundless dispersion" on the feminine side.

If we read the inscription of sexual difference in democratic citizenship in the context of my earlier discussion of the ethical saying and the said, then we might say that what is forgotten on the masculine side is an ethical saying, an asymmetrical encounter with the irreducible Other, whereas what is missing on the feminine side, as Lacan's diagnosis of the nonexistence and nonuniversality of The Woman suggests, is the mediation of the saying by the said. Let us recall at this point that for Levinas the relation between the said and the saying enables a passage from ethics to politics, from the singularity and asymmetry of the ethical relation to the generality and equality of all implied by democratic citizenship. Irreducible to dialectical mediation, the disjunctive relation between the said and the ethical saying provides a mode of commonality while maintaining a withdrawal, or excess, of alterity from discourse. By diagnosing a complicity between this lack of mediation and the exclusion of women from citizenship, Irigaray argues, that it is crucial to elaborate a synthesis, always marked by nonidentity, withdrawal of unity, and conflict, of the particular and the general for women. Without this mediation of the saying and the said, the singular and the general, private and public, for women and among women—a synthesis that entails, as we have seen, the labor of the negative, self-disappropriation, and I would add, antagonism—"we remain in the horizon in which man is the model of human kind, and within this human kind there are empirical women or there are natural entities without an identity of their own" (*ILTY*, 65).

My interpretation of sexual difference as the impossible mode of mediation exposing the limits of political identities and the disjunction between alterity and equivalence avoids the danger of universalization and "ontologization" of the heterosexual couple diagnosed in different ways by Drucilla Cornell and Judith Butler.[85] By stressing the distinction between sexual relations among the partners of the same or different sexes and sexual difference as the limit of a subject's positionality, I separate sexual difference from its connotations of heterosexuality and locate it instead in that precarious space of "in-between" that Chantal Mouffe considers to be an enabling condition of modern democracy: "Between the project of a complete equivalence and the opposite one of pure difference, the experience of modern democracy consist in acknowledging the existence of these contradictory logics and as well as the necessity of their articulation. . . . It is only in that precarious space 'in-between' that pluralist democracy can exist. Therefore such a democracy will always be a democracy 'to come,' . . . insisting . . . on the radical impossibility of a final achievement."[86] In so doing, I underscore not only the irreducible role of ethical responsibility—the inscription of the ethical saying within democratic politics—but also the impossibility of totalization of the political said, its nonteleological historicity so frequently ignored in Levinas's discussion of democracy. By exposing the impossibility of the full actualization of any universal, the political significance of sexual difference lies precisely in the fact that it underscores the radical futurity of democracy, which Irigaray associates with the defense of the impossible. As she claims in the preface to *I Love to You*, "I am, therefore, a political militant of the impossible [*une militante politique de l'impossible*], which is not to say a utopian. Rather, I want what is yet to be as the only possibility of a future" (*ILTY*, 10). To be a political militant of the impossible is to engage in a continuous struggle to displace the frontiers between the possible and impossible, between the present and the future. Within the horizon of the impossible, the inscription of sexual difference into democratic citizenship exposes a "groundless ground" of democracy and the unresolved tension between the constituted and constituting character of history.

This interpretation of sexual difference as the limit of political identities provides a more productive horizon for interpreting Irigaray's sexuate rights beyond what Penelope Deutscher sees as the split between the politics of recognition and the politics of performativity.[87] Growing out of Irigaray's engagement in social liberation movements,[88] the sexuate rights advocate political and economic changes to alleviate oppression of women in Western democracies, for instance, changes in the structure of the family (to challenge its institutional functions of the accumulation of property and reproduction), citizenship, law, religion, and in the modes of production and distribution of social goods. How can we understand the political justification of these rights? Are they based on the legal recognition of the truth of sexual identity, or, as Penelope Deutscher persuasively argues, on the performative power of the law " 'instituting' rather than 'recognizing' a culture of sexual difference"?[89] Drucilla Cornell's vacillation on this issue is an interesting illustration of this dilemma. As Deutscher points out,[90] in her more recent work, especially in *At the Heart of Freedom*, Cornell accuses Irigaray's rights of "naturalizing" sexual difference,[91] although in her earlier work she stresses the performative character of sexuate rights as both the possibility of remetaphorization of the feminine and the expression of equivalence within difference: "These rights are equivalent because they allow difference to be recognized and equally valued without women having to show that they are like men for legal purposes."[92]

I would like to suggest that we can exit the dilemma of performativity versus recognition by considering sexuate rights in the context of the limit of the political institution—that is, in the context of the constituted/constituting ambiguity dramatized by sexual difference. In my interpretation, sexuate rights neither naturalize sexual difference nor institute what they declare but foreground the very limits of the institution and full actualization of all human rights. As Claude Lefort argues, these limits of institution show that every act of proclamation of human rights is always already their reformulation. Consequently, the revision of human rights as "sexuate" stresses the fact that rights reflect not merely indeterminate subject but that this indeterminacy is linked with sexuality. In this context, I would like to refer again to Patricia Williams's politics of race and rights. I discussed in Chapter 3 the way Williams, in a manner similar to Levinas, advocates the reconfiguration of rights based not on "self-regard" but on the "regard for another's fragile, mysterious autonomy."[93] Here I want to stress another crucial point in her revision of rights, namely, the fact that "the recursive insistence of those rights is also defined by black desire for them."[94] By rejecting the replacement of rights by the discourse of needs proposed by critical legal studies, Williams links the possibility of the transformation of rights—the possibility of the "expanded reference of rights"—to the discourse of black desire. As Williams's interpretation suggests, the term "sexuate" rights cannot refer to the recognition of sexual identity, as Irigaray sometimes seems to imply, but rather to this mark of desire motivating the struggles for the redefinition of rights.

The comparison between Irigaray's and Williams's revision of rights brings us back to the question of race. Many of Irigaray's readers worry that Irigaray's "political economy" of sexual difference erases racial differences among women. In Gayatri Spivak's words, the ethico-political questions that are missing in Irigaray's theory are: "Who is the other woman? How am I naming her? How does she name me?"[95] As Amarpal K. Dhaliwal argues, the disregard of racial differences in democratic politics leads to serious doubts about whether the radical democracy "would deal with these social relations [of race] better than non-radical democracy has a history of doing."[96] These worries stem from Irigaray's refusal to engage the question of race in a more substantial manner than her proclamation of the abstract respect for "differences everywhere: differences between other races, differences between the generations, and so on" (JLI, 110). In this respect, Irigaray's work illustrates very well the type of feminist discourse in which, as Hammonds points out, "race is mentioned" but only as "a limited notion devoid of complexities."[97] Moreover, even this limited respect for differences among women is contradicted by statements that "the problem of race is, in fact, a secondary problem . . . and the same goes for other cultural diversities—religious, economic and political ones" (*ILTY*, 47). To make such a claim in the context of the feminist readings of Hegel is not only to ignore, as Paul Gilroy points out, a long tradition of the critical revisions of the master/slave dialectic by the black intellectuals but also to ignore the extent to which the discourse of rights is intertwined with racial differences.[98]

To redress the erasure of race in Irigaray's work, it is not enough to say, as many psychoanalytic critics do, that sex and race do not refer to the same type of difference because the first one describes the limits of the subject's position and the second supposedly refers to the historically specific form of identification.[99] It is precisely this thesis that needs to be complicated and called into question. As I have already shown in my discussion of Kristeva, it is precisely the intersection of race and sex that is at stake in the formation of racist fantasies underlying what bell hooks calls the psychosexual history of racial oppression. In the next chapter, I will continue the discussion of sex and race by engaging bell hooks's analysis of racial and sexual traumas. For now I want to say that the intersection between sex and race complicates Irigaray's work in two fundamental ways. First, thinking about the labor of the negative from a double perspective of sexuality and race allows us to negate the unquestioned presumption of whiteness in her work. According to hooks, this denial of racial differences by white feminists results in the crippling model of liberation based on the "profound narcissism," which undermines Irigaray's ethical project. Second, the intersection of sex and race allows us to reconsider the relation between the limits of identification and the conflicts among women. If we accept the thesis that sexual difference dramatizes the impossibility of achieving full gender, racial, or class identity, then we have to concede that it is inextricably linked to the contestation and refiguration of these identities.[100] Only this acknowledgment of the inequality and antagonistic differences among women can be a basis of a democratic "politics of solidarity."

To provide an analysis of sex as the limit of identifications in the context of antagonistic relations of race and gender, I would like to revisit Mae Gwendolyn Henderson's influential essay "Speaking in Tongues: Dialogics, Dialectics, and the Black Woman Writer's Literary Tradition." By bringing together the best insights of psychoanalysis and critical multiculturalism, Henderson's work shows that the political future of sexual difference is tied to the radicalized notion of diversity among women. If we read Henderson as a critique of Irigaray's theory, it becomes clear that what is missing in Irigaray's concept of sexual difference is the analysis of the way the impossible actualization of subjective identities reveals multiple and conflicting identifications along the lines of gender, race, and class. As I have already pointed out in Chapter 3, what is extremely suggestive in Henderson's analysis of the black female subjectivity is that she stresses not only the co-existence of agonistic relations of racial and gender differences with the "testimonial" relations of identification but also their limits represented by the experience of *jouissance* and, in a more sublimated fashion, by the ecstatic religious practice of speaking in tongues. Yet, although Henderson, like many other theorists of race and gender, stresses the concept of the divided and conflicted black female subjectivity constituted by the heterogeneous agonistic and testimonial speech acts, she ultimately places her analysis of antagonism in the context of the discursive limits of the subject positions foregrounded by sexuality. In her interpretation of Toni Morrison's *Sula*, Henderson reads Sula's sexual ecstasy as a rupture of the multiple discursive determinations of black female subjectivity: "It is through the howl of orgasm that Sula discovers a prediscursive center of experience that positions her at a vantage point outside of the dominant discursive order. The howl is a form of speaking in tongues and a linguistic disruption that serves as the precondition for Sula's entry into language."[101] By marking the limit of the antagonistic and testimonial articulations of racial and gender differences, the feminine *jouissance* is not only an expression of the ethical relation to the Other but also a moment of rupture and a "precondition" for the revision and contestation of the hegemonic power relations: "Disruption—the initial response to hegemonic and ambiguously (non)hegemonic discourse—and the subsequent response, revision (rewriting and rereading), together represent a progressive model for black and female utterance. . . . "[102] This notion of disruption and revision situates sexual difference in the context of the constituted/constituting ambiguity of history and links it to the possibility of invention of the new modes of life.

By considering sexual difference in the context of the ethics of dissensus—an ethics that theorizes responsibility for the Other in the context of the irreducible dimension of antagonism—I have proposed a more dynamic, more democratic, and more ethical theory of sexual difference capable of foregrounding not only the futurity of democracy and the antagonistic differences among women but also the ethical respect for alterity in all its forms. Such a theory of sexual difference stresses not a stable social position but the possibility of its transformation, not a normative identity but its contestation, not the unity of the subject but its internal heterogeneity, negativity, and incompleteness. It radicalizes Irigaray's concepts of the negative and the impossible in order to contest the often unquestioned presumption of whiteness and heterosexuality in her work. If the labor of the negative actualized through sexual difference can be a condition of ethical respect for alterity and difference, then it has to be mobilized continuously to negate not only the externalization of the internal conflicts onto the Other but also the perpetuation of the unspoken norms, marginalizations, and exclusions within feminism itself. Similarly, the disruptive potential of sexual difference—its disjunctive, *constituting* temporality—can be actualized only in the context of the specific historical genealogies *constituted* by race, class, and gender relations. Such an interpretation of the impossible of sexual difference in light of the constituting/constituted ambiguity of history allows me to link the future of sexual difference with the future of democratic politics. By contesting the disembodied notion of democratic citizenship and the exclusion of eroticism from ethics, I claim that the future of democracy—its precarious space "in-between"—cannot be explained only in terms of the antagonistic differences limiting collective identifications from without because it also depends on the limits represented by the sexed body, *jouissance*, ethical passions, and sexual love. As I will argue in the next chapter, only on this basis can we imagine coalition building and the democratic politics of solidarity.

## CHAPTER 6

# Postmodern Blackness/Visionary Feminism
## Paradigms of Subjectivity, Community, and Ethics in bell hooks's Work

IN THE PREVIOUS CHAPTERS I have argued that the feminist ethics of dissensus has to engage both sexual and racial difference in order to contest the persistence of white solipsism even in those discourses that claim to "negativize" narcissism and articulate responsibility for the Other. As this persistence suggests, the question of race still constitutes a site of the differend within postmodern and feminist discussions of ethics despite the fact that the phrase "gender, race, and class" has become, as Deborah McDowell sardonically remarks, "that mystical, holy trinity . . . a mantra to be uttered to mark (and mock) oppositional credentials."[1] Part of the difficulty, no doubt, lies in the slippage between the terms: gender and sexual difference, on the one hand, the politics of difference and ethics of alterity, on the other. If, thanks to the challenge of black feminism, the analysis of the political differences of race, gender, and class in the constitution of subjective identities, discourse, and power has become an established methodology, there still seems to be a great deal of uncertainty about how to pose the question of race in the context of the limits of identities and discourses marked by sexuality and the ethical concept of alterity.[2] And yet, it is precisely at these limits that the intersections of racial and sexual difference are most dense and invisible. By radicalizing what Irigaray describes as the labor of the negative, I have traced some of these intersections not only in the erasure of the damages of racism, the formation of racist fantasies, and in the persistence of antagonisms among women but also in the alternative ethical visions informing reformulations of human rights, resistance, and becoming.

In this chapter I would like to continue this line of investigation by turning to bell hooks, one of the most creative black feminist and postmodern theorists. hooks's work foregrounds three new aspects of the ethics of dissensus. First, her analysis of racial traumas allows us to rearticulate the "psychic life" of power in the context of racial terror. This discussion not only underscores the intersection of race and sexuality at the limit of discourse but also complicates the theories of resistance, performativity, and freedom. Second, she reformulates the ethical responsibility for the Other in terms of the accountability for racist, sexist, and economic oppression. Finally, her model of the multiracial solidarity, based on the "subject-to-subject encounter" and the desire for justice as the shared sensibility among oppressed groups, complicates hegemonic politics of radical democracy. For hooks, coalition politics requires not only the articulation of diverse forms of domination but also a cultivation of the ethical concern for the oppression of others.

Although hooks practices diverse genres and styles of writing, ranging from the critique of popular culture, feminist and race theory, and literary analysis to aesthetic theory, art criticism, and autobiographical texts, I focus in this chapter specifically on her theoretical and philosophical contributions to the postmodern discussions of subjectivity, ethics, and democracy.[3] In so doing, I want to challenge the way the theory/practice divide has been gendered and racialized, so that French feminism, for instance, is associated with theory and black feminism with practice, or with what hooks calls the analysis of "the experiential." As Deborah McDowell argues, all too frequently, black feminism "gets constructed as 'practice' or 'politics,' the negative obverse side of 'theory.' "[4] This construction has influenced the reception of hooks's work as well: although her critiques of white feminism and the postmodern discourse of the Other have been widely recognized and cited, her own theories of postmodernity, race, and feminism have received less attention. Occupying the position of "an outsider within" to use Patricia Hill Collins's apt term,[5] hooks challenges not only the erasure of the marginalized voices in postmodern theory but also the distrust of postmodernism by black intellectuals: "Confronting both the absence of recognition of black female presence that much postmodernist theory re-inscribes and the resistance on the part of most black folks to hearing about the real connection between postmodernism and black experience, I enter a discourse, a practice, where there may be no ready audience for my words" (Y, 24–25).[6] From this marginal position, hooks elaborates new conceptions of "radical black subjectivity," ethics, and democratic politics. What is unique about her paradigm of postmodernism is that it combines the structuralist critique of the interlocking relations of domination not only with the analysis of the psychic effects of oppression but also with an unapologetic commitment to ethical vision, which she sees as the necessary framework for both progressive feminist theory and democratic politics.

# The Politics of Radical Black Subjectivity:
# Performativity, Trauma, and the Ethos of Recovery

"Are you sure, sweetheart, that you want to be well?"

—Toni Cade Bambara

One of the crucial concerns in bell hooks's work on radical black subjectivity is a negotiation between the postmodern notion of power relations constitutive of subjective identities and the ethos of freedom. Referring to Paulo Freire's famous statement that "we cannot enter the struggle as objects in order to later become subjects," hooks argues that reclaiming the right to personhood, agency, and self-determination is an essential step in the liberation struggle: "Fundamental to the process of decentering the oppressive other and claiming our right to subjectivity is the insistence that we must determine how we will be and not rely on colonizing responses to determine our legitimacy" (Y, 22).[7] She concurs with Patricia Williams, for whom "owning the self in a disowned world" is an act of defense against the "spirit murder" inflicted by the crimes of racism.[8] Although this focus on the self-assertion of racial subjectivity reflects a central theme in African-American intellectual history, it might seem at odds with the postmodern critiques of the subject—critiques, which, for that very reason, have often been regarded as antithetical to liberation struggles. Yet, hooks suggests that some insights of postmodernism, especially the contestation of essentialism and the theory of performativity, might be reworked and deployed toward the formulation of the politics of "radical black subjectivity": "Postmodern critiques of essentialisms . . . can open up new possibilities for the construction of self and the assertion of agency" (Y, 28). As hooks's analysis of "postmodern blackness" suggests, worries about the incompatibility between postmodern critiques of the subject and liberation struggles often rest on the implicit confusion of the performative act of reclaiming personhood by subjugated groups with the metaphysics of the subject with which the postmodern critique is concerned. Consequently, postmodern critiques of essentialist identity and the assertions of "radical black subjectivity" represent different, but not necessarily mutually exclusive, political and philosophical projects. Although postmodernism deconstructs the dominant paradigm of the subject taken for granted in the discourse of modernity, the politics of black subjectivity emerges out of the struggle against the erasure of personhood under the conditions of white supremacy in which Western models of subjectivity are implicated.

hooks's concern with reclaiming the subjugated subjectivity as the basis of liberation struggle might also seem at odds with the structural analysis of power relations[9] and, for that reason, has been misread as a return to an unproblematic notion of experience.[10] Yet, instead of advocating a return to "the naked category of lived experience," as Sara Suleri has recently charged,[11] hooks argues that the reclaiming of subjectivity has to be understood as an act of resistance challenging patterns of racist domination. She grounds this act of resistance in the performative power of collective discourse, on the one hand, and in the recovery from the trauma of racial oppression, on the other: "We are rooted in language, wedded, have our being in words. Language is also a place of struggle. . . . Our words are not without meaning, they are an action—a resistance" (*TB*, 28). Although hooks affirms the notion of discourse as a form of action, she faults performative theory for not emphasizing strongly enough the function of race, which, under the conditions of white supremacy, determines who is granted the political and moral status of personhood and who is brutally excluded—in Hortense Spillers's words, "culturally 'unmade'"[12]—from the symbolic domain of signification. Since the racial hierarchy demarcates the boundaries of the symbolic and the political domain of the subject, race becomes a determining factor of performative acts for, as Mills argues, "it is because of race that one does or does not count as a full person, as someone entitled to settle, to expropriate, to be free, or as someone destined to be removed, to be expropriated, to be enslaved."[13]

By foregrounding race within the performative theory, hooks not only supplements the structural/institutional analysis of racist and sexist domination with "the psychic life of power"—with what Judith Butler defines as the processes of identifications with subject positions—but also changes our understanding of what the "psychic life of power" means in the conditions of racist and sexist oppression. As Gwen Bergner argues, the recent discourse on race and gender has tended to emphasize the institutional and ideological aspects of racism[14] (a necessary corrective of the liberal understanding of racism as a personal prejudice), paying less attention to "the processes through which the subject internalizes these cultural determinations. So, although W. E. B. Du Bois's term 'double consciousness' has become standard shorthand to describe African-American subjectivity, the condition of double consciousness remains relatively undertheorized."[15] Similarly, Claudia Tate claims that although the cultural, material paradigms of race and gender "can effectively describe the external conditions that produce personal experience, they cannot explain how individuals internalize . . . those conditions so as to construct personal meaning."[16] Yet, to theorize the internalization of the cultural determinations of race and gender, the discussion of the psychic life of power has to move beyond identifications with cultural norms and address the reality of the racial trauma. When the psychic life of power is considered in a double context of sexuality and race, then neither Butler's gender melancholia nor Kristeva's notion of fantasy are sufficient to account for what Paul Gilroy calls the history of racial terror.[17] It is this history that makes the experience of racial trauma—an unspeakable, unrepresentable event shattering the identity of the subject—a central figure of the psychic life of power in black modernity. As hooks argues, "Until African Americans, and everybody else in the United States, are able to acknowledge the psychic trauma inflicted upon black folk by racist aggression and assault, there will be no collective cultural understanding of the reality that these wrongs cannot be redressed simply by programs for economic reparation, equal opportunity . . . , or attempts to create social equality between the races" (*KR*, 137–38). Hortense Spillers describes the effects of such a trauma as the stripping of black subjectivity from its cultural, linguistic, sexual, and even bodily identity during the "Middle Passage": "They were culturally 'unmade,' thrown in the midst of a figurative darkness that 'exposed' their destinies to an unknown course. . . . Under these conditions, one is neither female, nor male, as both subjects are taken into 'account' as *quantities.*"[18]

How can we rethink reclaiming the subjugated subjectivity as a performative act of "struggle" under the conditions of racial terror? To answer this question, I would like to examine briefly three exemplary texts hooks frequently refers to in her writings—Martin Luther King Jr.'s *Where Do We Go From Here?*, Frantz Fanon's *Black Skins White Masks*, and Toni Morrison's *Beloved*. hooks's reading of these texts points to the necessity of reworking performative theory, in particular, the Althusserian model of interpellation, by taking into account the persistence of the unconscious racist and sexist fantasies, on the one hand, and the traumatic impact of racial oppression, on the other. The model of interpellation is nonetheless a useful starting point to explicate the import of hooks's claim that since our very "being" is "rooted in language" (*TB*, 28), discourse itself must be reconceived as a site of political struggle. As Judith Butler and Wendy Brown argue, the structure of interpellation complicates the traditional notions of agency, resistance, and freedom because it presents the constitution of the subject through the subjection to power relations.[19] In Althusser's paradigmatic example of the pedestrian hailed by the policeman, social recognition and identification with the address of the Other is coextensive with the subjection to its authority. If we take seriously the mutual co-implication of (mis)recognition and subjection, then the possibility of resistance cannot emerge from the politics of recognition[20] but, rather, from "restaging" and resignification of the injurious terms of public discourse, such as racist, sexist, or homophobic speech.[21]

hooks's theory of black subjectivity as a performative act of struggle against the very terms that constitute subjective identities is influenced by the powerful resignification of the racist discourse in Martin Luther King

Jr.'s collection of essays, *Where Do We Go From Here?* The importance of King's work for hooks lies in the fact that he not only describes the assertion of black subjectivity as a linguistic and political struggle against "cultural homicide" but also exposes the double and contradictory structure of racist interpellation:

> No Lincolnian Emancipation Proclamation or Kennedyan or Johnsonian civil rights bill can totally bring this kind of freedom. The Negro will only be truly free when he reaches down to the inner depth of his being and signs with the pen and ink of assertive selfhood his own emancipation proclamation. . . . This self-affirmation is the black man's need made compelling by the white man's crimes against him. *This is positive and necessary power for black people.*[22]

As this passage suggests, the ideological structure of racist interpellation is doubled in the aftermath of the 1965 Voting Rights Act into the democratic discourse of rights and the underlying criminal discourse of racism. What the political recognition by the white Other represents, therefore, is not only a "legitimate" acknowledgment of rights but also the reenactment of "the white man's crimes." This doubled discourse not only equates recognition with the subjection to white power but, in a more devastating way, links social life with social death,[23] which elsewhere King defines as the traumatic experience of the "reality of the black skin."[24] Because of the contradictory effect of racist interpellation, the black subject cannot regain agency from the Other's recognition, which according to Kelly Oliver repeats the structure of domination.[25] That is why hooks emphatically argues that "we are not looking to that Other for recognition" (*Y*, 22). Rather, black subjectivity gains agency, freedom, and, as King says, "positive" power from the performative act of self-assertion, which reverses the positions of the addressor and the addressee. This reappropriation of the discourse of rights changes the location of subjects in the pragmatics of the political discourse: by claiming the position of enunciation—by signing one's own "proclamation of emancipation"—the black subject puts the white Other into the position of an addressee of this performative act. As I have argued in my discussion of Patricia Williams's politics of race and rights, such an act of self-assertion reveals the performative character of rights discourse, that is, the fact that each proclamation of human rights can transform the rights' "frame of reference."

Although hooks finds the performative model of subjectivity extremely important for the revision of the models of liberation in the light of the linguistic constitution of the subject, in her later texts, especially in *Killing Rage*, *Sisters of the Yam*, and *Outlaw Culture*, she suggests that this model is incomplete since it does not address sufficiently that other scene underlying racist interpellation—the scene of fantasy and the racial trauma reflecting what

Cornel West calls "the physical terror and psychic horror of being black in America."[26] hooks's emphasis on the traumatizing effects of racist speech recalls the recent efforts of critical race theorists to redefine hate speech as words that "ambush, terrorize, wound, humiliate, and degrade."[27] Regardless of the controversial legal proposals to regulate "assaultive speech," this redefinition of hate speech offers nonetheless a more accurate analysis of the dehumanizing and traumatic effects of racist and homophobic language. Although in her recent work Butler proposes a reworking of the performative theory in the context of injurious speech acts, such as racist harassment or homophobia, where the address of the Other confers social recognition through wounding and injury, she does not diagnose sufficiently the effects of trauma inflicted by hate speech. As Kelly Oliver argues, those "who have been othered suffer from traumas directed at their subjectivity: traumas directed at their identities and sense of themselves as agents."[28]

To diagnose the unconscious mechanisms of racist fantasies and the traumatic impact of terror on black subjectivity, hooks turns to psychoanalysis despite her reservations about the shortcomings of both Freudian psychoanalysis and its feminist revisions. Referring to Frantz Fanon as a pioneer of the psychoanalytic analysis of racial trauma,[29] hooks deplores the paucity of attention to the traumatizing effects of racism in contemporary studies of "post-traumatic culture."[30] In *Black Skin, White Masks*, Fanon describes the effect of racist interpellation—"Mama, a Negro!"[31]—as a traumatic disintegration of the psyche and the painful fragmentation of the body culminating in a brutal dissociation and objectification of black subjectivity: "I took myself far off from my own presence, far indeed, and made myself an object. What else could it be for me but an amputation, an excision, a hemorrhage that spattered my whole body with blood?" (*BSWM*, 112).[32] In Fanon's text, trauma is triggered by a shocking confrontation with the racist fantasy supporting the ideological structure of domination—with the white child's phobia of being devoured by a black man. According to David Marriot, this violent and unexpected intrusion of racist fantasy into the black psyche shatters symbolic identifications, leaving "an empty space where before was arguably a self, or at least a proper name."[33] By conferring the injurious name, the racist interpellation in fact expels the black subject from the symbolic universe into the realm of "the unassimilable"—the term evoking Lacan's concept of the real (*BSWM*, 161). Since blackness embodies the threatening real in the racist fantasy, the expulsion of black subjectivity thus consolidates the false unity of the symbolic order and the ideological coherence of whiteness.

Referring to Fanon's work, hooks argues that any analysis of racist interpellation has to engage the traumatizing effects of the social fantasies structuring both the injurious speech acts and the political relations of domination. In her interpretations of popular culture, she calls attention to the persistence of racist fantasies underlying the relations of power and the ideological forms of interpellation. For instance, in her discussion of white phobia, hooks interprets the phantasmatic fear of the subjugated Other as a pernicious assertion of white privilege, which, although no less violent than more direct or conscious manifestations of hatred, allows the privileged group to disavow responsibility for racist oppression (KR, 268). Similarly to Kristeva's analysis of phobia as the metaphor of the "devouring mouth," hooks argues that white phobia is in fact an unconscious projection of aggression and cannibalistic fantasies on the black Other. As she points out in her essay, "Eating the Other," the obverse side of white phobia is the contemporary fascination with black sexuality, the appropriation of which seems to promise forbidden *jouissance*, transgression, and personal transformation (BL, 21–39). hooks's focus on racist fantasies and their traumatizing effects evokes Slavoj Žižek's argument that fantasy works as an obscene supplement of power, supporting its ideological framework and at the same time "serving as a screen against the direct intrusion of the real," that is, as a screen against trauma.[34] However, as Fanon and hooks point out, this relation between trauma and fantasy is reversed under the conditions of racist domination: while racist fantasy works as a screen for white subjectivity, it traumatizes the black subject by simultaneously interpellating and expelling her from the symbolic universe into an "unassimilable" zone of abjection (BSWM, 161).[35]

One of hooks's most original arguments is that unacknowledged racial trauma is frequently figured through the trauma of castration and reenacted through sexual violence. Although hooks is frequently credited for her analysis of racial and sexual difference as the interlocking relations of the power/knowledge, the relation between racial trauma and sexuality has been rarely explored in her work. For hooks, the intersections between racial trauma and sexual difference are particularly evident in the ways both racial domination and resistance have been sexualized in the social imaginary: "Sexuality has always provided gendered metaphors for colonization. Free countries are equated with free man, domination with castration, the loss of manhood, and rape . . . rape was a gesture of symbolic castration" (Y, 57). Ironically, the representation of the trauma of racial domination as an act of castration has been perpetuated in an inverse form in black nationalism, which, according to hooks, often equates liberation with the reclaiming of manhood: "The discourse of black resistance has almost always equated freedom with manhood, the economic and material domination of black man with castration, emasculation" (Y, 58). As Kobena Mercer remarks, hooks's critique of the fetishistic narratives of liberation shows that the "underlying racialized dualities of black nationalist discourses was a phallocentric identification with the other" expressed through the dominant trope of "having the phallus or losing it in castration."[36]

In her analysis of the confluence of race and sexuality, hooks argues that the castration anxiety can displace the trauma of racial oppression while simultaneously reinforcing the homosocial, or, in the case of Fanon, homophilial[37] ideal of liberation: "Accepting these sexual metaphors forged a bond between oppressed black man and their white male oppressors. They shared the patriarchal belief that revolutionary struggle was really about the erect phallus, the ability of men to establish political dominance that could correspond to sexual dominance" (*Y*, 58).[38] hooks's discussion of the figuration of the racial trauma in terms of castration precedes Daniel Boyarin's reading of Freud's castration complex as a defense mechanism against the feminized position of the colonized subject in the racist imaginary. Expressing Freud's own anxiety about the racist representation of Jewish masculinity in the anti-Semitic discourse, the Freudian castration complex, Boyarin argues, reveals the fundamental interconnection between race and sexuality: "In the context of postcolonial theory, Freud's universalized theories of subjectivity, all of them centered on the phallus . . . seem an elaborate defense against the feminization of the Jewish men. . . . His theories allowed him to claim that the 'real difference' is not between the Jewish and gentile penis but between having and not having a penis," that is, between masculinity and femininity.[39] Analyzing a similar displacement of racial humiliation onto the trauma of sexual difference, Gwen Bergner argues that the racial identifications of colonized subjects frustrate normative masculinity, producing in effect a negative version of the Oedipus complex in which the racialized Other assumes a "feminine attitude."[40]

Yet, what does it mean to say that the opacity of the racial trauma is represented as castration? In the case of such a representation, the necessary search for the figuration of trauma—the figuration of that shattering event which lacks the signifier in the symbolic—is arrested on the imaginary/phantasmatic level. The defensive elaboration of the racial trauma as the imaginary castration displaces the painful reality of the racial difference onto the black woman, who becomes the bearer of the double lack, while reducing the phallus to "the ultimate white mask."[41] Instead of being a signifier of lack, of the symbolic castration of every subjectivity, the phallus becomes in this fantasy an imaginary object of demand, the restoration of which could compensate for the traumatic event and recover the imaginary wholeness of the colonized subject—its "manhood." Ironically, by equating the liberation struggle with the demand for the phallus and manhood—that is, with "penis envy"—the colonized feminized subject equates "masculinity" with a "hysterical position," which is also characterized by the demand for an object that should fill the lack.[42] By revealing an intersection of politics and fantasy,[43] this demand for what hooks calls "the erect phallus" transforms the master/slave dialectic into the master/hysteric oscillation.[44] As hooks points out, the only solution of this impasse is to refuse the narcissistic consolation of manhood by "unmasking" the phallus itself and the imposture of white mastery it sustains.

hooks's analysis of racial trauma in the context of castration complicates not only black nationalist discourse but also French feminists' rereading of Freud, in particular, Irigaray's claim that the phallocentric construction of sexual difference reflects homosocial relations of men-among-themselves. As hooks suggests, this homosocial construction of sexual difference relies in fundamental ways on race since the imaginary reduction of the phallus to the object of demand structures the racial exchanges among men. hooks calls, therefore, for a critique of a different form of homosociality—what I propose to call "homo-raciality"—that Irigaray largely ignores in her work, namely, the erasure of racial differences of women-among-themselves. In her *Ain't I a Woman* (1981) and *Feminist Theory: From Margin to Center* (1984), hooks points out the parallel shortcomings in black nationalism and in white feminism produced by the inability to think race and sex together: if black nationalism contests racism but reproduces phallocentric constructions of sexual difference and the homosocial model of black liberation, white feminism rewrites sexual difference beyond its homosocial trappings but ignores inequalities among women: "Privileged feminists have largely been unable to speak to, with, and for diverse groups of women because they either do not understand fully the inter-relatedness of sex, race, and class oppression or refuse to take this inter-relatedness seriously. . . . They reflect the dominant tendency . . . to mystify woman's reality by insisting that gender is the sole determinant of woman's fate" (*FT*, 14).

This denial of racial differences by white feminists results in the crippling model of liberation based on "profound narcissism." hooks in fact argues that the emphasis on the commonality of "femininity" functions like a protective narcissistic shield against the deep-seated fear of differences, especially the fear of the subject's own internal division. In the context of hooks's discussion of trauma, we could say that white solipsism signifies a refusal to bear witness to the traumatic reality of racial difference. As Levinas reminds us, this refusal is a narcissistic defense against the traumatic experience that the encounter with the suffering of the Other invariably inflicts. Yet, by denying of Other's trauma, the defensive imaginary identification with a common "feminine" identity leads to the projection of fear and the aggressive rivalry with the other woman. By exposing the narcissistic compensations for the trauma of domination, hooks argues that thinking race, gender, and sexuality together requires not only a structural analysis of the interlocking patterns of domination but also "working through" fear, aggressivity, and the hatred of the self and the Other: "When women come together, rather than pretend union, we would acknowledge that we are divided and must develop strategies to overcome fears, prejudices, resentments, competitiveness, etc. . . . Women need to have the experience of working through hostility to arrive at understanding and solidarity" (*FT*, 63).

To overcome these impasses in the black and feminist struggle for liberation, hooks argues that the politics of resistance has to traverse phantasmatic consolations and address the trauma of oppression without either pathologizing black experience (*KR*, 135), or reproducing uncritically the narratives of "racial uplift": "For black folks to acknowledge that we are collectively wounded by racial trauma would require severing our attachment to an unproblematized tradition of racial uplift where that trauma had been minimized in the effort to prove that we were not collectively dehumanized by racist oppression and exploitation" (*KR*, 134). She repeatedly argues that denied traumas not only magnify the devastating impact of psychic damage but also block the possibility of resistance. In response to Cornel West's analysis of nihilism, hooks writes that the denial of racial traumas intensifies despair, hopelessness, and the "genocidal addiction" of its victims (*KR*, 143) and thus perpetuates the recurrence of traumatizing injury: "The reenactment of unresolved trauma happens again and again if it is not addressed" (*KR*, 144). hooks recalls here Freud's diagnosis that traumatizing events exceeding the bounds of experience and memory are compulsively repeated in nightmares, hallucinations, and symptoms.[45] By *repeating* "the repressed material as a contemporary experience instead of . . . *remembering* it as something belonging to the past,"[46] the injured subject remains arrested at the moment of trauma and thus cannot reenter history. As Dori Laub points out in the context of his work with Holocaust survivors, the wounded subject is thus ceaselessly subjected to the recurrence of traumatizing injury.[47]

It is precisely the untimely, unconscious reenactment and, thus, a continuing subjection to the traumatizing injury that complicate the struggle for liberation: it cannot be limited to the restructuring of the external relations of domination but has to address the reality of the psychic damage of racial and sexual violence. hooks's emphasis on the psychic recovery adds an often ignored therapeutic dimension to the performative theories of resignification. As Dominick LaCapra and Kelly Oliver argue,[48] the experience of trauma confronts the performative theory with the necessity of making a distinction between the compulsive "acting out" that continues to inflict the injury on the survivors even when the external threat is no longer present, and the therapeutic, interpretive process of "working through"—a process that breaks the cycle of unconscious repetitions and thus enables the recovery of the repressed painful event in memory.[49] hooks complicates the healing process of working through in two significant ways. First, she argues that the reclaiming of the injurious event in memory is a particularly difficult task for African-Americans not only because trauma represents, in Cathy

Caruth's words, an enigma of the "missed" experience exceeding the possibility of comprehension but also because in the racist culture it subjects the victims to the shame of victimization (OC, 204).[50] Second, as her critique of white feminism and black liberation suggests, "working through" has to traverse the compensatory narcissistic fantasies of manhood or common feminine identity and replace this imaginary elaboration of trauma with the symbolic figuration. As hooks's emphasis on "absences" in language suggests, the symbolic elaboration respects the opacity of the unspeakable experience while giving it inscription in language: "To cite them [gaps] at least is to let the reader know something has been missed" (Y, 147).

How can such an unclaimed experience of trauma possibly be reclaimed? For hooks the healing process of working through is intertwined with an attempt to construct a narrative, which, although it does not recover the losses, allows the traumatized subject to regain a symbolic position of enunciation through the inscription of the unspeakable event in language. Far from creating a "flat documentary," it is a difficult and painful effort to invent new modes of expression, to "create spaces where one is able to redeem and reclaim the past, legacies of pain, suffering and triumph in ways that transform the present reality. Fragments of memory are not simply represented as flat documentary but constructed . . . to move us into a different mode of articulation" (Y, 147). In the psychoanalytic context, this effort to create a representation for the unrepresentable is comparable to the creative work of sublimation. Given this close relation between recovery from trauma, sublimation, and the creation of the new means of expression, it is not surprising that for hooks it is easier to find the articulation of racial and sexual traumas in black women's fiction: "The breaking of this collective silence has its most sustained expression in the work of black women writers, particularly fiction writers. Works like Alice Walker's *The Color Purple* and Toni Morrison's first novel, *The Bluest Eye* . . . , as well as the more widely acclaimed *Beloved*, all address issues of psychic trauma" (KR, 138). As hooks suggests, Toni Morrison's *Beloved* can be read as a haunting example of the symbolic elaboration of trauma at the limits of language and memory[51]:

> Disremembered and unaccounted for, she cannot be lost because no one is looking for her, and even if they were, how can they call her if they don't know her name? Although she has claim, she is not claimed. . . .
> It was not a story to pass on.
> They forgot her like a bad dream. . . .
> The rest is weather. Not the breath of the disremembered and unaccounted for, but the wind in the leaves, or spring ice thawing too quickly. Just weather. Certainly no clamor for a kiss.[52]

This passage is one of the most stunning interpretations of trauma as an unclaimed experience, which, nonetheless, continues to have ethical claims on history. Naming the loss of memory, Morrison's *Beloved* is an effort to "re-memory" "the disremembered" sixty millions of black victims of slavery and racism to whom the book is dedicated. As the refrain of *Beloved*—"this is not a story to pass on"—suggests, the therapeutic writing of trauma endlessly grapples with the limits of both historical knowledge and subjective under-standing. In this confrontation with the erasure of representation and the impossibility of witnessing the unspeakable "psychic wounds inflicted by racist aggression" (*KR*, 137),[53] the novel nonetheless affirms the therapeutic and ethical power of aesthetics and language.

Yet, the importance of *Beloved* for hooks lies not only in the way it dis-plays the aesthetic dimension of the recovery from trauma but also in the way it links the complexity of the therapeutic process to collective mourn-ing and the ethical function of the community. Morrison emphasizes the therapeutic role of the community not only in the scene of Baby Suggs's ser-mon but also in the representation of the chorus of thirty women gathered outside Sethe's house because "rescue was in order" (*B*, 256). By breaking the limits of language, this cathartic singing enables Sethe to confront the loss of Beloved and to mourn her death: "The voices of women searched for the right combination, the key, the code, the sound that broke the back of the words. Building voice upon voice until they found it, and when they did. . . . It broke over Sethe and she trembled like the baptized in its wash" (*B*, 261). Referring to the representations of collectivity in the black women's texts, hooks argues that community is a place of recovery. The task of work-ing through racial trauma consists therefore not only in reclaiming the sym-bolic position of the subject through memory and the narration of losses but also in foregrounding the relation between the psychic work of recovery, community, and institutional change: "When I wrote *Sisters of the Yam: Black Women and Self-Recovery* the intent was to highlight the connections among psychological trauma, mental disorders, and the madness of forming self and identity in white supremacist capitalist patriarchy. While I wanted to em-phasize the importance of individual work for self-recovery, I wanted to link that work to progressive action for political change" (*KR*, 142).

By stressing both the aesthetic and the collective aspects of the therapeu-tic healing, hooks refuses the narcissistic compensations for racial trauma as the telos of the liberation struggle. She agrees with Fanon that the liberation struggle "must put an end to narcissism" (*BSWM*, 22). As Fanon points out, narcissistic compensations reinforce racial domination by maintaining the rigid ideological "either/or" divide between the races—"a Manichean delir-ium" of "dual narcissism" (*BSWM*, 10). Consequently, for Fanon the pro-ject of liberation would involve "nothing short of liberation of the man of color from himself [*Nous ne tendons à rien de moins qu'à libérer l'homme de couleur de lui-même*]" (*BSWM*, 8).[54] By rejecting both the imaginary manhood and the common feminine identity, hooks similarly argues that narcissistic compensations for trauma keep the subject in complicity with subjection and limit the question of freedom to the liberation of the imaginary ego, the counterpart of which is aggressive rivalry and the projection of the internal splitting onto the Other: "Psychoanalytically, it is clear that the unitary self is sustained only by acts of coercive control and repression" (KR, 249). Rather than reclaiming ego identity as an ethos of liberation, hooks suggests, therefore, that "owning a self in a disowned world" coincides, in a paradoxical way, with the liberation of the subject from the narcissistic ego. Although evocative of Kristeva's negativization of narcissism, hooks's critique of narcissism is far more complex because it engages not only sexuality but also the trauma of the oppressed subjectivity.

With the joined emphasis on performativity, trauma, and recovery, hooks reconfigures identity politics so that liberation no longer relies on narcissistic compensation, the overcoming of the internal splitting of the subject, or reclaiming the authority of experience.[55] Recalling Martin Luther King Jr.'s argument that the black subject is "a true hybrid, a combination of two cultures" (WDWGFH, 53), hooks argues that such a hybrid subjectivity is relational, decentered, and marked by internal division. Consequently, what is at stake in hooks's formulation of heterogeneous and "diasporic" subjectivity (KR, 249) is not only the multiplicity of the often antagonistic identifications but also, as the experience of trauma suggests, the intrinsic limit of these identifications. In a manner evocative of Mae Gwedolyn Henderson's dialogical black female subjectivity or Trinh T. Minh-ha's "infinite layers" of identity,[56] hooks's theory of postmodern blackness links therefore the ethos of liberation with an identity that is incomplete, "fluid, multiple, and always in process" (OC, 208). Although she affirms "identity politics as an important stage in liberation process,"[57] she also stresses the fact that "the ground we stand on is shifting, fragile, and unstable. We are avant-garde only to the extent that we eschew essentialist notions of identity, and fashion selves that emerge from diverse epistemologies, habits of being, concrete class locations, and radical political commitments" (Y, 19).

## "I Wish They Stopped Talking About the Other": The Ethos of Becoming and Social Accountability

At stake in hooks's reconfiguration of black subjectivity and liberatory praxis is a creation of an alternative ethics. Although the ethical implications of postmodern theory have been recognized only recently, the concern with ethics—with what Cornel West calls an "unapologetically moral" thought—constitutes an essential aspect of African-American culture and politics. As Manning Marable points out, "A pivotal feature of the African-American

Freedom Movement was the connection between black political objectives and ethical prerogatives. What was desired politically—the destruction of institutional racism—was simultaneously ethically and morally justified. This connection gave the rhetoric of Douglass, Du Bois, Robenson and King a moral grandeur and power of vision which was simultaneously particular and universal. . . . African-American Studies must perceive itself in this tradition, as a critical enterprise which educates and transforms the larger society."[58] For Katie Cannon, this tradition illustrates the difference "between ethics of life under oppression and established moral approaches which take for granted freedom and wide range of choices."[59] By continuing this line of inquiry, hooks elaborates an ethics that negotiates between commitments that are often thought to be mutually exclusive: between the ethos of freedom and the obligation to others, between the respect for difference and the creation of democratic community. What enables this negotiation is, first, the idea of marginality foregrounding the limits of discourse and, second, the ethical accountability for the conditions of oppression.

For hooks the logic of marginality points not only to external oppression but also to the internal limit of power, language, and the subject. As we have seen, according to hooks the process of decolonization involves simultaneously a political act of reclaiming the "personhood" by the oppressed groups and a liberation of subjectivity from narcissistic identity, which functions as a screen against the internal division of the subject. By contesting both the phantasmatic embodiment of the abject in the black body and the narcissistic compensations for the trauma of racist and sexist oppression, hooks transvaluates the meaning of marginality so that it not only means the violent exclusion of the oppressed but also signifies an internal limit of the symbolic order and all subjective positions. It is in the second sense that marginality can be an enabling condition of resistance. That is why hooks insists on the distinction "between that marginality which is imposed by oppressive structures and that marginality one chooses as a site of resistance—as location of radical openness and possibility. . . . We come to this space through suffering and pain, through struggle" (Y, 153). As this passage suggests, it is through the experience and the recovery from trauma that the black subjectivity transforms the limit of discourse into the possibility of resistance.

In order to avoid the frequent misreadings of hooks's notion of the margin, I propose to contrast it with the Lacanian concept of the real. As Slavoj Žižek writes, the real can be described as the radical incompleteness of the symbolic order, as "the internal limit preventing the symbolic field from realizing its full identity."[60] According to Žižek and Rey Chow, the relation to the real constitutes "an ethics of confrontation with the impossible," with the "traumatic kernel not covered by any *ideal*."[61] By contesting the phantasmatic embodiment of the threatening real in the black body, hooks's logic of marginality similarly aims to demystify the imaginary unity of every subjective identity and to expose its essential incompleteness. Yet, despite these analogies, hooks's reconfiguration of marginality suggests that Žižek's conception of ethics "after idealism" is insufficient because it neither addresses the becoming of the subject nor elaborates an ethical relation to alterity. By radicalizing the ethical implications of marginality, hooks, like Foucault and Irigaray, argues that the margin not only marks an impossibility of the unified identity but also exposes the limit of social regulation, and thus signifies the emergence of the new configuration of forces. As a limit of language and power, the margin can become a site of resistance, transformation, and change: "Understanding marginality as a position of resistance is crucial for oppressed, exploited, colonized people. If we only view margin as sign marking the despair, a deep nihilism penetrates in a destructive way the very ground of our being" (Y, 150). As a condition of nonteleological becoming, the margin opens a "radical perspective from which to see and create, to imagine alternatives, new worlds" (Y, 150).

Although she affirms resistance as fundamental for oppressed groups, hooks argues that the ethos of becoming has to be conceptualized beyond "reactive" opposition. As she writes, "Opposition is not enough. In that vacant space after one has resisted there is still a necessity to *become*—to make oneself anew. . . . It is different than to talk about becoming subjects" (Y, 15). Not only a struggle against dehumanization, the ethos of becoming "enables creative, expansive self-actualization" (Y, 15). Since she associates the nonteleological becoming with a creation of the new habits of being, social relations, and, ultimately, new models of democracy, hooks, like Foucault, defines this mode of relationality as "an aesthetics of existence." Irreducible to a theory of art, the "practical" and the political function of an aesthetics of existence is to enable the oppositional subject to envision new alternatives, "to imagine what is *possible*" (OC, 237). In a manner evocative of Fanon's conviction that "the real *leap* consists in introducing invention into existence" (BSWM, 229), hooks approaches the "aesthetics of existence" as a cultivation of the experimental, futural modes of being transcending the present configuration of power relations. If Foucault's aesthetics of existence is inspired by gay modes of life, then hooks's definition of "the aesthetics of being," which approaches the relation to oneself not as a suppressed identity to be liberated but rather as a task of transformation and "creative, expansive self-actualization," is indebted to the black women's artistic traditions, both vernacular and experimental: "I see how deeply my concern with aesthetics was shaped by black women who were fashioning *an aesthetic of being*, struggling to create an oppositional world view for their children. . . . We must not deny the way aesthetics serves as the foundation for emerging visions. It is, for some of us, critical space . . . (Y, 112).

Although both hooks and Cornel West stress the importance of "an im-provisational mode of protean, fluid, and flexible dispositions toward real-ity" (*RM*, 150), for hooks the transformative power of the aesthetic of exis-tence is conveyed not only by the metaphor of jazz but also by the black women's tradition of crazy quilts. Made from the reused scraps of material, discarded remnants, or worn-out clothes, crazy quilts are an embodiment of creative, hybrid, and polymorphic resignification. These quilts exemplify the performative act of renaming and remaking existence. At the same time, they are the work of memory that recovers the forgotten ordinary texture of history[62]: "These quilts were maps charting the course of our lives. They were history as life lived" (*Y*, 121). Contrary to some cultural critics' suspi-cions of aesthetics, hooks argues that this enlarged sense of the aesthetics of existence is a crucial component of oppositional politics because it enables the move beyond the critique of the status quo to the creation of alternative modes of life: "Our living depends on our ability to conceptualize alterna-tives, often improvised. Theorizing about this experience aesthetically, crit-ically is an agenda for radical cultural practice" (*Y*, 149).

Yet, hooks's logic of marginality—the limit of discourse and subjective identifications—stresses not only the futural becoming of the subject but also an ethical relation to the Other. As Žižek himself suggests, the relation to the real exposes the fact that "the negativity of the other which is prevent-ing me from achieving my full identity with myself is just an externalization of my own auto-negativity."[63] Although Žižek fails to account for the situ-ation of domination where the hegemonic white Other is irreducible to a mere "externalization" of the internal negativity of the oppressed, his point about the traversal of fantasy is similar to hooks's argument that the traver-sal of the defensive projections of the internal aggressivity is a crucial step that opens a possibility of an ethical relation to alterity. Only when the racialized others no longer function as the projection of the subject's own negativity or as the dialectical negation of the subject's freedom, then, per-haps, an ethical mode of intersubjective relations becomes possible. This concern with ethics suggests that liberation movements are mobilized not only by antagonism and the struggle against oppression but also by the hope of an ethical relation that is not based on domination.

hooks defines this ethical mode of relation in terms of a shift from the subject/object paradigm of representation to the ethical and democratic model of intersubjectivity—what she calls the "subject-to-subject" en-counter. Although she writes from a different theoretical and cultural loca-tion, hooks's concern with ethical intersubjective relations reaches conclu-sions similar to Levinas's contestation of Western philosophy: the discourse that reduces the Other's significance to the alienation of the subject, to an object of representation, or even to an occasion for a cultural critique of "the postmodern condition" in fact obliterates the subjectivity of the Other or masks the Other's absence: "Often this speech about the 'Other' is also a mask, an oppressive talk hiding gaps, absences, that space where our words would be if we were speaking, if there were silence, if we were there" (Y, 151). In place of "speaking about the Other," a position that assumes the mastery and authority of the subject, hooks elaborates alternative modalities of relation and responsibility across politicized differences: "We fear those who speak about us, who do not speak to us and with us" (Y, 152). In *Outlaw Culture* and elsewhere she describes subject-to-subject encounters in terms of "a lived practice of interaction" based on the recognition and re-spect for the alterity of the Other: "We must first be able to dialogue with one another, to give one another that subject-to-subject recognition . . . that is a part of the decolonizing, anti-racist process" (BB, 5). Such a notion of alterity includes the relations of race, class, gender, and sexual orientation but is not reduced to them: "We are always more than our race, class, or sex" (OC, 244). Thus, the subject-to-subject encounter neither assumes a common identity behind the differences nor reduces the alterity of the Other to the notion of a different subject position. What is required for such an ethical subject-to-subject encounter to take place is an attitude of "radi-cal openness," which hooks defines in terms of witnessing, listening, and meeting the Other at the site of resistance: "I am waiting for them to bear witness, to give testimony" (Y, 151).[64] If, as hooks and Levinas in different ways argue, anti-Semitism, racism, and capitalist exploitation destroy the very ability to respond to the Other, the task of contemporary ethics is to recreate it as the basis of an ethical obligation: "We invite all readers then to rejoice with us that this subject-to-subject encounter can be possible within a White supremacist, capitalist, patriarchal context that would, in fact, have us not be capable of talking to one another" (BB, 5).

hooks's emphasis on the ethical relation to alterity distinguishes her posi-tion from the majority of postmodern discourses of otherness. It is precisely because of the absence of a politically transformative ethics that these dis-courses fail abysmally to acknowledge the contributions of marginalized groups, in particular, the voices of black women. Without an ethical en-gagement with concrete others, postmodern theories of otherness become merely a gesture of political self-legitimation: "Postmodernist discourses are often exclusionary even as they call attention to, appropriate even, the ex-perience of 'difference' and 'Otherness' to provide oppositional political meaning, legitimacy, and immediacy when they are accused of lacking con-crete relevance" (Y, 23). hooks argues that even progressive postmodern theories of alterity risk reproducing the paradigms of colonialism where sub-jects of discourse belong to privileged groups and racialized others are turned into the objects of analysis: "Cultural studies re-inscribes patterns of colonial domination, where the 'Other' is always made object, appropriated, inter-preted, taken over by those in power, by those who dominate" (*Y*, 125). It is because of this "refusal to acknowledge accountability for racist conditions past and present" (*KR*, 17) that postmodern theory fails to challenge the po-litical reality of racial and sexual domination. What hooks finds most dis-turbing in postmodern theories of otherness is their blindness to conditions of inequality and the refusal of accountability for unjust power relations: "Contemporary white scholars writing about black people assume positions of familiarity, as though their work were not coming into being in a cultural context of white supremacy, as though it were in no way shaped and in-formed by that context" (*Y*, 124).

To underscore the originality of hooks's theory of the intersubjective en-counter, I would like to contrast her position with two white critics who at-tempt to articulate models of intersubjectivity in a postmodern, antiessential-ist perspective: Richard Rorty's ironic liberalism and Seyla Benhabib's communicative ethics. hooks's critique of Rorty's understanding of solidarity distinguishes her ethics from the postmodern liberal approach to difference.[65] Like many other postmodern philosophers, Rorty embraces the antiessential-ist position by stressing the historical contingencies of language, moral values, subjectivity, and community and argues that dialogue and solidarity have to be created rather than assumed. Yet, for Rorty such a creation is based on "the imaginative ability to see strange people as fellow sufferers,"[66] on the ability to disregard the differences of the "tribe, religion, race, customs, and the like" in favor of "similarities of pain and humiliation."[67]

Although hooks shares Rorty's antiessentialist position and his conviction that the historical contingencies of language and subjectivity do not prevent human solidarity, she takes him to task for reducing solidarity to the imagi-nary identification with a common identity:

[Rorty] argues that white people in America can be in solidarity with young black youth if they stop seeing them as "young black youth" and look at them as Ameri-can, and declare, "No American should have to live in this way." So it's the whole notion of "If you can find yourself in the Other in such a way as to wipe out the Otherness, then you can be in harmony." But a "grander" idea is "Why do we have to wipe out the Otherness in order to experience a notion of *Oneness?*" (*OC*, 234)

Furthermore, hooks's critique of "shared victimization" problematizes Rorty's desire for identification based on "the similarity of pain." Rorty's emphasis on pain leads to the assumption of the right to speak for the vic-tim: "There is no such thing as the 'voice of the oppressed' or the 'language of the victims.' . . . So the job of putting their situation into language is going to have to be done for them by somebody else."[68] Such an identi-fication with the nonwhite Other as a "fellow sufferer" not only renders him or her powerless but also obfuscates the reality of racist domination and leads to the abdication of responsibility for "the maintenance and perpetuation of sexism, racism, and classism" (FT, 46).

hooks's emphasis on obligation in the subject-to-subject encounter also distinguishes her position from the feminist articulation of communicative ethics, represented by Seyla Benhabib's work. Unlike Rorty's notion of solidarity, and unlike the Habermasian communicative rationality where consensus in dialogue is achieved through the departure from the particular experiences and the adoption of the impartial point of view, Benhabib's communicative ethics is based on the recognition of "the standpoint of the concrete other," who is "a unique individual, with a certain life history, disposition and endowment."[69] In contrast to Rorty's contingency, Benhabib's project attempts to reconcile differences with the "interactive universalism," which allows the participants in dialogue to challenge their situatedness.[70] This universalizable agreement can be created when the participants are willing to reverse their perspectives and to assume the Other's point of view: "To 'think from the perspective of everyone else' is to know 'how to listen' to what the other is saying, or when the voices of others are absent, to imagine to oneself a conversation with the other as my dialogue partner."[71]

Although hooks's communicative ethics is also based on the acknowledgment of the cultural-historical situation of concrete others, she questions the imaginative reversal of viewpoints, particularly, in the situation of inequality. As she argues again and again, the assumption that the members of privileged groups, for example, white women, can adopt, imagine, or represent the point of view of the marginalized groups obscures "the more crucial issues involved when a member of a privileged group 'interprets' the reality of the members of a less powerful, exploited, and oppressed group" (Y, 55). Stressing the asymmetrical differences among women, hooks's contestation of the universal category of woman can provide an insightful critique of Benhabib's model of communication: "I was saying that, in fact, women don't share a common plight solely because we're women—that our experiences are very, very different. . . . What about class differences between women? What about racial differences that in fact make some women more powerful than others?" (OC, 231). Yet, as hooks argues in Feminist Theory, the acknowledgment of asymmetrical differences not only does not negate the possibility of the subject-to-subject encounter but is in fact its precondition: "When women actively struggle in a truly supportive way to understand our differences, to change the misguided, distorted perspectives, we lay the foundation for . . . political solidarity" (FT, 64). As this interrogation of the feminist theory suggests, hooks is one of the first feminist critics to elaborate a relation to the Other on the basis of what Iris Young calls asymmetrical reciprocity: "While there may be many similarities and points of contact between them, each position and perspective transcends the others, goes beyond their possibility to share or imagine."[72]

What distinguishes hooks's model of the subject-to-subject encounter from the theories of communicative ethics (Benhabib), liberal solidarity (Rorty), or even from Young's asymmetrical reciprocity is her insistence on ethical accountability for the structures of domination. The irreversible differences in communicative ethics do not merely expose the limits of intersubjective understanding but primarily stress responsibility "for racist conditions past and present" (KR, 17). Influenced by Martin Luther King Jr.'s articulation of ethical and political responsibility in liberation struggle, hooks shifts the emphasis from intersubjective agreement to the collective and individual obligation. In Where Do We Go From Here, King argues that the vision of racial justice depends not only on the institution of just laws but also on the unenforceable obligations: "Court orders and federal enforcement agencies are of inestimable value in achieving desegregation, but desegregation is only a partial though necessary step. . . . True integration will be achieved by men who are willingly obedient to the unenforceable obligation" (WDWGFH, 100–101). For King, this sense of unenforceable obligation creates "a revolution of values," a change from the "I-centered" to "thou-centered" ethics: "From time immemorial men have lived by the principle that 'self-preservation is the first law of life.' But this is a false assumption. I would say that other-preservation is the first law of life . . . the universe is so structured that things go awry if men are not diligent in their cultivation of other-regarding dimension" (WDWGFH, 180). In the context of postmodern ethics, hooks's and King's emphasis on obligation resonates with Emmanuel Levinas's ethical project. In Totality and Infinity, Levinas similarly argues that the "face-to-face" encounter with the other "opens a primordial discourse whose first word is obligation"(TI, 201). As these thinkers claim, it is the relation to the Other that constitutes the irreplaceable dimension of the subject and not the other way around. According to King, "The self cannot be self without other selves" (WDWGFH, 180). "Stagnant, still, and stale," and ultimately without "life" (WDWGFH, 180), the conception of the isolated subject reflects not only a bankrupt philosophical idea but also an ideological support of domination, capitalist exploitation, and Western imperialism. Its frightening legacy is the history of racism, anti-Semitism, and slavery—in Levinas's words, "the millennia of . . . imperialism, of human hatred and exploitation, up to our century of world wars, genocides, the Holocaust, and terrorism, of unemployment, the continuing poverty of the Third world; of the pitiless doctrines and cruelties of fascism."[73]

The relation to the Other that Levinas, hooks, and King describe departs from both the subject/object structure of representation and the symmetrical structure of dialogue. By destroying the neutrality and symmetry of the usual conception of communication, the encounter with the Other is characterized, as Jill Robbins suggests, by the reversal from "the avid gaze" underlying representation to the structures of "generosity, responsibility, and language."[74] Drawing her inspiration from diverse sources, ranging from the writings of Martin Luther King Jr. to the Buddhist monk Thich Nhat Hanh, hooks argues that this reversal displaces the narcissistic ego of the subject: "The moment we are willing to give up our own ego and draw in the being and the presence of someone else, we are no longer 'Other-ing' them" (OC, 219). The asymmetrical encounter means that the Other is approached as an interlocutor who calls for a response. For hooks the emphasis on meeting the Other as an interlocutor, as a face that speaks, accuses, and obligates, not only intervenes into a presumptuous desire to speak for the Other but also prevents reification of the Other into a victim. As she points out, to regard the Other as a speechless victim obliterates the rage and militant resistance of the oppressed: "Only do not speak in a voice of resistance. Only speak from that space in the margin that is a sign of deprivation" (Y, 152). Approaching the oppressed Other as an interlocutor entails, therefore, meeting her in the site of resistance, creativity, and language: "Marginality as a site of resistance. Enter that space. Let us meet there" (Y, 152). hooks's refusal to reduce the alterity of oppressed people to the conditions of their deprivation is reflected in Levinas's double manifestation of the face in terms of destitution and eminence.[75] Thus, what makes the ethical relation to the Other irreversible is not just the historical situatedness of subjects and their specific cultural differences but the burden of responsibility, "the unenforceable obligation," imposed on the subject prior to his or her initiative. This irreversibility of perspectives means, according to Levinas, that "no one can answer in my place."[76]

The juxtaposition of hooks's subject-to-subject encounter, Martin Luther King Jr.'s "unenforceable obligation," and Levinas's face-to-face relation calls for a revision of ethical obligation so that it becomes inseparable from the accountability for the existing structures of domination. It is a matter, as Martin Luther King Jr. puts it, of bridging the gap between ethics and "freedom revolution." By arguing that the responsibility for the Other is always intertwined with a responsibility for the political structures of oppression, hooks likewise sees the ethical relation to the Other as "a part of the decolonizing, anti-racist process" (BB, 5). As she writes, "whenever there's the possibility for exploitation, what intervenes is recognition of the Other. Recognition allows a certain kind of negotiation that seems to disrupt the possibility of domination" (OC, 241). This recognition of the alterity of the Other can intervene into the political structures of domination only if it is a response to the Other's "call for an accounting that would really demand a shift in the structure of this society" (*KR*, 59). Fostering "a fundamental attitude of vigilance rather than denial" (*Y*, 55), the meeting with the Other across racial, class, and gender differences puts the subject into question in the sense that it demands an interrogation of one's privilege and possible complicity in the maintenance of oppression. By challenging the neutrality of both communication and knowledge, ethical responsibility requires from "scholars, especially those who are members of groups who dominate, exploit, and oppress others, to explore the political implications of their work without fear or guilt" (*Y*, 124). It is in this spirit that I propose to reread Levinas's claim that responsibility "empties the I of its imperialism" (TO, 353). For both hooks and Levinas, such a responsibility demands an active engagement in the struggle for democratic justice: for Levinas, it is the obligation to fight for the rights of Others; for hooks, it is the participation in the liberation struggle against racist, patriarchal, and capitalist domination.

In hooks's revisions of marginality and obligation, the ethos of responsibility ceaselessly crisscrosses the path of liberation. Just as the revision of marginality begins with the question of resistance and ends with the traversal of defensive fantasies blocking the ethical relation to the Other, so too the revision of obligation starts with the subject-to-subject encounter and ends with resistance understood as the participation in struggles against domination. We can say, therefore, that these revisions construct passages between heterogeneous and seemingly incompatible claims in postmodern discourse: between the freedom of the subject and the obligation for the Other, between the ethics of alterity and the politics of liberation. Although hooks's work does not aim to eliminate the productive tension between these claims, it proposes a different perspective from which they can be negotiated: when the ethical reflection begins with the situation of domination instead of taking the freedom of the subject for granted, the desire for freedom cannot be dismissed too quickly as ethically suspect or as antithetical to the accountability for the others' oppression.

## Toward a "Beloved Community": Hybridity, Solidarity, and the Politics of Multicultural Democracy

By stressing the ethical implications of the performative model of the black subjectivity, hooks claims that the obligation to others is inseparable from the articulation of the new basis of solidarity and democratic politics. As the sociologists John Murphy and Jung Min Choi argue, such an ethics is indispensable for the cultivation of the political ethos of a diverse and multicultural democracy: "In modern race relations this ethical imperative should be welcomed. Protecting the integrity of the other is translated as a challenge to cultural and racial supremacists."[77] What is at stake in bringing the ethics of respect for the Other to bear on the hegemonic politics of radical democracy is a reconfiguration of difference so that it no longer signifies liability, disorder, fear, or domination but represents instead "a call for inclusion without assimilation." As Audre Lorde argues, "We have *all* been programmed to respond to the human differences between us with fear and loathing and to handle that difference in one of three ways: ignore it, and if that is not possible, copy it if we think it is dominant, or destroy it if we think it is subordinate."[78] In contrast to the loathing and destruction of difference, the intervention of ethics I have been elaborating in this book allows us, to quote the words of Audre Lorde again, to "seek beyond history / for a new and more possible meeting."[79]

The role of ethical respect for unassimilable difference becomes even more important once the universal principles of justice transcending cultural differences of race, gender, and class are challenged in the name of a radicalized democratic pluralism. In hooks's work on radical multicultural democracy, the ethics of the "subject-to-subject encounter" not only contests the institutionalized patterns of dominations but also stresses the positive significance of difference as a condition of solidarity among diverse groups. On the basis of such solidarity, hooks hopes to reconcile two ideals—radicalized pluralism and the political community—that the protracted quarrel between liberals and communitarians has posited as incompatible.

hooks's rethinking of the political community in the light of the radicalized notion of social and cultural diversity goes against the grain of liberal democracy. Specifically, hooks contests the argument of liberal critics that the political ideal of community is incompatible with modern pluralism. In response to the communitarian conceptions of democracy, John Rawls, for instance, claims that democratic society is neither an association organized around common ends nor a community "governed by a shared comprehensive religious, philosophical, or moral doctrine."[80] In place of a substantive community, Rawls proposes an idea of a diverse democratic society, the structure of which is regulated by the political, rather than moral or philosophical, conception of justice expressing the minimum principles of fair cooperation among equal citizens. Yet, although Rawls affirms diversity and conflict as the irreducible dimension of democracy, his notion of pluralism is limited in two ways: on the one hand, it is separated from the analysis of domination; on the other, it is subordinated to the universal conception of justice abstracted from substantive differences of religion, belief, tradition, race, gender, or class.[81] Because modern democracy is conflicted and heterogeneous, consensus cannot be reached through intersubjective praxis or dialogue but only through the appeal to the universal principles of justice abstracted from the substantive differences among citizens.[82]

Like many other African-American and feminist political theorists—Iris

Young, Charles Mills, Patricia Williams, Lucius Outlaw, Seyla Benhabib, Chantal Mouffe, Manning Marable, and Cornel West, among others— hooks finds the liberal model of democracy insufficient. In particular, she is skeptical about the universal principles of color-blind justice, even if, as Rawls's "chastised political liberalism" suggests, these principles are limited to the minimal number. hooks argues that the abstraction from the differences of race, gender, sexuality, and class obliterates the acute historical contradiction between the histories of "Euro-American and New World African modernities,"[83] between the liberal ideal of equality and the actual global system of racial domination established by white supremacy: "The notion that differences of skin color, class background, and cultural heritage must be erased for justice and equality to prevail is a brand of popular false consciousness that helps keep racist thinking and action intact" (*KR*, 265).[84]

By contesting the exclusion of race, gender, sexuality, and class from mainstream political theory, African-American critics expose the confusion between the normative and descriptive levels of liberal theory.[85] Even though the abstract principles of justice are normative rather than descriptive (based on what "ought" to be rather than on what "is"), Rawls himself admits that they are derived from the implicit ideas of the dominant democratic culture: "Political philosophy does not . . . claim to discover what is true by its own distinctive methods of reason apart from any tradition of political thought and practice."[86] Despite this acknowledgment of the indebtedness of abstract justice to the historical democratic traditions, Rawls does not take into account the African-American contributions to political theory, even though it is possible to argue, as Marable does, that "the great gift of black folk to American politics and society has been that we have consistently fought for a more inclusive and humanistic definition of democracy."[87] Nor does Rawls investigate the impact of racism on the formation of the European and American political culture. That is why Paul Gilroy criticizes liberal justice as European particularism "dressed up as universal,"[88] and Lucius Outlaw sees it as a mask hiding interlocking forms of oppression.[89]

According to hooks, the liberal concept of abstract citizenship and universal justice transcending substantive differences not only impoverishes political culture but in practice entails the assimilation of minorities into the values of the dominant groups: "The notion that we should all forsake attachment to race and/or cultural identity and be 'just humans' within the framework of white supremacy has usually meant that subordinate groups must surrender their identities . . . and assimilate by adopting the values and beliefs of privileged class whites" (*KR*, 266). Consequently, the color-blind justice exacts the price of assimilation for the promise of equality. As Murphy and Jung Min Choi point out, when the color-blind democracy is upheld as an ideal of justice, the focus on race is increasingly perceived as a sign of the divisiveness and liability of the subjugated groups who are blamed for their failure to "adjust" to mainstream values.

hooks's critique of the false consciousness of abstract justice expresses doubts about whether such justice can redress wrongs and inequalities perpetuated by the domination based on race, gender, and class.[90] In order to contest racism, the theory of justice in democratic society cannot be restricted solely to universal formal principles abstracted from so-called historical contingent differences, but it has to start with a structural analysis of the institutionalized patterns of domination.[91] By disregarding the distinctive legacies of oppressed groups, and by failing to analyze the structural and institutional inequalities of race, gender, and class, the liberal theory of abstract justice, hooks claims, increases conflicts and divisions instead of generating consensus. In *Killing Rage*, hooks diagnoses a dialectical correlation between abstract justice transcending differences and the resurgence of nationalist fundamentalisms aiming to protect these differences. Reluctant to give up their cultural legacies for the sake of color-blind justice, subjugated groups, especially at the times of growing racial hostility and division, often embrace separatism as a refusal of assimilation to the white hegemonic culture: "As long as our society holds up a vision of democracy that requires the surrender of bonds and ties to legacies folks hold dear," separatism and fundamentalism will seem "the best or only way to either preserve our heritage or to make a meaningful political response to ending racism" (*KR*, 265–66). Consequently, hooks argues that an effective political challenge to fundamentalism requires a conception of democracy that not only contests the institutionalized patterns of domination but also protects differences without fear of anarchy, disorder, or destruction of culture.

Like Manning Marable, hooks sees a political alternative to both liberalism and separatism in the project of "radical multicultural democracy"[92]: "The goal of the radical democratic multiculturalists is not the liberal inclusion of representative number of blacks, Latinos, and others . . . but the radical democratic restructuring of the system of cultural and political power itself."[93] Marable associates the project of "radical multicultural democracy" with the work of such prominent black intellectuals as bell hooks, Patricia Williams, Lani Guinier, Michele Wallace, Patricia Hill Collins, James Jennings, and Cornel West. Despite the differences among these writers, the focus of this group as a whole is on the struggle with the interlocking systems of oppression, on restructuring existing institutions, on coalition building among the oppressed groups, and on the participatory conception of citizenship based on the interaction among diverse groups. As Cornel West writes, the democratic politics of difference "shuns narrow particularisms, parochialisms and separatisms, just as it rejects false universalisms. . . . Instead, the new cultural politics of difference affirms the perennial quest for the precious ideals of individuality and democracy by digging deep in the depths of human particularities and social specificities in order to construct new kinds of connections, affinities and communities."[94]

Confronted with the limitations of liberal democracy, its failure to redress racial injustice, and its excessive individualism, hooks suggests that the multiracial democracy has to confront a threefold challenge. First, the liberal concept of pluralism has to be radicalized so that it is neither separated from the structural analysis of domination nor confined to the status of private goods. Second, rather than seeing pluralism and community as incompatible, the notion of the political community has to be revised in light of the radicalized social and cultural diversity.[95] Finally, hooks is concerned with the active conception of participatory citizenship, its relation to ethics, and its implications for public discourse.

In *Killing Rage: Ending Racism*, hooks argues that the project of radical democracy requires a critical yet "generous" appreciation of the differences of race, gender, sexuality, and class. Since these differences are constitutive of the political identities of the citizens, they need to be taken into account in the disputes and policies concerning justice. According to hooks, this radicalization of difference can be associated with multiculturalism, provided that the meaning of this term is not limited to the separatist idea that "everyone should live with and identify with their own self-contained group" (*KR*, 201):

Beloved *community* is formed not by the eradication of difference but by its affirmation, by each of us claiming the identities and cultural legacies that shape who we are and how we live in the world. To form *beloved community* we do not surrender ties to precious origins. We deepen those bondings by connecting them with an anti-racist struggle which is at heart always a movement to disrupt that clinging to cultural legacies that demands investment in notions of racial purity, authenticity, nationalist fundamentalism. (*KR*, 265)

By elaborating a vision of democracy "where borders can be crossed and cultural hybridity celebrated" (*KR*, 272), hooks stresses the multiple differences not only between but also within racial and ethnic groups.[96] For Patricia Hill Collins, such a model of a hybrid democratic community is conveyed by the metaphor of the crazy quilt—a metaphor, which as we have seen, is also central in hooks's work: "Black women weave together scraps of fabric from all sorts of places. . . . Uniform size is not a criterion for membership in the quilt, nor is blending with all the other scraps."[97] The recognition of the heterogeneity of political and subjective identities, together with the commitment to a truly inclusive democracy, prevents these differences from deterioration into separatism, essentialism, or the false notions of racial or sexual purity. This ethos of radical multicultural democracy does not contradict the paradoxical negative notion of the universality I elaborated in Chapter 5—that is, the universal as the labor of negating any particular posing itself as the universal. What this ethos adds to the discussion of radical democracy is the notion of differences not only as the source of antagonism but also as the positive condition of coalition and solidarity.

The respect for differences and the rejection of both liberalism and separatism motivates hooks's critique of the traditional notions of community, associated with common values, unified traditions, or collective identities. Just as she criticizes white feminism for creating a false notion of sisterhood based on imaginary narcissistic identifications, so too she argues that black community does not express "the essential blackness": "I don't want to suggest that something magical took place there *because* everyone was black—it took place because of *what we did together* as black people" (*OC*, 227). These substantive notions of communities, even when they emerge as the marginalized communities of resistance, are constructed around "false frontiers" and thus risk reproducing oppression and violence (*OC*, 233). By repudiating the traditional notion of community on both local and national levels, hooks poses a challenge of reimagining a radically different community that cultivates respect for the irreducible difference and promotes politics of solidarity among diverse groups. Toward this end, she reconceptualizes Martin Luther King Jr.'s idea of "the beloved community." In his 1956 address, "Facing the Challenge of a New Age," King argues that the democratic struggles against racist segregation are not ends in themselves—"the end is creation of the beloved community."[98] Although she criticizes King's commitment to universalist liberalism and egalitarian Christianity in his early work,[99] hooks wants to preserve his idea of democratic community based on hope and solidarity born out of the revolutionary struggle against imperialism, poverty, and global racial domination: "The flaw . . . was not imagining a *beloved community*; it was the insistence that such a community could exist only if we erased and forgot racial difference" (*KR*, 263).[100]

The focus on the struggle against domination does not mean that a democratic community can be imagined only negatively, only "in reaction to" the interlocking mechanisms of oppression. On the contrary, hooks argues that such a community rests on the active conception of citizenship, solidarity, and participation in the diverse democratic struggles. Although the commonality of the hybrid community is not given in advance by the shared values or the common good, it emerges from the interaction and coalition building among diverse groups: between black and white women; between black men and black women; between people of color and progressive whites who are committed to antiracist struggles. As hooks writes, "A progressive politics of solidarity that embraces both a broad-based identity politics . . . as it simultaneously promotes a recognition of overlapping cultural traditions and values as well as an inclusive understanding of what is gained

when people of color unite to resist white supremacy is the only way to ensure that multicultural democracy will become a reality" (KR, 203).
According to Cornel West, such solidarity requires a new improvisational
thinking, which proceeds from particularities and arrives at contingent connectedness: "This connectedness does not signal a homogenous unity or
monolithical totality but rather a contingent, fragile coalition building in an
effort to pursue common radical libertarian and democratic goals."[101]
Irreducible to an overlapping consensus secured by the abstract principles of
justice, the commonality across differences is an effect of the hegemonic articulation and thus open to redefinition, contestation, and renegotiation in
the future. Its basis is political praxis, that is, an active participation in what
Lucius Outlaw calls "the unfinished American revolution."[102]

Pointing to the decline of Jesse Jackson's Rainbow Coalition, Marable argues that the politics of solidarity has been particularly difficult to pursue in
the last two decades, which were characterized by the resurgence of white
conservatism—a backlash against the legacy of civil rights and affirmative action, on the one hand, and the spread of separatist nationalist movements, on
the other. For hooks the renewal of solidarity politics requires not only a
hegemonic articulation of the common political goals among the oppressed
groups,[103] but also the cultivation of ethical concern for the oppression of
others: "If we are only committed to an improvement in that politic of
domination that we feel leads directly to our individual . . . oppression, we
not only remain attached to the status quo but act in complicity with it"
(OC, 244). As an alternative to the narrow view of coalition grounded in
"wounded narcissism," hooks cites the legacy of the civil rights movement,
which, as Martin Luther King Jr.'s metaphor of the inherited "world house"
suggests, fostered the vision of responsibility for "the planet, . . . for a world
beyond the self, the tribe, the race, the nation" (OC, 250).

Expanding "our capacity to care about the oppression and exploitation of
others" (OC, 244), hooks supplements hegemonic politics with the idea of
solidarity based on the respect for the irreducible difference of the Other.
Far more risky than the articulation of the common political goals, this sense
of solidarity does not confirm our identities but precisely puts them into
question and thus opens them to reconfiguration. As Bernice Johnson
Reagon graphically puts it, coalition work has nothing to do with comfort
or feeling at home; on the contrary, "most of the time you feel threatened
to the core."[104] Yet, as Levinas argues, this is a "fine" risk worth taking:
"The putting into question of the I by the other makes me solidarity with
the other in an incomparable and unique way—not solidarity . . . as an organ
is solidarity with the organism in which it has its function. Solidarity here is
responsibility—as though the whole edifice of creation rested on my shoul-
ders" (TO, 353). Evoking neither the organic unity of the community nor

the abstract principles of justice, ethical solidarity manifests itself in the political arena through the struggle for the rights of others. As Murphy and Choi suggest, what hooks's and Levinas's articulations of democratic solidarity have in common is the conviction that the respect for differences is a necessary condition of political praxis.[105] This respect for differences does not mean, however, that the politics of solidarity eschews dissent, negativity, and antagonism. On the contrary, as hooks argues, the communal ethos manifesting itself as a commitment to a diverse community involves building democratic spaces of critical dissent. Coalition politics articulates antagonism not only as a struggle against the external conditions of oppression but also as an internal debate over the interpretation of democratic vision, collective action, and the forms of liberation struggles. Progressive social movements, hooks claims, "must welcome and create a context for constructive conflict, confrontation, and dissent. Through that dialectical exchange of ideas, thoughts, and visions, we affirm the transformative power of feminist politics" (OC, 108).

One consequence of this negotiation between antagonistic politics of difference and the respect for alterity in intersubjective praxis is an extension of political discourse beyond rational communication. Indeed, hooks calls attention to the crucial role of affect, desire, and sensibility in the language of democratic politics. In my discussions of Levinas, Kristeva, and Lyotard, I linked these affective dimensions to the question of responsibility, the libidinal aspects of power, and the condition of reflective judgment respecting the particular. In hooks's work the affective dimension of politics—such as rage, fear, or yearning—is a correlative of the logic of marginality exposing the limits of discourse. Because the limits of discourse cannot be expressed otherwise than through affect and sensibility, hooks argues that the struggle for justice cannot be separated from passions, desires, and the rage of the oppressed people. As Paul Gilroy suggests, these "structures of feelings" not only sustain democratic struggles and shape intersubjective interactions but also express a utopian desire for a better future without domination—for the counterfactual "yet-to-come"—that transcends the present limitations and the capacities of articulation.[106] Emerging from the critical appreciation of differences, the affective intensities of discourse provide for hooks the only expression of solidarity based not on the common identity or even the common history of oppression but on the revolutionary hope for what is yet to come. As hooks writes, "Rather than thinking we would come together as 'women' in an identity-based bonding we might be drawn together rather by a *commonality of feeling*" (OC, 217). Referring to the title of her book, *Yearning*, hooks explains that the desire for freedom and a better future evokes "the idea that if we could come together in that site of desire and longing, it might be a potential place of community-building" (OC, 217).

Extending her analysis of the affective intensities of political discourse, hooks argues in *Killing Rage* that the negotiation between antagonism, solidarity, and utopian aspirations requires confronting and reconfiguring the ambivalence of rage and love. Starting her book with a positive reevaluation of rage in the context of Malcolm X's commitment to justice and closing it with Martin Luther King Jr.'s vision of the beloved community, hooks refuses to treat rage and love as mutually exclusive ethical and political choices.[107] Reminiscent of the psychoanalytic insight, hooks's emphasis on the ambivalence of love and rage not only contests the idealization of solidarity politics but also reinterprets this ambivalence in the context of the recovery from trauma and revolutionary hope for racial justice. Arguing against the pathologization of rage, hooks links it to the expression of the pain of traumatic injury and its transformation into the negativity implied in every revolutionary action. Similarly to Patricia Williams's discussion of "the gift of intelligent rage,"[108] hooks sees rage as a justified response to the conditions of oppression: "Renewed, organized black liberation struggle cannot happen if we remain unable to tap collective black rage. Progressive black activists must show how we take that rage and move it beyond fruitless scapegoating of any group, linking it instead to passion for freedom and justice" (*KR*, 20). By reclaiming the negativity of rage as a mobilization for the revolutionary struggle against racist, economic, and sexist oppression, hooks neither forgets what Slavoj Žižek calls the radical antagonism in the social field—that is, the internal negativity and impossibility of full identity expressed in the Lacanian concept of the real—nor assumes that the confrontation with that impossibility will automatically lead to the contestation of the political injustice. Rather, her work poses a challenge of rethinking the relation between the negativity of the real and social praxis in order to avoid the twin dangers of the internalization of racist violence or the projection of the internal negativity of the subject onto the Other.

To avert either crippling self-hatred or the destruction of the Other, the politics of radical democracy, hooks argues, has to link the negativity of rage with the nonnarcissistic concept of love. If rage is an essential moment in the expression and transformation of the pain of oppression into revolutionary action, then the sensibility manifesting itself in love is a reminder that the passion for justice cannot be divorced from the responsibility for the Other. Influenced by "the love ethics" of the civil rights movement, hooks regrets the absence of a political discourse of love in progressive leftist circles where it is mostly associated with naivete and depoliticized idealism. She contrasts this absence with King's concept of the "transformative power of love" that could mobilize and sustain oppositional political movement. As Cornel West suggests, King contests the insufficiency of the Christian love ethics because "it applied only to individuals' relationships—not to group, nation, or class conflicts." In response to Nietzsche's and Marx's critique of religion, King develops a love ethics informed by both "the combative spirituality" of the black church and the Gandhian nonviolent political resistance. As both hooks and West argue, King's love ethic is connected to "a way of struggle in which the oppressed people could fight for freedom without inflicting violence on the oppressor."[109] Based on the intertwined notions of desire for justice, liberation struggle, and responsibility for others,[110] King's idea of love refuses the dichotomies between the sentimental Christian love separated from struggle and the ruthless Nietzschean will to power, between the responsibility for the Other and the indifferent struggle of antagonistic forces:

One of the greatest problems of history is that the concepts of love and power are usually contrasted as polar opposites. Love is identified with a resignation of power and power with a denial of love. It was a misinterpretation that caused Nietzsche, the philosopher of the "will to power," to reject the Christian concept of love. It was the same misinterpretation that induced Christian theologians to reject Nietzsche's philosophy of the "will to power". . . . What is needed is a realization that power without love is reckless and abusive and that love without power is sentimental and anemic. Power at its best is love implementing the demands of justice. (*WDWGFH*, 37)

No longer opposed to power and struggle, this politicized notion of love and responsibility informs hooks's vision of public discourse and "beloved community." Contesting not only the ruthless domination of the Other but also the privatized Christian sentimentality, King's love, like Malcolm X's rage, is linked to political radicalism. As hooks writes, "That love was not sentimental. It did not blind us to the reality that racism was deeply systemic and that only by realizing that love in concrete political actions that might involve sacrifice, even the surrender of one's life, would white supremacy be fundamentally challenged" (*KR*, 265).

By refusing to separate love from rage, and ethical obligation from social antagonism, hooks's politics of solidarity provides an alternative to many postmodern and feminist theories of democracy, in particular, to Laclau's and Mouffe's hegemonic politics based exclusively on social antagonism and its obverse side, Habermas's and Benhabib's idealized communicative rationality, which fetishistically denies internal and external conflicts. Acknowledging the passionate and ambivalent dimensions of political community, hooks's notion of solidarity among diverse groups links nonnarcissistic love and ethical obligation not only to the engagement in the collective struggles against oppression but also to the necessary confrontation with the internal conflict, aggressivity, and division of the subject. Mindful of the projections of this internal negativity onto others, hooks's ethical vision and her project of multiracial democracy requires endless vigilance against the hatred of the self and violence against the Other. Although she affirms the indispensable role of the articulation of the interlocking forms of domination based on race, gender, and class, she supplements hegemonic politics of radical democracy with an ethical concern for the oppression of the Other. Like Cornel West and Patricia Hill Collins, she argues that political struggle without ethics cannot respond to the demand of justice, overcome nihilism, mobilize resistance, or offer hope.

• • •

hooks's critique of the postmodern discourse of the Other and her call for the alternative ethics point to the necessary intersection between feminist politics and ethics of difference. What is at stake in this intersection is neither the assimilation of ethics to politics nor a recovery of ethics as a new "ground" of politics but rather a redefinition of both in the context of the limits of discourse marked by the experience of trauma, marginality, and responsibility. Confronted with the reality of oppression, the feminist politics of difference has aimed to transform the institutional conditions of inequality and to demand the status of the subject for those who have been so "othered." Yet, as hooks argues, to challenge domination, it is necessary to supplement the structural analysis of power with the psychic consequences of the racial terror, on the one hand, and to transform the very nature of the self/Other relation, on the other. Preoccupied with discursive/institutional formations of race, gender, and class, feminist politics of difference cannot fulfill these tasks as long as it does not confront the configuration of race, sexuality, and alterity at the limits of discourse. Consequently, to respond to conflicts, injustice, and domination requires not only a critique of power/knowledge but also a therapeutic working through of the unspeakable racial traumas and the elaboration of an alternative ethics based on the responsibility for the Other's oppression. Without such responsibility, the politics of difference risks deteriorating into an indifferent struggle of antagonistic forces. By providing a blueprint for a more just and more democratic politics, hooks's ethics at the same time enables a more productive exchange among women across the "color line." It is the hope for such an exchange that has motivated the writing of this book.

# Afterword

MY ARTICULATION of an ethics of dissensus has grown out of a dissatisfaction with the two seemingly mutually exclusive prospects facing feminism today: either a politics of difference without ethical stakes—a politics that risks deterioration into an indifferent struggle of heterogeneous forces—or its opposite, the search for the normative criteria of justice transcending the antagonisms of race, class, sexuality, and gender. These oppositions manifest themselves, on the one hand, in a suspicion that the turn to ethics is an escape from politics and, on the other, in the worries that postmodern politics culminates in indifference to the injustices and suffering of others. I have been equally frustrated by the fact that some of the most interesting postmodern formulations of ethics avoid any substantive engagements with feminist and racial theories and thus, as bell hooks argues, reproduce a solipsistic discourse, despite all the talk about listening to the Other. To find an alternative to these impasses, and to avoid crippling moralism, the resurgence of which we see not only in ethics but also in self-righteous politics, I found it necessary to reformulate the postmodern turn to ethics in the context of multiple forms of antagonism characteristic of gender and race relations. Such a project has entailed a radical rethinking of ethical problematic, in particular of the question of freedom and obligation, by taking into account the historical constitution of subjectivity, the discursive operation of power, and the irreducible dimension of the external and internal antagonism, on the one hand, and the role of embodiment and sexual and racial differences, on the other. By bringing together discourses that rarely engage each other—poststructuralism, feminism, psychoanalysis, race theory, and the politics of radical democracy—this line of inquiry not only interrogates the role of ethics in democratic politics but also approaches ethics as a contested terrain.

As the term *ethics of dissensus* suggests, what is central to my theory of ethics is the notion of antagonism foregrounding the formative role of power in the constitution of identities, discourses, and bodies. Because it cannot be transcended by the appeal to consensus or higher moral principles, this concept of antagonism forces not only a radical reformulation of the questions of freedom and obligation but also a rethinking of the relationship between ethics and democratic politics. Stemming from the relational character of discourse and power, and reflecting the radical contingency of social relations in democracy, antagonism does not take place between agents with already established identities, but rather constitutes social relations, political identities, and the positions of agents themselves. This relational character and the ambiguity of the creative and destructive effects of power demonstrate that conflict, culture, and politics cannot be thought on the model of the totality still predominant in Levinas's work. I claim, however, that the concept of the formative antagonism in democratic politics has to be radicalized in two crucial ways: first, by taking into account the limit cases of the *polemos*—the differends—that lack the means of expression, and second, by analyzing the relation between power and embodiment. The existence of social conflicts that cannot be resolved because the wrong is not signifiable in the discourse in which the articulation and regulation of conflict takes place alerts us to the possible obliteration of wrongs in the process of forming hegemonic coalitions among diverse democratic movements. Although effective democratic politics requires hegemonic formations, which establish chains of equivalence among the interlocking patterns of oppression based on race, gender, and class, the notion of equivalence risks the effacement of certain forms of wrongs. As the proliferation of conflicts within feminism, ranging from the critiques of normative heterosexuality by queer theorists to the indictment of white solipsism by women of color, suggests, this radicalized sense of antagonism is particularly important for feminist politics because it exposes differends created by the hegemonic articulations of women's oppression.

By considering the relation between antagonism and embodiment, I stress the formative role of power not only in the construction of political identities but also in the materialization of bodies. This approach to racial and sexed bodies as the location of the political struggles is a necessary corrective to the disembodied character of political identities in many democratic theories, including Laclau and Mouffe's formulation of radical democracy. The relation between embodiment and power, however, raises the question not only of the political economy of bodies but also of the libidinal economy of politics. To articulate such a libidinal "surplus" of power, I rework the constitutive antagonisms and the instability of social relations in democracy in the context of fantasy, the negativity of the drive, and racial trauma. This reformulation of antagonism foregrounds both the unconscious mechanisms of sexual and racial fantasies consolidating power relations and the traumatic impact of racial terror and sexual violence.

By stressing the constitutive role of power in the formation of subjectivities, discourse, intersubjective relations, the sexed and racial bodies, and moral norms themselves, *An Ethics of Dissensus* radically changes the parameters of ethical reflection. Instead of elaborating normative criteria transcending antagonisms, this ethics is primarily *transformative*: it aims to change the unjust power relations and to assume an infinite responsibility for violence and the oppression of others. I call this double task the ethos of becoming and the ethos of obligation in order to underscore the necessity of redefining the questions of freedom and responsibility on an entirely new basis: on the "groundless ground" of the transformative encounters with alterity. This shift from moral law to the event locates responsibility in the always asymmetrical, embodied relation to the Other and redefines freedom as an engagement in the experimental praxis aiming to surpass historically sedimented identities and to create new modes of life.

Enabled by the "patiently documentary" genealogical research as well as the intensification of erotic pleasure, the ethos of becoming approaches freedom no longer as an attribute or a transferable possession of the subject, but instead as a possibility of change in power relations. Emerging from the tension between constituted and constituting character of society, between determination and rupture in history, freedom in this sense means not only the task of resistance to multiple forms of domination but also the creation of new modes of being, eroticism, social relations, and, ultimately, new models of democracy. This shift of emphasis from the liberation of repressed identities to the creation of new configurations of power relations stresses the radical futural dimension of democratic politics. Whether we refer to it in terms of Irigaray's politics of the impossible, Foucault's invention of the improbable, hooks's creation of the new "habits of being," or Kristeva's "new imaginary," the experimental ethos of becoming opens up an unpredictable relation to the future, which exceeds calculations, anticipation, and aspirations of the political agents.

My formulation of the ethos of becoming not only redefines ethics beyond the respect for the moral law but also provides a new basis for democratic politics. Irreducible either to the demand for the recognition or to the liberation of repressed identities, the goal of democratic struggles is redefined instead as the transformation of the existing power relations, discourses, and subjectivities. Although closely allied with the formation of democratic coalitions, the ethos of becoming supplements hegemonic politics in two crucial ways: first, it aims to restructure the external relations of domination and to address the libidinal aspects of power, in particular, the effects of fantasy and trauma in political life; second, it examines the relations among becoming, embodiment, and sexuality.

The analysis of the libidinal "surplus" of power confronts us with the fact that it is not only the unjust institutional arrangements and the configurations of power/knowledge that block the possibility of social and subjective transformation, but also the unconscious racist fantasies and the unacknowledged traumas of racial and sexual oppression. If fantasy thwarts the possibility of change by providing the means of satisfaction and compensation for the unstable sociosymbolic relations, then trauma continues to subject its victims to the devastating injury even when its external causes are no longer present. By taking into account the libidinal economy and the unconscious effects of power, my formulation of the ethos of becoming is, therefore, not limited to the restructuring of the external relations of domination, but rather confronts the double task of the traversal of racial fantasies consolidating power structures and the recovery from the traumatic damage of racial and sexual violence.

Finally, I argue that the ethos of becoming cannot be separated from eroticism, embodiment and pleasure. Indeed, if ethics is to intervene into modern power relations that operate on the level of the *bios*, then it also has to be conceptualized on that level. Consequently, I analyze sexed and racialized bodies not only as the materialization of disciplinary power but also as the productive condition of becoming, as the surpassing of the historical limits of action, knowledge, and discourse. By stressing the divergence and the discontinuity of power relations, I argue that the materialization of bodies is intertwined with the possibility of the event, and thus open to change, transformation, or the reversal of forces. Furthermore, this incomplete and temporal character of embodiment opens a different understanding of eroticism, which, by disrupting the identity of the subject, interrupts the disciplinary power's hold on the body. Paradoxically, Foucault himself begins to address the relation between becoming and sexual relations in his writings on the gay way of life, where he reformulates eroticism as "the attraction to the outside." Like Nietzsche's state of rapture, the attraction to the outside—what the Lacanian psychoanalysis in a different register analyzes as the relation to the "real"—provides an alternative to the subjugating reflexivity of sex. Following Leo Bersani, I suggest that this erotic "attraction of the outside" can be reinterpreted as the "self-shattering" *jouissance*, or "homo-ness." Ultimately, I examine the possibility of the relation to the outside in the context of sexual difference and bell hooks's theory of marginality. By radicalizing the theory of sexual difference in the light of race and queer theory, I interpret its negative and disappropriative character as both the limit of identity and the condition of social transformation. I argue, however, that if the ethics of sexual difference is to have a political future, then it has to negate the reification of the historical determinations of race, gender, and class into political or "natural" norms, and thus open them to contestation and change. In particular, it has to oppose the predominance of white solipsism and normative heterosexuality within postmodern and feminist theories.

By redefining the question of freedom and providing a new basis for emancipatory struggles, the ethos of becoming I proposed in this book is a crucial part of both feminist ethics and politics. However, no matter how important, this line of ethical inquiry reaches its limit because it cannot by itself elaborate nonappropriative relations to the Other, based on responsibility rather than on objectification, exclusion, and domination. Originating in the asymmetrical and traumatizing encounter with the Other, such an "anarchic" obligation does not produce the imaginary identifications of empathy, but to the contrary creates a profound disruption of the narcissistic identity, property, and mastery. If, as hooks and Levinas in different ways argue, anti-Semitism, racism, and capitalist exploitation destroy the ability to respond to the Other, then the task of contemporary ethics is to recreate it as the basis of ethical relations. Consequently, the second important task of the ethics of dissensus is to formulate an ethical model of intersubjective relations—or what I call the ethos of alterity—and to find the means of negotiation between the seemingly incompatible claims of freedom and obligation. What is at stake in working through the tension between the ethos of becoming and the ethos of alterity is the question of whether responsibility and respect for the Other can motivate democratic struggles against racial, patriarchal, and economic domination.

To develop such an emancipatory political vision that includes both a commitment to freedom and a commitment to the Other, it is necessary, I argue, to reconfigure the Levinasian concept of responsibility in the double context of sexuality and democratic politics. Consequently, my formulation of the ethos of alterity stresses first of all the embodied notion of responsibility that manifests itself as sensibility and erotic passion rather than as obedience to moral law. Despite his emphasis on the ethical significance of embodiment, Levinas fails to consider this crucial intersection between responsibility and Eros, because he lacks a theory of sexual difference that would allow him to approach sexual relations otherwise than as the manifestation of dual narcissism. However, if we approach sexual difference as the disappropriative labor of the negative revealing the incompleteness of the subject and the asymmetry of sexual relations, then the possibility of all ethical encounters, including erotic ones, depends not only on embodiment but, more specifically, on the condition of being a sexed subject. By exposing the internal division and the limitation of the subject for the sake of the Other's becoming, the labor of the negative prevents the reification of the Other either as the alienating opposite or as the compensatory complement of the subject. Consequently, the negativity of sexual difference does not sublate the Other into the same, but, by placing the limit on the subject, preserves the irreducible alterity. In sexual relations, this respect manifests itself in terms of indirection and intransitivity—that is, as an oblique "relation without relation" that neither objectifies the Other nor reduces her to the narcissistic substitute prop in fantasy.

Yet, if we accept the thesis that sexual difference dramatizes the impossibility of achieving full gender, racial, or class identity, then we have to concede that it is inextricably linked to the contestation and refiguration of these identities. Since the intersection between sexuality and conflict makes the Levinasian separation of ethics from all forms of violence untenable, it is necessary to reformulate the ethical relation by taking into account the multiple intersections between the internal antagonism within the subject represented by the libidinal economy of the drive and the conflicts generated by antagonistic differences in social relations. By considering the heteronomous logic of drive and affect, I argue that the possibility of ethical relation emerges from the traversal of fantasy and the sublimation of the death drive. A correlative of the disruption of narcissism, the traversal of fantasy unravels the defensive projections of the subject and reveals the fact that it is not the antagonistic relationship with the Other that prevents the accomplishment of full identity, but rather the internal splitting and antagonism. If the traversal of fantasy confronts the subject with the conflictual relation to the Other within, with what is irreconcilable within symbolic identifications, then sublimation redirects the aggressivity of the drive from the destruction of the Other toward the disruption and refigurations of the sociosymbolic order. By considering both sides of the ethical relation—the traversal of fantasy and the sublimation of the death drive—this model ceaselessly confronts the subject with the unassimilable otherness within herself and the exorbitant alterity of the Other while deflecting the violence of the death drive toward the transformation of the imaginary and symbolic structures. Consequently, it enables not only a nonviolent response to the Other but also a reconstruction of sociosymbolic relations.

By stressing the traversal of sexual and racist fantasies consolidating unjust power relations and by contesting the reification of antagonisms in the phobic construction of women and racialized others, my redefinition of responsibility foregrounds the interventions of ethics in political life. To challenge the existing order of power/knowledge, ethical responsibility, as bell hooks persuasively argues, has to be intertwined with the political accountability for the social structures of racist, sexist, and economic domination. Otherwise the postmodern "talk about the Other" risks political quietism or even complicity in the maintenance of unjust political systems. Such accountability not only demands an active engagement in democratic struggles against racism, gender discrimination, and economic exploitation but also reveals the necessity of judging the outcome of these struggles without the assurance of normative criteria. Expressing an ongoing concern with justice, such an indeterminate ethical judgment is crucial in democratic politics, first, because it obligates us to evaluate the unpredictable effect of democratic struggles, and second, because it enables us to bear witness and find the means of compensation for the obliterated wrongs—the differends—that lack the means of articulation within the existing hegemonic arrangements.

To elaborate a transformative political vision that includes commitments to both freedom and responsibility, I redefine the struggle for human rights in the context of Patricia Williams's, Emmanuel Levinas's, and Luce Irigaray's work. Following Lefort's claim that every act of proclamation of human rights is always already their reformulation, I stress the performative, future-oriented character of human rights. No longer grounded in the ideological fiction of the presocial human nature—a fiction in complicity with the disciplinary regime—the performative character of rights not only discloses the impossibility of the full actualization of political identities but also reveals their relational character. I argue that the indeterminacy and the incompleteness of social identities foregrounded by the performative politics of race and rights bears both a mark of sexual difference and a trace of the withdrawal of alterity from the existing political articulations. It is precisely these limits of articulation that make it possible to link the transformation of rights to the discourse of desire, on the one hand, and to the anarchic responsibility, on the other. Consequently, the ongoing reformulation of human rights expresses their social, relational character—the relations to Others based on desire, responsibility, and accountability for the history of domination—rather than a protection of private interests. When seen in the context of this double redefinition, the struggle for human rights is a powerful example of the transformative political praxis, motivated by both the desire for freedom and responsibility for others.

By making the questions of antagonism, sexuality, and race central to rethinking freedom and obligation, the ethics of dissensus not only intervenes into existing power relations but also redefines the task of democratic politics. First, my theory of ethics radicalizes the notion of antagonism by taking into account the libidinal economy of power, the effects of trauma, and the political function of fantasy consolidating hegemonic arrangements. Second, it argues that democratic politics should not only articulate and contest the interlocking patterns of domination based on the racial, gender, and class inequalities but also bear an obligation to respond and intervene into the erased conflicts in which victims cannot signify their damages. Although it contests normative discourse as an effect of hegemony, it nonetheless supplements the antagonistic politics with the necessity of an indeterminate ethical judgment and the responsibility for the articulation and compensation for obliterated wrongs. Third, the ethics of dissensus contests the reduction of all forms of alterity to the friend/enemy opposition and proposes instead an alternative model of intersubjective relations in which the respect for otherness is a necessary condition of solidarity and democratic community. Based on the accountability for the oppression of others, this notion of solidarity opens an alternative to the narrow view of coalition grounded in "wounded narcissism." Finally, by calling into question the depoliticized, desexualized subject of traditional morality, the ethics of dissensus also opposes the disembodied notions of citizenship. By challenging the thesis about the disincorporation of power in democratic regimes, it reveals passionate, ambivalent, anarchic dimensions of democratic politics. As these interventions suggest, I hope that this book will alter the optics of future discussions of both ethics and democratic politics so that the intertwined issues of antagonism, sexuality, and race are no longer excluded, or paid lip service, but rather constitute the prism through which the claims of freedom and obligation are negotiated.

# Notes

INTRODUCTION

1. In this book I will discuss the question of agency and resistance in the context of Foucault's, Butler's, and hooks's work. For postmodern accounts of agency in the context of struggle against racial and sexual oppression, see Janet R. Jakobsen, *Working Alliances and the Politics of Difference: Diversity and Feminist Ethics* (Bloomington: Indiana University Press, 1998), 3–20, 28–56.

2. See, for instance, Teresa L. Ebert's critique of feminist ethics as mystification obfuscating the reality of class struggle, in *Ludic Feminism and After: Postmodernism, Desire, and Labor in Late Capitalism* (Ann Arbor: University of Michigan Press, 1996), 113, 229–30.

3. Drucilla Cornell, "What Is Ethical Feminism?", in *Feminist Contentions: A Philosophical Exchange*, eds. Seyla Benhabib, Judith Butler, Drucilla Cornell, and Nancy Fraser (New York: Routledge, 1995), 78–80. See also Drucilla Cornell, "The Philosophy of the Limit: Systems Theory and Feminist Legal Reform," in *Deconstruction and the Possibility of Justice* (New York: Routledge, 1992), 69–91, and especially *The Philosophy of the Limit* (New York: Routledge, 1992), 109–69.

4. Lawrence Buell, "Introduction: In Pursuit of Ethics," *PMLA*, special issue, "Ethics and Literary Study," ed. Lawrence Buell, 114 (1999): 7.

5. Among the most influential discussions of postmodern ethics, see Zygmunt Bauman, *Postmodern Ethics* (Oxford: Blackwell, 1993); John D. Caputo, *Against Ethics* (Bloomington: Indiana University Press, 1993); John Rajchman, *Truth and Eros: Foucault, Lacan, and the Question of Ethics* (New York: Routledge, 1991); Charles Scott, *The Question of Ethics: Nietzsche, Foucault, Heidegger* (Bloomington: Indiana University Press, 1990); and Simon Critchley, *Ethics-Politics-Subjectivity* (London: Verso, 1998).

6. Linda J. Nicholson, ed., *Feminism/Postmodernism* (New York: Routledge, 1990); and Margaret Ferguson and Jennifer Wicke, *Feminism and Postmodernism* (Durham, N.C.: Duke University Press, 1994).

7. For an excellent critique of this split, see the editors' introduction to the collection of essays entitled *Daring to Be Good: Essays in Feminist Ethico-Politics*, ed. Bat-Ami On and Ann Ferguson (New York: Routledge, 1998), x–xvii. As they write, feminist critiques of "the liberal political discourse . . . are strangely silent on what kind of ethical values" postmodern feminism ought to be pursuing (xiv). Jakobsen persuasively argues that the distinction between ethics and politics is itself an effect of the disciplinary practices (*Working Alliances*, 16–17).

8. See, especially, Cornell, "What Is Ethical Feminism?", and *Beyond Accommodation: Ethical Feminism, Deconstruction, and the Law* (New York: Routledge, 1991); bell hooks, *Killing Rage: Ending Racism* (New York: Henry Holt, 1995), *Outlaw Culture: Resisting Representations* (New York: Routledge, 1994), *Sisters of the Yam: Black Women and Self-Recovery* (Boston: South End Press, 1993), and *Yearning: Race, Gender, and Cultural Politics* (Boston: South End Press, 1990); Tina Chanter, *Ethics of Eros: Irigaray's Rewriting of the Philosophers* (New York: Routledge, 1995); Rosalyn Diprose, *The Bodies of Women: Ethics, Embodiment and Sexual Difference* (London: Routledge, 1994); Rey Chow, *Ethics After Idealism: Theory, Culture, Ethnicity, Reading* (Bloomington: Indiana University Press, 1998); and Lynne Huffer, *Maternal Pasts, Feminist Futures: Nostalgia, Ethics, and the Question of Difference* (Stanford, Calif.: Stanford University Press, 1998). Other important feminist articulations of ethics include Linda A. Bell's Sartrean study of freedom, *Rethinking Ethics in the Midst of Violence: A Feminist Approach to Freedom* (Lanham, Md.: Rowman and Littlefield, 1993); Sarah Lucia Hoagland's study of value in distinction to norm, *Lesbian Ethics: Toward New Value* (Palo Alto, Calif.: Institute of Lesbian Studies, 1988); Sharon Welch's theologically inspired "ethic of risk," *A Feminist Ethic of Risk* (Minneapolis, Minn.: Fortress Press, 1990); and three collections of essays, Claudia Card, ed., *Feminist Ethics* (Lawrence: University Press of Kansas, 1991); On and Ferguson, eds., *Daring to Be Good*; and Elizabeth Frazer, Jennifer Hornsby, and Sabina Lovibond, eds., *Ethics: A Feminist Reader* (Oxford: Blackwell, 1992).

9. For the theory of "ethics of care," see Carol Gilligan, *In a Different Voice: Psychological Theory and Women's Development* (Cambridge, Mass.: Harvard University Press, 1982). For the most comprehensive collection representing the diverse voices in the debate about care and justice, see Moira Gatens, ed., *Feminist Ethics* (Dartmouth, N.H.: Dartmouth Publishing Company, 1998). See also Daryl Koehn, *Rethinking Feminist Ethics: Care, Trust, and Empathy* (London: Routledge, 1998); Virginia Held, ed., *Justice and Care: Essential Readings in Feminist Ethics* (Boulder, Colo.: Westview Press, 1995); and Diprose, *Bodies of Women*, 1–18.

10. For a defense of the moral project of Enlightenment against feminist postmodern theory, see, for instance, Alison Assiter, *Enlightened Women: Modernist Feminism in a Postmodern Age* (London: Routledge, 1996).

11. For the attempts to theorize ethics on the basis of women's experi-

ence, see, for instance, Gilligan, *In a Different Voice*; and Sara Ruddick, *Maternal Thinking: Toward a Politics of Peace* (Boston: Beacon Press, 1989).

12. For the most sophisticated defense of freedom from the existentialist perspective, which takes into account the existence of racial and sexual oppression, see Bell, *Rethinking Ethics*. My quarrel with Bell concerns her inadequate theory of power (which is often linked with the systems of oppression and is not seen as an element of discourse itself) and her postulation of "*ideals* of gender- and race-neutrality" (*Rethinking Ethics*, 3).

13. For the compelling example of the ethical visions of alternative communities, see the essays in the section "Identities and Communities," in On and Ferguson, eds., *Daring to Be Good*, 127–82.

14. For hooks's critique of the exclusionary practices within feminism, see her *Ain't I a Woman: Black Women and Feminism* (Boston: South End Press, 1981), *Feminist Theory: From Margin to Center* (Boston: South End Press, 1984), and *Talking Back: Thinking Feminist, Thinking Black* (Boston: South End Press, 1989). Similar criticisms have been made, among others, by Elizabeth V. Spelman, *Inessential Woman: Problems of Exclusion in Feminist Thought* (Boston: Beacon Press, 1990); Michele Wallace, *Invisibility Blues: From Pop to Theory* (London: Verso, 1990); Patricia Hill Collins, *Fighting Words: Black Women and the Search for Justice* (Minneapolis: University of Minnesota Press, 1998); Zillah R. Eisenstein, *The Color of Gender: Reimaging Democracy* (Berkeley and Los Angeles: University of California Press, 1994); and Katie Geneva Cannon, *Black Womanist Ethics* (Atlanta, Ga.: Scholars Press, 1988).

15. The important exceptions include, among others, Bell, *Rethinking Ethics*; Jakobsen, *Working Alliances*; Welch, *Feminist Ethic of Risk*; and Cynthia Willett, *Maternal Ethics and Other Slave Moralities* (New York: Routledge, 1995).

16. hooks, *Yearning*.

17. For the articulation of feminist ethics in the context of sexuality and embodiment, see, for instance, Diprose, *Bodies of Women*; for the rethinking of ethics in the context of sensibility and race, see Willett, *Maternal Ethics*.

18. For the rethinking of ethics in the context of conflict, see Bell, *Rethinking Ethics*; Jakobsen, *Working Alliances*; Welch, *Feminist Ethic of Risk*; and Willett, *Maternal Ethics*. Jakobsen's understanding of power as constitutive of discourse and identities is probably closest to my own. The main difference in our positions is that I supplement the Foucauldian understanding of power with Lyotard's notion of the differend—that is, the liminal case of antagonism that is not signifiable in the hegemonic discourse—on the one hand, and with the libidinal economy of the drive, on the other.

19. Gayatri Chakravorty Spivak, "French Feminism Revisited: Ethics and Politics," in *Feminists Theorize the Political*, ed. Judith Butler and Joan W. Scott (New York: Routledge, 1992), 81.

20. Moira Gatens, *Imaginary Bodies: Ethics, Power and Corporeality* (London:

Routledge, 1996), 102–3. For other attempts to rethink the division between politics and ethics, see Bell, *Rethinking Ethics*; Jakobsen, *Working Alliances*; and the collection of essays, On and Ferguson, eds., *Daring to Be Good*.

21. As Kelly Oliver argues, these dichotomies of subject/other, subject/object are symptoms of the pathology of oppression. See *Witnessing: Beyond Recognition* (Minneapolis: University of Minnesota Press, 2001).

22. Chantal Mouffe and Ernesto Laclau, *Hegemony and Socialist Strategy: Towards a Radical Democratic Politics* (London: Verso, 1994), 134–71. For a similar articulation of feminist alliances, see Jakobsen, *Working Alliances*, 58–97.

23. Oliver describes this model of relation based on "response-ability" and "addressability" as witnessing, but she is skeptical whether the ethical concept of the alterity derived from Levinas's ethics can provide a basis for this model. By contrast I argue that Levinas's ethical relation to the Other, in which it is the Other who calls the subject to responsibility, is indispensable to think witnessing as "the recognition of what is beyond recognition."

24. Caputo, *Against Ethics*, 60.

25. The asymmetry of this relation means, as Bauman argues, that we are "for the other" before being "with the other" (*Postmodern Ethics*, 13).

26. Patricia J. Williams, *The Alchemy of Race and Rights: Diary of a Law Professor* (Cambridge, Mass.: Harvard University Press, 1991).

27. For diverse interrogations of sexual difference in the context of race and queer theory, see, among others, hooks, *Feminist Theory*; and hooks, *Yearning*; Hortense J. Spillers, " 'The Permanent Obliquity of an In[pha]llibly Straight': In the Time of the Daughters and the Fathers," in *Daughters and Fathers*, ed. Lynda E. Boose and Betty S. Flowers (Baltimore, Md.: Johns Hopkins University Press, 1989); and Hortense J. Spillers, "Mama's Baby, Papa's Maybe: An American Grammar Book," *Diacritics* 17 (1987): 65–81; Valerie Smith, "Black Feminist Theory and the Representation of the Other," in *Changing Our Own Words: Essays on Criticism, Theory, and Writing by Black Women*, ed. Cheryl Wall (New Brunswick, N.J.: Rutgers University Press, 1989), 38–57; Spelman, *Inessential Woman*; Evelynn Hammonds, "Black (W)holes and the Geometry of Black Female Sexuality," *differences: A Journal of Feminist Cultural Studies* 6 (1994): 126–45, reprinted in *Feminism Meets Queer Theory*, ed. Elizabeth Weed and Naomi Schor (Bloomington: Indiana University Press, 1997), 136–56; Deborah E. McDowell, *"The Changing Same": Black Women's Literature, Criticism, and Theory* (Bloomington: Indiana University Press, 1995), 156–75; Ellen T. Armour, *Deconstruction, Feminist Theology, and the Problem of Difference: Subverting the Race/Gender Divide* (Chicago: University of Chicago Press, 1999); Judith Butler, *Bodies that Matter: On the Discursive Limits of "Sex"* (New York: Routledge, 1993); and the essays in the collection, Weed and Schor, eds., *Feminism Meets Queer Theory*.

28. Mae Gwendolyn Henderson, "Speaking in Tongues: Dialogics, Dialectics, and the Black Woman Writer's Literary Tradition," in *Feminists The-*

*orize the Political*, eds. Judith Butler and Joan W. Scott (New York: Routledge, 1992), 144–66.

29. For an excellent analysis and a critique of such a retreat from the politics of freedom in postmodern feminist theory, see Wendy Brown, *States of Injury: Power and Freedom in Late Modernity* (Princeton, N.J.: Princeton University Press, 1995), 3–21, 30–52. Brown's *States of Injury* and Drucilla Cornell's *At the Heart of Freedom: Feminism, Sex, and Equality* (Princeton, N.J.: Princeton University Press, 1998) represent two different attempts to reconceptualize freedom in postmodern feminist perspective.

30. Collins, *Fighting Words*; Cornel West, *Race Matters* (New York: Random House, 1993), 15–32; and Cornel West, *Keeping Faith: Philosophy and Race in America* (New York: Routledge, 1993), ix–xvii.

31. In addition to bell hooks and Rey Chow cited in note 8 above, see Kelly Oliver, *Subjectivity Without Subjects: From Abject Fathers to Desiring Mothers* (Lanham, Md.: Rowman and Littlefield, 1998); and Oliver, *Witnessing*.

CHAPTER I

1. For the discussion of freedom in Foucault as a contextualized practice rather than as an attribute of the subject, see Wendy Brown, *States of Injury: Power and Freedom in Late Modernity* (Princeton, N.J.: Princeton University Press, 1995), 3–30; and Jana Sawicki's excellent essay, "Feminism, Foucault, and the 'Subjects' of Power and Freedom," in *Feminist Interpretations of Michel Foucault*, ed. Susan J. Hekman (University Park: Pennsylvania State University Press, 1996), 159–78. For the notion of resistance as freeing of difference, see Susan J. Hekman, introduction to *Feminist Interpretations of Michel Foucault*, ed. Susan J. Hekman (University Park: Pennsylvania State University Press, 1996), 10–11; and Hekman's earlier *Gender and Knowledge: Elements of a Postmodern Feminism* (Boston: Northeastern University Press, 1990), 182–86.

2. Simon During argues, for instance, that Foucault's turn toward ethics is an expression of "futility and a new surge of aestheticism." See *Foucault and Literature: Towards a Genealogy of Writing* (London: Routledge, 1992), 11.

3. As James W. Bernauer, among others, argues, Foucault not only rejects moral experience based on religious revelation but also the modern project to ground morality in true knowledge. See *Michel Foucault's Force of Flight: Toward an Ethics for Thought* (Atlantic Highlands, N.J.: Humanities Press International, 1990), 17.

4. The following works by Michel Foucault will be cited parenthetically: *DP: Discipline and Punish: The Birth of the Prison*, trans. Alan Sheridan (New York: Random House, 1977).

DL: "The Discourse on Language," in *The Archeology of Knowledge and The Discourse on Language*, trans. A. M. Sheridan Smith (New York: Pantheon Books, 1972).

FWL: "Friendship as a Way of Life," in *Ethics: Subjectivity and Truth*, ed.

Paul Rabinow, trans. Robert Hurley et al. (New York: Pantheon, 1984).

GE: "On the Genealogy of Ethics: An Overview of Work in Progress," in *Ethics: Subjectivity and Truth*, ed. Paul Rabinow, trans. Robert Hurley et al. (New York: Pantheon, 1984).

*HS: The History of Sexuality*, vol. I, trans. Robert Hurley (New York: Random House, 1978).

MB: "Maurice Blanchot: The Thought from Outside," in *Foucault-Blanchot*, trans. Brian Massumi (New York: Zone Books, 1990).

NGH: "Nietzsche, Genealogy, History," in *Language, Counter-Memory, Practice*, ed. Donald F. Bouchard, trans. Sherry Simon (Ithaca, N.Y.: Cornell University Press, 1977).

SC: "Sexual Choice, Sexual Act," in *Michel Foucault: Politics, Philosophy, Culture*, ed. Lawrence D. Kritzman, trans. James O'Higgins (New York: Routledge, 1988).

UP: The Use of Pleasure, vol. 2 of *The History of Sexuality*, trans. Robert Hurley (New York: Random House, 1990).

WE: "What Is Enlightenment?" in *The Foucault Reader*, ed. Paul Rabinow, trans. Catherine Porter (New York: Pantheon, 1984).

5. Paul Gilroy, *The Black Atlantic: Modernity and Double Consciousness* (Cambridge, Mass.: Harvard University Press, 1993), 56.

6. Michel Foucault, "Sex, Power, and the Politics of Identity," in *Ethics: Subjectivity and Truth*, ed. Paul Rabinow, trans. Robert Hurley et al. (New York: Pantheon, 1984), 164.

7. Frantz Fanon, *Black Skin, White Masks*, trans. Charles Lam Markmann (New York: Grove Press, 1967), 222.

8. See, in particular, Hilary Radner's illuminating discussion of the contradictory interplay of the disciplinary technologies and the practices of self in feminine popular culture in *Shopping Around: Feminine Culture and the Pursuit of Pleasure* (New York: Routledge, 1995); the work of Susan Bordo on the eating disorders and the production of the slender body in *Unbearable Weight: Feminism, Western Culture and the Body* (Berkeley and Los Angeles: University of California Press, 1993); and Bordo's analysis of the normalizing function of the cultural images of beauty and physical perfection in the context of gender and race in *Twilight Zones: The Hidden Life of Cultural Images from Plato to O.J.* (Berkeley and Los Angeles: University of California Press, 1997); Sandra Lee Bartki's discussion of new disciplines regulating female bodies in "Foucault, Femininity, and the Modernization of Patriarchal Power," in *Feminism and Foucault: Reflections on Resistance*, ed. Irene Diamond and Lee Quinby (Boston: Northeastern University Press, 1988), 61–86; Jennifer Terry, "Body Invaded: Medical Surveillance of Women as Reproducers," *Socialist Review* 19 (1989): 13–43; and Naomi Zack for the discussion of

the differences in the sexualization of black and white female embodiment and reproduction in "The American Sexualization of Race," in *Race/Sex: Their Sameness, Difference, and Interplay*, ed. Naomi Zack (New York: Routledge, 1997). For an informative discussion of the feminist appropriations of Foucault to study the contemporary power relations, see Monique Deveaux, "Feminism and Empowerment: A Critical Reading of Foucault," in *Feminist Interpretations of Michel Foucault*, ed. Susan J. Hekman (University Park: Pennsylvania State University Press, 1996), 211–38.

9. For a discussion of possibilities and limitations of Foucault's discussion of modern racism inscribed in the technologies of normalizing state, see Ann Laura Stoller, *Race and the Education of Desire: Foucault's History of Sexuality in the Colonial Order of Things* (Durham, N.C.: Duke University Press, 1995), 55–93. See also Zack, "American Sexualization."

10. Honi Fern Haber, *Beyond Postmodern Politics: Lyotard, Rorty, Foucault* (New York: Routledge, 1994), 78.

11. Francis Bartkowski writes that Foucault exposes the irony of "movements of liberation, which, even as they operate, are constrained by the power-knowledge-pleasure apparatus." See "Epistemic Drift in Foucault," in *Feminism and Foucault: Reflections on Resistance*, ed. Irene Diamond and Lee Quinby (Boston: Northeastern University Press, 1988), 46. Foucault warns his readers in *Discipline and Punish* that "the man described for us, whom we are invited to free, is already in himself the effect of subjection much more profound than himself" (30).

12. Lois McNay, *Foucault: A Critical Introduction* (New York: Continuum, 1994), 102.

13. Bartkowski, "Epistemic Drift in Foucault," 44.

14. Foucault explains, "Where there is power, there is resistance, and yet, or rather consequently, this resistance is never in a position of exteriority in relation to power" (*HS*, I:95).

15. For an interesting contribution to the debate about the usefulness of Foucault for feminism, see, for instance, Amy Allen, "Foucault on Power: A Theory for Feminists," in *Feminist Interpretations of Michel Foucault*, ed. Susan J. Hekman (University Park: Pennsylvania State University Press, 1996), 265–81. However, because of the lack of an explicit discussion of how power is actualized in historical formations, Allen ends up with two contradictory notions of power in Foucault, neither of which in itself is useful for feminism: free circulation of forces, on the one hand, and the states of domination, on the other hand, in which individuals are unable to exercise power at all ("Foucault on Power," 277).

16. There are, of course, some notable exceptions, in particular the work of Judith Butler, devoted from the outset to the elaboration of the theory of agency within the Foucauldian framework.

17. For a critique of this reading of Foucault, see Judith Butler, *Bodies that Matter: On the Discursive Limits of "Sex"* (New York: Routledge, 1993), 8–10.

18. Nancy Hartsock, "Foucault on Power: A Theory for Women?" in *Feminism/Postmodernism*, ed. Linda Nicholson (New York: Routledge, 1989), 167. For a more recent critique of the limitation of Foucault's theory for the projects of liberation, see Nancy Hartsock, "Postmodernism and Political Change: Issues for Feminist Theory," in *Feminist Interpretations of Michel Foucault*, ed. Susan J. Hekman (University Park: Pennsylvania State University Press, 1996), 39–55.

19. Christopher Norris, *The Truth About Postmodernism* (Oxford: Blackwell, 1993), 33.

20. Axel Honneth, *The Critique of Power: Reflective Stages in Critical Social Theory* (Cambridge, Mass.: MIT Press, 1991), 189.

21. David M. Halperin, *Saint Foucault: Towards a Gay Hagiography* (Oxford: Oxford University Press, 1995), 22. In his trenchant criticism of the Anglo-American reception of Foucault, Halperin provides an excellent account of the importance of Foucault's work for gay activism.

22. Friedrich Nietzsche, *On the Genealogy of Morals*, trans. Walter Kaufmann (New York: Random House, 1969), 77–78.

23. Jacques-Alain Miller, "Jeremy Bentham's Panoptic Device," *October* 44 (1987): 5–6.

24. Joan Copjec, *Read My Desire: Lacan Against the Historicists* (Cambridge, Mass.: MIT Press, 1994), 41.

25. As Foucault writes, archaeological analysis compares discursive formations to "the non-discursive practices that surround them and serve as a general element for them": "an institutional field, a set of events, practices, and political decisions, a sequence of economic process . . . etc." (*Archeology of Knowledge*, 157).

26. As John Rajchman suggests, Foucault's emphasis on the organization of space serves "as a corrective to one tendency in the philosophy of time in Bergson, Heidegger, and Sartre—the tendency of putting 'space' on the side of the 'practico-inert,' while reserving for time the great questions of project and history." See "Foucault's Art of Seeing," *October* 44 (1988): 103.

27. Gilles Deleuze, *Foucault*, trans. Seán Hand (Minneapolis: University of Minnesota Press, 1988), 62. Subsequent references to this work will be cited parenthetically as *F*.

28. Peg Elizabeth Birmingham, "Arendt/Foucault: Power and the Law," in *Transitions in Continental Philosophy*, ed. Arleen B. Dallery, Stephen Watson, and Marya Bower (Albany: SUNY Press, 1994), 23–24.

29. Judith Butler, *The Psychic Life of Power* (Stanford, Calif.: Stanford University Press, 1997), 29.

30. Despite this similarity, Elizabeth Grosz describes the contrast between Nietzsche's and Foucault's approaches to the body in the following way: "Where for Foucault the body is the field on which the play of powers, knowledges, and resistances are worked out, for Nietzsche the body is the agent and active cause of knowledge." See *Volatile Bodies: Toward a Corpo-*

*real Feminism* (Bloomington: Indiana University Press, 1994), 146. Although indebted to Grosz's discussion of Nietzsche's concept of the body as both the social surface of inscription and a multiplicity of conflicting forces, my interpretation of the multiple modalities of materialization situates Foucault much closer to Nietzsche's legacy than Grosz does.

31. For an illuminating discussion of Nietzsche's concept of the body and its influence on Foucault, see Elizabeth Grosz, "Nietzsche and the Stomach for Knowledge," in *Nietzsche, Feminism and Political Theory*, ed. Paul Patton (London: Routledge, 1993), 49–70.

32. See Claude Lefort, *The Political Forms of Modern Society*, ed. John B. Thomson (Cambridge, Mass.: MIT Press, 1986), 239–306.

33. Butler, *Bodies that Matter*, 34.

34. Bordo, *Twilight Zones*, 9. See also Radner's analysis of the codification of the body parts in exercise routine (*Shopping Around*, 154).

35. As Stoller claims, "race is a theme" in *History of Sexuality*, vol. I, "but not the subject of analysis" (*Race and the Education of Desire*, 52). See also Robert J. C. Young, "Foucault on Race and Colonialism," *new formations* 25 (1995): 48–56.

36. Darrell Moore, "The Frame of Discourse: Sexuality, Power, and the Incitement to Race," *Philosophy Today* 42 (1998): 96. See also Stoller's discussion of the technologies of modern state racism in the context of Foucault's 1976 *The Collège de France* lectures (*Race and the Education of Desire*, 55–94).

37. Zack, "American Sexualization," 147–49.

38. Moore, "Frame of Discourse," 95.

39. Similarly, Abdul R. JanMohamed argues that "racialized sexuality refused or failed to develop a dense discursivity" but his explanation is different. He attributes this absence of discursivity to the fact that "white patriarchy's sexual violation of the racial border—the master's rape of the female slave—was an 'open secret'" that could not be admitted in the official pseudoscientific doctrine of racism. See "Sexuality on/of the Racial Border: Foucault, Wright, and the Articulation of 'Racialized Sexuality,'" in *DisCourses of Sexuality: From AIDS to Aristotle*, ed. Domna C. Stanton (Ann Arbor: University of Michigan Press, 1992), 104.

40. Butler, *Bodies that Matter*, 35.

41. Grosz, *Volatile Bodies*, 145–47.

42. Radner, *Shopping Around*, 173.

43. Ibid., 146.

44. Nietzsche, *Genealogy of Morals*, 58–59.

45. Michel Foucault, *The Order of Things: An Archaeology of the Human Sciences*, trans. Alan Sheridan (New York: Pantheon, 1971), 328.

46. McNay, *Foucault*, 102–3.

47. Butler, *Psychic Life of Power*, 86.

48. Grosz, *Volatile Bodies*, 124.

49. Nietzsche, *Genealogy of Morals*, 46.

50. For a discussion of the political function of fantasy, see Slavoj Žižek, *The Sublime Object of Ideology* (London: Verso, 1989), 118–24.

51. As Alan Schrift suggests in his discussion of Nietzsche's impact on Foucault's thought, the soul is the principle of the "hangman's metaphysics." See *Nietzsche's French Legacy: A Genealogy of Poststructuralism* (New York: Routledge, 1995), 48.

52. Brown, *States of Injury*, 118.

53. In adjudicating among many different readings of *Discipline and Punish*, Nancy Fraser claims that Foucault rejects humanism on both normative and strategic grounds without elaborating an alternative normative ethics. For her discussion, see "Michel Foucault: A 'Young Conservative?'" in *Unruly Practices: Power, Discourse and Gender in Contemporary Social Theory* (Minneapolis: University of Minnesota Press, 1989), 35–54.

54. For further discussion of the genealogy of the soul in Nietzsche, see Grosz, "Nietzsche and the Stomach for Knowledge," 49–70; Butler, *Psychic Life of Power*, 63–78; and Schrift, *Nietzsche's French Legacy*, 44–48.

55. Butler, *Psychic Life of Power*, 65.

56. Nietzsche, *Genealogy of Morals*, 161.

57. Louis Althusser, "Ideology and Ideological State Apparatuses," in *Lenin and Philosophy, and Other Essays* (New York: Monthly Review Press, 1970), 170–77.

58. Furthermore, disciplinary apparatus fails to produce the "ideological effect" Althusser describes as the obviousness of freedom. Although it is true that the law presupposes the freedom of will, delinquency introduces an involuntary causality, which explains the crime in terms of pathology: the criminal "is linked to his offence by a whole bundle of complex threads (instincts, drives, tendencies, character)" (*DP*, 253).

59. Friedrich Nietzsche, *The Will to Power*, trans. Walter Kaufmann (New York: Vintage, 1968), 270.

60. Michel Foucault, "Two Lectures," in *Power/Knowledge: Selected Interviews and Other Writings 1972–1977*, ed. Colin Gordon, trans. Colin Gordon et al. (New York: Pantheon, 1980), 108.

61. Foucault defines relational rights as "the right to gain recognition in an institutional sense for the relations of one individual to another individual, which is not necessarily connected to the emergence of a group." See "The Social Triumph of the Sexual Will," in *Ethics: Subjectivity and Truth*, ed. Paul Rabinow, trans. Robert Hurley et al. (New York: Pantheon, 1984), 162.

62. Lefort, *Political Forms*, 239–72.

63. bell hooks, *Yearning: Race, Gender, and Cultural Politics* (Boston: South End Press, 1990), 15, emphasis added.

64. For my discussion of Foucault's ethics, see " 'Straying Afield of Oneself': Risks and Excesses of Foucault's Ethics," *Symploke*, special issue, "The Histories of Michel Foucault," 3 (1995): 179–99.

65. Despite his emphasis on the creative, transformative, and utopian as-

pects of gay activism, Halperin's claim that "Foucault's aim . . . was not *liberation* but *resistance*" does not convey the full sense of the Foucauldian experimental ethos of progressive politics (*Saint Foucault*, 56–60).

66. FWL, 138.

67. Substituting "a history of ethical problematizations based on the practices of self, for a history of systems of morality based, hypothetically, on interdictions," Foucault changes the ethical problematic from the moral law to what Elizabeth Grosz calls "ethical self-production" (*Volatile Bodies*, 158).

68. Jacques Derrida, "Signature Event Context," in *Margins of Philosophy*, trans. Alan Bass (Chicago: University of Chicago Press, 1982), 321.

69. Butler, *Bodies that Matter*, 14.

70. Aristotle, *Nicomachean Ethics*, trans. Terence Irwin (Indianapolis, Ind.: Hackett, 1985), 151–54.

71. Among many Foucault interpreters who focus on the question of ethics there is more agreement about what his ethics refuses to do (it does not purport to establish a moral code or a new set of normative values) than on its positive content. For John Rajchman, the central category of Foucault's ethics is the notion of freedom: "There is the question of an ethic in which freedom would be modeled not on transgressive acts or on the liberation of repressed truth but on choosing forms of possible experience: the ethics in which forming ourselves would not be based on a prior knowledge of our nature." See "Ethics After Foucault," in *Michel Foucault: Critical Assessments*, vol. 3, ed. Barry Smart (New York: Routledge, 1994), 202; and John Rajchman, *Michel Foucault: The Freedom of Philosophy* (New York: Columbia University Press, 1985). For Bernauer, the most characteristic feature of Foucault's ethics consists in "the force of flight and escape" from the increasing confinements of human life and thought (*Michel Foucault's Force of Flight*, 1–23). For Sheridan the possibility of ethics emerges from the subversion of the regimes of truth; see *Michel Foucault: The Will to Truth* (New York: Tavistock, 1985). For further assessments, see also an excellent section, "Ethics and the Subject," in the collection of essays, *Michel Foucault Philosopher*, ed. Timothy J. Armstrong (New York: Routledge, 1992).

72. Richard Wolin, "Foucault's Aesthetic Decisionism," *Telos* 67 (1986): 71–86.

73. Michel Foucault, "On the Genealogy of Ethics: An Overview of Work in Progress," in *Ethics: Subjectivity and Truth*, ed. Paul Rabinow, trans. Robert Hurley et al. (New York: Pantheon, 1984), 258.

74. This formulation of diverse uses of pleasure also recalls Wittgenstein's analysis of language games. The point of analogy between Wittgenstein and Foucault is not only, as Rajchman argues, the analysis of the inner mental processes in terms of the public practices, but also a similar understanding of signification based on use rather than a code ("Ethics After Foucault," 193).

75. Bernauer suggests, for instance, that for Foucault the possibility of ethics emerges from the displacements effected by his type of historical analy-

sis: "What knowledge does (and not reads), how power constructs (and not represses), how a relation to self is invented (and not discovered)" (*Michel Foucault's Force of Flight*, 18).

76. Foucault, "Sex, Power," 166.

77. Grosz, *Volatile Bodies*, xii.

78. For an attempt to provide a theory of Foucault's approach to literature, see, for instance, During, *Foucault and Literature*. For an alternative strategy focusing on the effect of Foucault's specific readings of literary texts, see David Carroll, *Paraesthetics: Foucault, Lyotard, Derrida* (New York: Routledge, 1987).

79. Michel Foucault, "The Return of Morality," in *Michel Foucault: Politics, Philosophy, Culture*, ed. Lawrence D. Kritzman, trans. James O'Higgins (New York: Routledge, 1988), 250.

80. Martin Heidegger, *Nietzsche*, vol. I, *The Will to Power as Art*, trans. David Farrell Krell (San Francisco: Harper & Row, 1979), 123.

81. Fanon, *Black Skin, White Masks*, 229.

82. Heidegger, *Nietzsche*, I:136.

83. Foucault turns to Nietzsche to contest the separation of the critical and experimental force of modern art from other realms of existence. As Nietzsche writes, "One should not play with artistic formulas: one should re-model life so that it *has* to formulate itself" (*Will to Power*, 447).

84. Halperin, *Saint Foucault*, 76.

85. Cornel West, *Keeping Faith: Philosophy and Race in America* (New York: Routledge, 1993), 32.

86. FWL, 137.

87. Halperin, *Saint Foucault*, 18–20; and Leo Bersani, *Homos* (Cambridge, Mass.: Harvard University Press, 1995), 81.

88. FWL, 135–36.

89. Michel Foucault, "The Ethics of the Concern for Self as a Practice of Freedom," in *Ethics: Subjectivity and Truth*, ed. Paul Rabinow, trans. Robert Hurley et al. (New York: Pantheon, 1984), 283.

90. Foucault, "Sex, Power," 163.

91. Heidegger, *Nietzsche*, I:129.

92. Nietzsche, *Twilight of the Idols*, VII:122–23, quoted in Heidegger, 96–97.

93. Bersani, *Homos*.

94. Ibid., also quoted in Tim Dean, "Sex and Syncope," *Raritan* 15 (1996): 78.

95. Dean, "Sex and Syncope," 76. By negotiating between Bersani's (based on *jouissance*) and Halperin's (the cultivation of pleasure of the impersonal self) ethical positions, Dean argues that in the age of the AIDS epidemic "the reconstructive phase must follow self-shattering if the outcome is to be anything other than suicide" ("Sex and Syncope," 77). What I am arguing is that this tension between self-shattering and reconstruction of the

alterative mode of being is what is at stake in the Foucauldian experimental ethos.

96. For an extensive discussion of Foucault's understanding of S/M practices as both the parodic subversion of sexual norms and as an invention of a new relation to one's body, see Halperin, *Saint Foucault*, 85–91. For a critique of Halperin's interpretation, see Dean, "Sex and Syncope," 73–75.

97. Foucault, "Sex, Power," 163.

98. Ibid.

99. Moore, "Frame of Discourse," 96, 101.

100. John Rajchman, *Truth and Eros* (New York: Routledge, 1991), 14.

101. Michel Foucault, "A Swimmer Between Two Words," in *Aesthetics, Method, and Epistemology*, ed. James D. Faubion, trans. Robert Hurley (New York: The New Press, 1998), 173.

## CHAPTER 2

1. For an informative discussion of Levinas's influence, see Lawrence Buell, "Introduction: In Pursuit of Ethics," *PMLA*, special issue "Ethics and Literary Study," ed. Lawrence Buell, 114 (1999): 7–19.

2. Ibid., 9.

3. The following works by Emmanuel Levinas will be cited parenthetically:

*BPW*: *Basic Philosophical Writings*, ed. Adriaan T. Peperzak, Simon Critchley, and Robert Bernasconi (Bloomington: Indiana University Press, 1996).

*DF*: *Difficult Freedom: Essays on Judaism*, trans. Seán Hand (Baltimore, Md.: Johns Hopkins University Press, 1990).

*LR*: *The Levinas Reader*, ed. Seán Hand (Oxford: Basil Blackwell, 1990).

*OB*: *Otherwise than Being or Beyond Essence*, trans. Alphonso Lingis (The Hague: Martinus Nijhoff, 1981).

*OS*: *Outside the Subject*, trans. Michel B. Smith (Stanford, Calif.: Stanford University Press, 1994).

*TI*: *Totality and Infinity*, trans. Alphonso Lingis (Pittsburgh, Pa.: Duquesne University Press, 1969).

*TO*: "The Trace of the Other," trans. Alphonso Lingis, in *Deconstruction in Context*, ed. Mark C. Taylor (Chicago: University of Chicago Press, 1986).

4. Simon Critchley, *The Ethics of Deconstruction: Derrida and Levinas* (Oxford: Blackwell, 1992), 179. Subsequent references to this text will be cited parenthetically as *ED*.

5. Tina Chanter, *Ethics of Eros: Irigaray's Rewriting of the Philosophers* (New York: Routledge, 1995), 207.

6. Susan A. Handelman, *Fragments of Redemption: Jewish Thought and Lit-*

*erary Theory in Benjamin, Scholem, and Levinas* (Bloomington: Indiana University Press, 1991), 254.

7. Elizabeth Grosz, *Volatile Bodies: Toward A Corporeal Feminism* (Bloomington: Indiana University Press, 1994), 98.

8. Chanter, *Ethics of Eros*, 198.

9. As Alphonso Lingis suggests, it is a noncoincidence between the epistemological function of sense perception and an ethical significance of the exposure to exteriority. See "The Sensuality and Sensibility," in *Face to Face with Levinas*, ed. Richard A. Cohen (Albany: SUNY Press, 1986), 220–21.

10. Luce Irigaray, *An Ethics of Sexual Difference*, trans. Carolyn Burke and Gillian C. Gill (Ithaca, N.Y.: Cornell University Press, 1993), 133. Subsequent references to this text will be cited parenthetically as *ESD*.

11. For an excellent discussion of Levinas's relation to Merleau-Ponty, see Robert Bernasconi, "One-Way Traffic: The Ontology of Decolonization and its Ethics," in *Ontology and Alterity in Merleau-Ponty*, eds. G. Johnson and M. Smith (Evanston, Ill.: Northwestern University Press, 1990), 67–80.

12. Handelman writes that for Levinas "the body itself is a paradigmatic example of an exteriority not constituted by my consciousness" (*Fragments of Redemption*, 253). Levinas's discussion of anachronism of bodily constitution is, however, more complex: the body can always be constituted by consciousness (and reduced to the status of the objective body), but it is this act of constitution that reveals the prior embodiment of consciousness itself.

13. Maurice Merleau-Ponty, "An Unpublished Text," in *The Primacy of Perception and Other Essays*, ed. James M. Edie, trans. Arleen B. Dallery (Evanston, Ill.: Northwestern University Press, 1964), 5. Merleau-Ponty stresses his indebtedness to Lacan's "Mirror Stage" in the essay "The Child's Relations with Others," in *Primacy of Perception* (136).

14. Maurice Merleau-Ponty, *The Visible and the Invisible*, ed. James M. Edie, Claude Lefort, and John Wild, trans. Alphonso Lingis (Evanston, Ill.: Northwestern University Press, 1990), 133.

15. In the seminar devoted to the ethics of psychoanalysis, Jacques Lacan uses the term "extimacy," or "intimate exteriority," to describe an equally paradoxical relation to *das Ding*, which is at the center of ethical experience. See *The Ethics of Psychoanalysis*, ed. Jacques-Alain Miller, trans. Dennis Porter (New York: W. W. Norton, 1992), 139. For Derrida's "transcendence within immanence," see Jacques Derrida, *Adieu: To Emmanuel Levinas*, trans. Pascale-Anne Brault and Michael Naas (Stanford, Calif.: Stanford University Press, 1999), 138.

16. For further discussion of Fanon's epidermal schema of ethical responsibility developed in the context of the trauma of racial oppression, see my article, "Rethinking Dispossession: On Being in One's Skin," forthcoming in *Parallax*.

17. Frantz Fanon, *Black Skin, White Masks*, trans. Charles Lam Markmann (New York: Grove Press, 1967), 232.

18. Ibid., 231.

19. Handelman, *Fragments of Redemption*, 259.

20. Jean-François Lyotard, "Levinas's Logic," in *The Lyotard Reader*, ed. Andrew Benjamin (Oxford: Basil Blackwell, 1989), 294.

21. Lingis, "Sensuality and Sensibility," 224.

22. Slavoj Žižek, *For They Know Not What They Do: Enjoyment as a Political Factor* (London: Verso, 1991), 231.

23. Simon Critchley, *Ethics, Politics, Subjectivity: Essays on Derrida, Levinas, and Contemporary French Thought* (London: Verso, 1999), 206.

24. Luce Irigaray, "The Fecundity of the Caress," trans. Carolyn Burke, in *Face to Face with Levinas*, ed. Richard A. Cohen (Albany: SUNY Press, 1986), 241.

25. Ibid., 247.

26. Derrida, *Adieu*, 121.

27. Irigaray, "Fecundity of the Caress," 255.

28. Luce Irigaray, "Questions to Emmanuel Levinas," in *The Irigaray Reader*, ed. Margaret Whitford, trans. David Macey (Oxford: Basil Blackwell, 1991), 181.

29. Irigaray, "Fecundity of the Caress," 242.

30. For an illuminating discussion of the temporality of the body in Levinas's ethics, see Handelman, *Fragments of Redemption*, 253.

31. For an excellent criticism of the centrality of the father/son relation in contemporary ethical theory, including Levinas's ethics, see Kelly Oliver, *Subjectivity Without Subjects: From Abject Fathers to Desiring Mothers* (Lanham, Md.: Rowman and Littlefield, 1998), 25–42.

32. Irigaray, "Fecundity of the Caress," 232–33.

33. For a discussion of the political and religious character of the state of Israel as the embodiment of "a prophetic morality and its peace," see, in particular, the collection of essays grouped under the titles of "Difficult Freedom" and "Zionisms," in *LR*, 248–88.

34. For instance, there is no reference to Levinas in the work of the most influential theorists of democracy such as Lefort, Laclau, and Mouffe. For the examples of the work influenced by Levinas, see Jacques Derrida, "Force of Law: The Mystical Foundation of Authority," trans. Mary Quaintance, in *Deconstruction and the Possibility of Justice*, ed. Drucilla Cornell, Michel Rosenfeld, and David Gray Carlson (New York: Routledge, 1992), 3–67 (subsequent references to this text will be cited parenthetically as FL); *ED*, 200–40; Drucilla Cornell, "The Philosophy of the Limit: Systems Theory and Feminist Legal Reform," in *Deconstruction and the Possibility of Justice* (New York: Routledge, 1992), 69–91, and especially *The Philosophy of the Limit* (New York: Routledge, 1992), 109–69; Iris Marion Young, *Intersecting Voices: Dilemmas of Gender, Political Philosophy, and Policy* (Princeton, N.J.: Princeton University Press, 1997), 39–60; and Bernasconi, "One-Way Traffic."

35. For instance, Patricia J. Williams, writing from the position of the oppressed, would contest the notion of obligation for the Other, in particular,
when the Other is placed in the position of privilege and mastery, at the expense of self-protection. See *The Alchemy of Race and Rights: Diary of a Law
Professor* (Cambridge, Mass.: Harvard University Press, 1991), 64; subsequent
references to this text will be cited parenthetically as *ARR*.

36. Bernasconi, "One-Way Traffic," 75–79.

37. Levinas poses this question in his response to the Marxist critique of
the ideology of morality. As Levinas points out, the critique of ideology, including that of morality, is motivated not just by the suspicion of reason but
by a response to the cry of the destitute, which as an ethical response exceeds
the concept of Marxism as a science ("Ideology and Idealism," in *LR*, 237–
38).

38. Chantal Mouffe, *The Return of the Political* (London: Verso, 1993), 32.
Subsequent references to this text will be cited parenthetically as *RP*.

39. This point has been made by the communitarian critics (Michel
Sandel, Alastair MacIntyre, and Charles Taylor) of the new liberal paradigm
accommodating distributive justice proposed by John Rawls in *A Theory of
Justice* (Cambridge, Mass.: Harvard University Press, 1971). As Mouffe
points out in her summary of this critique, "The arguments of Sandel against
the disembodied subject found in liberal philosophy are really pertinent and
there is a clear contradiction in wanting to found a theory of distributive justice upon the premises of liberal individualism" (*RP*, 30). For a recent creative revision of Rawls for feminist purposes in terms of "equal protection of
minimum conditions of individuation," see Drucilla Cornell, *In the Imaginary
Domain: Abortion, Pornography, and Sexual Harassment* (New York: Routledge,
1995), 13–27.

40. For two different attempts to rearticulate the models of radical and deliberative democracy in the context of proliferating differences, see two excellent collections, Chantal Mouffe, ed., *Dimensions of Radical Democracy: Pluralism, Citizenship, Community* (London: Verso, 1992); and Seyla Benhabib,
ed., *Democracy and Difference: Contesting the Boundaries of the Political* (Princeton, N.J.: Princeton University Press, 1996).

41. Seyla Benhabib, "The Democratic Moment and the Problem of Difference," in *Democracy and Difference: Contesting the Boundaries of the Political*,
ed. Seyla Benhabib (Princeton, N.J.: Princeton University Press, 1996), 8.

42. See, in particular, "The Concept of Enlightenment," in Max
Horkheimer and Theodor Adorno, *Dialectic of Enlightenment*, trans. John
Cumming (New York: Continuum, 1989), 3–42.

43. *ARR*, 19.

44. For an illuminating discussion of Williams's critique of property, see
Kelly Oliver, *Witnessing: Beyond Recognition* (Minneapolis: University of Minnesota Press, 2001).

45. We can find such an interpretation even in Critchley's work, which

is otherwise concerned with elaborating the signification of ethics for politics: "The problem of politics is that of delineating a form of political life that will repeatedly interrupt all attempts at totalization" (*ED*, 223).

46. Derrida, *Adieu*, 73.

47. Ibid., 76.

48. According to Critchley, "The immediacy of the ethical is always already mediated politically" (*ED*, 231).

49. Young, *Intersecting Voices*, 49–60.

50. As Marx argues, "None of the so-called rights of men goes beyond the egoistic man, the man withdrawn into himself, his private interests and his private choice, and separated from the community as a member of civil society." Rights are then "the justification of the egoistic man, man separated from his fellow men and from the community." See "On the Jewish Question," in *Writings of the Young Marx on Philosophy and Society*, ed. and trans. Loyd D. Easton and Kurt H. Guddat (New York: Doubleday, 1967), 236–37.

51. Jürgen Habermas, "Three Normative Models of Democracy," in *Democracy and Difference: Contesting the Boundaries of the Political*, ed. Seyla Benhabib (Princeton, N.J.: Princeton University Press, 1996), 26.

52. Levinas's and Williams's critique of liberalism reminds me here of Michael Sandel's point: "To view citizens first and foremost as objects of treatment, however fair, rather than agents of self-rule is to concede from the start a certain disempowerment, or loss of agency." See his *Democracy's Discontent: America in Search of a Public Philosophy* (Cambridge, Mass.: Harvard University Press, 1996), 27.

53. As Laclau and Mouffe argue, "It is never possible for individual rights to be defined in isolation, but only in the context of social relations which determine subject positions. . . . It is in this sense that the notion of 'democratic rights' must be understood, as these are rights which can only be exercised collectively." See *Hegemony and Socialist Strategy: Towards a Radical Democratic Politics* (London: Verso, 1985), 184.

54. bell hooks, *Outlaw Culture: Resisting Representations* (New York: Routledge, 1994), 244.

55. Isaiah Berlin, "Two Concepts of Liberty," in *Four Essays on Liberty* (Oxford: Oxford University Press, 1969). For the discussion of Berlin's notion of freedom, see *RP*, 37–38.

56. Lefort, *The Political Forms of Modern Society*, ed. John B. Thomson (Cambridge, Mass.: MIT Press, 1986), 260. Subsequent references to this text will be cited parenthetically as *PFMS*. Similarly, Chantal Mouffe claims that the framework of democracy makes it possible "for new rights to be claimed, and new meanings, new uses and new fields of application to be created for the ideas of liberty and equality." See "Democratic Politics Today," in *Dimensions of Radical Democracy: Pluralism, Citizenship, Community*, ed. Chantal Mouffe (London: Verso, 1992), 2.

57. Levinas's understanding of rights is similar to Drucilla Cornell's

analysis of the ethical assessment and reassessment of legal principles through the projection of the regulative ideal in the process of reconstruction of the law. See her *Transformations: Recollective Imagination and Sexual Difference* (New York: Routledge, 1993), 37–39.

58. Wendy Brown, *States of Injury: Power and Freedom in Late Modernity* (Princeton, N.J.: Princeton University Press, 1995), 99–134.

59. The "extra-territoriality" of rights repeats, therefore, what Derrida diagnoses as the aporia between infinite justice and calculable law (FL, 22).

60. As Drucilla Cornell argues, "iterability . . . makes consistency with precedent as exact replication *impossible* and, therefore, interpretation, change, and innovation *inevitable*" (*Transformations*, 38). For further discussion of the relevance of Derrida to legal theory, see her *Philosophy of the Limit*, 111, and "Philosophy of the Limit: Systems Theory and Feminist Legal Reform," 68–91.

61. Butler writes, "The law is no longer given in a fixed form, but is produced through citation as that which precedes and exceeds the mortal approximations enacted by the subject." See her *Bodies that Matter: On the Discursive Limits of "Sex"* (New York: Routledge, 1993), 14.

62. Jacques Derrida, "Signature, Event, Context," in *Margins of Philosophy*, trans. Alan Bass (Chicago: University of Chicago Press, 1982), 317.

63. Critchley notes, "One must not restrict oneself to conceiving of democracy as an existent political form (and, once again, certainly not as an apologetics for Western Liberal democracy). Rather, one must begin to think of democracy as a task, or project, to be attempted" (*ED*, 240).

64. For a discussion of Levinas's "messianic conception of justice," see Cornell, "Philosophy of the Limit: Systems Theory and Feminist Legal Reform," 87; and especially Handelman, *Fragments of Redemption*, 319–35.

65. Butler, *Bodies that Matter*, 193.

66. Derrida similarly argues, "Every time that . . . we placidly apply a good rule to a particular case, . . . we can be sure that law [*droit*] may find itself accounted for, but certainly not justice. Law is not justice. Law is the element of calculation, and it is just that there be just law, but justice is incalculable . . ." (FL, 16).

67. For an excellent discussion of the relationship between the absolute future and the past in Levinas's work, see Jill Robbins, *Altered Reading: Levinas and Literature* (Chicago: University of Chicago Press, 1999), 20–32.

68. Cornell, *Philosophy of the Limit*, 167.

69. For a discussion of a temptation and the ethical impossibility of murder, see Jill Robbins, *Prodigal Son / Elder Brother: Interpretation and Alterity in Augustine, Petrarch, Kafka, Levinas* (Chicago: University of Chicago Press, 1991), 130–31, 142–43; and Robbins, *Altered Reading*, 63–72.

70. For a lucid presentation of Levinas's position on violence, see John Llewelyn, *Emmanuel Levinas: The Genealogy of Ethics* (New York: Routledge, 1995), 142–45.

71. For further discussion of performative force in the context of Levinas's justice, see FL, 13, 26–27.

72. Jacques Derrida, "Violence and Metaphysics," in *Writing and Difference*, trans. Alan Bass (Chicago: University of Chicago Press, 1978), 117. Subsequent references to this text will be cited parenthetically as VM. For an excellent discussion of the relation between Derrida and Levinas, see the numerous essays by Robert Bernasconi, in particular, "Levinas and Derrida: The Question of the closure of Metaphysics," in *Face to Face with Levinas*, ed. Richard A. Cohen (Albany: SUNY Press, 1986), 181–202; Robert Bernasconi, "The Trace of Levinas in Derrida," in *Derrida and Difference*, ed. David Wood and Robert Bernasconi (Evanston, Ill.: Northwestern University Press, 1988), 13–29; and Robert Bernasconi, "Deconstruction and the Possibility of Ethics," in *Deconstruction and Philosophy*, ed. John Sallis (Chicago: University of Chicago Press, 1987), 122–39. See also Cornell, *Philosophy of the Limit*, 68–72, 105–12.

73. Robbins, *Altered Reading*, 11.

74. This interpretation is suggested by Seán Hand in his useful introduction to Levinas's essay, "Ideology and Idealism": "If ethics should be a victim of youthful rebellion, this is perhaps because rebellion is an eminently ethical activity" (*LR*, 235).

75. For this argument, see Derrida, *Adieu*, 92–95.

76. hooks, *Outlaw Culture*, 234.

77. Young, *Intersecting Voices*, 50. Young draws on Levinas and Irigaray in order to respond to Benhabib's model of communicative ethics and deliberative democracy based on the reversibility of perspectives and to propose an alternative model based on asymmetrical reciprocity.

78. For a discussion of the theme of paternity and ethics in Levinas's, Ricoeur's, and Derrida's work, see Kelly Oliver, "Fatherhood and the Promise of Ethics," *Diacritics* 27 (1997): 45–57. For a difference between Levinas's paternity and the Oedipal mode, see Handelman, *Fragments of Redemption*, 206.

79. For examples of maternal feminism, see Jean Bethke Elshtain, "Antigone's Daughters," *Democracy* 2 (1982): 46–59; and Sara Ruddick, "Maternal Thinking" *Feminist Studies* 6 (1980): 342–67. For a useful critique of this concept of citizenship, see Mary Dietz, "Context is All: Feminism and Theories of Citizenship," in *Dimensions of Radical Democracy: Pluralism, Citizenship, Community*, ed. Chantal Mouffe (London: Verso, 1992), 63–85.

80. For an excellent critique of both fraternity and sisterhood as models of political solidarity, see Anne Phillips, *Democracy and Difference* (University Park: Pennsylvania State University Press, 1993), 23–35.

81. hooks, *Yearning: Race, Gender, and Cultural Politics* (Boston: South End Press, 1990), 13.

82. Cornell, *Transformations*, 169.

83. hooks, *Outlaw Culture*, 244.

CHAPTER 3

1. Emmanuel Levinas, *Totality and Infinity*, trans. Alphonso Lingis (Pittsburgh, Pa.: Duquesne University Press, 1969), 21.

2. David Carroll, "Rephrasing the Political with Kant and Lyotard: From Aesthetic to Political Judgements," *Diacritics* (1984): 74–88, quote on 75.

3. Ernesto Laclau and Chantal Mouffe, *Hegemony and Socialist Strategy: Towards a Radical Democratic Politics* (London: Verso, 1994), 134–71.

4. For an excellent discussion of coalition politics from a feminist point of view, see Janet R. Jakobsen, *Working Alliances and the Politics of Difference: Diversity and Feminist Ethics* (Bloomington: Indiana University Press, 1998).

5. The following works by Jean-François Lyotard will be cited parenthetically:

CTGWB: "Can Thought Go on Without a Body?" *The Inhuman: Reflections on Time*, trans. Geoffrey Bennington and Rachel Bowlby (Stanford, Calif.: Stanford University Press, 1991).

D: *The Differend: Phrases in Dispute*, trans. Georges Van Den Abbeele (Minneapolis: University of Minnesota Press, 1988).

JG: *Just Gaming*, trans. Wlad Godzich (Manchester, England: Manchester University Press, 1985).

LL: "Levinas' Logic," trans. Ian McLeod, *Lyotard Reader*, ed. Andrew Benjamin (Oxford: Basil Blackwell, 1989).

TSWS: "One of the Things at Stake in Women's Struggles," trans. Deborah Clarke with Winifred Woodhull and John Mowitt, in *The Lyotard Reader*, ed. Andrew Benjamin (Oxford: Basil Blackwell, 1989).

PC: *The Postmodern Condition: A Report on Knowledge*, trans. Geoff Bennington and Brian Massumi (Minneapolis: University of Minnesota Press, 1984).

SH: "The Sign of History," trans. Geoff Bennington, in *Post-structuralism and the Question of History*, ed. Derek Attridge, Geoff Bennington, and Robert Young (London: Cambridge University Press, 1987).

6. Bill Readings defines differend as "the clash" of heterogeneous language games. See *Introducing Lyotard: Art and Politics* (New York: Routledge, 1991), 188.

7. The most drastic injustice occurs in the case of the victim, who in addition to the suffered wrong is divested of the means to argue his case. The differend marks here not only the incompatibility between the victim's idiom and the idiom of the judge but also the violent suppression of this incompatibility by the genre of litigation.

8. Readings aptly puts it, "Lyotard's later work is very much concerned with the distinction of the eventhood of the event (the 'it happens,' the *quid*) from its meaning or content ('what happens,' *quod*)" (*Introducing Lyotard*, xviii).

9. Stephen Watson, "The Adventures of the Narrative: Lyotard and the Passage of the Phantasm," in *Philosophy and Non-Philosophy Since Merleau-Ponty*, ed. Hugh Silverman (London: Routledge, 1988), 187–88.

10. Allen Dunn, "A Tyranny of Justice: The Ethics of Lyotard's Differend," *Boundary* 2, no. 20 (1993): 197.

11. Carroll, "Rephrasing the Political," 76.

12. Niklas Luhmann, "Speaking and Silence," *New German Critique*, special issue on Niklas Luhmann, 61 (1994): 25–37. What Luhmann means by "victimology" here, as William Rasch and Eva M. Knodt aptly put it, is Lyotard's attempt to link silence and the differend to the ethical imperative. William Rasch and Eva M. Knodt, "Systems Theory and the System of Theory," *New German Critique* 61 (1994): 3–7. In contrast, in Luhmann's purely descriptive framework, silence "serves the autopoiesis of communication," that is, its self-reproduction, because "it is recursively linked up to the network, that is, included" ("Speaking and Silence," 35).

13. Lyotard explains, "By terror I mean the efficiency gained by eliminating, or threatening to eliminate, a player from the language game one shares with him" (*PC*, 63).

14. For the incisive yet illuminating discussion of Lyotard's place in the debates over the status of modernity, in particular with respect to Habermas and Apel, see Wlad Godzich, "Afterword: Reading against Literacy," in Jean-François Lyotard, *The Postmodern Explained: Correspondence 1982–1985*, trans. Don Barry et al. (Minneapolis: University of Minnesota Press, 1993), 114–23.

15. The debate between Habermas and Lyotard has dominated many discussions of postmodernity and thus produced vast secondary literature. For insightful discussions of this debate, see, especially, Emilia Steuerman, "Habermas vs. Lyotard. Modernity vs. Postmodernity?" in *Judging Lyotard*, ed. Andrew Benjamin (London and New York: Routledge, 1992), 99–118; and Mark Poster, "Postmodernity and the Politics of Multiculturalism," *Modern Fiction Studies* 38 (1992): 567–80.

16. As Steuerman points out, Habermas wants to keep communicative action separate from strategic action, and thus from *polemos* ("Habermas vs. Lyotard," 105).

17. For the charges of victimology, see, for instance, Luhmann, "Speaking and Silence," 25–37. For the opposite criticism of indifference, see Dunn, "A Tyranny of Justice," 192–220.

18. See, for instance, Honi Fern Haber, "Lyotard and Pagan Politics," *Philosophy Today* (1995): 142–56. Haber writes that Lyotard's notion of justice does not necessarily "give voice to difference," because he disregards the fact that "since not all language games are equally empowered and language games are not pacific, they usually . . . entail the intrusion into another's space" (147).

19. Patricia J. Williams, *The Alchemy of Race and Rights: Diary of a Law Professor* (Cambridge, Mass.: Harvard University Press, 1991), 121.

20. Ibid., 48.

21. Michel Foucault, *Power/Knowledge: Selected Interviews and Other Writings 1972–1977*, ed. Colin Gordon, trans. Colin Gordon et al. (New York: Pantheon, 1980), 91.

22. As Lyotard writes in *The Postmodern Condition*, one can find a Nietzschean problematic already in Kant if one rereads antinomies as Kant's acknowledgment of the irreducible conflict of Reason with itself.

23. Levinas, *Totality and Infinity*, 23.

24. For a lucid discussion of the relation between the sublime and the sign of history, see Geoffrey Bennington, *Lyotard: Writing the Event* (New York: Columbia University Press, 1988), 165–69.

25. Dunn, "A Tyranny of Justice," 203–5.

26. Terry Eagleton, *The Ideology of the Aesthetic* (Oxford: Blackwell, 1994), 398. A similar, although much more nuanced, critique can be found in Honi Fern Haber's "Lyotard and the Problems of Pagan Politics," *Philosophy Today* (1995): 142–56. See also Haber's critique of Lyotard's politics in *Beyond Postmodern Politics: Lyotard, Rorty, Foucault* (New York: Routledge, 1994), 9–42.

27. Frederic Jameson, *The Political Unconscious: Narrative as a Socially Symbolic Act* (Ithaca, N.Y.: Cornell University Press, 1981), 35.

28. For a discussion of the limits of historical knowledge emphasized by Lyotard's revision of the sign of history, see Carroll, "Rephrasing the Political," 78.

29. Immanuel Kant writes, the "event would have to be considered not itself as the cause of history, but only as an intimation, an historical sign (*signum rememorativum, demonstrativum, prognostikon*)." See "An Old Question Raised Again: Is the Human Race Constantly Progressing?" in *Kant on History*, trans. Lewis White Beck et al. (New York: Bobbs-Merrill, 1963), 143.

30. Hannah Arendt writes, "The condition *sine qua non* for the existence of the beautiful objects is communicability; the judgment of the spectator creates a space without which no such objects would appear at all. The public realm is constituted by the critics and the spectators, not by the actors or the makers." See her *Lectures on Kant's Political Philosophy*, ed. Ronald Beiner (Chicago: University of Chicago Press, 1982), 63. For an illuminating comparison of Arendt's and Lyotard's positions, see David Ingram, "The Postmodern Kantianism of Arendt and Lyotard," in *Judging Lyotard*, ed. Andrew Benjamin (London: Routledge, 1992), 119–44.

31. Lyotard writes, "That, in a phrase universe, the referent be situated as a sign has a corollary that in this same universe the addressee is situated like someone who is affected" (*D*, 57).

32. To mark the inappropriateness of the term enthusiasm for "our history," Lyotard exposes the limits of the very concept of the sign and necessitates its revision as the differend. "Other names are now part of our history ... the preliminary question would be: are 'we' today still able to give cre-

dence to the concept of the sign of history?" In response to this question that occurs in the last chapter of *The Differend*, Lyotard claims that "[The differend] is not a sign. But it is to be judged, all the way through to its incomparability" (*D*, 181).

33. As Readings aptly puts it, the prescription to be just is incommensurable with the description of the true (*Introducing Lyotard*, 108). Furthermore, "the confusion of prescriptive justice" with "the descriptive *justification*" leads to injustice (*Introducing Lyotard*, 112).

34. While the logical critique contests the equivalence established between the specific obligation ("act in such a way") and the universal norm ("so that the maxim of your will will be valid as the principle of the universal legislation"), the pragmatic analysis criticizes the false correspondence between the addressee of obligation and the subject of enunciation, between "you ought to" and "I am able to."

35. Seyla Benhabib, *Situating the Self: Gender, Community and Postmodernism in Contemporary Ethics* (New York: Routledge, 1992), 204.

36. Ibid., 213.

37. Ibid., 229.

38. Seyla Benhabib, "Democracy and Difference: Reflections on the Metapolitics of Lyotard and Derrida," *The Journal of Political Philosophy* 2 (1994): 1–23.

39. Gayle Rubin, "The Traffic in Women," in *Toward an Anthropology of Women*, ed. Rayna R. Reiter (New York: Monthly Review Press, 1975), 160, also quoted in Nancy Fraser and Linda J. Nicholson, "Social Criticism Without Philosophy," in *Feminism/Postmodernism*, ed. Linda J. Nicholson (New York: Routledge, 1990), 28.

40. Fraser and Nicholson, "Social Criticism," 25.

41. Ibid., 24.

42. bell hooks, *Yearning: Race, Gender, and Cultural Politics* (Boston: South End Press, 1990), 21.

43. Fraser and Nicholson, "Social Criticism," 35.

44. hooks, *Yearning*, 26.

45. Ibid., 55.

46. Jean-François Lyotard, *Peregrinations: Law, Form, Event* (New York: Columbia University Press, 1988), 15.

47. For an excellent discussion of the shift in Lyotard's thought from the libidinal economy to the question of justice, see Watson, "Adventures of the Narrative," 174–89. While I agree with Watson's argument, I think we need to take into account the opposite movement in Lyotard's work, characteristic of the essays in *The Inhuman*, which seeks the analogon for the complexity of justice in the sexed body.

48. Jacques Lacan, *On Feminine Sexuality: The Limits of Love and Knowledge: Encore 1972–73*, trans. Bruce Fink (New York: W. W. Norton, 1998), 79.

49. Emmanuel Levinas, *Outside the Subject*, trans. Michel B. Smith (Stanford, Calif.: Stanford University Press, 1994).

50. For Lyotard, this concept of the body changes the relation between transcendence and immanence. What opens the possibility to transcend the given is no longer the fiction of metalanguage abstracted from the body and limited only by the needs of survival, but rather by the possibility of desire.

51. Mae Gwendolyn Henderson, "Speaking in Tongues: Dialogics, Dialectics, and the Black Woman Writer's Literary Tradition," in *Feminists Theorize the Political*, eds. Judith Butler and Joan W. Scott (New York: Routledge, 1992), 148. Subsequent references to this text will be cited parenthetically using the abbreviation ST.

CHAPTER 4

1. Judith Butler, *The Psychic Life of Power: Theories in Subjection* (Stanford, Calif.: Stanford University Press, 1997), 2–10.

2. Slavoj Žižek, *The Sublime Object of Ideology* (London: Verso, 1989), 124. Subsequent references to this text will be cited parenthetically as *SO*.

3. References to the following texts by Julia Kristeva will be cited parenthetically:

*DL: Desire in Language: A Semiotic Approach to Literature and Art*, ed. Leon S. Roudiez, trans. Leon S. Roudiez et al. (New York: Columbia University Press, 1980).

*PH: Powers of Horror: An Essay on Abjection*, trans. Leon S. Roudiez (New York: Columbia University Press, 1982).

PP: "Psychoanalysis and the Polis," trans. Margaret Waller, in *The Kristeva Reader*, ed. Toril Moi (New York: Columbia University Press, 1986).

*RPL: Revolution in Poetic Language*, trans. Leon S. Roudiez (New York: Columbia University Press, 1984).

*ST: Strangers to Ourselves*, trans. Leon S. Roudiez (New York: Columbia University Press, 1991).

*TL: Tales of Love*, trans. Leon S. Roudiez (New York: Columbia University Press, 1987).

WT: "Women's Time," trans. Alice Jardine and Harry Blake, in *The Kristeva Reader*, ed. Toril Moi (New York: Columbia University Press, 1986).

Subsequent references to Jacques Lacan, *The Seminar of Jacques Lacan: Book VII, The Ethics of Psychoanalysis*, ed. Jacques-Alain Miller, trans. Dennis Porter (New York: W. W. Norton, 1992) will be cited as *SVII*.

4. For a similar analysis of the psychic structure of racist ideology, see Juliet Flower MacCannell, "Fascism and the Voice of Conscience," in *Radical Evil*, ed. Joan Copjec (New York: Verso, 1996), 46–73, quote on 47.

5. Claude Lefort, *The Political Forms of Modern Society: Bureaucracy, Democracy, Totalitarianism*, ed. John B. Thompson (Cambridge, Mass.: MIT Press, 1986), 285. Subsequent references to this text will be cited parenthetically as *PFMS*.

6. As Rene Tostain similarly argues, "Anxiety is not the fear of an object but the confrontation of a subject with the lack of an object." See "Fetishization of a Phobic Object," in *How Lacan's Ideas Are Used in Clinical Practice*, ed. and trans. Stuart Schneiderman (London: Jason Aroson, 1993), 247–60, quote on 256.

7. Frantz Fanon, *Black Skin, White Masks*, trans. Charles Lam Markmann (New York: Grove Press, 1967), 154–55. Subsequent references to this text will be cited parenthetically as *BSWM*.

8. For a discussion of fascism as an integral part of the French intellectual tradition, see Zeev Sternhell, *Neither Right nor Left: Fascist Ideology in France*, trans. David Maisel (Berkeley and Los Angeles: University of California Press, 1986). For an excellent analysis of French nationalist fascism, see David Carroll, *French Literary Fascism: Nationalism, Anti-Semitism, and the Ideology of Culture* (Princeton, N.J.: Princeton University Press, 1995), 99–124.

9. For a discussion of the complexity of the reception of Céline among the fascist and leftist intellectuals, see Carroll, *French Literary Fascism*, 180–95; and Alice Yaeger Kaplan, *Reproductions of Banality: Fascism, Literature, and French Intellectual Life* (Minneapolis: University of Minnesota Press, 1986), 107–21. Kaplan points out that Simone de Beauvoir and Sartre "memorized passages from *Voyages au bout de la nuit* and chanted them to each other, much as the fascists . . . chant passages from *Bagatelles*" (118).

10. Despite crediting Kristeva for being one of the first critics to analyze Céline "with a sensitivity to both his poetry and his racism" (*Reproductions of Banality*, 10), Kaplan nonetheless argues that by "canonizing Céline with the modern primitivists, Kristeva saves him from fascism without having to deny his fascism or apologize for it" (*Reproductions of Banality*, 109). Similarly, Carroll claims that Kristeva's "powerful analysis of Céline's anti-Semitism and fascism and their intimate links" with his style "are limited by the privilege she assigns to literature and poetic language" (*French Literary Fascism*, 185). In my reading, Kristeva's interpretation of Céline is more complicated—rather than "rescuing" modernism or poetic language from fascism, she focuses on the collapse of avant-garde art into fascist ideology.

11. Kristeva's discussion of the phallic fantasy of the fusion with the maternal body supporting fascist ideology explains why "the maternal" and the "paternal" aspects of fascism cannot be separated. As Kaplan writes, "One can't 'decide' between the mother-bound and father-bound elements in fascism. They get bundled up in fascism's totalizing machinery" (*Reproductions of Banality*, 24).

12. Carroll, *French Literary Fascism*, 174.

13. Kristeva's discussion of "symptom" is similar here to Lacan's analysis

of "sinthome"—in both cases it is a signifying formation linked to enjoyment. For the interpretation of sinthome, see *SO*, 75–79.

14. For the Lacanian interpretation of the uncanny as the encounter with the real, see, for instance, Joan Copjec, *Read My Desire: Lacan Against the Historicists* (Cambridge, Mass.: MIT Press, 1994), 117–39; and Mladen Dolar, " 'I Shall Be with You on Your Wedding-Night': Lacan and the Uncanny," *October* 58 (1991): 6–23.

15. See, for instance, Dolar, " 'I Shall Be with You,' " 7.

16. This formulation recalls Lacan's argument that with the death of God, the prohibition of *jouissance* manifests itself dialectically in the horror of the *jouissance* of one's neighbor (*SVII*, 167–90).

17. The famous 1989 incident *"l'affaire du foulard"*—the expulsion from public school of the three young women from North African families who insisted on wearing head-scarves—is but one instance of the tensions accumulating around immigrants in France, especially around Islamic immigrants from North Africa. For a detailed discussion of the role of this incident as a background for Kristeva's texts, see Norma Claire Moruzzi, "National Abjects: Julia Kristeva on the Process of Political Self-identification," in *Ethics, Politics, and Difference in Julia Kristeva's Writing*, ed. Kelly Oliver (New York: Routledge, 1993), 136–42. My argument, however, in many ways opposes Moruzzi's reading, which, by ignoring the leading role of the Freudian concept of the uncanny in the structure of Kristeva's text, accuses her of "resorting to the traditional comforts of Enlightenment humanism" (140).

18. Copjec points out, "According to this reasoning . . . that which is impossible must also be negated" (*Read My Desire*, 121).

19. Slavoj Žižek, *Tarrying with the Negative: Kant, Hegel, and the Critique of Ideology* (Durham, N.C.: Duke University Press, 1993), 202.

20. Ibid., 222.

21. Benedict Anderson, *Imagined Communities: Reflections on the Origin and the Spread of Nationalism* (London: Verso, 1991), 141.

22. As Alice Jardine writes, Kristeva's "work intervenes at the intense intersection between this actively informed *fear* and our naively passive *belief* that Fascism and Stalinism cannot possibly return." See "Opaque Texts and Transparent Contexts: The Political Difference of Julia Kristeva," in *Ethics, Politics, and Difference in Julia Kristeva's Writing*, ed. Kelly Oliver (New York: Routledge, 1993), 25.

23. For an interesting discussion of "the negativization of narcissism," see ibid., 26.

24. The importance of the Kristevan ethics has been stressed, among others, by Drucilla Cornell, *Beyond Accommodation: Ethical Feminism, Deconstruction and the Law* (New York: Routledge, 1991), 42–73; Jardine, "Opaque Texts"; Jacqueline Rose, "Julia Kristeva—Take Two," Jean Graybeal, "Kristeva's Delphic Proposal: Practice Encompasses the Ethical," and Marilyn Edelstein, "Toward a Feminist Postmodern *Poléthique*: Kristeva on Ethics and

Politics," all found in *Ethics, Politics, and Difference in Julia Kristeva's Writing*, ed. Kelly Oliver (New York: Routledge, 1993). For a discussion of different models of "the outlaw" ethics in Kristeva's work—ethics of poetic language, ethics of maternal body, and ethics of psychoanalysis—see Kelly Oliver, *Reading Kristeva* (Bloomington: Indiana University Press, 1993), 8, 181–90. See also my "At the Limits of Discourse: Heterogeneity, Alterity, and the Maternal Body in Kristeva's Thought," *Hypatia* 7 (1992): 91–108.

25. I have initiated the negotiation between the ethics of psychoanalysis and the Levinasian ethics of responsibility in my "Kristeva and Levinas: Mourning, Ethics, and the Feminine," in *Ethics, Politics, and Difference in Julia Kristeva's Writing*, ed. Kelly Oliver (New York: Routledge, 1993), 62–78.

26. For a representative scope of this discussion, see the collection of essays, Sarah Harasym, ed., *Levinas and Lacan: The Missed Encounter* (Albany: SUNY Press, 1998).

27. Hans-Dieter Gondek, "*Cogito* and *Séparation*: Lacan/Levinas," in *Levinas and Lacan: The Missed Encounter*, ed. Sarah Harasym (Albany: SUNY Press, 1998), 31–32.

28. Emmanuel Levinas, "The Trace of the Other," trans. Alphonso Lingis, in *Deconstruction in Context: Literature and Philosophy*, ed. Mark Taylor (Chicago: University of Chicago Press, 1986), 346.

29. For a fine discussion of Lacan's figure of the stranger in the context of Levinas's ethics, see Kenneth Reinhard, "Kant with Sade, Lacan with Levinas," *Modern Language Notes* 110 (1995): 785–808; and Kenneth Reinhard, "Freud, My Neighbor," *American Imago* 54 (1997): 165–95.

30. Jacques Lacan, *Le Seminar, Livre VII: l'éthique de la psychanalyse* (Paris: Seuil, 1986), 70.

31. Although the relation between Lacan and Kristeva has not been sufficiently studied in Kristeva scholarship, the question of ethics provides a productive context for the engagement between these thinkers.

32. Silverman defines the active gift of love in the following way: "The active gift of love . . . implies both idealizing beyond the parameters of the 'self,' and doing so with a full understanding of one's own creative participation. . . . It means to *confer* ideality, not to *find* it." See *The Threshold of the Visible World* (New York: Routledge, 1996), 78.

33. Cornell writes, "Ironically, there is less room in the later Kristeva for the break-up of the symbolic through her subversive power of the feminine than there is in Lacan, precisely because the identification with the imaginary father is pushed back to the pre-Oedipal phase" (*Beyond Accommodation*, 69). Similarly, Rose sees the concept of the imaginary father "as race back into the arms of the law" ("Julia Kristeva," 48). In response, Kelly Oliver argues that the primary father is a screen for maternal love ("Kristeva's Imaginary Father and the Crisis in the Paternal Function," *Diacritics* 21 (1991): 43–63; and Oliver, *Reading Kristeva*, (69–90).

34. Judith Butler, "The Body Politics of Julia Kristeva," in *Gender Trou-*

*ble: Feminism and the Subversion of Identity* (New York: Routledge, 1990), 86–87. Although I fully agree with Butler's critique of "the hetero-pathos that pervades the legacy of Lacanian psychoanalysis and some of its feminist reformulations" as well as with her diagnosis that this privilege can be countered by making the symbolic more open to "the transformations under the pressure of social practices." See "Against Proper Objects," in *Feminism Meets Queer Theory*, ed. Elizabeth Weed and Naomi Schor (Bloomington: Indiana University Press, 1997), 23. I am more hesitant to locate the source of the problem in Kristeva's theory of the drives. Rather, the task for me is to think through the relation between the negativity of the drives and social practice as it is suggested in different ways by Kristeva, Irigaray, and Castoriadis.

35. For a critique of the ideological division between the maternal semiotic and the paternal symbolic, see Rose, "Julia Kristeva," 50.

36. Oliver, *Reading Kristeva*, 61. See also Rose's critique of the idealization and degradation of women ("Julia Kristeva," 51).

37. For a suggestive interpretation of Levinas's alterity in the context of *das Ding*, see Simon Critchley, *Ethics-Politics-Subjectivity* (London: Verso, 1998), 200–204, and "The Original Traumatism: Levinas and Psychoanalysis," in *Questioning Ethics: Contemporary Debates in Philosophy*, ed. Richard Kearney and Mark Dooley (London: Routledge, 1999), 230–42.

38. Emmanuel Levinas, *Otherwise than Being or Beyond Essence*, trans. Alphonso Lingis (The Hague: Martinus Nijhoff, 1981), 115.

39. As Lacan writes, sublimation allows the subject to fashion a signifier "in the image of the Thing, whereas the Thing is characterized by the fact that it is impossible for us to imagine it" (*SVII*, 125).

40. Critchley, *Ethics-Politics-Subjectivity*, 204.

41. Joan Copjec, "The Body Immortal," plenary address at the American Lacanian Link Conference, "The Subject-*Encore*," University of California, Los Angeles, Mar. 5–7, 1999.

42. As Rose puts it, *Tales of Love* "is no idyll" because of the ambivalence of love and hate that it emphasizes ("Julia Kristeva," 55).

43. See Rose, "Julia Kristeva." Similarly, Oliver argues that Kristeva's "concern is to link the ethical with negativity so that it won't degenerate into either conformity or perversion" (*Reading Kristeva*, 181).

44. Since Kristeva redefines drive in terms of the negativity of force, her discussion of the irruption of the death drive within the symbolic provides a certain mediation between what Foucault describes as the relation to the outside and Lacan as the relation to the real.

45. Butler, "Against Proper Objects," 23.

46. Chantal Mouffe, "Democratic Politics Today," in *Dimensions of Radical Democracy: Pluralism, Citizenship, Community*, ed. Chantal Mouffe (London: Verso, 1992), 11.

47. Slavoj Žižek, "Beyond Discourse Analysis," in Ernesto Laclau, *New Reflections on the Revolution of Our Time* (London: Verso, 1990), 249–60; and

Rey Chow, *Ethics After Idealism: Theory, Cultures, Ethnicity, Reading* (Bloomington: Indiana University Press, 1998), 33–54.

48. Karl Marx, "On the Jewish Question," in *Writings of the Young Marx on Philosophy and Society*, ed. and trans. Loyd D. Easton and Kurt H. Guddat (Garden City, N.Y.: Anchor Books, 1967), 217.

49. Joan Copjec, "The Subject Defined by Suffrage," *Lacanian Ink* 7 (1993): 47–58. Wary that the predominant discourse of historicism might reduce the subject of democracy merely to the number of discursive positions it occupies, Copjec argues that Lefort's formulation of the "right to have rights" "is strictly equivalent to the Lacanian notion of the 'desire to desire.'" She concludes, "A democracy can be defined, then, as that form of society that continuously inscribes the impossibility of inscribing the subject" ("Subject Defined," 53). For further comparison of Lefort's and Lacan's conception of the symbolic character of power, see Copjec, *Read My Desire*, 160–61.

50. Mouffe, "Democratic Politics Today," 9–10.

51. William E. Connolly, *Why I Am Not a Secularist* (Minneapolis: University of Minnesota Press, 1999).

52. As if echoing Kristeva's logic of abjection, Mouffe similarly argues that modern radical democracy occupies a precarious and ambiguous space of in-between: "Between the project of a complete equivalence and the opposite one of pure difference, the experience of modern democracy consists in acknowledging the existence of these contradictory logics and as well as the necessity of their articulation. . . . It is only in that precarious space 'in-between' that pluralist democracy can exist" ("Democratic Politics Today," 43–44).

53. In a sense, Paul Smith is right that there is a certain shift in Kristeva's work away from the dialectical understanding of practice, although I do not agree with the political consequences he draws from it. See *Discerning the Subject* (Minneapolis: University of Minnesota Press, 1988), 130. I articulate this shift as a move from determinate negation to reflective judgment. We have to note, however, that even in her early work Kristeva criticizes the closed nature of the dialectic and the subordination of negativity to totality.

54. Dominick LaCapra, *Representing the Holocaust: History, Theory, Trauma* (Ithaca, N.Y.: Cornell University Press, 1994), 208–14.

55. For my earlier discussion of the relation between Arendt and Kristeva, see "The Uncanny Style of Kristeva's Critique of Nationalism," *Postmodern Culture* 5 (1995).

56. Hannah Arendt, *Lectures on Kant's Political Philosophy*, ed. Ronald Beiner (Chicago: University of Chicago Press, 1982).

57. Arendt argues, "The it-pleases-or-displeases-me, which as a feeling seems so utterly private and noncommunicative, is actually rooted in a community of sense and is therefore open to communication once it has been transformed by reflection, which takes all others and their feelings into account" (*Lectures*, 72). For an excellent discussion of Arendt's concept of cit-

254 NOTES TO CHAPTER 4

izenship, see Maurizio Passerin d'Entrèves, "Hannah Arendt and the Idea of Citizenship," in *Dimensions of Radical Democracy: Pluralism, Citizenship, Community*, ed. Chantal Mouffe (London: Verso, 1992), 145–68.

58. Julia Kristeva, "Hannah Arendt: Life as Narrative," plenary address, International Association of Philosophy and Literature, Hartford, Conn., May 11–15, 1999.

59. Ibid.

60. Jean-Luc Nancy, *The Inoperative Community*, ed. Peter Connor, trans. Peter Connor et al. (Minneapolis: University of Minnesota Press, 1991).

61. For an interesting discussion of Arendt's theory of judgment and of the controversies her theory has created, see Passerin d'Entrèves, "Hannah Arendt," 101–38.

62. Kristeva's work has produced many controversies and debates among feminist critics, who vary greatly in the assessment of the usefulness of her theory. While acknowledging the limitations of Kristeva's work, Rose, like Kelly Oliver and Tina Chanter, argues that "Kristeva gives to women the privilege of the central dilemma . . . : how to challenge the very form of available self-definition without losing the possibility of speech." See Rose, "Julia Kristeva," 54; Oliver, *Reading Kristeva*, 2–16; and Chanter, "Kristeva's Politics of Change," in *Ethics, Politics, and Difference in Julia Kristeva's Writing*, ed. Kelly Oliver (New York: Routledge, 1993), 179–95. In contrast, Judith Butler and Ann Rosalind Jones see Kristeva's politics as "self-defeating." See Butler, *Gender Trouble*, 80–81; and Jones, "Julia Kristeva on Femininity: The Limits of a Semiotic Politic," *Feminist Review* 18 (1984): 46–73. Nancy Fraser is concerned that Kristeva's negative approach to social relations "cannot figure in the reconstruction of the new, politically constituted, *collective* identities and solidarities that are essential to feminist politics." See "The Uses and Abuses of French Discourse Theories for Feminist Politics," *Boundary 2*, no. 17 (1990): 98. For Drucilla Cornell the limitation of Kristeva's semiotic is that it collapses the distinction between the feminine and the mother; see her *Transformations: Recollective Imagination and Sexual Difference* (New York: Routledge, 1993), 81. Lynne Huffer argues that Kristeva's works "in fact conform to a conservative ideology of individual possession and imperialist expansion," in *Maternal Pasts, Feminist Futures: Nostalgia, Ethics, and the Question of Difference* (Stanford, Calif.: Stanford University Press, 1998), 76. This argument has been made most strongly by Gayatri Chakravorty Spivak in "French Feminism in an International Frame," *Yale French Studies* 62 (1981): 154–84. For a synopsis of Kristeva's relation to feminism, see Oliver, *Reading Kristeva*, 152–62; and Martha J. Reineke, *Sacrificed Lives: Kristeva on Women and Violence* (Bloomington: Indiana University Press, 1997), 33–48.

63. Juliet Flower MacCannell, *The Regime of the Brother: After the Patriarchy* (London: Routledge, 1991).

64. For an insightful synopsis of the dilemmas of egalitarian feminism, see,

for example, Elizabeth Grosz, *Volatile Bodies: Toward a Corporeal Feminism* (Bloomington: Indiana University Press, 1994), 15–16.

65. Nancy Fraser, *Justice Interruptus: Critical Reflections on the "Postsocialist" Condition* (New York: Routledge, 1997).

66. See, for instance, Mouffe, "Democratic Politics Today," 1–10.

67. Butler points out, "Kristeva does not challenge the structuralist assumption that the prohibitive paternal law is foundational to culture itself" and she restricts the function of this law to prohibition (*Gender Trouble*, 86).

68. I see this task elaborated in a number of recent books rethinking the body beyond the sex/gender divide. See, among others, Judith Butler, *Bodies that Matter: On the Discursive Limits of Sex* (New York: Routledge, 1993); Moira Gatens, *Imaginary Bodies: Ethics, Power and Corporeality* (London: Routledge, 1996); and Grosz, *Volatile Bodies*. In this context it is interesting to consider Chanter's diagnosis that the widespread reluctance to accept Kristeva's distinction between the semiotic and the symbolic stems from "an unspoken feminist commitment to the ideology of sex and gender" ("Kristeva's Politics of Change," 185).

69. For a discussion of the imaginary and revolt, see Julia Kristeva, "Revolt Today," in *Questioning Ethics: Contemporary Debates in Philosophy*, ed. Richard Kearney and Mark Dooley (London: Routledge, 1998), 220–29.

70. In contrast to these criticisms, Iris Young advances quite a different interpretation of Kristeva's politics. In her influential essay, "The Ideal of Community and the Politics of Difference," Young focuses precisely on what kind of a reconstruction of social relations could emerge from Kristeva's notion of the subject as a heterogeneous process. According to this reading, Kristeva's theory allows for a reconceptualization of group solidarity and political community beyond the notion of collective identity. For Young this different sense of belonging together corresponds to a politics of difference.

71. Kristeva, "Revolt Today," 227.

72. Smith, *Discerning the Subject*, 130; and Paul Smith, "Julia Kristeva ET AL; or Take Three or More," in *Feminism and Psychoanalysis*, ed. Richard Feldstein and Judith Roof (Ithaca, N.Y.: Cornell University Press, 1989), 84–104.

73. Fraser, "Uses and Abuses," 98.

74. Rose, "Julia Kristeva," 53.

75. Žižek, "Beyond Discourse Analysis," 249–60; and Chow, *Ethics After Idealism*, 33–54.

## CHAPTER 5

1. For the discussion of Luce Irigaray's ethics in the context of sexual difference and relations to others, see Rosalyn Diprose, *The Bodies of Women: Ethics, Embodiment and Sexual Difference* (London: Routledge, 1994), 32–37.

2. For the diverse critiques of sex/gender divide, see Judith Butler, *Gen-*

*der Trouble: Feminism and the Subversion of Identity* (New York: Routledge, 1990), and *Bodies that Matter: On the Discursive Limits of "Sex"* (New York: Routledge, 1993); Tina Chanter, *Ethics of Eros: Irigaray's Rewriting of the Philosophers* (New York: Routledge, 1995), 21–45; Moira Gatens, *Imaginary Bodies: Ethics, Power and Corporeality* (London: Routledge, 1996), 3–20; and Lynne Huffer, *Maternal Pasts, Feminist Futures: Nostalgia, Ethics, and the Question of Difference* (Stanford, Calif.: Stanford University Press, 1998), 96–114.

3. For diverse interrogations of sexual difference in the context of race and queer theory, see, among others, bell hooks, *Feminist Theory: From Margin to Center* (Boston: South End Press, 1984), and *Yearning: Race, Gender, and Cultural Politics* (Boston: South End Press, 1990); Hortense J. Spillers, " 'The Permanent Obliquity of an In[pha]llibly Straight': In the Time of the Daughters and the Fathers," in *Daughters and Fathers*, ed. Lynda E. Boose and Betty S. Flowers (Baltimore, Md.: Johns Hopkins University Press, 1989), and "Mama's Baby, Papa's Maybe: An American Grammar Book," *Diacritics* 17 (1987): 65–81; Valerie Smith, "Black Feminist Theory and the Representation of the Other," in *Changing Our Own Words: Essays on Criticism, Theory, and Writing by Black Women*, ed. Cheryl Wall (New Brunswick, N.J.: Rutgers University Press, 1989), 38–57; Elizabeth V. Spelman, *Inessential Woman: Problems of Exclusion in Feminist Thought* (Boston: Beacon Press, 1988); Evelynn Hammonds, "Black (W)holes and the Geometry of Black Female Sexuality," *differences: A Journal of Feminist Cultural Studies* 6 (1994): 126–45, reprinted in *Feminism Meets Queer Theory*, ed. Elizabeth Weed and Naomi Schor (Bloomington: Indiana University Press, 1997), 136–56; Deborah E. McDowell, *"The Changing Same": Black Women's Literature, Criticism, and Theory* (Bloomington: Indiana University Press, 1995), 156–75; Ellen T. Armour, *Deconstruction, Feminist Theology, and the Problem of Difference: Subverting the Race/Gender Divide* (Chicago: University of Chicago Press, 1999); Butler, *Bodies that Matter*; Gayle Rubin, "Thinking Sex: Notes for a Radical Theory of the Politics of Sexuality," in *The Lesbian and Gay Studies Reader*, ed. Henry Abelove, Michèle Aina Barale, and David M. Halperin (New York: Routledge, 1993), 3–44; and the essays in the collection *Feminism Meets Queer Theory*, ed. Elizabeth Weed and Naomi Schor.

4. Pheng Cheah and Elizabeth Grosz, "Of Being-Two: Introduction," *Diacritics*, special issue, "Irigaray and the Political Future of Sexual Difference," ed. Pheng Cheah and Elizabeth Grosz, 28 (1998): 3.

5. Ann DuCille, "The Occult of True Black Womanhood: Critical Demeanor and Black Feminist Studies," in *Female Subjects in Black and White*, eds. Elizabeth Abel, Barbara Christian, and Helene Moglen (Berkeley and Los Angeles: University of California Press, 1997), 21–55; hooks, *Yearning*, 21, 23–31; Smith, 38–57; and McDowell, *"Changing Same"*, 156–75. Like McDowell and Smith, hooks argues that white feminism appropriates black feminist thought either by relegating it to "the realm of the experiential" or by limiting it only to the discussion of race (*Yearning*, 21).

6. Elizabeth Abel, "Race, Class, and Psychoanalysis," in *Conflicts in Feminism*, ed. Marianne Hirsch and Evelyn Fox Keller (New York: Routledge, 1990), 184–204; Rosi Braidotti, *Nomadic Subjects: Embodiment and Sexual Difference in Contemporary Feminist Thought* (New York: Columbia University Press, 1994); Joan Copjec, *Read My Desire: Lacan Against the Historicists* (Cambridge, Mass.: MIT Press, 1994); Slavoj Žižek, *Tarrying with the Negative: Kant, Hegel, and the Critique of Ideology* (Durham, N.C.: Duke University Press, 1993), 45–80; Slavoj Žižek, *The Ticklish Subject: The Absent Center of Political Ontology* (London: Verso, 1999), 247–400; Chanter, *Ethics of Eros*, 21–45; Drucilla Cornell, *Beyond Accommodation: Ethical Feminism, Deconstruction, and the Law* (New York: Routledge, 1991), 119–206, and *Transformations: Recollective Imagination and Sexual Difference* (New York: Routledge, 1993), 170–94; Jacqueline Rose, *Sexuality in the Field of Vision* (London: Verso, 1986), and "Introduction II," in *Feminine Sexuality: Jacques Lacan and the École Freudienne*, ed. Juliet Mitchell and Jacqueline Rose, trans. Jacqueline Rose (New York: W. W. Norton, 1983), 27–59.

7. Spillers, "Mama's Baby, Papa's Maybe," 65–81; Hammonds, "Black (W)holes," 136–56; and Claudia Tate, *Psychoanalysis and Black Novels: Desire and the Protocols of Race* (Oxford: Oxford University Press, 1997). See also the collection of essays in Christopher Lane, ed., *The Psychoanalysis of Race* (New York: Columbia University Press, 1998).

8. The earlier version of this section, entitled "Toward a Radical Female Imaginary: Temporality and Embodiment," appeared in *Diacritics* 28 (1998): 60–75. My inquiry into Irigaray's ethics has been inspired by Elizabeth Grosz's keynote address, "Thinking the New: Of Futures Yet Unthought," delivered at the 1996 American Comparative Literature Association, University of Notre Dame, and published in *Future Crossings: Literature Between Philosophy and Cultural Studies*, ed. Krzysztof Ziarek and Seamus Deane (Evanston, Ill.: Northwestern University Press, 2000).

9. References to the following texts by Luce Irigaray will be cited parenthetically:

*ESD*: *An Ethics of Sexual Difference*, trans. Carolyn Burke and Gillian C. Gill (Ithaca, N.Y.: Cornell University Press, 1984).

*ÉDS*: *Éthnique de la différence sexuelle* (Paris: Les Éditions de Minuit, 1984).

*ILTY*: *I Love to You: Sketch of a Possible Felicity in History*, trans. Alison Martin (New York: Routledge, 1996).

*JA*: *J'aime á toi* (Paris: Grasset, 1992).

*JLI*: " 'Je-Luce Irigaray': A Meeting with Luce Irigaray," Interview with Elizabeth Hirsh and Gary O. Olson, trans. Elizabeth Hirsh and Ga'ton Brulotte, *Hypatia* 10 (1995): 93–114.

*TS*: *This Sex Which Is Not One*, trans. Catherine Porter (Ithaca, N.Y.: Cornell University Press, 1984).

Subsequent references to Jacques Lacan, *The Seminar of Jacques Lacan: Book VII, The Ethics of Psychoanalysis*, ed. Jacques-Alain Miller, trans. Dennis Porter (New York: W. W. Norton, 1992) will be cited as *SVII*.

10. See Copjec, *Read My Desire*.

11. Valerie Smith points out, "Male-authored Afro-Americanist criticism assumed a conception of blackness that concealed its masculinist presuppositions; Anglo-or-Euro-centered feminism relied upon a notion of gender that concealed its presumption of whiteness." See her "Split Affinities: The Case of Interracial Rape," in *Conflicts in Feminism*, ed. Marianne Hirsch and Evelyn Fox Keller (New York: Routledge, 1990), 271. For related criticism, see, among others, Spelman, *Inessential Woman*, 75; Armour, *Deconstruction*, 166–67; and hooks, who diagnoses a widespread "failure to recognize a critical black presence in culture and in most scholarship and writing on postmodernism" (*Yearning*, 24).

12. hooks, *Yearning*, 54.

13. Armour argues, "White feminism has erected itself in and through the exclusion of its raced others and its own race" (*Deconstruction*, 166).

14. Žižek, *Ticklish Subject*, 273.

15. Both Copjec and Rose stress the fact that sexual difference indicates the direction of the failure of meaning (Copjec, *Read My Desire*, 204–7; and Rose, "Introduction," 43).

16. Judith Butler, "Against Proper Objects," in *Feminism Meets Queer Theory*, ed. Elizabeth Weed and Naomi Schor (Bloomington: Indiana University Press, 1997), 23.

17. Even though I concede the persistence of the heterosexual pathos in Irigaray's work, I disagree with Butler's claim that Irigaray's later work offers merely a theory of heterosexuality; see Butler, "The Future of Sexual Difference: An Interview with Judith Butler and Drucilla Cornell," *Diacritics* 28 (1998): 19–42.

18. For one of the most suggestive discussions of the numerous sources of Irigaray's revision of the imaginary, see Margaret Whitford, *Luce Irigaray: Philosophy in the Feminine* (London: Routledge, 1991), 53–74. As Whitford points out, "Castoriadis's theoretization of the imaginary as a primordial creative source or magma, and the imaginary as social formation is probably closest to Irigaray's imaginary" (56). For a sustained discussion of the "imaginary" as "images, symbols, metaphors, and representations" through which "we make sense of social bodies and which determine, in part, their value," see Gatens, *Imaginary Bodies*, viii–xiv, 146–51.

19. Whitford suggests, "Like Castoriadis . . . [Irigaray] is arguing that radical transformation in the social imaginary *could* take place" (*Luce Irigaray*, 69).

20. Referring to the rather protracted debate of essentialism in Irigaray's work, the term "language of essence" comes from Diana Fuss, *Essentially Speaking* (New York: Routledge, 1989), 55.

21. Jacques Lacan, "Some Reflections on the Ego," *The International Jour-*

*nal of Psycho-analysis* 34 (1953): 15, quoted in Richard Boothby, "The Psychological Meaning of Life and Death: Reflections on the Lacanian Imaginary, Symbolic, and Real," in *Disseminating Lacan*, ed. David Pettigrew and François Raffoul (Albany: SUNY Press, 1996), 350.

22. Jacques Lacan, *Écrits: A Selection*, trans. Alan Sheridan (New York: W. W. Norton, 1982), 21.

23. Boothby, "Psychological Meaning of Life and Death," 349.

24. Cornelius Castoriadis, *The Imaginary Institution of Society*, trans. Kathleen Blamey (Cambridge, Mass.: MIT Press, 1987), 145. Subsequent references to this text will be cited parenthetically as *IIS*.

25. Žižek, *Tarrying with the Negative*, 215.

26. Slavoj Žižek, *The Sublime Object of Ideology* (London: Verso, 1989), 124.

27. For the discussion of becoming, see Rosi Braidotti, "Of Bugs and Women: Irigaray and Deleuze on the Becoming-Woman," in *Engaging with Irigaray*, ed. Carolyn Burke, Naomi Schor, and Margaret Whitford (New York: Columbia University Press, 1994), 111–39.

28. Christine Holmlund, "The Lesbian, the Mother, and the Heterosexual Lover," *Feminist Studies* 17 (1991): 296.

29. For an informative discussion of the reception of Irigaray, see Naomi Schor, "Previous Engagements: The Reception of Irigaray," in *Engaging with Irigaray*, ed. Carolyn Burke, Naomi Schor, and Margaret Whitford (New York: Columbia University Press, 1994), 3–14. For an analysis of utopianism in Irigaray feminist practice, see Cornell, *Beyond Accommodation*, 106, 167–69; and Margaret Whitford, "Irigaray, Utopia, and Death Drive," in *Engaging with Irigaray*, ed. Carolyn Burke, Naomi Schor, and Margaret Whitford (New York: Columbia University Press, 1994), 379–400. For a critique of Irigaray's disregard for the differences among women, see Butler, *Bodies that Matter*, 48–49. Butler repeats Gayatri Spivak's criticism that French feminism fails to address the other articulations of differences; see Gayatri Chakravorty Spivak, *In Other Worlds: Essays in Cultural Politics* (New York: Routledge, 1988), 150. Similar problems in Irigaray's work can be observed in the context of lesbian politics. For an informative analysis of this issue, see Holmlund, "The Lesbian, the Mother"; and Elizabeth Grosz, "The Hetero and the Homo: The Sexual Ethics of Luce Irigaray," in *Engaging with Irigaray*, ed. Carolyn Burke, Naomi Schor, and Margaret Whitford (New York: Columbia University Press, 1994), 335–50.

30. For W. E. B. Du Bois's famous discussion of seeing oneself through the look of the white other, see *The Souls of Black Folk* (New York: Signet, 1989), 2–3. See also Frantz Fanon's discussion of the traumatic effects of the white gaze in *Black Skin, White Masks*, trans. Charles Lam Markmann (New York: Grove Press, 1967), 109–40; Hortense J. Spillers's discussion of specularity of race in "All the Things You Could Be by Now If Sigmund Freud's Wife Was Your Mother," *Critical Inquiry* 22 (1996): 726; Patricia J. Williams,

*The Alchemy of Race and Rights: Diary of a Law Professor* (Cambridge, Mass.: Harvard University Press, 1991); and bell hooks, *Black Looks: Race and Representation* (Boston: South End Press, 1992). For the account that links Irigaray's critique of the specular economy of female sexuality with the specular economy of race, see Armour, *Deconstruction*, 103–36.

31. Fanon, *Black Skin, White Masks*, 160.

32. See Michele Wallace, *Invisibility Blues: From Pop to Theory* (London: Verso, 1990); and Charles W. Mills, *Blackness Visible: Essays on Philosophy and Race* (Ithaca, N.Y.: Cornell University Press, 1998), 10–19.

33. For a discussion of this oppressive "hypervisibility," see, for instance, Hammonds, "Black (W)holes," 145.

34. For the different constructions of white and black women's sexuality, see, in particular, Patricia Hill Collins, *Black Feminist Thought: Knowledge, Consciousness, and the Politics of Empowerment* (London: Harper Collins Academic Press, 1990); Spillers, "Mama's Baby, Papa's Maybe"; and Smith, "Split Affinities," 271–87. For the "psychosexual history" of race rooted in slavery, see hooks, *Yearning*, 57–65.

35. Smith, "Split Affinities," 275.

36. Hammonds, "Black (W)holes," 142.

37. As Debra Bergoffen suggests, for Irigaray the move from the imaginary violence to its symbolic mediation under the Name of the Father, means that "aggression is transformed . . . to a subtle war of men against women." "Queering the Phallus," in *Disseminating Lacan*, ed. David Pettigrew and François Raffoul (Albany: SUNY Press, 1996), 287.

38. Fanon, *Black Skin, White Masks*, 218.

39. For a critical assessment of the essentialism/antiessentialism debate in the reception of Irigaray, see, among others, Fuss, *Essentially Speaking*, 55–65; Naomi Schor, "Previous Engagements: The Receptions of Irigaray," 3–14, and Naomi Schor, "This Essentialism Which Is Not One: Coming to Grips with Irigaray," 57–78, both in *Engaging with Irigaray*, ed. Carolyn Burke, Naomi Schor, and Margaret Whitford (New York: Columbia University Press, 1994); Cornell, *Beyond Accommodation*, 167–85; Jane Gallop, *Thinking Through the Body* (New York: Columbia University Press, 1988), 92–99; and Chanter, *Ethics of Eros*, 21–46. For the relevance of this debate to the rethinking of racial difference, see Armour, *Deconstruction*, 16–30, 38–44, 102–11.

40. See Gallop's eloquent argument stressing the rhetoricity of the body (*Thinking Through the Body*, 92–100).

41. For an illuminating discussion of Irigaray's reading of Plato, see Butler, *Bodies that Matter*, 36–49; and Huffer, *Maternal Pasts, Feminist Futures*, 55–69. Chanter offers an insightful interpretation of Irigaray's reading of Aristotle's concept of space (*Ethics of Eros*, 151–59).

42. For an illuminating discussion of Foucault and Irigaray, see Diprose, *Bodies of Women*, 18–37.

43. For a discussion of Irigaray's engagement with Heidegger, see Joanna Hodge, "Irigaray Reading Heidegger," 191–210, and Ellen Mortensen, "Woman's Untruth and *le feminin*: Reading Luce Irigaray with Nietzsche and Heidegger," 211–28, both in *Engaging with Irigaray*, ed. Carolyn Burke, Naomi Schor, and Margaret Whitford (New York: Columbia University Press, 1994); and Chanter, *Ethics of Eros*, 127–45, 167–69. For an interpretation of the importance of the event in Irigaray and Heidegger, see Krzysztof Ziarek, "Between *Techne* and *Poiesis*: Irigaray on Sexuate Experience," in the 1996 IAPL volume, *Thinking Culture, Thinking Drama* (Chicago: Northwestern University Press, forthcoming).

44. For an illuminating discussion of the revolutionary rupture as model of repetition, that is, as the retrospective fulfillment of the failed revolutionary attempts in the past, see Žižek, *Sublime Object*, 137–42. Žižek's interpretation of the temporality of the future perfect in both Benjamin's notion of history and in the transferential situation would contest Irigaray's argument about Freud's forgetting of the disruptive temporality of the event.

45. For an illuminating discussion of the difference between gender and sexual difference, see Charles Shepherdson, "The *Role* of Gender and the *Imperative* of Sex," in *Vital Signs: Nature, Culture, Psychoanalysis* (New York: Routledge, 2000), 85–115.

46. Margaret L. Andersen and Patricia Hill Collins, "Preface," in *Race, Class, and Gender*, 2d ed., ed. Margaret L. Andersen and Patricia Hill Collins (Belmont, Calif.: Wadsworth PC, 1995), xiv.

47. Ibid., xiv, xv.

48. For an interesting discussion of this disjunction in postmodernism, see John D. Caputo, *Against Ethics* (Bloomington: Indiana University Press, 1993), 60.

49. For a critique of the primacy of the heterosexual model in Irigaray's work, see "The Future of Sexual Difference: An Interview with Judith Butler and Drucilla Cornell"; for an alternative reading of Irigaray, see Huffer, *Maternal Pasts, Feminist Futures*, 55–69, 110–14.

50. Butler, "Future of Sexual Difference," 28.

51. As Pheng Cheah and Elizabeth Grosz suggest, sexual difference does not exclude same-sex desire but poses the following question: "What would same-sex desire be like if it were based on the ethical acknowledgment of sexual difference?" ("Of Being-Two," 14).

52. Ibid., 13.

53. Jacques Lacan, *The Four Fundamental Concepts of Psychoanalysis, Seminar XI*, ed. Jacques-Alain Miller, trans. Alan Sheridan (New York: W. W. Norton, 1981), 276. Subsequent references will be cited parenthetically as *SXI*.

54. Emmanuel Levinas, *Totality and Infinity*, trans. Alphonso Lingis (Pittsburgh, Pa.: Duquesne University Press, 1969), 266. Subsequent references will be cited parenthetically as *TI*.

55. Jacques Lacan, *Encore: On Feminine Sexuality, The Limits of Love and Knowledge: Encore 1972–73*, trans. Bruce Fink (New York: W. W. Norton, 1998), 6. Subsequent references will be cited parenthetically as *E*.

56. As Chanter and Cornell have argued, Irigaray's ethics of sexual difference is deeply influenced by Levinas's work (Chanter, *Ethics of Eros*, 170–224; and also Cornell, *Beyond Accommodation*, 183–86).

57. Emmanuel Levinas, *Otherwise than Being or Beyond Essence*, trans. Alphonso Lingis (The Hague: Martinis Nijhoff, 1981), 5–8, 37–38. Subsequent references to this work will be cited parenthetically as *OB*. For a detailed discussion of the signification of alterity in Levinas's work, see, for instance, Krzysztof Ziarek, "Semantics of Proximity: Language and the Other in the Philosophy of Emmanuel Levinas," *Research in Phenomenology* 19 (1989): 213–47; and Chanter, *Ethics of Eros*.

58. For an illuminating discussion of Lacan's "para-being" in the context of Heidegger, see Krzysztof Ziarek, "Love and the Debasement of Being: Irigaray's Revision of Heidegger and Lacan," *Postmodern Culture* 10 (1999).

59. As a mark of withdrawal and interruption, indirection can be compared to Lacan's *significance*. As Jacqueline Rose remarks, "The concept of *jouissance* (what escapes in sexuality) and the concept of *significance* (what shifts within language) are inseparable." See "Introduction. II," in *Feminine Sexuality: Jacques Lacan and the École Freudienne*, ed. Juliet Mitchell and Jacqueline Rose, trans. Jacqueline Rose (New York: W. W. Norton, 1982), 52.

60. Žižek, *Ticklish Subject*, 281.

61. Ibid., 294.

62. Ibid., 279.

63. As Cornell argues, for Irigaray "the carnality of the feminine 'sex'" represents "the embodiment of a proximity that is not appropriation" (*Beyond Accommodation*, 185).

64. Gayatri Chakravorty Spivak, "French Feminism Revisited: Ethics and Politics," in *Feminists Theorize the Political*, ed. Judith Butler and Joan W. Scott (New York: Routledge, 1992), 80.

65. Without a vision of political justice, Irigaray argues, market-driven liberalism will turn money into our "only civil mediator" (*TD*, 86)—which means, as Anna Yeatman points out, that any political valuation of difference will be converted "into the assertion of market preferences." See *Postmodern Revisionings of the Political* (New York: Routledge, 1994), 91.

66. See, for instance, Luce Irigaray, "The Eternal Irony of the Community," in *Speculum of the Other Woman*, trans. Gillian C. Gill (Ithaca, N.Y.: Cornell University Press, 1985), 214–26; and Luce Irigaray, "An Ethics of Sexual Difference," in *ESD*, 118–20. For an excellent discussion of "Hegel's restricted economy" of sexual difference, see Diprose, *Bodies of Women*, 38–64.

67. Luce Irigaray, "How to Define Sexuate Rights?" trans. David Macey, *The Irigaray Reader*, ed. Margaret Whitford (Oxford: Basil Blackwell, 1991),

207. Although irreducible to the politics of recognition, Irigaray's negotiation between economic equality and the culture of sexual difference is similar to Nancy Fraser's recent formulation of political justice, which combines economic politics of redistribution with the cultural claims of difference: "We should see ourselves as presented with a new intellectual and practical task: that of developing a *critical* theory of recognition, one that identifies and defends only those versions of the cultural politics of difference that can be coherently combined with the social politics of equality." See *Justice Interruptus: Critical Reflections on "Postsocialist Condition"* (New York: Routledge, 1997), 12.

68. Etienne Balibar, "Culture and Identity (Working Notes)," trans. J. Swenson, *The Identity in Question*, ed. John Rajchman (New York: Routledge, 1995), 191.

69. Ibid., 190, 192. Balibar is working here with the terminology of the symbolic and the imaginary classes proposed by Jean-Claude Milner, *Les noms indistincts* (Paris: Éditions du Seuil, 1983).

70. For the examples of the critiques of the presumed whiteness and heterosexuality of gender identities, see Diprose, *Bodies of Women*.

71. For the feminist critique of the liberal concept of citizenship, see, among others, Chantal Mouffe, *The Return of the Political* (London: Verso, 1993); Carole Pateman, *The Sexual Contract* (Stanford, Calif.: Stanford University Press, 1988); Yeatman, *Postmodern Revisionings*; Iris Marion Young, "Impartiality and the Civic Public," in *Feminism as Critique*, eds. Seyla Benhabib and Drucilla Cornell (Minneapolis: University of Minnesota Press, 1987), 57–76; and Williams, *Alchemy of Race*.

72. Cheah and Grosz, "Of Being-Two."

73. " 'Representation and Democracy': An Interview with bell hooks and David Trend," in *Radical Democracy: Identity, Citizenship, and the State*, ed. David Trend (New York: Routledge, 1996), 231.

74. Ernesto Laclau, "Universalism, Particularism and the Question of Identity," in *The Identity in Question*, ed. John Rajchman (New York: Routledge, 1995), 99.

75. Ibid., 104.

76. Chantal Mouffe, "Feminism, Citizenship and Radical Democratic Politics," in *Feminists Theorize the Political*, ed. Judith Butler and Joan W. Scott (New York: Routledge, 1992), 377.

77. Chantal Mouffe, "Democratic Politics and the Question of Identity," in *The Identity in Question*, ed. John Rajchman (New York: Routledge, 1995), 42.

78. Ibid., 44–45.

79. For a critique of this externalization of the internal antagonism, see Slavoj Žižek, "Beyond Discourse-Analysis," in *New Reflections on the Revolution of Our Time*, ed. Ernesto Laclau (London: Verso, 1990), 249–60.

80. Chanter, *Ethics of Eros*, 109–11. For a similar argument, see Drucilla Cornell, *The Philosophy of the Limit* (New York: Routledge, 1992), 48.

81. G. W. F. Hegel, *Phenomenology of the Spirit*, trans. A. V. Miller (Oxford: Claredon Press, 1977), 272–73.

82. In the context of Irigaray's critique of the political value of war, we may wonder whether certain readings of Lacan are not an heir to this kind of Hegelianism. Consider, for instance, the complicity in Žižek's argument between his emphasis on the "mortification" of the body by the symbolic and his location of the subject of psychoanalysis at this moment when the Hegelian subject internalizes the revolutionary terror. Žižek writes that "the symbolic order 'stands for death' in the precise sense of 'mortifying' the real of the body, of subordinating it to a foreign automatism . . . : the very symbolic machine which 'mortifies' the living body produces by the same token the opposite of mortification, the immortal desire, the Real of 'pure life' which eludes symbolization" (Žižek, *Tarrying with the Negative*, 179, 27).

83. For an informative discussion of Irigaray's critique of Hegel, in particular, of his "anthropocentric conception of nature," see Cheah and Grosz, "Of Being-Two," 8–10. As they point out, women in the Hegelian dialectic are deprived of both singularity and universality and thus are excluded from the spiritual real of culture.

84. Žižek, *Tarrying with the Negative*, 58.

85. Butler, "Future of Sexual Difference," 19–42.

86. Mouffe, "Democratic Politics," 43–44.

87. For an excellent discussion of the split between the politics of recognition and performativity in the interpretation of Irigaray's sexuate rights, see Penelope Deutscher, "Luce Irigaray's Sexuate Rights and the Politics of Performativity," in *Transformations: Thinking Through Feminism*, ed. Sara Ahmed et al. (London: Routledge, 2000); and Penelope Deutscher, "Is This a Question of Can Saying Make It So?: The Declaration of Irigarayan Sexuate Rights," in *Feminist Perspectives on Law*, ed. Ralph Sandland and Janice Richardson (London: Cavendish Press, 2000).

88. As Irigaray explains in one of her interviews, "Why do I approach juridical problems more concretely? Because, since 1970, I have often worked with women or groups of women belonging to liberation movements . . ." See "How to Define Sexuate Rights?" trans. David Macey, *The Irigaray Reader*, ed. Margaret Whitford (London: Basil Blackwell, 1991), 204.

89. Deutscher, "Luce Irigaray's Sexuate Rights."

90. Deutscher, "Is This a Question?"

91. Drucilla Cornell, *At the Heart of Freedom: Feminism, Sex, and Equality* (Princeton, N.J.: Princeton University Press, 1998), 30.

92. Drucilla Cornell, "Gender, Sex, and Equivalent Rights," in *Feminists Theorize the Political*, ed. Judith Butler and Joan W. Scott (New York: Routledge, 1992), 293. For an excellent discussion of Cornell's notion of legal equality based on the "equal protection of the minimum conditions of in-

dividuation," see Kelly Oliver, "Recognition, Witnessing, and Identity: Drucilla Cornell on Family Law," in *Subjectivity Without Subjects: From Abject Fathers to Desiring Mothers* (Lanham, Md.: Rowman and Littlefield, 1998), 79–95.

93. Williams, *Alchemy of Race*, 164.

94. Ibid. The question of desire is precisely what is missing in Wendy Brown's discussion of Williams's concept of rights; see her *States of Injury: Power and Freedom in Late Modernity* (Princeton, N.J.: Princeton University Press, 1995), 163–69. For a psychoanalytic discussion of desire in the context of rights, see Joan Copjec, "The Subject Defined by Suffrage," *Lacanian Ink* 7 (1993): 47–58.

95. Spivak, *In Other Worlds*, 150.

96. Amarpal K. Dhaliwal, "Can the Subaltern Vote? Radical Democracy, Discourses of Representation and Rights, and the Questions of Race," in *Radical Democracy: Identity, Citizenship, and the State*, ed. David Trend (New York: Routledge, 1996), 56–57.

97. Hammonds, "Black (W)holes," 137.

98. Dhaliwal, "Can the Subaltern Vote?" 56–57.

99. For this argument, see Copjec, *Read My Desire*.

100. At this point, my analysis differs from Kelly Oliver's argument that proposes to rethink intersubjectivity outside conflict and struggle. While I share Oliver's critique of the Hegelian concept of war and recognition, I accept conflict as the irreducible dimension of democracy. For Oliver's critique of recognition and struggle, see her forthcoming book, *Witnessing: Beyond Recognition* (Minneapolis: University of Minnesota Press, 2001).

101. Mae Gwendolyn Henderson, "Speaking in Tongues: Dialogics, Dialectics, and the Black Woman Writer's Literary Tradition," in *Feminists Theorize the Political*, ed. Judith Butler and Joan W. Scott (New York: Routledge, 1992), 158.

102. Ibid., 160.

## CHAPTER 6

1. Deborah E. McDowell, *"The Changing Same": Black Women's Literature, Criticism, and Theory* (Bloomington: Indiana University Press, 1995), xiii.

2. In her recent study, Claudia Tate provides an insightful analysis of these difficulties in terms of the conflict between the demands of racial politics and the movement of desire, which "includes and exceeds racial liberation." See *Psychoanalysis and Black Novels: Desire and the Protocols of Race* (Oxford: Oxford University Press, 1998), 3–21, quote from 5.

3. As Marilyn Edelstein points out, hooks's engagement with postmodernism, like her previous work with feminist theory, is dialogic and contestatory; see her "Resisting Postmodernism; or, 'A Postmodernism of Resistance': bell hooks and Theory Debates," in *Other Sisterhoods: Literary Theory*

*and U.S. Women of Color*, ed. Sandra Kumamoto Stanley (Urbana: University of Illinois Press, 1998), 86–118.

4. McDowell, *"Changing Same,"* 158. While McDowell credits hooks for challenging the divide of theory and practice, she argues that hooks nonetheless ends up "valorizing 'theory' in the process" (171). I think this criticism does not take fully into account the style of hooks's writing, which crosses the institutional divide not only between theory and practice, but also between philosophy and literature, high and popular culture, personal and political.

5. Patricia Hill Collins defines the term "outsider within" as "the border spaces marking the boundaries between groups of unequal power" and associates this location with the production of black feminist critical knowledge. See her "Learning from the Outsider Within: The Sociological Significance of Black Feminist Thought," in *Social Problems* 33(6) (1986): 14–32; and also her *Fighting Words: Black Women and the Search for Justice* (Minneapolis: University of Minnesota Press, 1998), 3–10, 279. Subsequent references to *Fighting Words* will be cited parenthetically as *FW*.

6. The following works by bell hooks will be cited parenthetically:

*BB: Breaking Bread: Insurgent Black Intellectual Life* (with Cornel West) (Boston: South End Press, 1991).

*BL: Black Looks: Race and Representation* (Boston: South End Press, 1992).

*FT: Feminist Theory: From Margin to Center* (Boston: South End Press, 1984).

*KR: Killing Rage, Ending Racism* (New York: Henry Holt, 1995).

*OC: Outlaw Culture: Resisting Representations* (New York: Routledge, 1994).

*SY: Sisters of the Yam: Black Women and Self-Recovery* (Boston: South End Press, 1993).

*TB: Talking Back: Thinking Feminist, Thinking Black* (Boston: South End Press, 1989).

*Y: Yearning: Race, Gender, and Cultural Politics* (Boston: South End Press, 1990).

7. Collins sees three components of the passage from objectification to "full human subjectivity" in bell hooks's texts: "breaking silence about oppression, developing self-reflexive speech, and confronting or 'talking back' to elite discourses" (*FW*, 47).

8. Patricia J. Williams writes, "We need to elevate what I call spirit-murder to the conceptual, if not punitive level of a capital moral offense." See her "Spirit-Murdering the Messenger: The Discourse of Fingerpointing as the Law's Response to Racism," in *Critical Race Feminism: A Reader*, ed.

Adrien Katherine Wing (New York: New York University Press, 1997), 234.

9. For different assessments of this rift between postmodernism and black feminism, see, among others, Gwen Bergner, "Politics and Pathologies: On the Subject of Race in Psychoanalysis," in *Frantz Fanon: Critical Perspectives,* ed. Anthony C. Alessandrini (New York: Routledge, 1999), 219–34; Barbara Christian, "Race for Theory," in *Gender and Theory: Dialogues on Feminist Theory,* ed. Linda Kauffman (New York: Basil Blackwell, 1989), 225–37; Edelstein, "Resisting Postmodernism," 87–97; and Marianne H. Marchand and Jane L. Parpart, eds., *Feminism/Postmodernism/Development* (London: Routledge, 1995), 127–76. Patricia Hill Collins summarizes this debate in the following way: "Postmodernism neither gave African-American women license to decenter the authority of privileged White males nor planted the idea to do so. Rather, postmodernism provides powerful analytical tools and a much-needed legitimation function for those Black women . . . whose struggle takes place in academic arenas" (*FW,* 153–54).

10. For this kind of misinterpretation of hooks's work, see, for instance, Sara Suleri, "Woman Skin Deep: Feminism and the Postcolonial Condition," *Critical Inquiry* 18 (1992): 756–69. Suleri charges that hooks's and Trinh Minh-ha's attempt to articulate the intersection of race and gender "illustrates the hidden and unnecessary desire to resuscitate the 'self' " and the body as "testimony for lived experience" (762–63). My focus on hooks's performative rewriting of the structures of interpellation and the recovery from trauma points to the ongoing problematization of "experience" in hooks's work. I am grateful to my colleague, Cyraina Johnson-Roullier, for the reference to Suleri's article.

11. Ibid., 762–63.

12. Hortense J. Spillers, "Mama's Baby, Papa's Maybe: An American Grammar Book," *Diacritics* 17 (1987): 72. As Spillers argues, under the conditions of "Middle Passage," "one is neither female, nor male, as both subjects are taken into 'account' as *quantities*" (72).

13. Charles W. Mills, *Blackness Visible: Essays on Philosophy and Race* (Ithaca, N.Y.: Cornell University Press, 1998), 134. Subsequent references to this edition will be cited parenthetically as *BV.*

14. For a representative example of the social analysis of race, gender, and class as interrelated structures of domination, see the influential anthology, Margaret L. Andersen and Patricia Hill Collins, eds., *Race, Class, and Gender,* 2d ed. (Belmont, Calif.: Wadsworth PC, 1995). The editors write, "Analyzing race, gender, and class is more than 'appreciating cultural diversity.' It requires analysis and criticism of existing systems of power and privilege" (xii).

15. Bergner, "Politics and Pathologies," 220–21.

16. Tate, *Psychoanalysis and Black Novels,* 15.

17. Paul Gilroy, *The Black Atlantic: Modernity and Double Consciousness* (Cambridge, Mass.: Harvard University Press, 1993), 41–71.

18. Spillers, "Mama's Baby, Papa's Maybe," 72. As Spillers argues, under the conditions of "Middle Passage," one is even robbed of one's body—"a willful and violent . . . severing of the captive body from its motive will, its active desire" (67).

19. Judith Butler, *Excitable Speech: A Politics of the Performative* (New York: Routledge, 1997), 24–41; Wendy Brown, *States of Injury: Power and Freedom in Late Modernity* (Princeton, N.J.: Princeton University Press, 1995), 18–29.

20. For a critique of the politics of recognition implicated in the pathology of oppression, see Kelly Oliver, *Witnessing: Beyond Recognition* (Minneapolis: University of Minnesota Press, 2001).

21. Butler writes, "The interval between instances of utterances not only makes the repetition and resignification of the utterance possible, but shows how words might through time become disjoined from their power to injure and recontextualized in more affirmative ways" (*Excitable Speech*, 15).

22. Martin Luther King Jr., *Where Do We Go From Here: Chaos or Community?* (New York: Harper and Row, 1967), 43–44, emphasis added. Subsequent references to this text will be cited parenthetically as *WDWGFH*.

23. The term "social death" is used by Orlando Paterson to describe the "forced alienation" and the dehumanizing erasure of subjectivity imposed by slavery; the significance of this term can be extended to include the effects of hate speech. See *Slavery and Social Death: A Comparative Study* (Cambridge, Mass.: Harvard University Press, 1982), 5–7.

24. King writes that because of the cruelty of racism, "every Negro child suffers a traumatic emotional burden when he encounters the reality of the black skin" (*WDWGFH*, 109).

25. Oliver, *Witnessing*, 14 (MS. pages).

26. Cornel West, *Race Matters* (New York: Random House, 1994), 146. Subsequent references to this text will be cited parenthetically as *RM*.

27. Mari Matsuda, Charles Lawrence III, Richard Degaldo, and Kimberle Crenshaw, eds., *Words that Wound: Critical Race Theory, Assaultive Speech, and the First Amendment* (Boulder, Colo.: Westview Press, 1993), I. For a useful discussion of the hate speech controversy, see *FW*, 79–94; and Samuel Walker, *Hate Speech: The History of American Controversy* (Lincoln: University of Nebraska Press, 1994).

28. Oliver, *Witnessing*, 12 (MS. pages). That is why Oliver argues that Butler's theory of the performative is insufficient because it does not engage the healing process of "working-through." See "The Transformative Power of Working-Through," in *Witnessing*; and Kelly Oliver, "What's Transformative about the Performative? From Repetition to Working-Through," *Studies in Practical Philosophy* 2 (1999): 144–66.

29. hooks writes of Fanon that "more than any other thinker, he provided me with a model for insurgent black intellectual life that has shaped my

work." See "Feminism as a Persistent Critique of History: What's Love Got to Do With it," in *The Fact of Blackness: Frantz Fanon and Visual Representation*, ed. Alan Read (Seattle, Wash.: Bay Press, 1996), 77–85, quote on 85. At the same time, hooks criticizes Fanon for "a profound lack of recognition of the presence of the mothering body" (81) and for his model of liberation as a kind of "homophilia" (83).

30. I take the term "post-traumatic culture" from Kirby Farrell's study, *Post-Traumatic Culture: Injury and Interpretation in the Nineties* (Baltimore, Md.: Johns Hopkins University Press, 1998).

31. Frantz Fanon, *Black Skin, White Masks*, trans. Charles Lam Markmann (New York: Grove Press, 1967), 113. Subsequent references to this edition will be cited parenthetically as *BSWM*.

32. For an illuminating discussion of Fanon's treatment of racial trauma, see E. Ann Kaplan, "Fanon, Trauma and Cinema," in *Frantz Fanon: Critical Perspectives*, ed. Anthony C. Alessandrini (New York: Routledge, 1999), 146–57; and David Marriot, "Bonding over Phobia," in *The Psychoanalysis of Race*, ed. Christopher Lane (New York: Columbia University Press, 1998), 419–21. For an evaluation of the complex relation of Fanon to psychoanalysis, see Hortense J. Spillers, " 'All the Things You Could Be by Now If Sigmund Freud's Was Your Mother': Psychoanalysis and Race," *Boundary* 2, no. 23 (1996): 75–142.

33. Marriot, "Bonding over Phobia," 426.

34. Slavoj Žižek, "Love Thy Neighbor? No, Thanks!" in *The Psychoanalysis of Race*, ed. Christopher Lane (New York: Columbia University Press, 1998), 162.

35. That is why Kelly Oliver describes Fanon's analysis of the psychic damage of colonization as "the reversed mirror stage" (*Witnessing*, 43, MS. pages).

36. Kobena Mercer, "Busy in the Ruins of a Wretched Phantasia," in *Frantz Fanon: Critical Perspectives*, ed. Anthony C. Alessandrini (New York: Routledge, 1999), 207. For a discussion of the conjunction of the phallus and whiteness, see, for instance, Kalpana Seshadri-Crooks, "The Comedy of Domination: Psychoanalysis and the Conceit of Whiteness," in *The Psychoanalysis of Race*, ed. Christopher Lane (New York: Columbia University Press, 1998), 358; and Bergner, "Politics and Pathologies," 228.

37. hooks, "Feminism as a Persistent Critique," 83. For a discussion of the complicated sexual politics of liberation in Fanon's work, see Kobena Mercer, "Decolonization and Disappointment," 114–31; and Lola Young, "Missing Persons: Fantasizing Black Women in *Black Skin, White Masks*," 86–102, both in *The Fact of Blackness*, ed. Alan Read; and Rey Chow, *Ethics After Idealism: Theory, Culture, Ethnicity, Reading* (Bloomington: Indiana University Press, 1998), 55–73. For a nuanced discussion that takes into account the historical context of the conflicts and affinities between Fanon's work and

radical black feminism, see T. Denean Sharpley-Whiting, *Frantz Fanon: Conflicts and Feminisms* (Lanham, Md.: Rowman and Littlefield, 1998).

38. For the recent attempts to redress the relative silence of psychoanalysis on the question of race, see Elizabeth Abel, "Race, Class, and Psychoanalysis," in *Conflicts in Feminism*, eds. Marianne Hirsch and Evelyn Fox Keller (New York: Routledge, 1990), 184–204; Claudia Tate, *Psychoanalysis and Black Novels*; Elizabeth Abel, Barbara Christian, and Helene Moglen, eds., *Female Subjects in Black and White: Race, Psychoanalysis, Feminism* (Berkeley and Los Angeles: University of California Press, 1997); and Christopher Lane, ed., *The Psychoanalysis of Race* (New York: Columbia University Press, 1998).

39. Daniel Boyarin, "What Does a Jew Want?; or, The Political Meaning of the Phallus," in *The Psychoanalysis of Race*, ed. Christopher Lane (New York: Columbia University Press, 1998), 229.

40. Gwen Bergner, "Myths of Masculinity: The Oedipus Complex and Douglass's 1845 *Narrative*," in *The Psychoanalysis of Race*, ed. Christopher Lane (New York: Columbia University Press, 1998), 254.

41. Boyarin, "What Does a Jew Want?" 224.

42. Paul Verhaeghe writes, "This explains a certain monotony in hysteria: everything is reduced to the demand for an object that should fill up the lack, yet it is never enough." See *Does the Woman Exist? From Freud's Hysteric to Lacan's Feminine*, trans. Marc du Ry (New York: Other Press, 1997), 245. Needless to say, in the context of my discussion, the question in the title of Verhaeghe's book could be rephrased as "Does the Master Exist?"

43. For the discussion of the gap between personal fantasy, desire, and the demand of racial politics, see Tate, *Psychoanalysis and Black Novels*, 4–21. hooks's analysis of the representation of racial trauma as castration points out how this gap is ceaselessly crossed.

44. For a discussion of master/slave dialectic in a "black idiom," see Gilroy, *Black Atlantic*, 58–71. For a discussion of master/slave dialectic in a "hysterical idiom," see Verhaeghe, *Does the Woman Exist?*, 104–15. The disjunction between these two texts is one more illustration of the difficulty of thinking sex and race together.

45. As Cathy Caruth points out, the belated recurrence of trauma in nightmares is intimately connected to the fact that the unexpected occurrence of the traumatic event resists comprehension and thus is not available to experience. A traumatic event "is experienced too soon . . . to be fully known and is therefore not available to consciousness until it imposes itself again, repeatedly, in the nightmares and the repetitive actions of the survivor." See *Unclaimed Experience: Trauma, Narrative, and History* (Baltimore, Md.: Johns Hopkins University Press, 1996), 4.

46. Sigmund Freud, *Beyond the Pleasure Principle*, trans. and ed. James Strachey (New York: W. W. Norton, 1961), 12.

47. Shoshana Felman and Dori Laub, M.D., *Testimony: Crisis of Witnessing in Literature, Psychoanalysis, and History* (New York: Routledge, 1992), 69.

48. Dominick LaCapra writes, "Working through, as it relates both to the rebuilding of lives and to the elaboration of a critical historiography, requires the effort to achieve critical distance on experience . . . through a reconstruction of larger contexts that help to inform and perhaps transform experience." See *Representing the Holocaust: History, Theory, Trauma* (Ithaca, N.Y.: Cornell University Press, 1994), 200.

49. In *Beyond the Pleasure Principle*, Freud writes that the goal of working through is "to force as much as possible to the channel of memory and to allow as little as possible to emerge as repetition" (13). In his 1914 "Remembering, Repeating and Working-Through," he defines the goal of working through in the following way: "Descriptively speaking, it is to fill in the gaps in memory; dynamically speaking, it is to overcome resistances due to repression." See *The Standard Edition of the Complete Psychological Works of Sigmund Freud*, trans. and ed. James Strachey (London: Hogarth Press, 1958), 148.

50. Bergner credits hooks's work for diagnosing persistent difficulty of African Americans to acknowledge "the psychic damage" of racism in the aftermath of the long history of the racist stereotypes pathologizing black experience ("Myths of Masculinity," 223).

51. For a discussion of trauma and haunting in *Beloved*, see, among others, Avery Gordon, *Ghostly Matters: Haunting and the Sociological Imagination* (Minneapolis: University of Minnesota Press, 1997); and Sharon P. Holland, *Raising the Dead: Readings of Death and (Black) Subjectivity* (Durham, N.C.: Duke University Press, 2000).

52. Toni Morrison, *Beloved* (New York: Penguin, 1988), 274–75. Subsequent references will be cited parenthetically as *B*.

53. As Marriot points out, the traumatizing impact of this interpellation is intensified by the absence of the witness to the black pain: "This derelict and evacuated psychic space . . . attests to a loss for which the black subject has no witness" ("Bonding over Phobia," 426).

54. Frantz Fanon, *Peau Noire, Masques Blancs* (Paris: Seuil, 1952), 26.

55. Although the emphasis on the intersubjective and relational aspects of performative subjectivity is evocative of Habermas's "communicative reason," bell hooks's postmodern blackness contests nonetheless his rigid division between modernity and postmodernity, rationality and irrationality, politics and pleasure, public and private. See Jürgen Habermas, *The Philosophical Discourse of Modernity: Twelve Lectures*, trans. Frederick G. Lawrence (Cambridge, Mass.: MIT Press, 1992), 294–326. For hooks postmodern blackness is irreducible to the "communicative reason," since it encompasses affective and aesthetic modalities of discourse and the experimentation with the body, pleasure, and sex: "It was also important to claim the body as a site of pleasure . . . our bodies were the occupied countries we liberated" (*OC*, 74).

56. Trinh Minh-ha writes: " 'I' is, therefore, not a unified subject, a fixed identity, or that solid mass covered with layers of superficialities one has grad-

ually to peel off before one can see its true face. 'I' is, itself, *infinite layers.*" See *Woman, Native, Other: Writing Postcoloniality and Feminism* (Bloomington: Indiana University Press, 1989), 94. For the discussion of the dialogical structure of black female subjectivity, see Mae Gwendolyn Henderson, "Speaking in Tongues: Dialogics, Dialectics, and the Black Woman Writer's Literary Tradition," in *Feminists Theorize the Political*, ed. Judith Butler and Joan W. Scott (New York: Routledge, 1992), 144–66. Similar models of the decentered black female subjectivity are advocated by Deborah E. McDowell, "Boundaries: Or Distant Relations and Close Kin," in *Afro-American Literary Study in the 1990s*, ed. Houston A. Baker and Patricia Redmond (Chicago: University of Chicago Press, 1989); and Karla Holloway, *Moorings and Metaphors: Figures of Culture and Gender in Black Women's Literature* (New Brunswick, N.J.: Rutgers University Press, 1992).

57. For a complex analysis of the identity politics in the modality of the "perhaps," see Kenneth Mostern, *Autobiography and Black Identity Politics* (Cambridge: Cambridge University Press, 1999). Mostern approaches black identity politics as "the many and complicated ways in which intellectuals from a community both already constituted and always being reconstituted have attempted to work with existing racial positions in the formation of their political identities" (6).

58. Manning Marable, *Beyond Black and White: Transforming African-American Politics* (London: Verso, 1995), 116.

59. Katie Geneva Cannon, *Black Womanist Ethics* (Atlanta, Ga.: Scholars Press, 1988), 5–6. For Cannon the uniqueness of this ethical perspective lies in the fact that "throughout the history of the United States, the interrelationship of white supremacy and male superiority has characterized the Black woman's moral situation as a situation of struggle—a struggle to survive in two contradictory worlds simultaneously, 'one white, privileged, and oppressive, the other black, exploited and oppressed'" (6–7).

60. Slavoj Žižek, "Beyond Discourse-Analysis," in *New Reflections on the Revolution of Our Time*, ed. Ernesto Laclau (London: Verso, 1990), 253.

61. Ibid., 259.

62. For an insightful discussion of the specificity of the aesthetic practices in African-American women's quilts and their relation to history, see Elsa Barkley Brown, "African-American Women's Quilting: A Framework for Conceptualizing and Teaching African-American Women's History," *Signs* 14 (1989): 921–29. For the discussion of the crazy quilt as a metaphor for the innovative fictional form and political praxis, see Madhu Dubey, *Black Women Novelists and the Nationalist Aesthetic* (Bloomington: Indiana University Press, 1994), 126–44.

63. Žižek, "Beyond Discourse-Analysis," 252–53.

64. According to Patricia Hill Collins, hooks's interviews and dialogues with Cornel West, published in the collection *Breaking Bread: Insurgent Black Intellectual Life*, are a stunning illustration of "the postmodern notion of mul-

tiple voices." See her review of *Breaking Bread: Insurgent Black Intellectual Life,* by bell hooks and Cornel West, and *Segregated Sisterhood: Racism and the Politics of American Feminism,* by Nancie Caraway, *Signs* 20 (1994): 176–79.

65. For a similar critique of Rorty's position on ethnocentrism, see Drucilla Cornell, *Transformations: Recollective Imagination and Sexual Difference* (New York: Routledge, 1993), 172–77.

66. Richard Rorty, *Contingency, Irony, and Solidarity* (Cambridge: Cambridge University Press, 1989) xvi.

67. Ibid., 192.

68. Ibid., 94.

69. Seyla Benhabib, *Situating the Self: Gender, Community and Postmodernism in Contemporary Ethics* (New York: Routledge, 1992), 10. For a critique of the reversibility of perspectives, see Iris Marion Young, *Intersecting Voices: Dilemmas of Gender, Political Philosophy, and Policy* (Princeton, N.J.: Princeton University Press, 1997), 39–59.

70. Benhabib, *Situating the Self,* 8.

71. Ibid., 137.

72. Young, *Intersecting Voices,* 50.

73. Emmanuel Levinas, *Basic Philosophical Writings,* ed. Adriaan T. Peperzak, Simon Critchley, and Robert Bernasconi (Bloomington: Indiana University Press, 1996), 173. Subsequent references will be cited parenthetically.

74. Jill Robbins, *Prodigal Son / Elder Brother: Interpretation and Alterity in Augustine, Petrarch, Kafka, Levinas* (Chicago: University of Chicago Press, 1991), 102.

75. Robbins notes, "The face speaks to me from a height and also in utter destitution" (*Prodigal Son / Elder Brother,* 143).

76. Emmanuel Levinas, "The Trace of the Other," trans. Alphonso Lingis, in *Deconstruction in Context,* ed. Mark Taylor (Chicago: University of Chicago Press, 1986), 353. Subsequent references will be cited parenthetically TO.

77. John W. Murphy and Jung Min Choi, *Postmodernism, Unraveling Racism, and Democratic Institutions* (Westport, Conn.: Praeger, 1997), 79.

78. Audre Lorde, *Sister Outsider* (Freedom, Calif.: Crossing Press, 1984), 115.

79. Audre Lorde, "Outlines," in *Race, Class, and Gender,* 2d ed., ed. Margaret L. Andersen and Patricia Hill Collins (Belmont, Calif.: Wadsworth, 1995), 540.

80. John Rawls, *Political Liberalism* (New York: Columbia University Press, 1993), 42.

81. For a critique of pluralism from the perspective of radical multicultural democracy, see Marable, *Beyond Black and White,* 177–84; Murphy and Choi, *Postmodernism,* 71–80, 121–22; and especially, the collection of essays in Andersen and Collins, eds., *Race, Class, and Gender.* As that collection's ed-

itors, Margaret L. Andersen and Patricia Hill Collins, write, "The very term *diversity* implies that understanding race, class, and gender means only recognizing the plurality of views and experiences in society . . . [it] requires analysis and criticism of existing systems of power and privilege" (xiii).

82. Rawls, *Political Liberalism*, 46.

83. For the discussion of Euro-American and New World African modernities, see Cornel West, *Keeping Faith: Philosophy and Race in America* (New York: Routledge, 1993), xii–xiii.

84. As Mills points out, abstract liberalism is in fact supported by the "*Herrenvolk* moral theory appropriate for a white supremacist polity, in which the difference race makes is to demarcate persons from subpersons" (*BV*, 109).

85. Murphy and Choi, *Postmodernism*, 93.

86. Rawls, *Political Liberalism*, 45.

87. Marable, *Beyond Black and White*, xiv.

88. Gilroy, *Black Atlantic*, 190.

89. Lucius T. Outlaw Jr., *On Race and Philosophy* (New York: Routledge, 1996), 40.

90. As Mills similarly contends, when race is considered to be irrelevant to citizenship, "policies prescribed on this basis will not be sufficient in the real-life, nonideal polity of the United States, to redress past inequalities" (*BV*, 108).

91. As Ann DuCille similarly concludes in her book, *Skin Trade*, the future of democracy in America depends on "a head-on collision with the deep structures and historical roots of its social and economic problems. . . . It means acknowledging racism as a fundamental element of American condition, from the seeming innocence of Barbie dolls to the assumed guilt of O.J. Simpson, from interpersonal relationships to public policy." See *Skin Trade* (Cambridge, Mass.: Harvard University Press, 1996), 172–73.

92. Marable distinguishes three different political orientations among African-American intellectuals: pragmatic integration / liberalism; separatism / black nationalism; and the transformative project of multicultural democracy (*Beyond Black and White*, 209).

93. Ibid., 124.

94. West, *Keeping Faith*, 29.

95. Drawing on the work of W. E. B. Du Bois, Outlaw defines this project as a "conservation" of differences in the context of radicalized democratic pluralism (*Race and Philosophy*, 150). As Chantal Mouffe similarly argues, the main question is how to defend the radical pluralism "without destroying the very framework of the political community." See "Democratic Politics Today," in *Dimensions of Radical Democracy: Pluralism, Citizenship, Community* (London: Verso, 1992), 3.

96. Similarly, Cornel West associates cultural hybridity with "democratic sensibility," which "flies in the face of any policing of borders and boundaries of 'blackness,' 'maleness,' 'femaleness' or 'whiteness'" (*RM*, 151).

97. *FW*, 248.

98. Martin Luther King Jr., "A Challenge of a New Age," in *A Testament of Hope: The Essential Writings and Speeches of Martin Luther King, Jr.*, ed. James M. Washington (San Francisco: Harper, 1986), 140.

99. For a discussion of the religious influences in King's thought, see Cornel West, *Prophetic Fragments* (Grand Rapids, Mich.: William Eerdmans Publishing Company, 1988), 3–12.

100. In *Outlaw Culture* (243–50), hooks concurs with Cornel West that Martin Luther King Jr. remains "the most significant and successful organic *intellectual* in American history" (West, *Prophetic Fragments*, 3).

101. West, *Keeping Faith*, 31.

102. Outlaw, *Race and Philosophy*, 33.

103. As David Trend argues, "hooks's work is of particular relevance to ongoing debates in radical democracy in the way it seeks out common political goals among diverse movements." See "Representation and Democracy: An interview with bell hooks," in *Radical Democracy: Identity, Citizenship, and the State*, ed. David Trend (New York: Routledge, 1996), 228.

104. Bernice Johnson Reagon provides a sobering yet witty analysis of the difficulties and risks involved in coalition building: "Coalition work has to be done in the streets. And it is some of the most dangerous work you can do. And you shouldn't look for comfort." See "Coalition Politics: Turning the Century," in *Race, Class, and Gender*, 2d ed., ed. Margaret L. Andersen and Patricia Hill Collins (Belmont, Calif.: Wadsworth, 1995), 520.

105. Murphy and Choi, *Postmodernism*, 74.

106. For the reformulation of Raymond Williams's term "structures of feelings" to express the utopian aspirations of the black culture, see Gilroy, *Black Atlantic*, 36–38, 74–76.

107. For a discussion of the difference in King's and Malcolm X's articulations of rage and love, see West, *Race Matters*, 144–45. While crediting Malcolm X for crystallizing the complex relation between rage, black affirmation and love, and the desire for freedom, West is critical of Malcolm X's "Manichean" mentality and his suspicion of black cultural hybridity.

108. Williams, "Spirit-Murdering the Messenger," 234.

109. West, *Prophetic Fragments*, 10.

110. For a discussion of the relationship between love and justice in King's work, see Cannon, *Black Womanist Ethics*, 21–24, 165–67.

# Index